# Immigration, Incorporation & Transnationalism

# Immigration, Incorporation & Transnationalism

*Elliott R. Barkan, editor*

Transaction Publishers
New Brunswick (U.S.A.) and London (U.K.)

Copyright © 2007 Immigration and Ethnic History Society.

All rights reserved under International and Pan-American Copyright Conventions. No part of this book may be reproduced or transmitted in any form or by any means, electronic or mechanical, including photocopy, recording, or any information storage and retrieval system, without prior permission in writing from the publisher. All inquiries should be addressed to Transaction Publishers, Rutgers—The State University, 35 Berrue Circle, Piscataway, New Jersey 08854-8042. www.transactionpub.com

This book is printed on acid-free paper that meets the American National Standard for Permanence of Paper for Printed Library Materials.

Library of Congress Catalog Number: 2007006106
ISBN: 978-0-7658-0386-3
Printed in the United States of America

Library of Congress Cataloging-in-Publication Data

Immigration, incorporation, and transnationalism / Elliot R. Barkan, editor.
    Includes bibliographical references.
    ISBN 978-0-7658-0386-3
    1. Assimilation (Sociology). 2. Transnationalism. 3. United
States–Ethnic relations. I. Barkan, Elliott Robert.

JV6342.I475   20007
304.8'73—dc22                                                    2007006106

# Contents

## PART III: RECENT DEVELOPMENTS

# Introduction: Immigration, Incorporation, Assimilation, and the Limits of Transnationalism

*ELLIOTT R. BARKAN*

ON JULY 5, 2005, four young men from Leeds, England, three of whom were born to middle-class Pakistani parents in Britain and the fourth from Jamaica, went to London and blew themselves up on three trains and a double-decker bus. Asked his reaction, a twenty-two-year-old Muslim in Leeds commented, "I don't approve of what [they] did, but I understand it. You get driven to something like this; it doesn't just happen." A few days later a *New York Times* reporter compared Muslim experiences in Leeds with those of Muslims in Jersey City, in the New York metropolitan region. In the former, extensive unemployment, lack of job skills, and uncompleted education both reflected and compounded the years of mistreatment of South Asians in this formerly quite homogeneous nation. The mistreatment had left many of these newcomers, and especially their English-born children, marginalized, frustrated, and, for some, sufficiently alienated to have become susceptible to radical Muslim terrorist appeals. Evidently, the processes of incorporation, whereby they might have been better integrated into mainstream English society, had eluded them.[1]

## EXPLORING THE THEMES AND ISSUES

Of course, one can find failures and alienated individuals and groups in America and even those native-born Americans, such as Timothy McVeigh and Terry Nichols, who are willing to resort to extreme acts of violence. But, immigrants coming to America have entered a nation where by and large ethnic diversity was readily acknowledged and newcomers felt themselves less obviously visible because of their differences and where expectations of mobility—the presence of opportunities—seemed synonymous with the new nation. It is likewise true that the disaffected, disenchanted, and defeated could—and often did—move on or return home, just as it was true that immigrants were probably involved in the Chicago Haymarket bombing that killed nine policemen in 1889, in various riots sparked by the Industrial Workers of the World (Wobblies), and much later on in the 1992 Los Angeles Riot. America all along has been largely identified with opportunity and yet there have been episodes of disaffection and alienation resulting in such actions, or in the formation of gangs, or, as Nina Bernstein reported, second-generation Muslims, who also feel "victimized, resentful, and alienated" as well as politically excluded. Clearly, they felt bypassed by the forces and opportunities for entry into mainstream opportunity or, in other words, incorporation. And yet, observed Bernstein, in Jersey City, New Jersey, "more than a third" were foreign-born but "there are no hard edge ethnic enclaves."

"Hard edge"—as in boundaries markedly defining ethnic turf. Gangs define boundaries; whites long demarcated boundaries setting apart African Americans from whites and, in places, Chinese and Mexicans from whites. In contrast, most (European) immigrant groups have encountered borders rather than boundaries, separations that eventually blurred, giving way to those who crossed those less rigid lines for economic, cultural, social, and then political motives. With so many peoples and communities in the United States, boundaries and borders have varied considerably in their permeability, durability, and origins, whether they were of the group's making, such as for religious purposes, or the host society's doing, especially against racially-defined populations. Many variables come into play here, which could be summed up as the context of migration (or of exit)— what drove a people to emigrate—and the context of reception—the political, economic, social, cultural, and racial conditions shaping the responses to the newcomers in the host/settlement society.[2]

And there are also the critical intervening variables, such as the transportation and communication facilities most readily accessible. The state of the global economy and military conditions likewise affect the extent of contact that people are able to establish and maintain with their homelands or with sister communities located in other countries, or the ties between themselves and those who never left.

The combination is critical in shaping the fundamental processes of "incorporation" as experienced particularly by immigrants and their children (as well as by such others as Native Americans, African Americans, and Puerto Ricans, who, though all American nationals, have migrated, respectively, from reservations, out of the South, and from their island homeland). Gary P. Freeman posed the questions, does such incorporation include "economic, social, political, and cultural processes" and are they "fundamentally interactive," to which he suggested, "Interactive yes, but not necessarily correlated as part of a more cohesive process."[3] Is this incorporation being defined as synonymous as assimilation? While that occasionally has been the case in recent discussions regarding models of assimilation, far more commonly incorporation is used more broadly—to define steps individuals (and then groups) take to move out of their enclaves, or ethnic communities, and into the mainstream.[4]

But those measures come with the understanding that such actions are taken initially by individuals and their families and *cumulatively* impact the group.

That is, collectively they come to form group patterns in the same manner that assimilation is basically the consequence, or outcome, of actions taken by individuals. Groups do not assimilate, people do. Thus, in defining my own model of assimilation, I point out that "Integration and assimilation are foremost the actions of individuals, although there are clearly consequences for their ethnic groups." Moreover, "ethnic groups have not advocated the assimilation of their group members (although particular community leaders sometimes do), for that would represent a community decision to dissolve itself." These points apply as well to the broader process of incorporation. The prominent sociologist, Alejandro Portes, more recently made a similar observation regarding transnationalism that likewise applies here to incorporation: The combination of actions of transnational activists and other migrants "adds up to a social process of significant economic and social impact for communities and even nations."[5]

Incorporation therefore involves ever widening circles of contact and interaction and frequently begins in job settings and then moves outward to informal and less structured encounters, such as in schools, sports, and religious institutions, as well as on to foods and observance of holidays. Over time, this process of incorporation (if not thwarted, aborted, or encountering resistance) may come to include social and institutional connections through membership in non-ethnic organizations, attendance at pan-ethnic activities or festivals of other ethnic or mainstream groups, political participation (or at least voting), and social interactions leading to inter-ethnic dating and marriage.

On the one hand, incorporation does involve more accessibility, initially in terms of surmounting less formidable boundaries, and may not (for some time, or for a generation) involve more intimate contacts or more hegemonic roles. In that sense, borrowing from my model, incorporation initially embraces acculturation, adaptation and integration before the more comprehensive stage of assimilation.[6] At many of these points in time in the adjustment process other external factors can profoundly affect the access individuals have to incorporate, including a changing political or economic climate that drains away the welcoming spirit or legislative and policy decisions that thwart people's best intentions. International crises or serious disruptions and upheavals in the homeland can likewise readily divert men and women from focusing on their incorporation into the host society.

On the other hand, as the stages of incorporation increasingly approach full assimilation, it is important to emphasize that assimilation is ultimately a two-way process. It requires a willingness of minority group members to leave aside more and more of their ethnic traditions and ethnic exclusivity (without, as historically argued, having to do so completely) and the willingness of members of other groups (in the case of segmented assimilation—that is, integration with another ethnic group and not necessarily mainstream society) or of the general society to accept such individuals in more equal and/or more intimate settings and encounters. That can lead to access to avenues of mobility, influence, and political power.

Five components of incorporation have become more apparent in recent years. We more clearly recognize that, as bonds develop across communities, transcending prior divisions, boundaries between groups and communities become borders—less permanent, more permeable, more negotiable. Understanding the transitional stages enables us to make better cross-group comparisons and contrasts. First, as the proportion of both single and married women in the work force increases, we are more likely to witness women as well as men engaging in activities that involve more incorporation beyond their own immigrant/ethnic group or their own traditional mores. Second, it is still quite obvious that incorporation could commence among immigrants with limited reciprocity among mainstream Americans. However, the transition processes from the initial stages to the more assimilative phases frequently extend beyond the first generation before being further advanced. Third, as long as migration from a group's homeland continues, it is most likely that one will find individuals within the immigrant/ethnic community (or enclave) at different stages, or degrees, of incorporation. Affecting the speed and extent of such incorporation are the variables of recentness of arrival, age, gender, education, linguistic aptitude, occupation, long-term goals, cultural disparity, religion, the strength of homeland ties, the individuals' (or community's) location, and host society perceptions.

Fourth, we recognize that assimilation is an end-stage process of incorporation that traditionally (so states the canon) was thought to culminate in the outsiders (newcomers and/or their children) shedding older identities and pronounced customs and cultural practices either forbidden or discouraged by the mainstream host society (or host minority).[7] It is now more commonly acknowledged that the enhanced toleration of diversity and pluralism in American society has made the inclusion (even integration) of minorities more acceptable without the earlier mandatory caveat that prior cultures and identities had to be abandoned entirely as a condition of "admission" (sometimes even as a condition of being regarded as "white"). That kind of transformation is not painless or effortless and is even a harder and less available option for peoples of color. The earlier expectations also assumed that ties to homelands would be effectively severed, which, in actual practice, were often not so completely disengaged, especially by the late nineteenth and early twentieth centuries. The extent of such connections certainly varied but often survived intermittently and symbolically.

Now, many peoples had harsh encounters and pressures to conform, especially during wartime and other domestic crises. That so much accommodation and toleration is now quite visible is a testament to the decades when such (more open) attitudes were first evolving; to the vast distances within America that have enabled many peoples to set themselves apart and thereby preserve

Old World traditions; to the movements that persuaded state and federal governments to modify, even repeal, the institutionalized obstructions to minority incorporation and mobility; to the urban forges wherein so many different groups were cast that newcomers were able to achieve relative invisibility or a degree of toleration; or the extent to which they were simply ignored or given time and space to redefine and resolve differences with mainstream Americans and, in the process, even to strive to become more "white." However, not all were so privileged and the particular causes or needs of such marginalized groups (principally peoples of color or explicitly sectarian groups) were ignored or overlooked, or rebuffed.

Fifth, contemporary multiculturalism (native and imported); globalization of communications, travel, and trade; and the redefinitions of citizenship that now overlook or forebear condemning dual citizenship have together resulted in a phenomenon where the economic as well as social and even political bonds with homelands are tolerated if not welcomed, especially for economic and diplomatic reasons. Indeed, Peter Kivisto argues that "No adequate theory of assimilation can be developed that does not account for [such] globalization."[8] We would maintain the same argument for incorporation. We now better recognize that homeland ties do range from the intense, on-going, multi-level transnationalism, financially committed (through remittances), to the more moderate, periodic, limited, less comprehensive, less financially involved translocalism.[9] The new understanding is that cross-border connections need not be seen as a barrier to incorporation or even substantial assimilation (unless they created conflicts of interest or principles). Frequently, the processes are now concurrent—links to the homelands and incorporation into the host society—with elements of this duality present even among the second generation.[10]

The historic reality behind all this is that such parallelism of incorporation and on-going homeland ties not uncommonly was present earlier in both rural and urban settings until the political crises arising from World War One and the Americanization programs. Widespread pressures were put on immigrant minorities to advance their incorporation by moderating, if not abandoning, their original practices and identities that had set them apart (suspiciously, it seemed)—especially those whose roots were in Germany or the Austro-Hungarian Empire. Moreover, for cultural, religious, political, and historical reasons, certain groups have resisted the latter stages of integration and, among some, reaffirmed their homeland commitments and interests, only to see them begin to fade as those homelands achieved independence, as U.S. immigration laws severely narrowed the gateway for new immigrants, and as those expressions or actions of homeland affiliation were perceived as signs of questionable loyalties to America.

Many communities found that international and domestic events compelled them to recognize that there were (and still are) limits to American's tolerance for diversity and ultimately an insistence that groups explicitly commit to (that is, publicly endorse) the fundamental political principles binding the nation together. Pragmatic responses to such conditions have nudged immigrant/ethnic groups to make compromises regarding their traditional ties and some traditional practices and mores in order to preserve the extent of incorporation and acceptance they had achieved. Then and now.

In fact, the government's response during the late 1910s and 1920s, a renewed immigration, and disillusionment with the war's outcome and with many immigrant communities' reassertion of homeland ties and involvement—was to use immigration policy as, notes Reed Ueda, "a device for social engineering" plus a "racially restrictive naturalization policy" by which "the state [could constrict] the boundary of American nationality." There would be serious consequences not only for the groups then present but also for immigration and citizenship policies for more than a generation afterwards. The lesson learned was that incorporation has had its advantages and benefits but it has also had its price. However, most groups (quite recently, Muslims since September 2001) have come to recognize that the common sorts of changes are worth the price of "admission," as if the alterations made by second-generation persons did not usually make that almost a moot choice.[11]

In sum, there have been no single formulas or paths that minority persons have followed, because the permutations of home, host, and intervening variables are too numerous. Moreover, as Deborah Dash Moore points out in her essay, "Ethnicity is interactive" both in terms of the dynamics within ethnic groups and between different ones. It is not, we now appreciate, entirely a matter of minority versus mainstream but includes the presence of other groups and their (positive or negative) influence, which can have a bearing on the decisions individuals make. Those decisions sometimes are made out of duress, or for pragmatic reasons, or in response to the greater weight of various loyalties, or as a consequence of specific goals set forth earlier (and the success or failure to achieve them), or, especially, in the context of ineffable feelings of attachment or alienation. Thus, as has been so often noted, if migrants vote with their feet, so, too, many newcomers and their children assess their transnational or translocal ties and the demands and expectations associated with incorporation into American society and vote with their hearts.

Early twentieth century scholars in the Chicago School of sociology (Robert E. Park and his colleagues) theorized that assimilation was a rather straight-lined, even inevitable process—for most whites—in which it was assumed that newcomers would shed past allegiances and customs and embrace Americanization. Beginning in World War Two, under the federal government's public relations prodding, Americans began to recognize the merits of pluralism (as opposed to a melting pot of Anglo-American conformity). The immigration reforms beginning in 1965 unleashed (or, some would say, accelerated) a demographic revolution in terms of the groups soon being admitted from Southeast, South, and Western Asia, Latin America and the Caribbean, Eastern Europe, and Africa.

Those reforms and the parallel civil rights movement (followed soon by the feminist movement) also sanctioned an ideological revolution by legitimizing and institutionalizing multiculturalism, group rights, women's rights, and immigrant rights.

As Ueda points out, the federal government, having used immigration and naturalization laws and policies to manage immigrants' incorporation, now liberalized those boundaries that Americans had been defining so narrowly. The 1965 legislation restored "the central role of immigration" and "the cosmopolitan belief in the capacity of all individuals for membership in the American nation"[12]—thereby facilitating their further integration into American society. That prompted various groups and communities to reassess their own boundaries, frequently pushing outward the physical, cultural, and even social ones. Many individuals took advantage of the new opportunities and new protections to move outside their established neighborhoods and communities.

At the same time that these dramatic changes in the civic culture were taking place—notably in the norms and values of inter-group relations and in the rights of access and equal treatment—many institutions also began to reevaluate their boundaries, especially economic (by businesses and unions), religious, educational, and political ones. In turn, these startling and dramatic developments sparked the Black Power and Brown Power (and, to a smaller extent, the Pan-Asian American) movements and the ethnic heritage revivals among European ethnic communities. There were profound consequences for the more than twenty-six million legal immigrants who began arriving in the mid-1960s (through 2004), plus the estimated eleven million more arriving and remaining illegally (as of March 2005).[13] They soon recognized that their options in terms of how rapidly and how extensively they chose to integrate into the American mainstream, or with other groups, had been considerably expanded and become quite flexible. The types and depth of responses to these changes were being affected by social class, gender, and racial, religious, educational, and occupational factors as well as by the broader shifts in institutional, legal, and governmental environments.

Moreover, scholars have recognized as part of these developments the reassertion, indeed expansion, of homeland connections, a trend of major significance.[14] Indeed, by the early 1990s, transnationalism had become the term of choice to describe the multi-level, sustained, intensive financial connections to families and/or communities in the homelands. By 2004 the scale of remittances had reached $32 billion dollars just from those in the United States, and those immigrants (and, to a lesser degree, their children) have become a critical source of national revenues for such countries as the Philippines, El Salvador, and Mexico. Indeed, El Salvador adopted the U.S. dollar as its national currency. So many countries have come to appreciate this remittance phenomenon that close to one hundred have granted their nationals the right of dual citizenship—urging them to become American citizens while retaining their original nationality.

Although the United States does not formally recognize dual citizenship, ever since the major 1967 U.S. Supreme Court decision in *Afroyim v. Rusk*, the federal government has accepted a ruling that severely limits the grounds upon which it could denaturalize citizens. For the most part—leaving aside fraud in the petitions for naturalization— citizens must explicitly renounce their U.S. citizenship in order to be divested of it.[15]

However, while these developments appeared to reinforce, or facilitate, transnational behaviors, many writers either confounded the meaning of the term transnationalism (using it as a synonym for internationalism) or described it as if *all* foreigners were transnationals engaged in extended, on-going activities with their homelands. By 2003–04 a number of scholars at last recognized, or acknowledged, or made the case that transnationalism had been vastly overstated in terms of the numbers maintaining such ties. I elsewhere suggest that, as with a Bell curve, most immigrants fall into the middle range, maintaining only limited, intermittent, episodic, financially uneven ties, which, as noted, I label translocalism. At one end, some entirely disengage; on the other, some are thoroughly involved. Thus, clear transnational behaviors could be seen, for example, in the involvement of Colombians and Dominicans in homeland elections and the campaigns of Mexican hometown clubs to provide services and infrastructures that, in many cases, their villages never had had. Yet, among most newcomers these actions have been limited, frequently fading over time as the immigrants put roots down in America. They are scarcely being carried over to the second generation, although some evidence of that is now being assembled. Still, Alejandro Portes recognized that it remains essentially a grass-roots phenomenon and, he now acknowledges, "Not all immigrants are transnationals" and "regular involvement in transnational activities characterizes only a minority of immigrants and . . . even occasional involvement is not a universal practice."[16]

The incorporation of immigrants remains a dramatic issue for scholars and students of immigration and ethnicity because, as indicated, the extent and rapidity of it have been affected by the interaction of critical changes globally as well as in American society and by the dramatic awakening of sensibilities among newcomers to the desirability, feasibility, and practicality of their shifting borders and transcending boundaries—within America and between America and their homelands. It is that which prompted Peter Kivisto to emphasize recently that such globalization of trade, travel, and communication has accelerated the reduction of the old boundaries and borders and enabled immigrants simultaneously to forge more extended bonds in their new host (or settlement) society while preserving many older homeland ones.

Researchers are also better understanding that all these phenomena are not mutually exclusive, as if in a zero sum game: Implicit here, too, is that incorporation, transnationalism, translocalism, and assimilation can take place concurrently within ethnic communities, be they Hmong, Muslim, or Mexican. Identity issues, citizenship choices, settlement destinations, gender roles, residential concentrations, occupational options, educational objectives, organizational memberships, regularization of immigration statuses, acquisition of citizenship and political participation, and even intermarriage continue to confront immigrants and their children, much as they did the earlier generations. At the same time, these very factors continue to be in flux and certainly, though alike, are not uniform from group to group. Consequently, one must emphasize that these conceptual tools are invaluable for understanding critical features of immigrant experiences, outlining many factors that one could (or should) look for. But, there is thus far no single pattern or path to incorporation among the first generations of newcomers, just as there is no single one for measuring the attainment of assimilation. Similarly, there is no single model representing the elements of translocalism, just as there is no fixed definition of the threshold at which actions constitute transnationalism. We have been witnessing complex processes in both domains of those experiences because, on the one side, as there is no single, definitive response that establishes that incorporation is underway, there can be no single outcome (end point) that all peoples will achieve. On the other side, as there is no single model of engagement or involvement by a person, or group, in both home and host societies, there is as yet no definitive measure of the point at which a person's (or group's) translocalism becomes transnationalism (or vice versa).

Notwithstanding these qualifications, public opinion studies have shown that Americans have not been entirely comfortable with these trends toward an uncertain unity. During economic downturns and during the recent terrorist threats and attacks, misgivings have been expressed and American ambivalence has been heard again, although, most interestingly, nothing like that during the 1920s and 1930s.[17] Not only did President George W. Bush in September 2001 urge Americans not to blame all Muslims for the attacks on September 11—as President Franklin D. Roosevelt should have done for the Japanese in December 1941—but there was also no serious groundswell of nativist sentiment or concerted demands for closing the borders. Indeed, debates have focused more on our porous borders and inconsistencies regarding temporary workers and undocumented aliens. Lamentations and political expediencies continue to be offset by economic realities in terms of who still seeks the jobs Americans will not take but which they need to have done.[18]

Illustrating some of the contemporary dilemmas and uncertainties is the story of four young Mexican Americans, now in their early twenties, who did indeed incorporate into American society, who did participate well in high school in Arizona, who were applauded in 2002 for their science project and rewarded with a trip to Niagara Falls. There they were detained as illegal aliens, for they had been brought into the country as youngsters between two and seven years of age. They had not made the migration choices but they had been successful in school, were defended by their teacher and principal, and in July 2005 the U.S. government's case for their deportation was thrown out, by which time three of the four either were in college or had graduated and hoped to acquire U.S. citizenship. The *Los Angeles Times* applauded the judge's "sensible step blocking their deportation." The extent of incorporation by these four young men proved more compelling to the judge than the government's argument that, as illegals, they should be deported whatever the circumstances.[19]

On the other hand, as Carolle Charles and Ester Hernandez document, the abysmal treatment of Haitian, Salvadoran, and Guatemalan refugees and asylees, who, with a few exceptions, have faced nearly insurmountable barriers to gaining permanent residence, has certainly demonstrated how, in reality, isolated cases of compassion have commonly been far more outweighed and overshadowed by the many instances where political and diplomatic priorities have trumped humanitarianism. The four boys (like Elián González earlier) make for good, short-term media stories, while others, in far greater numbers, remain invisible, insecure, and desperate.

Our objective with this collection of essays is to bring to the reader's attention the fact, long unacknowledged, that "immigration researchers . . . are increasingly crossing disciplinary boundaries . . .," which has been "creative and empowering" because it has been so enlightening.[20] At least six disciplines are represented in these twelve essays: history, sociology, criminology, women's studies, Chicano Studies, and anthropology. Six of the essays were presented in earlier form at the October–November 2003 conference sponsored by the Immigration and Ethnic History Society and New York University and held at NYU, "Transcending Borders: Migration, Ethnicity, and Incorporation in an Age of Globalism"; four were given at the 2005 meeting of the Social Science History Association in Portland, Oregon; one was read at the Fall 2005 conference in Toronto, "Labouring Feminism and Feminist Working Class History in North America and Beyond," and one was delivered at the May 2005 conference at the University of Minnesota honoring Rudolph Vecoli.

Thus, these works are recent, interdisciplinary, and exciting and they have been divided into three sections: Broad Perspectives, Case Studies, and Recent Developments. While three are more general and multi-group in their coverage, the essays cover more than ten ethnic groups. I believe the reader will find them particularly fascinating not only because of their disciplinary and ethnic breadth but also because some are not here presented in traditional (orthodox?) academic style, thereby providing still another dimension to the collection. I especially sought that because, to borrow from Louise Cainkar's essay, I want readers to think "outside the box" and to recognize that we can effectively draw our information from census, immigration, and naturalization data; surveys, overviews, interviews; media and government sources; and traditional archives, news reports, and oral histories. This is especially relevant because more recent developments compel us to turn to a greater variety of academic and nonacademic resources. The additional fact that ten of the thirteen contributors are women scholars further delights me because many of them share important perspectives that had, until the last quarter century, conventionally been minimized or overlooked.

Taken all together, we hope in this way to demonstrate how dramatically the field of immigration/ethnic studies has been changing and how our thinking about these issues has shifted. The debates continue over government policies and controls, illegal aliens, guest worker programs, legislation for tracking potential terrorists (e.g., USA Patriot Act), the regular admission of between seven hundred thousand and over one million immigrants annually, and the processes by which the more than thirty-four million (legal and illegal) immigrants present (as of November 2004) struggle to determine what strategies, if any, to employ in order to incorporate into American society—and how far to go.[21] At different rates and with different degrees of difficulty, the great majority of them will move through the stages of acculturation and accommodation, and perhaps even integration. Some may assimilate, or their children may. Others will resist, or fail to negotiate the changes, or emigrate. The research continues in an effort to document and better understand these unceasing dynamics. Precisely because they are likely to continue for the foreseeable future, the interdisciplinary research represented here will continue to provide important contributions to our understanding of contemporary, and earlier, American society—and some of the on-going debates over these complex issues.

## AN OVERVIEW OF THE ESSAYS

In the opening essay, Nancy Foner builds upon some of her recent work focusing on a comparison of immigration patterns some one hundred years ago and during the past few decades. She highlights several key themes that we need to keep before us as we delve into the other essays. The comparison over time reminds us that what some often dramatize as novel developments in the present, such as the varied means of international communications, may be technologically innovative but a century or so ago letters sent overseas, or even across the country, often had a powerful effect within the context of that period, opening up worlds to the recipients and luring many into migrating as well. Once in motion, networks for social ties and job searches likewise played key roles then and now in helping individuals reach their destinations, get settled, and perhaps, eventually, identify a potential marriage partner. Foner's analysis raises questions about the central issue of how much of traditional cultures is transplanted and how much transformed. While we know the immigrant experience traditionally included such choices and changes, even the presence today of instant global communications does not mean those same processes of balancing retention versus incorporation and accommodation are not experienced by newcomers. Thus, immigrant experiences (internally or internationally) continue to involve a blend of continuity and change, not just during the earlier and contemporary periods but as well during the years in between those two "periods." Consequently, we take note of the rapidity of events such that *now* is the first decade of the twenty-first century and *then* is not just the 1900s but already the 1970s and even 1980s.

Christiane Harzig offers us the most global perspective of the essays in this collection. Her work is included because she introduces issues that provide another perspective to the usual paradigm of immigration followed by settlement or emigration. In fact, most of the essays here do focus on settlers rather than sojourners. Harzig emphasizes that the migrating male— *"homo migrans"*— does not represent "the universal experience of migration" because "migration is a profoundly gendered process. . . ." The motivations, strategies, and impact of women do leave their mark on home and host societies, even though a disproportionate number of them are migrating to countries in Europe, Asia, Africa, North America, and Australia as service providers—domestics—and even though many (perhaps most) are, in the final analysis, sojourners. Harzig details how such sojourning female workers, especially those who are wives and mothers, engage in transnational activities, particularly through their remittances and material goods sent home and the close contact maintained with family members left behind. In addition, coming with plans to work for specific periods of time, they are not seen as individuals exceptionally concerned about incorporation into the host societies and, yet, because they most often work in the homes of middle-class, dual-working couples in most destinations they have a vested interest in learning the language and various customs and foods that would increase their effectiveness and marketability.

Moreover, contends Harzig, these women frequently come due to many of the same motives as do males—with perhaps a somewhat greater emphasis on achieving independence and escaping the traditional controls of defined marriage and gender roles. They, too, rely upon networks; they, too, seek to learn about the urban environment and culture into which they are thrust. And they, too, will return home—unless they find spouses or simply decline to go back, which is more common in North America. There they frequently acquire new skills, new knowledge, and a new awareness of rights, freedoms, and shared responsibilities and family decision-making. Thus, this essay on domestic workers in the global context introduces themes that go beyond the confines of the one principal occupation. It suggests that even sojourning women have frequently partaken of transnational experiences and, notably in North America, are clearly exposed to important aspects of incorporation. Collectively, their impact is greater than the sum of their numbers, and we are reminded that in the ethnic accounts presented here we see that women are active players and, when they return home (as with returning men), often important agents of change. Just as the validity of addressing the issues of transnationalism and incorporation should not be time-bound, so the broader perspective should be able to extend beyond one (or just a few) emigration centers in a nation, one host destination, or any one set of variables influencing the migration and adjustment of newcomers.

The richness of these broadly drawn essays can be found in the layering of factors that affect the lives of newcomers. Val Johnson takes us from the federal level discussed by Roger Daniels to the local one of New York City politics, the interaction of class, gender, and ethnic origin, and the way issues of sexual morality (prostitution) were defined so as to appeal to particular immigrant voters (particularly German Jews) and, through them (with great difficulty), to the newer Jewish arrivals from Southern and Eastern Europe. A major player was Tammany Hall, the dominant force in the Democratic Party there for decades. It skillfully nurtured ties with the newer immigrants, who welcomed the assistance Tammany could provide them rather than condemning its corruption or even its support (via protection) of prostitution, which was precisely what a coalition of native-born American elites and German Jews was hoping to achieve. While Johnson's essay seems, on one level, like a straightforward foray into local politics, it is actually an elaborate analysis of the role that women—though non-voters—played in bringing certain issues to the forefront and compelling men to address them. Johnson discusses the early divisions between German and East European Jews and the speed with which some relatively recently-arrived groups, especially in the highly charged political environment of New York City, could learn about American politics and take those first steps toward political incorporation. Thus, precursors of later Americanization programs and reformers' disenchantment with the "new" immigrants were already evident by the 1890s, as was the reality that conditions in America, when combined with the diverse backgrounds of peoples of supposedly a shared ethnicity (in this case the Jews), could produce conflicts and schisms that polarize the community. There have been a multitude of subsequent examples of other such schisms, including, as we see in Carolle Charles's essay, among Haitian Americans.

Roger Daniels concentrates on World War Two. His specific theme of government policies that fundamentally altered the lives of particular ethnic groups adds to our general tools of analysis, namely that the expansion of government regulations and bureaucracy become key variables influencing the incorporation of newcomers and even their children, most especially among the Nikkei—the Japanese American communities. The power to define and treat a whole people as if they were enemy aliens even though more than two-thirds were native-born citizens was profound, all the more so in that this was accomplished without statutory authority. Required registration, mandatory notification of address changes, and internment and incarceration as well as the extension of naturalization rights to Chinese and then Asian Indians and Filipinos all left indelible marks. The latter development (citizenship for Asians) and the special postwar admissions legislation literally changed the course of history for the Chinese and then for the other Asian populations, making the 1943 repeal of both Chinese exclusion and their ineligibility for naturalization a watershed event. In addition, the refusal to develop a refugee policy before the war and the radical shifts afterward underscored not only the immense consequences of federal legislation but also the singularly important role of presidential leadership—or the lack thereof—in determining the fates of specific peoples. Events of the 1940s had an impact on a number of groups at that time and certainly many more thereafter. Nonetheless, one finds disturbing parallels between responses then to the war, global crises, and the presence in America of peoples associated with the nation's enemies and post-September 11 events, which is Daniels's implicit point.

The next eight essays offer case studies of specific immigrant and ethnic groups, extending back to the 1920s and 1940s and forward to contemporary events whose outcome we cannot yet know. With these essays we see more concretely those factors that define homeland ties and those facilitating or obstructing ethnic incorporation.

Diane Vecchio's study of the migration of Italian men and women to Cortlandt prior to the Depression is a remarkable community study because it is based on a sound reading of the literature, extensive interviews, and trips she made to the villages in Italy from which her sample population came, including her own ancestors. We learn most directly of the personal and family decisions behind those who first migrated, those who followed, and those few who returned to Italy. In very specific ways we learn of the networks through which newcomers were able to secure jobs in factories on the day they arrived, because Italians were already working there and could provide the language environment in which the newcomers could adjust to America. Vecchio discusses the patterns of incorporation and especially the changing notions about gender appropriateness that took place when Italian wives quickly adopted the unprecedented practice (for Italian wives) of taking in boarders and working seasonally in the packing houses as well as opening grocery stores and restaurants on the first floor of their residences. Networks were nurtured among the women; family and village links were preserved and used for arranging marriages; and remittances were sent home by many persons—and for many years. But, if there were unquestionably transnational family bonds, there were also examples of responses to homeland politics. With newfound national pride, many Italians would admire Mussolini for his reforms in Italy, but Donato Vecchio, for one, would not return precisely because he would not abide Mussolini's fascist regime.

Roland L. Guyotte and Barbara M. Posadas have written much about Filipinos in the Midwest, and their exceptional essay analyzes here over four hundred Filipino applicants for citizenship in Chicago in 1946, the year in which they first became eligible. They gleaned a considerable amount of data from naturalization petitions, comparing those married with those divorced and those never married. A significant number—more than 87% of the over three hundred who married—wed white women. Once again we see how laws and regulations affect individuals, this time in terms of the freedom to select marriage partners, or not. Certainly, such a preponderance of Filipino men marrying white women represented a significant measure of incorporation. Occupations and family size are other measures used, comparing, for example, American-Filipino unions with those involving Filipinas and those with families still in the Philippines. The wives' cultural differences and perhaps the economic goals of their husbands quite likely influenced decisions concerning the number of children they wished to have. Thus, we have here an interesting case study where a group's cultural predilections carry over into the very specific actions of individual men who felt they had the right, through marriage at least, to be part of American society and took what steps they could to attain their goal.

Deborah Dash Moore focuses our attention on second-generation Jews following World War Two, offering an interesting perspective on the distinctive characteristics of this population and the dynamics of generation, urbanization, mobility, and ethnicity. The quest of this generation was, as the title of her well-known book puts it, "being at home in America." In general, the major thrust of incorporation efforts by newcomers and their offspring was precisely to attain that level of acceptance and comfort. Part of the issue of accommodation is here broadened to the challenge facing the children of those immigrants who specifically maintained transnational ties to their homelands. The question arose concerning the degree to which such children became socialized to those transnational bonds. Estrangement between the generations often occurred as the children responded to America's opportunities for further mobility and integration, moving off into worlds that differed from their parents'. In New York City, for example, the process of "becoming American," some scholars contend, has been almost interchangeable with becoming a New Yorker, an identity shared across comparable groups and a consequence of the dynamics of this singular urban environment.

Connected with that is Moore's observation that strains arose over questions related to traditions maintained and identities preserved, in large part because each generation's community setting was different and their life experiences therefore also differed, especially in terms of what they considered "old" and what "new." In the case of young New York Jews the population was so concentrated and attained such a "critical mass" that part of their incorporation involved elements of American culture becoming integral parts of their overlapping urban and Jewish-American culture. Their Judaism also changed, but not as much as did their sense of their Jewish-ness. Consequently, the argument has been made that the outcome of the second generation's integration was an "acculturation without assimilation," a parallel universe between their subculture and the American mainstream culture. A fusion of the urban and urbane enabled the postwar American-born generation to feel "at home in America." Not surprisingly, the third generation did not always embrace the kind of fusion created by their second-generation parents.

Sharron P. Schwartz's illuminating essay about Cornish Americans adds several interesting facets to the discussions here. She describes a group that has received relatively scant attention, and certainly not for being a particularly large or viable people during the course of the last century. (They are not, for example, listed among the ancestry choices in the 2000 Census.) By approaching this from the perspective of a scholar in England, Schwartz offers the reader a far more nuanced view of an immigrant group's migration patterns, their efforts to preserve their ties with communities in Cornwall, and the effects of those efforts on the Cornish who remained behind in southwestern England or had returned there from America. We see, too, the consequences for those connections of the newcomers' gradual incorporation into American society, with Schwartz detailing the transition of those Old World bonds from transnational to translocal. Her description of that transformation results in a fine case study of the evolution of ethnicity, especially within the context of changing economic fortunes in America. The impact of such macro-variables was compounded by the dramatic ethnic defection of second-generation men and women, who found more appeal in the opportunities to integrate into American society than to maintain distant relations that appeared to have little relevance for them.

But, remarkably, the story does not end on that note, for the Cornish in Great Britain are a Celtic minority with their own enduring identity. Gradually, beginning in the second quarter of the twentieth century, an ethnic revival began to take place on both sides of the Atlantic, a dual revivalism that eventually connected, overlapped, and reinforced one another. Cornish-American ethnicity, although the expression of a rather small population, had not disappeared but, instead, experienced a renaissance—an almost classic return and rediscovery of ethnic roots that was facilitated by the parallel revival in Cornwall itself. It is not readily feasible to determine what proportion of these Cornish-American descendants are actively involved. It also remains to be seen whether the activities we do see (most recently in 2004, Schwartz notes) represent a true transnational reawakening or only the expression of symbolic ethnicity and the echoes of past transnationalism. Nonetheless, the dynamic inter-relationship between transnationalism, translocalism, and immigrant incorporation is well illustrated in this essay.

The four remaining essays, in Part III, focus on contemporary developments with such significant political import that one must set them apart from the others. On the one hand, Part I presents essays exploring the contextual dynamics—home, host, and intervening conditions—which have confronted new peoples who have struggled to fit in to American society. Both official and non-governmental institutions have defined certain parameters and boundaries, some potentially impeding or confining the newcomers and others facilitating incorporation and ties to the homelands, transnational as well as translocal. Part II includes studies of diverse groups—first- and second-generation—responding to a variety of conditions, opportunities, and experiences covering most of the twentieth century. They illustrate how such peoples responded to government policies, cultivated homeland ties in varying degrees, and especially seized a host of economic opportunities to set their roots in America, with consequences for traditional roles and both inter-generational and gender relations. On the other hand, Part III provides four case studies where political conditions have powerfully impacted Haitians, Cubans, Central Americans (Salvadorans, in particular), and Arab Americans, spanning nearly the last five decades of the twentieth century. In fact, the responses by Cubans and Haitians to the political environment are so starkly different that they serve as a reminder of how important it is not to allow generalities to obscure the particulars of specific group experiences. Different cultural and political backgrounds and different policy contexts have profoundly affected their homeland ties and their opportunities for incorporation and acceptance in America.

Carolle Charles dramatically details how government policies and their implementation at both the sending and receiving ends can define or label a migrant population, thereby adversely affecting their ability both to enter and remain in the host country and to maintain unbroken lines of communication with family and community members left behind. We see very clearly, as with Salvadoran and Guatemalans, how a desperate people can become pawns in larger global or diplomatic contexts or contestations. As would happen with many Southeast Asians, conditions forcing people to flee versus (usually economic) conditions inclining people to relocate become the variables differentiating potential refugees or asylees from immigrants. Moreover, the convergence of deteriorating homeland conditions and U.S. geopolitical policies influence who gets in, how they are treated and the assistance given them, and even how sizeable their remittances might be. With such homeward-bound funds reaching thirty-five percent of Haiti's gross national product (GNP), the incorporation of Haitian immigrants and refugees (especially with regard to their economic status) profoundly influences them and those left behind. Not only does Charles lay out the evolution of U.S. policies concerning Haitians but she also emphasizes the presence of the different waves of Haitian arrivals and the economic, social, and educational/professional differences separating earlier from later newcomers. These class divisions have contributed to the outbreak of schisms that have hampered the establishment of concerted Haitian-American strategies. The result is a population among whom many continue to struggle to secure a foothold in America while continuing to honor their obligations to relatives still on their island homeland.

Guillermo J. Grenier's essay shows that the contrast of Haitians with the other principal Caribbean refugee population, Cubans, could not be starker. Useful symbols in the Cold War, Cubans fleeing Castro since 1959 have for decades received special treatment, financial and other support through special U.S. legislation, and, despite more recent policy changes to discourage Cuban refugees, have benefited from a federal policy referred to as "wet foot/dry foot." If they are trying to sneak in the country and touch American soil, they technically become asylees and are permitted to enter; those not so lucky are returned. Desperation to reach American shores has resulted in numerous deaths at sea in many frail and contrived sailing "vessels." Still, many times more Cubans have been admitted since 1959 than Haitians and Central Americans. Furthermore, many among the very early waves of Cubans were middle-class, relatively affluent and educated, frequently entrepreneurs or professionals—in many cases people with resources and/or special skills (or entrepreneurial experiences) and quite familiar with Florida from prior trips.

The first waves of Cubans proceeded with much assistance to establish a unique enclave that has transformed Miami specifically and Florida more generally. Predominantly, they not only incorporated themselves into American society to an extraordinary degree (notwithstanding the pronounced enclave conditions) but also have preserved deep transnational ties to Cuba—stemming from the failed 1961 Bay of Pigs invasion, the 1980 Mariel boatlift, the frequent plots against Castro, the extensive cash remittances to family members in Cuba, and even the sizeable number of return visits (less so by first-wave persons than by more recent arrivals). Although recent refugees have been more racially mixed, less educated, less commonly of the middle class, and obviously familiar with life under Castro, Grenier reports that they have been less wedded to the isolation of Cuba and less intransigent about Castro's overthrow than the surviving members of the first waves of refugees. The latter's fixation with ousting Castro has thoroughly colored their political integration in America and their measure of all candidates for political office, particularly in the Miami-Dade County area and even beyond.

But, argues Grenier, such resistance may not be reflected in the changes taking place among the newest asylees, the legally admitted immigrants, and the American-born. His 2004 poll among Cubans in Miami found that attitudes were much more divided on many issues than community leaders acknowledged, especially regarding selling food and medicine to Cuba, opening a dialogue with Cuba, and reestablishing diplomatic relations. Many of the variables already discussed converge in this case, for host and homeland policies combined with the intense sentiments among many older Cuban exiles to demonstrate how government policies, transnational bonds, and strong in-group hostilities have affected Cubans and non-Cubans—a distinctive case of incorporation producing consequences for both the minority and mainstream populations.

If the treatment of Haitian and Cuban refugees exhibits sharply contrasting U.S. policies and the very different push factors driving men and women to flee, the Central American nations offer another scenario, beset as they have been by civil wars, earthquakes, hurricanes, and other natural and man-made disasters—with El Salvador at the center of the resulting foreign policy/immigration policy morass. Ester E. Hernandez presents a compelling analysis of the various policies developed to deal with the legal, illegal, and refugee populations that have felt compelled to emigrate due to the frail conditions there. Some relief came from the novel TPS (Temporary Protected Status) provisions—first legislated in 1990—which provide for an exemption-from-deportation form that has needed to be renewed periodically (for a fee) and NACARA (Nicaraguan Adjustment and Central American Relief Act, November 1997), which granted relief (admission as permanent residents) for up to two hundred thousand Salvadorans, 150,000 Nicaraguans, and 50,000 Guatemalans. Salvadorans in particular have been able to remain in the United States and obtain work permits. Earning far more than they could in El Salvador, the Salvadorans remain so close to their homeland families and send so much in remittances that those moneys have now come to exceed all foreign aid to that country and revenues from the principal coffee crops. These circumstances have made laborers that small nation's principal export and preventing their forced return the top priority of El Salvador's foreign policy.

For many decades Arabs were relatively few in number compared to the major immigrant populations arriving during the first decades of the twentieth century. Although many were traders or small businessmen and many others worked in factories, for railroads, etc., alongside those of different backgrounds, they tended to remain socially among themselves— even when embarking on new business ventures. While they experienced a limited amount of discrimination, their claims to "whiteness" were not always successful, and in several cases U.S. courts were divided on their eligibility for citizenship. But the situation for Arabs began to change with the Arab-Israeli Wars (1947–73) and their aftermath in the region, official and media sympathies in the United States for Israel, skyjackings (early 1970s), the Arab-dominated oil embargo (1973–74), and the seizure of American hostages in Teheran (1979–80). These events were described in increasingly negative and stereotypical terms that depicted Arabs as backwards, barbaric, and possessing a culture that did not respect human life. All that in turn fueled the mounting hostility across America to this relatively unknown people in the nation's midst. The stereotypes crystallized into a racialization of Arabs, and of Muslims generally—America's first *large* population of non-Judaic-Christian immigrants (with some parallels to the treatment of the first waves of Asian migrants).

As Louise Cainkar strongly conveys in the final essay, periodic patterns of hostile behaviors toward "others" were now being directed at Arabs and any Muslims thought to be associated with Arabs. Such hostilities marginalized them, delegitimized them as non-whites, and fastened negative traits on them as an undifferentiated people (or "group")—thus portraying them as monolithic and collectively responsible for the actions of any extremists among them (or elsewhere, but identified with them). Such attitudes would pose significant hurdles to Arab incorporation into American society, in effect reversing it and undoing decades of their efforts to integrate.

Moreover, under the "right" circumstances since 1970, such attitudes have triggered coercive and selective governmental actions against Arabs. And, having come with generally non-Western backgrounds that left them largely unfamiliar with the traditions of participatory democracy, political mobilization, and the systematic cultivation of favorable public and political opinions—as was true of other immigrant groups usually from peasant backgrounds—these newer Americans were slow to emulate those who better knew those techniques and how to marshal them effectively against Arabs. And even where such Arab or Muslim organizations did exist, they were usually geographically concentrated and often found during these years that the American public was not very receptive to their efforts to offer alternative perspectives.

Before 9/11, Arab and Muslim communities were rather scattered— aside from Los Angeles and a few Midwestern ones, such as Dearborn and Detroit, Michigan—and relatively few Americans overall had direct contact with them. Whatever was the resulting mix of sentiments and images as outlined here, they thereafter rapidly hardened, compounded (despite the president's initial call for tolerance) by harsh, selective, and sometimes over-zealous actions by federal agencies desperate to respond to terrorist threats—now synonymous with Muslims and "Arab"- (or "Middle Eastern") looking persons.

Cainkar carefully explains how the array of investigatory actions by federal officials between 2001 and 2003 (some constitutionally questionable) reinforced public concerns that where among such persons there was smoke, there might also be some fire—perhaps Al Qa'eda fire. They also made Muslims increasingly defensive and apprehensive. In reaction, these developments finally convinced them of the need to improve their collaboration and to organize in their communities not only for mutual support but also to counter negative, stigmatizing public images. Furthermore, organizations that had previously tended to distance themselves from Arabs and Muslims were now sufficiently concerned about post-9/11 federal policies to lend their support.

At the same time, these stereotypes and tendencies by both mainstream Americans and American non-white minorities to marginalize Muslims as a "race" apart began to convince more and more Arab Americans (and other non-Arab Muslims) that perhaps they did not share enough of European culture to warrant classifying themselves as white. As Cainkar illustrates, many Arab Americans are defensive but now hopeful that they can overcome the stigmatization that Arab Muslims are essentially— inherently—different from other (white) Americans. Some subgroups among them are concentrating on presenting their identity, culture, and values as those of just another American religious community—as opposed to classifying them as ethnic or national ones. What we have, then, are peoples who are, in many cases, recent enough newcomers to still maintain ties with their homelands but also to incorporate into American society as a strategy that could alter the negative perceptions of them as a monolithic group of outsiders. Finally, for those whose families have been in America for several generations and who felt that events of the past four decades had marked a setback to their efforts to integrate, recent actions in this direction hold out the prospect that the processes of incorporation can be renewed or advanced.

Collectively, the contributors in this volume offer broad perspectives and an array of both historical and contemporary ethnic case studies. They will afford the reader an opportunity to examine various facets of transnationalism and translocalism, past and present, as well as some one dozen illustrations of how ethnic groups and individuals have explored, and continue to explore, alternative paths to incorporation into a host society. The essays make it abundantly clear that these processes were evident earlier and are not solely the product of modern developments, even if many technological and political innovations have reshaped and speeded up the means by which they now take place. The essays likewise illustrate the fact that there are numerous degrees of response to the options of transnationalism and translocalism and to the time frames in which they can take place. They further underscore the reality that there is no one path to incorporation, or integration, into a host society and certainly no one outcome. And, finally, several of these essays make it clear that discussions about groups should not blind us to the impact public events and policies can have on specific individuals, for it is far more often a case of individuals and families taking action with respect to homelands and host societies than of collective decisions by immigrant and ethnic communities.

Although American public opinion with respect to minorities, especially immigrant minorities, has fluctuated over the years, as have specific government policies affecting them, both the spectrum of alternative behaviors and attitudes involving connections with homelands old and new and that concerning the paths of incorporation have persisted and will continue to do so as long as the ethnic communities endure and still newer peoples arrive.

## NOTES

1.  Hassan M. Fattah, "Anger Burns on the Fringe of Britain's Muslims," *New York Times*, 16 July 2005; Sarah Lyall, "Lost in Bombings, Diverse and Promising Lives," *New York Times*, 17 July 2005; Nina Bernstein, "In American Cities, No Mirror Image of Muslims of Leeds," *New York Times*, 21 July 2005.
2.  Alejandro Portes in particular developed the models of the contexts. The third context would be international conditions as well as globalization, which certainly affect the avenues between homeland and host land. See Portes, "Conclusion: Theoretical Contingencies and Empirical Evidence in the Study of Immigrant Transnationalism," *International Migration Review* 37, no. 3 (Fall 2003): 879, and Portes and Rubén G. Rumbaut, *Legacies: The Story of the Immigrant Second Generation* (Berkeley, CA, 2001), 46–49.
3.  Gary P. Freeman, "Immigrant Incorporation in Western Democracies," *International Migration Review* 38.3 (Fall 2004): 947.
4.  Philip Kasinitz, John H. Mollenkopf, and Mary C. Waters, "Worlds of the Second Generation," in *Becoming New Yorkers: Ethnographies of the New Second Generation*, ed. Philip Kasinitz, John H. Mollenkopf, and Mary C. Waters (New York, 2004), 4.
5.  Elliott R. Barkan, " Race, Religion and Nationality in American Society: A Model of Ethnicity—From Contact to Assimilation," *Journal of American Ethnic History* 14, no. 2 (Winter 1995): 49, and reprinted in *Incorporating Diversity: Rethinking*

*Assimilation in a Multicultural Age*, ed. Peter Kivisto (Boulder, CO, 2005), 190–91; and Portes, "Conclusion," 877.

6.  Barkan, 54–58; and, in Kivisto, *Incorporating Diversity,* 194–98.
7.  Peter Kivisto, "The Revival of Assimilation in Historical Perspective," 5–14, in *Incorporating Diversity*, ed. Kivisto.
8.  Ibid., 25.
9.  The limits of transnationalism and the alternative model of translocalism are developed by Elliott R. Barkan in "America in the Hand, Homeland in the Heart: Transnational and Translocal Immigrant Experiences in the American West," *Western Historical Quarterly* 35, no. 3 (Autumn 2004): 335–41.
10. This does not rule out the possibility that such dualities existed earlier; it was simply more challenging for immigrants to do so. See Peggy Levitt, Josh DeWind, and Steven Vertovec, "International Perspectives on Transnational Migration: An Introduction," *International Migration Review* 37 no. 3 (Fall 2003): 567–71, and especially 571.
11. Reed Ueda, "Historical Patterns of Immigrant Status and Incorporation in the United States," 305, in *E Pluribus Unum? Contemporary and Historical Perspectives on Immigrant Political Incorporation*, ed. Gary Gerstle and John Mollenkopf (New York, 2001).

    Kivisto (22) also cites Will Kymlicka's point that the four prerequisites for the functioning and integration of a multicultural society—in effect, the ground rules groups and mainstream society both must accept—are "public spiritedness," a "sense of justice," "civility and tolerance," and a "shared sense of solidarity or loyalty." Akin to this has been the recent pressures on American Muslims to demonstrate their commitment to American principles by explicitly disavowing terrorism as a legitimate part of Islamic teachings. In July 2005, American Muslim leaders did issue a *fatwa*, judicial ruling, following the bombings in London, and declared that Islam condemns extremism and violence against civilians. Laurie Goodstein, "From Muslims In America, A New Fatwa On Terrorism," *New York Times*, 28 July 2005.
12. Ueda, "Historical Patterns," 313.
13. U.S. Office of Immigration Statistics, Department of Homeland Security, *2003 Yearbook of Immigration Statistics* (Washington, September 2004), Table 2; and Jeffrey S. Passel, "Estimates of the Size and Characteristics of the Undocumented Population," Pew Hispanic Center, 21 March 2005, 1.
14. Transnationalism sometimes is employed in reference to trade policies, commercial ties, even inter-governmental relations, but the term was taken up to describe the actions of individuals and, collectively, their groups and not institutions' *international* practices. Such formal links may well influence the transnational behaviors and attachments of individuals, but they are not synonymous. Such a distinction helps keep clear the thinking about this phenomenon of transnationalism.
15. Betsey Cummings, "Cash Flow Across Border Starts to Get More Savvy," *New York Times*, 28 July 2005; Celia W. Dugger, "Study Finds Small Developing Lands Hit Hardest by 'Brain Drain,'" *New York Times*, 25 October 2005; *Afroyim v. Rusk*, 387 US 253 (1967), and Ester Hernandez's essay in this collection.
16. Portes, "Conclusion," 876–77; and Kivisto, *Incorporating Diversity*, 23.
17. For example, see Elliott R. Barkan, "Return of the Nativists? California Public Opinion and Immigration in the 1980s and 1990s," *Social Science History* 27, no. 2 (Summer 2003): 229–83; and David M. Reimers, *Unwelcome Strangers: American Identity and the Turn Against Immigration* (New York, 1998).
18. Eric Lipton, "Report Finds U.S. Failing on Overstays of Visas," *New York Times* 23 October 2005; Jonathan Peterson, "Bush Polishes His Guest Worker Plan,"

*New York Times*, 23 October 2005; Editorial, "Broken border, broken record," *Los Angeles Times*,22 October 2005; and "Kennedy discusses comprehensive immigration reform with Mexican Foreign Minister [Luis Ernesto] Derbez," *The Congressional Desk*, 26 October, 2005, reprinted in U.S. Immigration News, Center for Immigration Studies, October 26, 2005, center@cis.org. The latter includes the key provisions of the proposed McCain-Kennedy legislation, "Secure America and Orderly Immigration Act."

19.  Nicholas Ricardi, "Judge Rules Students Can Stay in U.S.," *Los Angeles Times*,22 October 2005.

20.  Quote is from Nancy Foner, Rubén G. Rumbaut, and Steven J. Gold, "Immigration and Immigration Research in the United States," 6, in *Immigration Research for a New Century*, ed. Foner, Rumbaut, and Gold (New York, 2000).

21.  Steven A. Camarota, "Economy Slowed, But Immigration Didn't: The Foreign-Born Population, 2000–2004," Washington: Center for Migration Studies, November 2004, 1.

# 1

# Then *and* Now or Then *to* Now: Immigration to New York in Contemporary and Historical Perspective

*NANCY FONER*

THE TITLE OF THIS ARTICLE—"Then *and* Now or Then *to* Now"— hinges on a conjunction and preposition: "and" and "to." Two very simple words, but whether we use one word or the other makes a world of difference in how we understand and analyze immigration and the immigrant experience in the United States over time. In what follows I focus on what difference it makes and on the benefits and drawbacks of both the "and" and "to" approaches. Or to put it another way, I consider the relative merits of comparing immigration "then and now," on the one hand—that is, a comparative approach—and, on the other hand, analyzing changes over time in a "then to now" manner, what one might call a historical "becoming" approach.

I come to this issue as what one might call a "then and now" person—as a social scientist who has focused, in my own work, on comparisons between today's immigrants and those a hundred years ago. I became especially sensitive, however, to the limits of this kind of comparative approach in the course of running a series of interdisciplinary workshops on immigration, race, and ethnicity to the United States with the historian George Fredrickson.[1] It was our intention that the papers, and resulting volume, would compare the impact of the large-scale contemporary immigration with that of the great immigrant inflow of the late nineteenth and early twentieth centuries. Indeed we initially subtitled the workshop, "then and now." We ended up changing the subtitle. Not only was the periodization problematic when it came, for example, to the West Coast and Mexican migration but also many of the authors, especially the historians, told a story of immigration and its impact as it proceeded over time rather than comparing two different eras.

And this has led me to think more closely and critically about the implications of a comparative vs. "over-time" approach to immigration—and to reflect on what each approach has to offer. I am not, I want to make clear, arguing for the primacy of one over the other. Both approaches, I would argue, can—in different ways—help us to understand the impact of immigration in the contemporary era as well as in earlier periods.

In developing this argument, the spotlight here is on New York City, America's classic immigrant destination. It is the city I have written about and where I have conducted research on present-day and earlier immigrants, and the place where I grew up and where I now live. As in my earlier work, the period under consideration is, roughly speaking, the last hundred years, from the end of the nineteenth century to the beginning of the twenty-first.

## THEN AND NOW COMPARISONS

First, consider systematic then-and-now comparisons. One of the reasons I wrote *From Ellis Island to JFK: New York's Two Great Waves of Immigration*—a then-and-now comparison if ever there was one!—was to set the record straight.[2] A series of popular myths and images has grown up about the massive immigration to New York City around the turn of the twentieth century, myths that deeply color how the newest arrivals are seen. In one sense, therefore, a "then-and-now" perspective is simply a response to popular discourse and popular comparisons, a way of showing what really happened then and what is happening today as against nostalgic memories of immigrant folk heroes and heroines of the past, which inevitably put the latest arrivals in an unflattering light.

But there are other reasons for a then-and-now comparison. It can deepen our understanding of migration by raising new questions and research problems and can help modify and evaluate theoretical perspectives and formulate explanations that could not be made on the basis of one case—or one time period—alone.

As the historian George Fredrickson has observed, a comparative approach undermines two contrary but equally damaging presuppositions— the illusion of total regularity and the illusion of absolute uniqueness.[3] In other words, it enables us to see what is unique to a specific situation and what is more general to the migration experience. Of course, to some degree it is a matter of emphasis. Or of finding what you are looking for: if you look for similarity across time, you find it; if you look for differences across time, you also find them. And then there are disciplinary predilections. As Nancy Green notes, historians are more inclined to emphasize historical parallels in understanding today's migration and settlement patterns than sociologists, who see contemporary detail with disciplinary eyes, that emphasize newness.[4]

In emphasizing what is distinctive today, social scientists studying immigration often give insufficient weight to similarities with the past. Frequently, there is only a brief nod to the past—usually to emphasize how different it is from the present—before proceeding to an analysis of the current era. For their part, historians, according to Gary Gerstle and John Mollenkopf, have not "risen to the challenge" of applying lessons from the past to the present immigration.[5]

Regardless of discipline, the great benefit of comparisons of immigration in different periods is that they bring out *both* the similarities and differences between past and present. What comparisons lead us to do is to try to explain the similarities and differences—a process which is useful "in enlarging our theoretical understandings of the kinds of institutions and processes being compared, thereby making a contribution to the development of social scientific theories and generalizations."[6]

With regard to similarities, a comparison with the past can show whether, and in what ways, we have been there before—whether we are currently witnessing variations on long-standing themes that characterize the immigrant experience in the United States, or in particular cities like New York.

Clearly, there are a host of resemblances between immigrant New Yorkers then and now. Many immigrants, arriving with little or no English and few transferable skills, still endure terrible working conditions in jobs nobody else wants. The underlying processes of niche development— elaborated most notably by Roger Waldinger—also still operate to create ethnic job concentrations.[7] As before, immigrants tend to flock into fields where settlers have established a solid foothold. Lacking information about the broader labor market and dependent on the support of their own kind, new arrivals typically learn about and get help finding jobs through personal networks in the immigrant community. For their part, employers often prefer applicants who are recommended by existing employees. Ethnic businesses are another perennial feature of the American immigrant scene, if only because they emerge to serve the special tastes and needs of the ethnic market.

In what also seems like a timeless feature, many newcomers today, as in the past, cluster in ethnic neighborhoods with their compatriots, partly owing to economic constraints and prejudice from established New Yorkers, but also because they seek comfort and security among kinfolk and friends. Immigrant women still experience burdens and disabilities as members of the "second sex." It is a sociological truism that conflicts between the generations stem, in large part, from the fact that parents are steeped in old-country traditions and values while their children have grown up in an American social and cultural world. And now, after several years of scholarship on transnationalism, it is widely recognized that living trans-nationally—having a foot in two societies, as social scientists often write— is not altogether new, and that many migrants in the past also maintained ties with, and participated in economic and political activities in, their communities of origin at the same time as they were involved in life in New York.[8]

But of course it is not just the same old story or a timeless immigrant saga, as everybody knows. There are different immigrant groups today with different characteristics—and New York City, to say nothing of the United States as a whole, is a dramatically different place than it was a hundred years ago. Comparisons with the past, as I have written elsewhere, can show what and how much is really new about the new immigration.[9]

Consider a few of the differences as a counterpart to the parallels I just mentioned. Because many immigrants arrive today with college degrees and speak fluent English, a higher proportion are able, right from the start, to get decent, often high-level, jobs in the mainstream economy. (In 2000, 23 percent of foreign-born New Yorkers, ages 25 and over, had a college degree or more; 26 percent of employed foreign-born men and 30 percent of employed foreign-born women in New York City were in managerial and professional occupations.)[10] The latest arrivals are also more likely to begin life in New York outside the classic ethnic neighborhood, in many cases in polyethnic neighborhoods of extraordinary diversity and sometimes in bedroom suburbs amidst middle-class native-born whites. If contemporary immigrant women still suffer from gender inequalities, they benefit from dramatic improvements that have altered the lives of all women in American society over the last hundred years—among them, the right to vote, the expansion of educational and employment opportunities for women, liberalized legislation concerning divorce and gender discrimination, and social welfare programs that have made it easier for them to manage on their own. And, finally, much is new about transnationalism due to, among other things, new transportation and communication technologies, the new global economy and culture, and new laws and political arrangements. Migrants can now maintain more frequent and more intimate contact with their home societies than was possible, or even imaginable, a hundred years ago.[11]

Looking at differences between then and now brings into sharper focus aspects of today's immigration that might be overlooked or minimized— or simply taken for granted—in our own era. Indeed, certain contemporary patterns, like improvements in the position of married immigrant women (who now routinely go out to work and earn an independent wage whereas in the past they were more tied to the home) and the critical role of education in immigrant mobility (compared to the past when secondary and college education was less critical for getting ahead) stand out in sharper relief when set against patterns among earlier arrivals.

And it is not just a matter of identifying what is new and what is not. It is also a question of analyzing what accounts for the "newness" or the "sameness," thereby shedding light on the factors that shape the immigrant experience and pushing forward our ability to make generalizations, or develop frameworks or theories, about broader processes associated with immigration, from the construction of racial and ethnic identities to the nature and impact of transnational relations.

A historical comparison raises questions about whether models and concepts elaborated in light of today's immigration only apply to the current period or whether they also pertain to the past. Moreover, applying theoretical perspectives developed in one era to immigration in another can lead to a rethinking, re-evaluation, and modification of these perspectives.

Historians, for example, are now going back to examine transnational ties in the last great immigration wave. To be sure, historians have long documented the existence of transnational ties in the past even if they did not use the term transnationalism—for example, they have written extensively about return migration. But historians are now revisiting the past in light of writings and theoretical conceptualizations about transnationalism among present-day immigrants.[12] So far historians' emphasis has been on the first, or immigrant, generation, but given concerns about the fate of transnationalism among the current second generation, historical studies of second-generation transnationalism can help to identify what factors help to sustain—or, alternatively, undermine—it.[13]

Then there is segmented assimilation, a perspective that looms large in discussions about the contemporary second generation. Indeed, the segmented assimilation perspective was developed specifically to explain dynamics in the present-day period, when, among other things, many children of immigrants are growing up in inner cities in the midst of poor native-born minorities and where they are at risk—according to the segmented assimilation model—of being influenced by the oppositional counterculture said to be widespread among inner-city minority youth. Segmented assimilation, as developed and elaborated by Alejandro Portes and his colleagues, implies a diversity of outcomes among today's second generation, with some moving rapidly upward due to their parents' high human capital and favorable context of reception, others doing well because of their parents' dense networks and cohesive ethnic communities, and still others, whose parents have fewer resources and who are exposed to the lifestyles and outlooks in inner-city schools and neighborhoods, experiencing downward assimilation.[14]

One question is how extensive an oppositional outlook or ethos really *is* among today's native-born minority and immigrant youth. Assumptions about the pervasiveness of an oppositional ethos that devalues academic achievement have, to date, been based on only a few ethnographic studies. It also has been argued that the discussion of oppositional culture among the children of immigrants may confuse style for substance: listening to hip-hop music and affecting a "ghetto" presentation of self should not be taken as evidence of joining a subordinated "segment" of society that engages in self-defeating behavior.[15]

A comparison with the past reminds us, as Joel Perlmann and Roger Waldinger have noted, that an oppositional culture can emerge from the working-class experience without exposure to a "proximal host" of visible, stigmatized, native-born minorities.[16] Nor are the consequences necessarily so dire. In the mid-twentieth century, an oppositional outlook flourished among the working-class sons of southern European immigrants that involved a cynicism about and hostility to school and teachers. This oppositional stance, however, did not spell economic disaster. Despite not doing well in school, Italian American working-class young men could enter the unionized, blue-collar labor force through the help of friends and relatives and earn enough to support a stable and secure middle-class life style. However, in today's economic and occupational context, doing badly in school is much more problematic, and the kind of tough-guy and antiauthoritarian stance that was acceptable, indeed encouraged, in the work culture of the factory floor would be a problem, to put it mildly, in most service jobs that dominate the contemporary landscape.

The segmented assimilation literature also emphasizes the role of strong families and ethnic communities in protecting today's immigrant children from negative Americanizing influences, particularly from disaffected minority youth. The message is that immigrant children should stay involved with their ethnic community and ethnic culture as a way to get ahead. Certainly, this sounds very different from the past. Early in the twentieth century there was no concern that immigrants would absorb values of African Americans that would prevent them from joining the mainstream. In fact, educators then worried that among some groups, like Italians, the cultural values and close families in their *own* communities were preventing the second generation from making educational progress. To what extent is this past-present difference due to the fact that New York a hundred years ago was a European American city, where African Americans formed a tiny minority, under two percent of the population, whereas today Latinos and blacks make up more than half of the city's population? Or to the fact that education is now much more important in getting ahead? Or even to the values and aspirations that contemporary immigrant parents bring with them to the United States?

These questions point to the need for more extensive analyses of the pathways of mobility of the second generation in the past—against the backdrop of segmented assimilation's claims about second-generation mobility today. Such analyses will enrich not only our understanding of the past. They can also help in critically examining the relevance of segmented assimilation in the present era.[17]

In a parallel fashion, frameworks and analyses elaborated with earlier immigrants in mind can illuminate aspects of immigrant integration today. For example, the growing historical literature on how southern and eastern European immigrants went from being disparaged as racial inferiors and outsiders to becoming part of the racial majority in the mid-twentieth century dramatically highlights the elasticity and changeability of racial perceptions and raises questions about whether immigrant groups viewed as "nonwhite" today will continue to be seen this way several decades from now. This literature also points to factors involved in changed racial perceptions in the past, such as the economic successes of Jewish and Italian immigrants and their children, which are likely to be pertinent in the future. (Note that in light of critiques of the whiteness literature, I do not speak of Jews and Italians becoming white—since European immigrants were, from the start, considered in many contexts, particularly political and legal contexts, in Thomas Guglielmo's phrase, "white on arrival.")[18]

Or take David Roediger's and James Barrett's analysis of Irish hosts and white panethnicity. On the one hand, Roediger and Barrett acknowledge that they have been influenced by studies of contemporary immigrants that examine how newcomers learn about race in America. On the other hand, Roediger and Barrett add a new perspective by analyzing how, a hundred years ago, Irish American hosts taught southern and eastern European newcomers about the racial order and the possibilities for joining in a panethnic alliance as whites. Roediger and Barrett call on social scientists to carry out similar kinds of analyses in the contemporary context—exploring how racial knowledge is conveyed by modern-day hosts, including who the hosts are, what knowledge they convey, and how encounters with hosts shape the thinking of the most recent immigrants.[19]

Let me just mention two more areas where social scientists can benefit from analytic insights of historical studies. One is labor histories of unionization among early twentieth-century immigrant workers, which, among other things, have explored the social bases of unionization as well as sought to explain the reasons for the successes and failures of various union struggles and campaigns. Another is studies of historical memory—such as Hasia Diner's on the memories of the Jewish Lower East Side that developed among the children, grandchildren, and great-grandchildren of turn-of-the-twentieth-century immigrants.[20] Indeed, by now, at the beginning of the twenty-first century—as gentrification continues apace on the Lower East Side—we may be ready for studies that examine memories of the 1970s and 1980s, when the Lower East Side, much of it now fashioned the East Village, was a decidedly different place for new immigrants than it is today.

In this vein, a couple of years ago, the *New York Times* ran a story about how a different neighborhood in the city—Brighton Beach—had become a tourist attraction for post-1990 Russian Jewish immigrants who say that visiting Brighton Beach felt like going back in a time machine to a place that was too much like the Russia of the Brezhnev era. According to Annelise Orleck, whereas Russian Jews, who came from the Soviet Union in the 1970s and 1980s, reveled in the glitter of Brighton Beach's newly-renovated stores and restaurants, the latest arrivals, coming from a transformed Russia, now view Brighton Beach as provincial or, as one newcomer said, a "cartoon of Russia. It hasn't changed since the 1970s. It's like a museum."[21]

## A THEN-TO-NOW APPROACH

This leads to some of the limitations of a comparative then-and-now approach. One drawback, which I alluded to earlier, is the problem of periodization—an essentialized "then" and "now" that have a tendency to ignore or pay too little attention to the years that straddle or do not neatly fit into the defined "then" and "now" periods. Also, because a "then-andnow" approach compares the immigrant experience in two distinct periods, it may miss or minimize the importance of changes that take place *over* time. And so I come to what I call a "then-*to*-now" or "becoming" approach. The kind of approach I have in mind analyzes how, in a dialectical process, migrant inflows in one period change the very social, economic, political, and cultural context that greets the next wave.

New York City is a perfect site for analyzing this process. A hundred years ago, Jews and Italians entered a city that had been dramatically changed by the massive German and Irish immigration of earlier decades and where, as Roediger and Barrett put it, Irish Americans were frequently the hosts who taught newcomers lessons about racial and ethnic boundaries.[22] And, of course, it was a city where Irish Americans had had a significant impact on the structure and nature of political and religious institutions.

In turn, Jewish and Italian immigrants left their own stamp on New York, to say nothing of the many thousands of Puerto Ricans from the Caribbean and African Americans from the South who entered and transformed the city in the mid-twentieth century. Indeed, a then-and-now approach that focuses on the two great immigration waves at both ends of the twentieth century may pay insufficient attention to the huge influx of Southern blacks and Puerto Ricans that occurred in between and that, among other things, transformed New York's racial and ethnic order. As Matthew Guterl argues in *The Color of Race in America*, the children of Jewish and Italian immigrants who came of age in the 1920s, 1930s, and 1940s, did so in a city where the massive inflow of African Americans had shifted the racial order from a multiplicity of white races to race as color, focusing in particular on whiteness and blackness.[23]

At the same time, the children of Jewish and Italian immigrants, like the second generations before, were, in Richard Alba and Victor Nee's phrase, remaking the mainstream.[24] Their very incorporation into American society created, as Philip Kasinitz puts it, a white society that was self-consciously pan-European rather than Anglo-Saxon in its origins, where an assumed common Protestant heritage was replaced by newly invented "Judeo-Christian traditions" in religious life. [25]

Today's Asian, Latin American, and Caribbean immigrant New Yorkers are, once again, changing the city's ethno-racial landscape and the very way that race is constructed. Yet, like immigrants before, they do so in a context that is a product of the past. The whites whom current-day immigrants encounter are, in the main, descendants of Italian, Irish, and Jewish immigrants of years gone by. And many immigrants' immediate hosts are the children and grandchildren of African American and Puerto Rican internal migrants. A good number of today's second-generation New Yorkers operate in contexts where American generally means African American and Puerto Rican—and where native blacks and Puerto Ricans, as Philip Kasinitz, John Mollenkopf, and Mary Waters write, "are in the strange position of managing the ethnic succession of second-generation individuals in colleges, labor unions, and political groups while continuing to see themselves as outsiders to these power structures."[26]

Certainly, the presence of a huge African American and Puerto Rican population in New York City—about two million people in 2000—has played a role in how racial and ethnic identities are formed among today's immigrants and their children. Among other things, immigrants often seek to distance themselves from African Americans and Puerto Ricans as a way to avoid the stigma associated with these groups. Much has been written about West Indians' attempts to assert an ethnic identity— in terms of their country of origin or as West Indian—in order to make a case that they are culturally different from and superior to African Americans.[27] Mexican immigrants in New York emphasize that they are "not black" and "not Puerto Rican"; Dominican New Yorkers, it has been argued, often choose the Hispanic or Latino label as a form of racial identification to position themselves as non-black; and many Asian Indian immigrants, whose darker skin color puts them at risk of being confused with black Americans, stress their ethnic identity and distinctive history, customs, and culture as a way to avoid such mistakes.[28]

If immigrants often attempt to distinguish themselves from African Americans and Puerto Ricans, there are also many instances of cooperation, and, particularly in the case of black and Latino immigrants, identification with native minorities. Indeed, for many contemporary second-generation New Yorkers—to come back to critiques of the segmented assimilation model—becoming part of the Latino or black community can be beneficial in that it may provide entry points into mainstream institutions and access to institutions controlled and dominated by native minorities, such as unions, political groups, and community-based social services.

Thanks to the gains of the civil rights movement of the 1950s and 1960s, there is also a considerable African American middle class; incorporation into what has been called the African American middle-class minority culture of mobility provides resources for upward mobility for black immigrants and their children, including black professional and fraternal associations and organizations of black students in racially integrated high schools and universities.[29] Recent research in New York City high schools reveals a fascinating dimension to this dynamic: some academically successful Mexican youth identify and socialize with their black counterparts as a way to become incorporated into the black middle-class culture of mobility and facilitate their own upward path.[30]

A final point about the value of a then-to-now or becoming approach. The "now" is currently a forty-year period—dating from the 1965 Hart-Celler immigration reforms, which were so important in ushering in the "new" immigration—and therefore actually not so new anymore. (In fact, another distinguishing feature of the recent immigration to New York— compared to the immigration of Italians and Jews a hundred years ago— is that it continues to be replenished by new recruits; the Italian and Jewish immigration was reduced to a trickle after immigration restriction legislation in the 1920s, followed by the Great Depression and World War Two.) As time passes, one question concerns the way the immigration of the 1960s, 1970s, and 1980s has changed the context that the very latest arrivals find when they enter New York in the early twenty-first century— a context, by the way, in which the second and, indeed, the third generation of post-1965 immigrants is growing up and entering adulthood. And to come back to a "then-*and*-now" approach of a very different variety than I have discussed in this essay, comparisons of a 1970s and 1980s "then" with an early twenty-first century (one might say post-September 11) "now" can contribute to understanding the changing dynamics of the immigrant experience in recent times.

Thus, immigrants arrive in New York today to a city with a four-fold classification system—white/black/Hispanic/Asian—that is a product of the post-1965 influx and affects how they are seen and come to see themselves. Within each ethnoracial category there are also new divisions that have become important in the last thirty or forty years. When Dominicans began arriving en masse in the late 1960s and 1970s, for instance, Puerto Ricans were one of the city's two minority groups (the other was blacks) and, by far, the largest Latino group. By 2000, Puerto Ricans were only a little more than a third of the city's Hispanic population, down from 64 percent in 1970. Mexicans—one of the "new players" in the city's immigrant scene, whose census numbers quadrupled from 33,000 in 1990 to 123,000 in 2000—now take their place alongside Dominicans, Colombians, Ecuadorians, and other Latin Americans in a much more variegated Hispanic population. The Mexican case also illustrates how ethnic succession has taken new twists in the last decade as recently-arrived low-skilled Mexicans have become an important component of New York's low-wage work force, toiling in low-level and undesirable jobs, while members of many longer-established post-1965 immigrant groups have been moving slowly upward.

The enormous growth in New York City's immigrant population in the past three decades, from 1.4 million foreign-born in 1970 to 2.9 million in 2000, has given rise to dense ethnic neighborhoods—Dominican Washington Heights in Upper Manhattan, for example, and West Indian sections of central Brooklyn—which provide many of the newest arrivals with initial housing as well as established communities with familiar institutions and friends and relatives from the home country. Births to immigrant mothers, according to a recent report, have dramatically increased their share of all births so that children of immigrants are now likely to have considerably more contact with other children whose mothers have come from abroad than was the case thirty years ago, a situation that has far-reaching ramifications for the children's sense of identity and social relations. In Queens, for example, 28 percent of births in 1970 were to immigrant mothers compared to 68 percent in 2002; in Brooklyn, the percentage went from 21 in 1970 to 51 in 2002; in the Bronx, from 16 to 49.[31]

By now, many immigrant groups have gained a foothold in New York City politics, so that Dominicans, Jamaicans, and Chinese newcomers who get off the plane now often are represented by elected officials from their nationality group on the City Council. And all of the present-day arrivals enter a city that has created new programs and services in response to the post-1965 Caribbean, Latin American, and Asian influx, including special immigrant schools, language programs, and translating services in hospitals that were either not available, or less available, to those who came several decades ago. Obviously, there are many more ways that New York City has been transformed by the post-1965 immigration, and just how this altered context affects the latest arrivals and distinguishes their experiences from immigrants in the earlier 1970s and 1980s cohorts are topics that require further study.

## CONCLUSION

Clearly, bringing together past and present—and historical and social science research—is of enormous value in the study of the immigrant experience, yet, as I have shown, it makes a difference just how this is done. The argument here is that both a then-*and*-now comparative approach and a then-*to*-now becoming approach can, in different ways, enrich our understanding of how immigration transforms immigrants themselves as well as the places where they settle.

Thus, as we try to figure out what is new about the immigrant experience today, historian David Kennedy reminds us of the importance of looking back to the past with a *comparative* then-and-now lens: "The only way we can know with certainty," he writes, "as we move along time's path that we have come to a genuinely new place is to know something of where we have been."[32] At the same time, it is essential to appreciate, in a then-to-now *becoming* manner, the way successive waves of immigrants continually have reshaped New York and the country as a whole—or, as the economist Joseph Schumpeter once put it, how "every social situation is the heritage of preceding situations."[33] Combining the study of past and present in these two ways can, in short, provide new insights and new ways of thinking about immigration that, in the end, are fundamental to our understanding of immigration's impact in the past and in the present. Because large-scale immigration is likely to continue for a good while to come, these approaches may also provide clues as to what lies in store in the years ahead.

## NOTES

This article is a revised version of the keynote address delivered at the November 2003 conference on "Transcending Boundaries: Migration, Ethnicity and Incorporation in the Age of Globalism," sponsored by the Immigration and Ethnic History Society and New York University.

1.    Nancy Foner and George Fredrickson, eds., *Not Just Black and White: Historical and Contemporary Perspectives on Immigration, Race and Ethnicity in the United States* (New York, 2004).

2. Nancy Foner, *From Ellis Island to JFK: New York's Two Great Waves of Immigration* (New Haven, CT, 2000).
3. George Fredrickson, *The Comparative Imagination: On the History of Racism, Nationalism, and Social Movements* (Berkeley, CA, 1997), 65.
4. Nancy Green, "Comments on Transnationalism and Diaspora," paper presented at Workshop on Transnational Ties and Identities: Past and Present, Wassenar, Netherlands, November 2002.
5. Gary Gerstle and John Mollenkopf, "The Political Incorporation of Immigrants, Then and Now," in Gary Gerstle and John Mollenkopf, eds., *E Pluribus Unum? Contemporary and Historical Perspectives on Immigrant Incorporation* (New York, 2001), 3.
6. Fredrickson, *The Comparative Imagination*, 23.
7. Roger Waldinger, *Still the Promised City? African Americans and New Immigrants in Postindustrial New York* (Cambridge, MA, 1996).
8. See, for example, Foner, *From Ellis Island to JFK*; Ewa Morawska, "Immigrants, Transnationalism and Ethnicization: A Comparison of This Great Wave and the Last," in Gerstle and Mollenkopf, eds., *E Pluribus Unum?* 175–212.
9. See Foner, *From Ellis Island to JFK*.
10. Arun Peter Lobo and Joseph Salvo, *The Newest New Yorkers 2000* (New York, 2004).
11. See Nancy Foner, *In a New Land: A Comparative View of Immigration* (New York, 2005); and Foner, *From Ellis Island to JFK*.
12. See, for example, Elliot Barkan, "America in the Hand, Homeland in the Heart: Transnational and Translocal Immigrant Experiences in the American West," *Western Historical Quarterly* (Autumn 2004): 331–54; Madeline Hsu, *Dreaming of Gold, Dreaming of Home: Transnationalism and Migration Between the United States and South China, 1882–1943* (Stanford, CA, 2000).
13. Foner, *In a New Land*, chapter 3.
14. Alejandro Portes and Rubén Rumbaut, *Legacies: The Story of the Immigrant Second Generation* (Berkeley, CA, 2001); and "Conclusion—The Forging of a New America: Lessons for Theory and Policy, in Rubén Rumbaut and Alejandro Portes, eds., *Ethnicities* (Berkeley, CA, 2001), 301–17. Also see Alejandro Portes and Min Zhou, "The New Second Generation: Segmented Assimilation and Its Variants among Post-1965 Immigrant Youth," *The Annals of the American Academy of Political and Social Sciences*, vol. 530: 74–96.
15. Philip Kasinitz, John Mollenkopf, and Mary C. Waters, eds. *Becoming New Yorkers: Ethnographies of the New Second Generation* (New York, 2004), 396.
16. Joel Perlmann and Roger Waldinger, "Second Generation Decline? Children of Immigrants, Past and Present: A Reconsideration," *International Migration Review* (Winter 1997): 893–923.
17. For a recent attempt see Joel Perlmann, *Italians Then, Mexicans Now: Immigrant Origins and Second-Generation Progress, 1890–2000* (New York, 2005).
18. Thomas Guglielmo, *White on Arrival: Italians, Race, Color, and Power in Chicago, 1890–1945* (New York, 2003). See Foner, *In a New Land* for a discussion of this issue as well as forecasts about how racial boundaries may change in the future.
19. David Roediger and James Barrett. "Making New Immigrants 'Inbetween': Irish Hosts and White Panethnicity, 1890 to 1930," in Foner and Fredrickson, eds. *Not Just Black and White*.
20. Hasia Diner, *Lower East Side Memories: A Jewish Place in America* (Princeton, 2000).

21. Annelise Orleck, "The Soviet Jews: Life in Brighton Beach, Brooklyn," in Foner, ed., *New Immigrants in New York* (New York, 1987), 297–300. Quote from Sabrina Tavernise, "To Young, A Russian Enclave is Too Much the Old Country," *New York Times*, October 8, 2003.

22. Roediger and Barrett, "Making New Immigrants 'Inbetween,'" passim.

23. Matthew Pratt Guterl, *The Color of Race in America, 1900–1940* (Cambridge, MA, 2001).

24. Richard Alba and Victor Nee, *Remaking the American Mainstream* (Cambridge, MA, 2003).

25. Philip Kasinitz, "Race, Assimilation and 'Second Generations,' Past and Present," in Foner and Fredrickson, eds., *Not Just Black and White*, 281.

26. Philip Kasinitz, John Mollenkopf, and Mary C. Waters, "Becoming American/ Becoming New Yorkers: Immigrant Incorporation in a Majority Minority City." *International Migration Review* 36, no. 2 (Winter 2002): 1032.

27. See, for example, Foner, *In a New Land*; Milton Vickerman, *Crosscurrents: West Indian Immigrants and Race* (New York, 1999); and Mary Waters, *Black Identities: West Indian Immigrant Dreams and American Realities* (Cambridge, MA, 1999).

28. Robert C. Smith, "Mexicans: Social, Educational, Economic, and Political Problems and Prospects in New York," in Nancy Foner, ed. *New Immigrants in New York*, rev. ed. (New York, 2001), 286; Jose Itzigsohn and Carlos Dore-Cabral, "The Manifold Character of Panethnicity," in Agustin Lao-Montes and Arlene Davila, eds., *Mambo Montage: The Latinization of New York* (New York, 2001); Johanna Lessinger, *From the Ganges to the Hudson* (Boston, 1995); Margaret Abraham, *Speaking the Unspeakable:
Marital Violence among South Asian Immigrants in the United States* (New Brunswick, NJ, 2000).

29. See Foner, *In a New Land*.

30. Robert C. Smith, "Mexican New York," Presentation at Baruch College School of Public Affairs, New York, April 2004.

31. Steven A. Camarota, "Births to Immigrants in America, 1970 to 2002," *Backgrounder, Center for Immigration Studies* (Washington, DC, July 2005).

32. David Kennedy, "Can We Still Afford to Be a Nation of Immigrants?" *Atlantic Monthly* (1996), 68.

33. Joseph Schumpeter, *Imperialism and Social Classes* (New York, 1955), 111.

# 2

# Domestics of the World (Unite?): Labor Migration Systems and Personal Trajectories of Household Workers in Historical and Global Perspective

## CHRISTIANE HARZIG

WOMEN WHO MIGRATE to take up waged domestic labor[1] form the largest single female category of migrant labor, not only in the twentieth and twenty-first century but in fact throughout the history of migration. This is accounted for by economic restructuring processes (mainly agrarian and in the textile industry), by an uneven distribution of wealth between regions and nations, and by changes in the international division of labor. Different parts of the world are connected and related by various domestic workers' migration systems, however, their exact volume, trends and developments over time are almost impossible to determine.[2] Cynthia Enloe provides for a compelling cultural-political analysis to explain today's migration of women into domestic service, situating it appropriately at the juncture of international politics, its domestic political implications, and the historical role of women in society:

> International debt politics has helped create the incentives for many women to emigrate, while at the same time it has made governments dependent on the money those women send home to their families. The International Monetary Fund [which pressures] . . . indebted governments to adopt politics which will maximize a country's ability to repay its outstanding loans with interest, has insisted that governments cut their social service budgets. Reductions in food-price subsidies are high on the IMF's list of demands. . . . Keeping wages down, cutting back public works, reducing the numbers of government employees, rolling back health and education budgets—these are standard IMF prescriptions for indebted governments. . . .
> These politics have different implications for women and men in the indebted countries, because women and men usually have such dissimilar relationships to

family maintenance, waged employment, public services and public policy-making. If a government does decide to adopt the IMF package, feeding a family and maintaining its members' health will become more taxing. . . . Thus policy makers make their own calculations: they need the IMF loans to maintain international credibility; but if they swallow the IMF pill whole, they may not be around to benefit from that credibility. Crucial to this political calculation, though not acknowledged, is the absorption capacity of individual households: how much financial belt-tightening can each family tolerate. . . . This question depends on the skill and willingness of women—as wives and single mothers.[3]

Whether migration into domestic service is regarded as an exception to the male rule or whether it is acknowledged as a worldwide phenomenon depends very much on the perspective of one's analysis. Mainstream international migration studies still pay little theoretical attention to single female labor migrants. However, when migration is conceptionalized as a profoundly gendered process, the migrating domestic worker has become a major trope. Nevertheless, gendered data on migration flows are seldom obtained on a global and comparative basis;[4] migration into domestic service tends to be "invisible" to indifferent governments; and often it progresses illegally, clandestine, in short, undocumented.

By the same token, studies only slowly begin to grasp the profound impact women who migrate into domestic service have on societies, the one they leave behind as well as the one they enter. In the (Western) receiving societies, the presence of migrant or foreign domestic workers and the availability of their labor ignited a number of discussions addressing issues of political, social and cultural organization. Society's concern over reproductive labor (child and old people's care, domestic chores, emotional and educational support work); othering processes and the fixation of racial hierarchies; unity and diversity of feminist movements and demands; acknowledgment of value and skill of reproductive and domestic labor; and, last but not least, immigration policies are topics in the debate. Though the debate started over the presence of foreign domestic workers, it moved on to address core issues of social organization today.

The debate has its mirror issues in the sending countries. Women migrate into domestic service because they see the need and the opportunity to financially provide for the family. More often than not, they are in control over the decision to move and are supported by family members. The ability to go abroad and become family providers may raise their status in the family and affect their self-esteem. They perceive an increase in skill and experience. This, together with shifting domestic responsibilities, has an impact on gender roles and gender relations. Their absence as primary caregivers to their own children negatively affects their children's upbringing. However, it has been argued, in the long run it has a positive impact because of growing financial means invested into the children's education.[5] Providing for better education and the future of children was one of the most prominent motivating aspects for women who emigrated in the past and has remained to be so for women who migrate into domestic service. The volume of remittances sent home so profoundly influences national economies that states provide for easy venues of money transfer. State economies depend on it for their international currency balance.[6] So far, remittance monies are invested mainly into consumer goods and do little in support of long-term financial and economic security. Various policies suggest investments in an attempt to rectify the situation.

The paper will first outline the various migration systems created and maintained by domestic workers in their historical and contemporary dimension and then proceed to analyze the positionality and agency of the women within the varying discourses on servitude.

## MIGRATION SYSTEMS

Regional and local sociological, anthropological and historical studies provide us with a good understanding of what constitutes a migration system, how migration systems emerge, how they are maintained, and who participates in them.[7] A migration proceeds along a system when it involves a sizable number of persons and when it is sustained over a longer period. Emerging migration systems are as much determined by structural aspects as they are initiated and maintained by the activities of those who are involved. Dependencies of national economies, inequalities (i.e., U.S.Mexico, Germany-Poland), center-periphery relations, as well as historical ties stemming from colonialism, traditions of emigration and immigration, cultural affinities, and just plain proximity facilitate the growth of migration systems. However, in order for them to flourish, these structural factors have to be compounded by personal and discursive relationships. Moments of recognition and memory are a constitutional aspect of migration systems; they are maintained by people who travel within the system, by the discourse and information that travel along and serve to recruit new migrants into the scheme. Stories of success outnumbering stories of failure and personal contacts are as vital to the maintenance of a migration system as are state policies and recruitment agencies that facilitate movement. Migration systems may be very encompassing, such as relating South Asia to the Gulf states or North America; or they may be very specific in historical time and space, as with German girls migrating to the Netherlands in the 1920s, Polish women going to Chicago at the turn of the nineteenth century, or Slovene women migrating to Egypt.[8]

Roberta Espinoza, in *Global Woman*, has mapped four major migration "trends," as she calls them:[9]

1. South Asia to the Gulf
2. South Asia to Europe
3. Eastern Europe and Africa to Western Europe
4. Mexico and Central America to North America.

In order to understand how these trends function as migration systems, and to access the experience of women who "work" the system, the trends need to be differentiated and historicized. We will then gain a better understanding about how the trends emerge and how the systems are maintained.

The system of which we, at the moment, are most knowledgeable relates the various Asian labor exporting and important countries and the Gulf States. It is most likely the one that involves the largest number of people, though from a Northern hemispheric perspective it does not draw the most attention, nor is considered politically, socially and economically the most relevant. This system relates Bangladesh, Burma, Indonesia, the People's Republic of China, the Philippines, Sri Lanka, and Thailand as sending countries to Brunei, the Gulf States, Hong Kong, Malaysia, Pakistan, Singapore, and Canada as receiving countries.[10] Within the system, some countries (e.g., Pakistan) are at the same time sending and receiving countries. The most prominent aspect that distinguishes the sending and the receiving countries is the striking wealth disparities. It is estimated that in the 1980s, one million to 1.7 million women migrated as domestic workers in the system.[11]

A second system provides European households with domestic labor. Women may come from the former colonies to Britain and France, or from neighboring Central and East European countries to Germany (Poland) and Austria (Czech Republic, Slovakia). Most recently, Spain began to attract women from Latin America.[12] Italy and Greece also rely on women from Ethiopia and Somalia as well as from Albania, if they can make it across the border and across the Adriatic Sea.[13] Italy has been shown also to have relationships with the Philippines.[14] Internal European south-north migration also ensures labor market input. Women who seek out domestic service are either brought into the European Union by agencies; they may have come as asylum seekers or they negotiate tourist visas. Very often they have to be considered as "illegal" or "undocumented."[15]

A third system feeds into the North American labor market, also drawing from the Philippines but including Latin American countries and the Caribbean, such as the Dominican Republic, Jamaica, El Salvador, Guatemala and, most of all, the neighboring Mexico.

In Spanish America/Latin America, however, migration into domestic service is largely a self-contained system where most women move within their own country, though the richer countries attract migrant labor from the poorer countries on the continent. As in the past, women continue to move from the rural countryside and the periphery to urban areas. Culturally mediated push-pull factors keep the system in motion. In the 1970s and 1980s, around 20 percent of the female workforce in Latin America were employed as domestic workers.[16] In Bogotá in the 1980s, domestic workers made up 17.4 percent of the population and 98.2 of them were women. This figure only accounts for live-in workers.[17] In Buenos Aires the percentage dropped from 30.5 in 1947 to 20.6 in 1980; but in real numbers it expressed an increase from around 376,000 in the

1940s to 567,000 in the 1980s.[18] Despite predictions to the contrary, domestic work, often constructed as a pre-modern type of employment, was and is not on the decline in Latin America.

Similar to South America, in Africa migration into domestic service is historically and culturally grounded, often functioning on kinship networks (fostering) when children are sent from rural areas to a relative in the city in order to provide services and learn a trade.[19] It mainly involves internal migration, that is, migration within national or culturally constructed boundaries, from the rural periphery to urban centers. In southern Africa employment has been and still is closely linked with migration; in fact, because of the spatial division and separation of the "races" migration is a function of employment and vice versa. This was, and is, true as much for mineworkers, when temporary employment and rotation between the village and the mines was intentional, as it is in the case for domestic workers. In the late 1990s in South Africa, domestic work was considered the fifth largest source of formal employment.[20] Whether moving from rural areas to the city or living in the outskirts of urban centers, the lack of adequate transportation and long working hours force women into to live-in arrangements, or make living-in seem like the best option.

Colonial historical ties also generate domestic migration systems out of Africa to Europe, such as Ethiopians, Eritreans, and Somali to Italy, women from Senegal to France and from Nigeria and Ghana to Britain. Quebec, Canada, is also actively recruiting among French-speaking Africans for its immigration scheme. Some of those movements may have started out as refugee and asylum migration, but since many of the women awaiting their decision on refugee status in Europe and North America try to earn money by working as a domestic, the line between the two movements should not be marked too strongly.

## HISTORICAL CONTEXT AND DISCURSIVE CONSTRUCTION OF DOMESTIC SERVICE MIGRATION

In Germany, domestic service has always been closely related with mobility. From the mid-eighteenth century to the mid-twentieth century, Germany experienced out-migration on a large scale. Women made up 35–45 percent of the movement; when single they most likely migrated into domestic service. Their history may serve here as an example for the historical complexity of domestic service migration.

Mobility of domestic workers is not a modern day phenomenon, as Wierling shows in her historical study on domestics in Germany. She points out that domestic service was the most mobile occupational category at the turn from the nineteenth to the twentieth century. Mobility was characterized by a migration from the countryside to nearby towns, by moves to urban centers, and by changes in positions. "The mobility of servant maids did not so much depend on economic cycles as did the mobility of other workers, and thus it did not vary so much. For them, every change of jobs also implicated a change of abode. However, changes were frequent. In 1895 in Berlin, 61,063 servants were accounted for; during the same year, there were 82,948 changes of jobs." These moves so characterized the profession that domestics were branded by contemporary observers as "gypsies of the nation."[21]

From the women's point of view, these moves were motivated by the desire to find better, more suitable positions, to escape loneliness and isolation, to seek the more anonymous environment of the urban landscape, or to connect with friends or relatives. Conversely, the decision to remain came from the desire to grow roots and to maintain contacts, for example, with a fiancé. Every move expressed the hope to find better wages, better food and nourishment, shorter work hours, and a less heavy workload. Less tangible motives included ill-humored work relationships with colleagues, harassment from employers, tyranny from the children, and disrespectful treatment. All of these reasons are equally relevant today.

Though for many single young women work in domestic service was the most obvious option to independently pursuing a livelihood, despite its involving migration, for others migration was the end and domestic service the means.[22] Since knowing how to maintain a household and perform reproductive work was the most marketable skill for women on an international gender-segregated labor market even in the nineteenth century, every young woman in Europe most likely "knew" that if she were willing to take up domestic employment she could find work almost everywhere. Therefore, for women service and long-distance migration became as closely linked as service, marriage, and short-distance migration. Regional studies have shown that among those single women who registered for legal emigration from nineteenth-century Germany and who gave an occupation, 80 percent named domestic service or maid, other occupations being seamstress, day laborer, spinner, and midwife.[23] These studies also demonstrated that having previous experience as a servant maid made emigration as a single woman a viable option.[24]

Domestics were part of all the various migrations from Germany. According to U.S. statistics, between 1875 and 1880 six hundred German servants immigrated per year; from 1880 to 1885, the annual figure rose to 2644, then increased to 3344 by 1890 and to 4189 by 1895; after the turn of the century the number declined, and between 1900 and 1912 a total of 30,602 servants arrived in the United States. Domestic servants made up almost one-tenth of all German emigrants between 1899 and 1910.[25] In the U.S. labor market, domestics constituted the majority of all gainfully employed German immigrant women. Their placement in the labor market was aided by being stereotyped positively as laborious, clean, and unassuming; being Protestant and having a (professional) reputation for child care[26] were additional advantages.

In the 1920s migration systems for domestics expanded to include cross-border migrations. Germany after World War One experienced unprecedented hardships marked by unemployment, inflation, food shortage and subsequent

hunger. When seeking employment across the border in the Netherlands, perceived then as the land of milk and honey, women could follow long established
migration systems of agricultural workers, miners, and construction crews. In addition, families of German industrialists and businessmen who successfully had
established themselves in the Netherlands were responding to what was labeled
as a severe "servant crisis" in the 1920s by seeking out women from Germany
to work in their households. Thus, the push factor of economic desperation and
the pull factor of adequate nourishment and an understaffed labor market in the
1920s and 1930s drew around twenty-four thousand German women across the
border. According to official statistics in 1920, around 9,100 foreign women
worked in the Netherlands, in 1930 the number had grown to 30,500. Twenty-
four thousand were from Germany.[27] Fluctuation in the profession was as great
as in Germany. The number of servants who passed across the border from 1920
to 1924 is estimated between one hundred and three hundred. Soon a network of
peers and relatives together with women's groups and state employment agencies provided employees for the Dutch middle-class households. Even though
the migration was considered by German contemporary officials as temporary
or voluntary migration, the women who left a society marked by a skewed sex
ratio, due to the great losses of men during the war, often either stayed in the
Netherlands and married or considered further migration overseas. In the cities,
English courses were offered. "On average three years passed before the servant
maids either returned to Germany, continued migration to another country or
gave up their German citizenship as well as their employment as a domestic
by marrying a Dutch man."[28]

A very little studied migration network related the German countryside to
Paris, as has been shown by Mareike König. Throughout the second half of the
nineteenth century young women from Germany made up the largest group
of foreign domestics seeking employment in the French metropolis. In 1901,
they made up 43 percent.[29] Liberation, to live a self-determined life at least for
a couple of years, excitement and adventure, and the desire to learn the language and better their chances on the marriage market were push factors in this
movement. Higher wages, a high market value, their good reputation among the
French bourgeoisie, and the lure of nice clothes were the matching pull factors.
Those who came with knowledge and connections, possibly a position, had a
better head start for a working life in Paris; those who took their chances often
had to spend weeks and months to find appropriate employment. Though no
passports or immigration restrictions limited their movement, finding a job,
nevertheless, depended on the right papers, most importantly references, ide-
ally from French families. Lack of language, references, and experience were
detrimental in the subsequent job search. Once positioned successfully, long
working hours, lack of contact with French peers or families, and isolation
marked their working experience. A system of very controlling German church
affiliated charity services, Catholic and Protestant, tried to help the women in

difficult times, mainly when being ill, unemployed, and homeless.[30] This migration system ended with the beginning of World War One.

Transporting or encouraging working-class women to immigrate to the "colonies" to work as domestics, with the civilizing mission to tame men's rugged pioneering behavior and to become mothers of the nation, has been a prominent theme in British and Canadian history.[31] For the German colonies, a slightly different story evolves. German women participated in the imperial colonial project (1880 to 1914) in so far as they supported nursing associations training to work in the colonies and established schools to educate middle-class and professional women to work and to function productively in the colonies (Southwest and East Africa). Their efforts served the dual purpose of solving the German "woman's question," that is, providing educated middle-class women with means to support themselves in a class-acceptable fashion and at the same time function as preservers and maintainers of the superior status of the white, and more specifically *German* race. Only minimal efforts were made to bring working-class women to the German colonies. "In 1898 the [German Colonial Society] sponsored twelve domestic servants. By 1907 it had given free passage to 111 unmarried German women." Much as Hansen has described for Zambia, German colonists took recourse to African male servants to do their reproductive and dirty work.[32]

## DISCURSIVE CONSTRUCTION OF SERVITUDE

Migration systems are not only accounted for by the structural movement of "bodies" but also by discourses on servitude and the role of women in society. This is as much the case for trans-border systems as it is for internal ones. These discourses are historically grounded and specific to the respective societies.

Domestic service in the United States and Canada has predominantly been a function of migration and otherness. Both being white settler societies, the "institution" shows a number of similarities there. However, due to different historical trajectories and immigration policies, form, content, and discourse of domestic service also differ. In the United States, indentured servitude, immigration, slavery, racial hierarchies and segregation, illegal cross-border migration, and green-card policies signify the historically changing social and political relations in domestic service.

Canada's domestic service is marked by *engagé(e)s* from France; by single women recruited from Britain to civilize pioneer society and, as mothers of the nation, to secure the white future of the dominion; by immigrant women recruited from northern and western European countries; and by forty years of live-in-care-giver programs, i.e., immigration policies bringing in women mainly from the Caribbean and Philippines to enable dual career families and to cover for an inadequate state-supported child-care program.[33]

In Spanish America, as Kusnesof's historical account points out,[34] domestic service is as much a function of the colonial lifestyle as it is of rural-to-urban migration. The ideologies prescribing the patriarchal household as the central unit of control and referring women to the tutelage of men evolved in the colonial period with implications way into the twentieth century. These ideologies had an impact on women's ability to work and made domestic service appear as the ideal type of employment for poor single women. It provided adequate protection under the supervision of the male head of household and offered education and preparation for married life. The colonial household of the sixteenth to the nineteenth century being a major site of production[35] and the low level of technology and urban services in the colonial setting accounted for the employment of large number of servants. In the metropolitan areas (Buenos Aires, Mexico City, Caracas), one out of five households employed one or more domestic servants.[36]

Despite its ubiquitous presence, or maybe because of it, the relationship expressed in domestic service was marked by processes of "othering" as much as by paternalism. While in the seventeenth century Spanish immigrant women came as indentured servants, indigenous women also were engaged, being kept under quasi-slavery conditions; later blacks and ex-slaves entered the households and migrants from the rural periphery were always available. An original paternalistic relationship fostered by kinship relations changed over time when working-class and "other" women began to dominate the profession, and domestic service became associated with "the lower end of the class/caste/color system that so dominated Spanish American society [and] caused a gradual alienation between employers and servants, as well as a loss of status for the occupation of service."[37]

In the twentieth century, domestic service at first appeared to decline due to improved household technology and urban services and better wages and employment opportunities for men. However, growing white-collar employment opportunities for women after World War Two again created a growing demand for domestic workers, while declining prospects in agriculture ensured a continuing supply of migrant women seeking employment in the cities. Since female unskilled industrial employment also declined, domestic work has remained a viable option.[38]

In Latin America, as elsewhere, economic as well as socio-cultural reasons account for the mobility of domestic workers. On the one hand, agrarian restructuring processes induce out-migration or, put differently, push women out of the countryside. Changes in landholding policies regularly exclude women from land tenure, as has been shown by Pappas-Deluca for Chile.[39] Restricted access to land is considered one of the most important forces inducing women to leave for the city.[40] Other factors include reduced employment rates of men, which force women to take up gainful employment and a reduction of employment opportunities for women in the countryside. In the prevailing discourse on the migration of domestic workers, these economic aspects are compounded with ideological-cultural aspects, drawing on concepts of modernization, emancipation, and self-fulfillment in addition to women's traditional role under patriarchy. Chilean women always have made use of rural-to-urban migration to overcome limitations and constraints. Women are also pulled to the cities by the confidence that they will be able to find employment as domestic workers and that they will be able to gain economic and social independence from parents, escape boredom at the periphery and find peers to socialize with. The move into domestic service may be regarded as liberating, albeit in a culturally sanctioned context.[41] At times, domestic work even enables women to negotiate and/or escape marital status and to manage single motherhood. According to Radcliffe, women in Ecuador also experience migration into domestic service as a process of becoming "white," i.e., to take up a more urban, "white" identity.[42] In rural Andean townships, she points out, "whiteness is not phenotypical, but rather constituted through a combination of dress codes, possessions of cash and Spanish-language use."[43]

In *southern Africa* migration into urban areas and into domestic service is also closely related to the restructuring of the agrarian economy and landholding patterns. With men leaving rural areas, either in pursuit of employment or with the intention of deserting their families (often both go hand in hand), women are left with the necessity to care for their children alone and no means of waged employment available. Migration into urban areas to seek employment as domestic worker often is the only option. At the same time as rural restructuring processes supply the urban labor market with women willing to work as domestics, the entry of educated, middle-class women into wage-earning employment has increased the demand for household services.

During the apartheid regime, the relationship between white employer woman and black servant woman was signified by the trope of "maids and madams" as captured in a film by the same title by writer/director Mira Hameresh.[44] While in the first part white women are interviewed addressing their role as employers, the second part picks up the concerns of black women and their double fight against racism in the white community and sexism in their own community. It also discusses (feminist) women's awareness, rather than activism, in dealing with the unequal power relations. In the post-apartheid regime, the relationship is satirized in the cartoon "Madam and Eve," where the power relationship of maid/madam is cunningly turned around. Today, the cartoon is used to inform household workers about their rights.[45]

Due to a degree of economic upswing, though manifested unevenly, in postcolonial southern African society the potential employer class has grown and diversified. Since governments often consider domestic service as a marginal and invisible occupation, wages are unregulated and employers may set wages and working conditions at will.[46] Working conditions depend on race and type of household: working for a male-headed household the domestic worker may be confronted with sexual harassment, while in a female-headed household she may be treated either "like one of the children" or as a companion. In white, usually expatriate, households wages tend to be better and a degree of privacy is made possible by being relegated to sleep in the servant quarters;[47] working in a black household the domestic worker often is treated as "one of the family" which usually is a euphemism for more informal and invisible exploitation.[48]

Women who seek out domestic work in southern Africa (research is available for South Africa, Swaziland; in Zambia male servants dominated in the immediate post-colonial era) operate according to a number of rationales:

- Domestic service provides accommodation and food and thus it enables them to save on food and rent.
- Living with the employer family also provides a degree of safety and security, as opposed to living in "informal housing" or squatter homes on the urban periphery.[49]
- The women hope that they can provide their children with an education and eventually break the cycle of poverty.
- For themselves they may consider domestic service as a "waiting zone" until better employment opportunities open up or until they are able to buy a sewing machine to establish themselves in business; in Ghana parallel career moves into street vending are most likely.[50]

In the absence of formal employment agencies, which may actually be a blessing since they often skim off women's wages, employment is found through women's networks of referrals. "Unless women knew somebody in the city, who knew somebody else who needed a domestic worker, it was difficult to get a job."[51]

Networks of friends also constitute coping strategies. Based on the understanding that domestic work is done to support and educate the children they help to maintain a sense of dignity. "For the sake of the children, domestic workers have devised coping strategies that compensate, to some extent, for the Government's failure to ensure adequate sustainable development in Swaziland."[52] Working as domestic servant also generates conflicting feelings. Being employed away from home and leaving children without adequate care creates stress and anxiety; being able to earn income and support the family, despite men's neglect, brings about the joy of independence.[53] In southern Africa, domestic service is situated at the crossroads of conflicting sensations and trajectories: of escaping rural depression and embracing the prospects of urban opportunities, or of experiencing oppression and poverty and feeling competent and hopeful for a better future for the children.

In Britain, the homeland of the prototypical, classical, servant, the profession has undergone fundamental changes in the post-World War Two era not so much with regard to the labor performed, but with regard to the social profile of the employer and the way the work is organized. Being once an intricate and constitutive part of the Victorian and Edwardian upper- and middle-class household and one of the most important occupational categories in Britain, it declined in the 1950s. The number of women doing domestic work rose again in the 1980s, now mainly servicing the middle class, typically the two-career household with small children; and two types of services predominate: nannying and cleaning. As a study conducted in the 1980s shows: "30 to 40 per cent of dual career households in contemporary Britain employ a nanny; and three-quarters of those dual career households employing waged domestic labor employ a cleaner. Moreover, as our findings show, a minority of dual-career households (less than 15 percent) employ more than one waged domestic (typically a cleaner and a nanny). Waged domestic labor therefore is revealed to be a vital facet of daily social reproduction amongst the middle classes of contemporary Britain (that is, domestics contributing to the family's emotional and social maintenance).[54] Aside from living-in and living-out domestic workers, much of the services are provided by business/cleaning services, an industry largely expanding in the 1980s.

Australia, once very closely linked, culturally and socially, to Britain, seems to be situated outside the most prevalent contemporary household workers' migration systems. Unlike Canada, it does not have caregiver recruitment policies; and its restrictive immigration policy only targets what is traditionally perceived as the high-skill sector. Little is known about illegal migration to Australia. However, like Canada, it relied on immigrant women from Britain to perform the necessary "civilizing tasks" in a pioneer society. Thanks to Higman we have a fairly good understanding about the position of domestic service in Australian history.[55] While being absent as an occupation before the arrival of European settlers in 1788, it quickly rose to its peak in 1860. During the "pastoral age" of the 1820s and 1830s, which saw large-scale free migration and the amassing of great wealth by squatters/settlers, domestic servants were not only useful to perform the necessary labor but also helped to provide the proper status in the creation of an emerging Australian gentry. After 1860 domestic service steadily declined in relation to other occupational categories for women till it almost faded away in the 1970s. In the following years "it experienced revival but remained at low level."[56]

Three major moments in the history of Australia help to categorize the women (and sometimes men) who found employment in domestic service. In the formative years most of the convict women sent between 1790s and 1840s were assigned to work in private households. Putting women to productive use and assuming some correctional impact of household work were the operative ideologies of the time. This concept of correctional domesticity also stood behind the idea of assimilating aboriginal people by putting children into household apprenticeships. "Thus Aboriginal children removed from their communities, orphans, wards of the state and inmates of industrial schools were all coerced to perform domestic labor long after the broader exploitation of child labor had been limited by the introduction of compulsory schooling in the 1880s."[57] Orphanages in Ireland also were tapped to provide female laborers for the burgeoning middle class. But by far the largest group of women came through the assisted passage programs, which brought single women from the British Isles to the colony. New South Wales even advertised as "A Land of Opportunity for Domestic Servants."[58] During the 1940s and 1950s, when migrants from Britain ceased to move to the colonies, refugee women used short-term employment in domestic service as a starting point for a new life in Australia.

## WHAT'S IN IT FOR THE WOMEN?

[R]esearch often fails to contextualise the personal perspectives of research subjects. Only by incorporating these perspectives in our research may we observe the ways in which migrating for work in the household labour sector gives women an opportunity to challenge societal constraints on their mobility and (. . .) to "continue moving forward."[59]

Hardly any other theme in migration studies depends in its analysis so much on the position taken by the respective researcher. Women can be seen either as being moved around in a structurally imposing system, as victims of exploitation and inequalities, or as subjects with agency. All three approaches have their validity and advantages: while a structural approach seeks necessary information such as volume and social composition, a victims approach may lead to efforts to improve working and living conditions and legal status. Looking at the women's agency provides us with an understanding of the meaning they attach to the migration experience and the way in which they negotiate constraints and opportunities that characterize their mobility.

A structural-functionalist approach emphasizes the restructuring processes in agriculture and industry, most notably the limited access to land and the decline of textile production as locally based cottage industry, which pushes women into waged domestic labor. It points to the impact on national economies by listing the positive but limited effect of remittances and the negative aspects of brain drain[60] and the unbalanced development of consumer culture and materialism.[61] It also engages in a discussion on whether migration into domestic service can be seen as a modernizing impulse for women from rural and peripheral areas or whether domestic service itself is a pre-modern, feudal type of employment which should have no place in an enlightened, democratic society based on equality.

The question remains: Can migration into domestic service actually have an emancipatory effect on women? In the past as in the present, working in service is, more than any other employment for women, shaped by female dominated contexts. With few exceptions—the British butler, the Chinese laundry man and the colonial male servant—domestic work is woman's work and the principal employer of domestic work is the woman in a household. To take up domestic work or to migrate into domestic service is a decision over which the woman has a large amount of control. She can assume some familiarity with the work she is expected to do (this is not to argue that domestic work is unskilled labor, which, in fact, it is not) and generally there is little or no patriarchical or traditionally informed opposition against such form of female labor and waged employment. In addition, she can assume that jobs are readily available.

The different migration systems are generated and maintained by various push and pull factors, i.e., different incentives and motives to take up this type of employment; and the various systems have different demographic profiles. Internal, short-distance, rural-to-urban migration into domestic service, as is common in Africa and Latin America, attracts younger women and sometimes even children.[62] Younger women and children also are drawn into traditional, kinship-related apprentice or fostering systems, when well-to-do urbanized households take in poorer relatives or families to whom they feel an obligation.[63] International domestic migrants tend to be older, often married or single mothers with families of their own who frequently are the sole provider of their household.[64] The notable exception is southern Africa, where periphery-to-center migration for domestics predominates and where the domestics also tend to be married women with children.

Though all women who migrate into domestic service seek employment and higher wages, they do not necessarily come from the poorest strata of society and they usually have an above average education. This is particularly true for women from the Philippines[65] and Sri Lanka, but can also be shown for women who migrate from the periphery to urban centers. Cultural and social resources in the form of education, knowledge how the migration system functions, financial means to pay the recruitment agency, and family or household support, emotional and material, particularly in taking care of the children while abroad, are necessary when embarking on the "domestic journey."[66] "The process of migration favours those who can afford to go and not necessarily those who need to go."[67]

Women who migrate into domestic service are motivated by various sets of reasons and circumstances. In Latin America, where domestic service is part of the culturally and historically manifested class structure and a function of the rural-urban, center-periphery relationship, young women may experience migration to town to find employment as a domestic as a rite of passage and liberation. They may leave their hometown to escape patriarchal constraints and parental control. The entrenched cultural tradition of domestic service prevents gross stigmatizations and allows women to consider domestic service as a valid option on a trajectory towards an urban life style and into "whiteness." Well-established and culturally secure employer-employee relationships within fixed and rather stable class boundaries provide room for negotiations over control, freedom, and workloads. Public urban spaces allow for social encounters with peers, they as much defy stigmatization as they break through the isolation of the household. Domestic service, beyond stigmatization, also presents better opportunities for cooperation. In the 1960s and 1970s, union-type organizations generated enough impact to influence wages and working conditions. Institutionalized gathering space was provided for by the Catholic Church. Though the Church generally advocated employer-friendly policies, it at least provided shelter and support in times of personal needs.

A second set of reasons relates to the need of support for the family and the maintenance and security of a middle-class life style. In well-established migration systems, such as Filipinas to Hong Kong and North America and Sri Lankan and Indonesian women to the Middle East, it is the firm knowledge about better earning opportunities abroad that motivates out-migration. Being able to provide more consumer goods, to finance the construction of a house for parents and siblings, and to pay for the children's higher education are reasons that induce Filipinas to give up their skilled, low white-collar employment as clerks or teachers to seek employment in domestic service in Hong Kong or Canada. This also can be argued for Muslim women migrating to the Middle East. To prevent the family from slipping into poverty[68] by taking up employment, on the one hand, motivates women to venture onto that route and, on the other hand, provides for the cultural-religious justification to move beyond the traditional confines of female Muslim space. For a female member to migrate into waged domestic labor may be acceptable to the household only because it implies a transcultural move outside the confines of the home culture.[69]

While international migration may be motivated by the desire to achieve or maintain an economically more secure or even prosperous family and household existence, short-distance periphery-to-center migration in southern Africa often is initiated out of the very necessity of survival. However, even here the future-oriented goal of providing an education for the children is a powerfully motivating factor.[70]

However, whatever set of reasoning may predominate, the women inevitably will experience a sense of being in control, taking up responsibilities for the household. They even may seek the initiative to bring upward economic mobility to themselves and their families. Even when succumbing to family pressures, they realize that the family depends on them and that their earnings secure the future of the household and the next generation. This empowering perception also may aid in the decision to return into domestic service and re-enter situations, which are often experienced as oppressive, exploitive, and abusive.[71]

What happens next? How many and who returns and what happens to those who decide not to return but to settle? From history we know that women had a much lower return rate (from the United States) than men;[72] for the post-World War Two period we need more research to attempt to answer these questions. Much of it depends on the respective migration system and, of course, on the women's own trajectories. Legal migration to Hong Kong and to the Middle East is based on temporary contracts, where women are expected to return or have their contracts extended, though not indefinitely. Immigration, as a rule, is not an option, though some women are able to move beyond domestic work to establish businesses providing services for their former fellow workers (selling telephone cards or home food, running travel agencies and remittance services). Many return with a sense of having earned enough money to buy property or build a house, nourishing a perception of security for self, family, and parents.

Since Canada's live-in-caregiver program is the only program of its kind providing legal, landed immigrant status after two years, becoming a regular immigrant and then re-uniting the family through sponsoring is a very strong trajectory in this system. In the United States, whether women are able to bring in family members and to pursue further employment options depends to a great extent on immigration status (legal or illegal), on language skills, and on support networks. Often they are able to move into the ever-expanding (and somewhat more regulated) care industry: old-age care, home nursing, or hospital employment. Spending their working years in the receiving society with the idea of returning home upon retirement is a thought nurtured by transnational migrants since late nineteenth century.

## OTHERNESS AS CULTURAL RESOURCE

Within the trade in domestic workers, foreignness or otherness is one of the most substantial and tangible forms of socio-cultural capital. This may seem a strange assertion in light of the fact that foreignness is also the major reason for extreme exploitation. Most obviously in the case of nannies and au pairs, women are hired precisely because they carry a different cultural baggage. The au pair's desire to learn the language and experience the life-style of the receiving culture meets the interest of the employer's household to profit from either the foreign/British professional training of the nanny or the language skills of the au pair. These matching interests lie at the core of this particular hiring choice. As in the case of foreign domestic workers, their cultural otherness may not be recognized as an asset to household care and child rearing (though it could and should), but it is their foreignness which leads to their employment in the first place. Foreign women are available, as opposed to native, indigenous, domestic women who are not available, at least not for the price the employer household believes it can afford. Their otherness, while it enhances the opportunities for extreme exploitation, also hides the unequal power relationship and hierarchy because it takes place outside the system of classed social reality of which the employer household is a part. The foreign worker's need for wages, shelter (security and protection), and aid in negotiating the new cultural experience coincides with the employer household's need for inexpensive, live-in, around-the-clock service.[73]

By the same reasoning, the domestic worker may situate herself outside the very same culture with its specific hierarchical power relationships, which inevitably places her at the bottom. She may take comfort in the knowledge about her own social position at home and her being essential to the family's survival. She may also have a strong sense about her own culture's superior food habits and child rearing practices.[74]

The race-class-gender systems of "importing" cultures (North America, Europe, the Middle East) provide for ready access to stereotypes in order to structure and organize historical "knowledge" and present "experience." Cultural markers are attached to the women as they relate to their performance as domestic workers. While British women seem to be forever connected to the "nanny" image,[75] historically Dutch, Scandinavian, and German women were considered clean, honest, and competent, as opposed to Irish women, who were viewed as sleazy and Catholic, or Finnish women, who were considered clean but also unruly.[76] This is the North-American frame of reference.

This stereotyping hardly has changed in today's hiring system. Women from the Caribbean are considered uppity and lazy. Jamaican women in particular are seen as aggressive, but they have the advantage of the English language. Filipinas are seen as good housekeepers, competent, and sociable; and women from Latin America have a "natural," caring, and friendly way with children. Employment agencies make use of this system of stereotypes to cater to the needs of the market and to target their clientele. Providing special profiles arguably makes better "matches."[77] Women seeking employment, conversely, may use the stereotyping to enhance their value on the labor market.

Cultural-religious preferences clearly work in favor of Muslim women migrating to the Middle East. Malaysian women from Sri Lanka may use their cultural capital of being Muslim in a number of ways. They find it easier to secure employment; they receive travel benefits from the local recruiters and have to pay only nominal recruitment fees; once employed they may use their ability to participate in religious practices to renegotiate their position in the household. "These maids, then, make use of their identity as Muslims and, when it suits them, as foreigners, to gain greater psychological and physical access and mobility in a new society."[78]

Can migration into domestic service thus be seen not only as a mechanism to overcome economic/financial difficulties of the household but also as a means to surpass personal/individual limitations and constraints? How one answers this question actually depends very much on how domestic service is situated in the traditional discourse on women's role in society and culture and, maybe even more so, on the position and opinion of the researcher and writer. If migration into domestic service is seen as an essential move to guarantee the family's survival or to enhance its well-being, it inevitably will have an empowering effect on women. Being away from direct patriarchal and parental control, controlling her own money, allocating savings likely will enhance self-esteem. Having a public space in which to socialize, stepping out of the isolation and invisibility of the private household workplace, helps to take the stigma and degrading effects out of being foreign and a domestic worker. The same is true for organizational efforts in support of better wages and working conditions. Since lack of recognition, appreciation, and respect are some of the main complaints of women working in domestic service, anything that supports domestic workers in their recognition as skilled laborers and important service providers will support the emancipatory effect of the migration experience.

In order to appreciate this development one has to look into the extent to which returning women act as agents of change in their home cultures. This change would be at the same time particularly subtle and effective because it would start in the most immediate context of the family and the household and then have an effect upon power negotiations and personal relationships.

The women operate within a spectrum of options, which, even when encountering exploitative conditions, exhibit agency. Migration into domestic service usually is only a condition in pursuit of other life goals and personal trajectories. However, it is a means readily available towards reaching these goals and a method that the women are able to control. Thus I argue that, yes, migration into domestic service may have an emancipatory effect upon women.

## CONCLUSION

The experience of domestic workers . . . serve[s] to underscore how simplistic the First World/Third World split is, and how inadequate it is to make sense of today's international politics. Literally hundreds of thousands of women from Third World countries are cleaning the homes and minding the children of *other*, more affluent Third World women. In China today the government and the Communist Party's own Women's Federation are officially encouraging urban households to hire maids as a way of reducing the housework responsibilities of other women. As in Britain and the United States, maids are being seen as the solution to the career woman's "double burden." In Latin America, "domestic worker" is the single largest job category for women. Most of the women are working for other women. Most of those women working in the Gulf States and Filipino women in Singapore and Hong Kong are employed in what we still refer to as "'Third World" societies.[79]

This is Cynthia Enloe's analysis of the global impact of domestic workers' migration. And we may pick up from there. The existence of domestic workers, their migration systems, their participation in the world economy, their life trajectories and their work patterns question a number of assumptions and point toward a number of pressing issues. Not unlike the male workers in the past, whose internationalism was evoked by socialist and communist movements, domestic workers have not been able to build up large, encompassing unions or organizations speaking out in their interests. However, they have found ways to insert themselves into a process of awareness and claim human rights through non-governmental organizations (NGOs) and feminist-inspired interest groups. When seeking information about the live-in-caregiver programs listed on a Canadian government website, potential migrants are informed about self-help and interest groups acting on their behalf in Canada. This is clearly the result of feminist activism in conjunction with those concerned.

Looking into domestic service migration, it can be seen that the unattached, single, male *homo migrans* does not adequately reflect the universal experience of migration. Migration is a profoundly gendered process, and experience and should be analyzed as such. In the past as in the present, migration into domestic service has been an opportunity available to (single) women, and women continue to make ample use of it. Though their migration systems are very much structured by economic constraints and financial incentives, the women insert their agency into the system and thus maintain it, alter it, and make it work for them. Their entrepreneurship also affects the existing systems by altering the migration direction and expanding, increasing, or limiting the migration flow. Their activities affect governments, state economies and social discourses. Through their individual moves the global comes close to home and their presence creates transcultural spaces in the receiving household. Through remittances and packages sent home, their absence inserts the global into the sending household, making televised images of the world somewhat more real. On both ends of the trajectory, they will have a much more profound impact on civil society than we are ready to recognize.

## NOTES

1. A note on terminology: the most commonly used term to refer to today's women is domestic workers, household workers, or, as in the British context, women doing waged domestic labor, this most likely being the most precise term. In historical context, "domestic servants" most adequately indicates the occupation and the person. I will use "domestic servants" in historical context and "domestic workers" in present-day context. When referring to the institution, "domestic service" is used.
2. Noeleen Heyzer and Vivienne Wee, "Domestic Workers in Transient Overseas Employment: Who Benefits, Who Profits," in *The Trade in Domestic Workers*, ed. Noeleen Heyzer, et al. (London, 1994), 31–102. The authors point out (39) that "[m]any official statistics under-report the actual numbers of workers involved [in the 'maid trade'] especially for illegal migrants."
3. Cynthia Enloe, *Bananas, Beaches and Bases: Making Feminist Sense of International Politics* (Berkeley, CA, 1989), 184.
4. The statistics which exist are often inconsistent and not up to date, the efforts of some international research institutions and economic think tanks not withstanding. The OECD (2004) in its latest report makes a strong effort to produce comparable statistics on migration trends but has very little to say on female migration, let alone on the migration of household workers. This, however, is mainly due to the deficiency of national statistics and reports. See also Migration Policy Institute (mpi) data.
5. Sri Harijati Hatmachji, "Gender Dimension of International Migration: the Indonesian Case," Economic and social commission for Asia and the Pacific, Ad Hoc expert group meeting on migration and development, Bangkog, August 2003.
6. Eight percent (6.3 mio in 2001) of the Philippine's Gross Domestic Product comes from remittances. Information is based on IMF Statistics. Stalker's Guide to International Migration, http://pstalker.com/migration/mg_5.htm.
7. Jan Lucassen and Leo Lucassen, eds., *Migration, Migration History, History: Old Paradigms and New Perspectives* (Bern, 1997); and James Jackson, Jr., and Leslie

P. Moch, "Migration and Social History in Modern Europe," in *European Migrants: Global and Local Perspectives*, ed. Dirk Hoerder and Leslie Page Moch (Boston, 1996), 52–69.

8. Barbara Henkes, *Heimat in Holland: Deutsche Dienstmädchen 1920–1950*. (Niedesthein, 1989); Maria Anna Knothe, "Land and Loyalties: Contours of Polish Women's Lives," in *Peasant Maids—City Women: From the European Country Side to Urban America*, ed. Christiane Harzig (Ithaca, NY, 1997), 143–82; Marilyn Barber, *Immigrant Domestic Servants in Canada: Canada's Ethnic Groups* (Ottawa, 1991); and Ana Barbicˇ and Inga Miklavcˇicˇ-Brezigar, "Domestic Work Abroad: a Necessity and an Opportunity for Rural Women from the Gorisˇka Borderland Region of Slovenia," in Janet Henshall Momsen, *Gender, Migration* (London, 1999), 164–77.

9. For a graphic visualization of the various migration systems, see Barbara Ehrenreich and Arlie Russell Hochschild, eds., *Global Woman. Nannies, Maids, and Sex Workers in the New Economy* (New York, 2002), 276–79.

10. Canada is included in this list because it "imports" a large number of women from the Philippines. See also Heyzer and Wee, *Trade in Domestic Workers*, 36.

11. Ibid., 40. The following figures are given:

| Sending countries | Lowest estimates | Highest estimates |
| --- | --- | --- |
| Bangladesh | 2,000 | 15,000 |
| Indonesia | 100,000 | 240,000 |
| Philippines | 275,567 | 275,569 |
| Sri Lanka | 100,000 | 175,000 |
| **Total** | **477567** | **(mistake in the book) 705,584** |

| Receiving countries | | |
| --- | --- | --- |
| Bahrain | 40,383 | |
| Oman | 1,345 | |
| Kuwait | 28,833 | |
| Saudi Arabia | 750,000 | |
| Hong Kong | 65,924 | |
| Malaysia | 27,912 | |
| Filipina Workers | (8,000) | 10,000 |
| Indonesians | (19,912) | |
| Singapore | 65,000 | |
| **Total** | **979,397** | **981,397** |

12. OECD (Organization for Economic Cooperation and Development), *Trends in International Migration*, Annual Report, 2004 Edition, OECD Publishing (online-read only version), 55.

13. Emigration from Albania into Italy is particularly contested and thus dangerous for the migrants. The respective horror stories of desolate boat people regularly make the news in Europe, accusing Italy of not doing enough to protect its borders.

14. Rhacel Salazar Parreñas, *Servants of Globalization: Women, Migration, and Domestic Work* (Stanford, CA, 2001).

15. Bridget Anderson, *Doing the Dirty Work? The Global Politics of Domestic Labour* (London, 2000).

16. Janet Henshall Momsen, *Gender, Migration and Domestic Service* (London, 1999), 81; and Katina Pappas-Deluca, "Transcending Gendered Boundaries: Migration for Domestic Labour in Chile," in ibid., 100.

17.  Mary Garcia Castro, "What is Bought and Sold in Domestic Service? The Case of Bogotá: A Critical Review," in *Muchachas No More: Household Workers in Latin America and the Caribbean*, ed. Elsa M. Chaney and Mary Garcia Castro (Philadelphia, 1989), 106.

18.  Mónica Gogna, "Domestic Workers in Buenos Aires," in Chaney and Castro, *Muchachas No More*, 84.

19.  Roger Sanjek, "Maid Servants and Market Women's Apprentices in Adabraka," in *At Work in Homes: Household Workers in World Perspective*, ed. Roger Sanjek and Shellee Colen, American Ethnological Society Monograph Series, No. 3. (Washington, DC, 1990), 35–62.

20.  Tessa LeRoux, "Home is Where the Children Are: A Qualitative Study of Migratory Domestic Workers in Mmotla Village, South Africa," in Momsen, *Gender, Migration*, 185.

21.  Dorothee Wierling, *Mädchen für alles: Arbeitsalltag und Lebensgeschichte städtischer Dienstmädchen um die Jahrhundertwende* (Berlin and Bonn, 1987), 70.

22.  See Wierling's discussion of childhood experiences and socialization of women who entered domestic service (Chapter II, Kindheit.)

23.  Silke Wehner-Franco, *Deutsche Dienstmädchen in Amerika, 1850–1914* (Münster, 1994).

24.  Harzig, *Peasant Maids—City Women*.

25.  Wehner-Franco, *Deutsche*, 129. She refers to a 1912 study indicating 279,006 German immigrants during this period, with 25,614 domestics (9.2 per cent) among them.

26.  The majority of emigrants from Germany were Protestant; reference is made to the development of Froebel Kindergardens.

27.  Henkes, *Heimat in Holland*, 33–48, and here 33.

28.  "Im Durchschnitt vergingen drei Jahre, bevor die Dienstmädchen nach Deutschland zurückkehrten, in ein anderes Land weiterzogen oder durch die Eheschließung mit einem Niederländer die deutsche Staatsbürgerschaft und ihre Arbeit als Dienstmädchen aufgaben." Translated by author from ibid., 48.

29.  Mareike König, "'Bonne à tout faire' Deutsche Dienstmädchen in Paris im 19. Jahrhundert," in *Deutsche Handwerker, Arbeiter und Dienstmädchen in Paris: Die vergessene Migration im 19. Jahrhundert*, ed. Mareike König (München, 2003). 71.

30.  Since König had to rely mainly on church and charity sources, the victimization paradigm dominates in her account, and the dangers lurking around every corner, luring or forcing domestics into prostitution are (over)emphasized.

31.  For a brief summary and comparison with Britain, see Enloe, *Bananas, Beaches, and Bases,* 181–84. On Canada, see Adele Perry, *On the Edge of Empire: Gender, Race and the Making of British Columbia, 1849–1871* (Toronto, 2001).

32.  Lore Wildenthal, *German Women for Empire, 1884–1945.* (Durham and London, 2001), 91; and Karen Tranberg Hansen, *Distant Companions: Servants and Employers in Zambia, 1900–1985* (Ithaca, NY, 1989), 24–84.

33.  The literature on domestic service for both countries is large. On the United States see for example, David M. Katzman, *Seven Days a Week: Women and Domestic Service in Industrializing America* (New York, 1978); Mary Romero, *Maid in the U.S.A.* (New York, 1992); and Evelyn Nakano Glenn "From Servitude to Service Work: Historical continuities in the Racial Division of Paid Reproductive Labor," in *Unequal Sisters: A Multicultural Reader in U.S. Women's History*, ed. Vicki L. Ruiz and Ellen Carol Dubois, 3rd ed. (New York, 2000), 436–65. On Canada, see

Barber, *Immigrant Domestic Servants*; Patricia Margot Daenzer, *Regulating Class Privilege: Immigrant Servants in Canada, 1940–1990s* (Toronto, 1993); and Abigail B. Bakan and Daiva Stasiulis, eds., *Not One of the Family: Foreign Domestic Workers in Canada* (Toronto, 1997).

34. Elizabeth Kuznesof, "A History of Domestic Service in Spanish America, 1492–1980," Chaney and Castro, eds. *Muchachas No More*, 17–36.

35. On the presence of domestic servants in household production in early modern Europe, a system emulated by the colonists, see Louise Tilly and Joan Scott, *Women, Work and Family* (New York, 1978). Servants made up 15–30 percent of the population in preindustrial European cities (pp. 16–65).

36. Kuznesof, "History of Domestic Service in Spanish America, in Chaney and Castro, *Muchachas No More*, 25.

37. Ibid., 22.

38. The historiography on domestic work in Latin America is very much influenced by Margo Smith's research, which first appeared in her Ph.D. dissertation. Smith argues that domestic service can indeed be seen as a modernizing chance for rural women. Subsequent research often takes up this emancipatory notion of domestic service, and domestic work in Latin America is less often constructed as victimizing. See Margo L. Smith, "Domestic Service as a Channel of Upward Mobility for the Lower-Class Woman: the Lima Case," in *Female and male in Latin America: Essays*, ed. Ann Pescatello (Pittsburgh, 1973), 192–207; as well as Sarah Radcliffe, "Race and Domestic Service: Migration and Identity in Ecuador," in Momsen, *Gender, Migration and Domestic Service*, 83–97; and Pappas-Deluca, "Transcending Gendered Boundaries," 98–113. Women's agency is more forcefully argued.

39. Ibid.

40. See also Radcliffe, "Race and Domestic Service."

41. Pappas-Deluca, "Transcending gendered Boundaries."

42. "In the city of Quito, as in other urban areas, whiteness is articulated as one facet of the progress, civilization and incorporation expressed in the city, particularly by the élite in their literary and visual representations of the capital city of Quito and its centrality in the nation." Radcliffe, "Race and Domestic Service," 91.

43. Ibid., 92.

44. *Maids and Madams*, film by Mira Hamermesh (Capetown, 1985).

45. http://www.southafrica.info/public_services/citizens/your_rights/domestic rights. htm.

46. This has been argued for Swaziland in the 1980s. See Miranda Miles, "Working in the City: The Case of Migrant Women in Swaziland's Domestic Service Sector," in Momsen, *Gender, Migration*, 208. In South Africa today, wages are regulated to a degree, but compliance with the law is not necessarily enforced.

47. Working for a Western household in Jakarta brings fundamental spatial and cultural adjustments, and the Western life style is looked down upon. Rebecca Elmhirst, "'Learning the Ways of the *priyayi*': Domestic Servants and the Mediation of Modernity in Jakarta, Indonesia," in Momsen, *Gender, Migration*, 251.

48. Miles, "Working in the City."

49. Ibid., 204.

50. Sanjek, "Maid Servants and Market Women's Apprentices in Jakarta."

51. Miles, "Working in the City," 207.

52. Ibid., 208.

53. LeRoux, "Home Is Where the Children Are," 192.

54. Nicky Gregson and Michelle Lowe, *Servicing the Middle Classes: Class, Gender and Waged Domestic Labour in Contemporary Britain* (New York, 1994), 50.

55. Brian W. Higman, *Domestic Service in Australia* (Melbourne, 2002).
56. Ibid., 20.
57. Ibid., 74.
58. Immigration propaganda, 1910. Cover of a leaflet produced by the New South Wales Immigration and Tourist Bureau. See Higman, *Domestic Service in Australia*, 92.
59. Pappas-DeLuca, "Transcending Gendered Boundaries," 112.
60. The women who migrate seldom come from the poorest stratum of society and usually have an above average education.
61. The positive and negative impacts on receiving and sending cultures can be summarized in tables. A good and very informative table is provided by Patricia Licuanan, "The Socio-economic Impact of Domestic Workers Migration: Individual, Family, Community, Country," in *The Trade in Domestic Workers: Causes, Mechanisms, and Consequences of International Labor Migration*, ed. Noeleen Heyzer, Geertje Lycklama á Nijeholt, and Nedra Weerakoon (London, 1994), 112.
62. Sanjek, "Maid Servants and Market Women's Apprentices in Jakarta."
63. "Among Java's indigenous élite, the employment of servants was closely associated with the system of patronage that tied élite *(priyayi)* families to particular families of the rural poor.. . . Systems of patronage and obligation ran between the two families, and into arenas beyond the domestic. . . . Working as a servant was represented discursively as a privilege: a way of learning the way of the *priyayi* and of charting a course of upward mobility, though in practice this was rarely the case." Elmhirst, "'Learning the Ways of the *priyayi*,'" in *Gender, Migration, and Domestic Service*, ed. Momsen, 246.
64. The minimum age of women migrating to the Middle East is thirty, as prescribed by the agencies, which place the job. Munira Ismail, "Maids in Space: Gendered Domestic labour from Sri Lanka to the Middle East," in *Gender, Migration, and Domestic Service*, ed. Momsen, 235.
65. Nicole Constable, Maid to Order in Hong Kong: Stories of Filipina Workers. (Ithaca, NY, 1997), 77–79.
66. "Compared to the average migrant, Muslim women where found to come from smaller families with a higher household income and a higher education, coupled with a greater determination to overcome economic hardship by making use of the opportunities migration provided." Ismail, "Maids in Space," in *Gender, Migration*, ed. Momsen, 232.
67. Ibid.
68. Often due to declining employment opportunities for men and women (for example destruction of local textile industry by the liberalism paradigm of world trade).
69. Ibid., 1999, 232; and Hatmachji, "Gender Dimensions of International Migration."
70. Miles, 1999.
71. Sri Lankan Muslim women often make circular moves of three to four trips to the Middle East. Ismail, "Maids in Space," in *Gender, Migration*, ed. Momsen, 235. See also Hatmachji, "Gendered Dimensions of International Migration."
72. Donna Gabaccia, "Women of the Mass Migrations: From Minority to Majority, 1820–1930," in *European Migrants*, ed. Hoerder and Moch, 90–111.
73. Sympathetic employer-women often help in negotiating bureaucracies and in language acquisition.
74. Pierrette Hondagneu-Sotelo, *Doméstica. Immigrant Workers Cleaning and Caring in the Shadow of Affluence* (Berkeley, CA, 2001).
75. See the television show *"Supernanny,"* which features a homely woman with a British accent, a Union Jack umbrella, and a quaint British-looking car, who takes care of unruly children.

76. All of these images have been taken up in literature. See for example Mary Mc-Clung, *Painted Fires* (Toronto, 1925), whose heroine is a Finnish immigrant woman working as a domestic.

77. Bernadette Stiell and Kim England, "Jamaican Domestics, Filipina Housekeepers and English Nannies: Representations of Toronto's Foreign Domestic Workers," in *Gender, Migration*, ed. Momsen, 43–61.

78. Ismail, "Maids in Space," in *Gender, Migration*, ed. Momsen, 232.

79. Enloe, *Bananas, Beaches, and Bases*, 193.

# 3

# "The Moral Aspects of Complex Problems": New York City Electoral Campaigns against Vice and the Incorporation of Immigrants, 1890–1901"[1]

*VAL JOHNSON*

THIS ESSAY ARGUES that the intersection between immigrant incorporation and the construction of municipal politics and citizenship is crucial to understanding either phenomenon in late-nineteenth- and early-twentieth-century New York City. In so doing, it demonstrates that what Elliott Barkan terms "translocalism" historically has included the multiple ways in which international migration and immigrant incorporation shape the cultures and politics of receiving nations and how the hybrid results in turn affect the experience of migration and incorporation. The essay also explores how the ethnic and racialized, national, and class relations that characterized the intersection between immigration and local politics were gendered and sexualized in complex ways.[2]

At the turn of the last century, native-born New Yorkers were dependent on immigrants for the construction of their own identities, citizenship, and politics: because they defined their identities in connection with those of immigrants; because of the demographics, politics, and cultures through which immigrants shaped migration and activism; and because of their intersection with the municipal electorate and governing apparatus. Despite and in reaction to this dependence, many privileged, native-born political reformers acted on the assumption that nativity, mass migration, ethnicity, and class created hierarchical capacities for political decision-making that rendered the *native born* stewards of immigrant identity and politics. This dance of dependence and hierarchy, and immigrant New Yorkers' varied engagement with it, were particularly evident in the municipal electoral campaigns of 1894 through 1901. Elite male reformers played leading roles in these contests, but their victories required the mobilization of both bourgeois women reformers and various groups of immigrant men and women.

I am especially interested here in how the prominence of moral issues in these campaigns—specifically the alleged links between municipal politics and prostitution—meant that a key conduit for this interdependence was the gender, class, ethnic, and racialized relations among two sets of social groups: 1) privileged Gentile and Jewish Americans of Anglo and Northwestern European heritage and 2) Eastern European Jewish and German immigrants who were predominantly of the working classes. Many of us take for granted that ethnicity and class shape migration and relations among immigrants and the native born, but how are national, ethnic, racialized, and class relations around immigration and incorporation gendered? The analysis of immigration too often has provided an unself-conscious gendered analysis of men. Centering women and gender relations among women and men, I undertake an analysis of the dynamics around immigration, politics, and citizenship.[3]

A useful tool in this undertaking is an analytical focus on sexual morality as a measure of personal and social worth, safety, and danger. Sexual morality is about the regulation of boundaries. It provides an ideal lens for examining the construction of gender and sexuality but also class, ethnicity, nation, and politics. Gender and sexualized relations and norms inflected immigrant and native-born struggles around migration, incorporation, and citizenship because of a number of factors: anxieties around how the political economy of industrialization affected gender relations; the demographics of migration and incorporation in conjunction with receiving populations; the ways gender and sexual relations shaped the tenuous status and mobility of migrants and their incorporation into the United States; and relatively privileged women's limited access to formal politics and their use of alternate routes to socio-political participation.[4]

This essay reveals both that gender was central to relations among immigrant and native-born women and men and that these inter- and intragroup gendered dynamics were as much about formal politics, class, ethnicity, and race as they were about relations between men and women. By way of example, when working-class men expressed hostility toward native-born women campaigning for political reform in immigrant neighborhoods, they were not acting solely on perceived gender interests. Bourgeois, native-born women acted as liminal figures in multi-faceted political conflict not just cooperation. These complex social relations that unfolded via citizenship construction and electoral politics importantly shaped New York City as well as immigrants' experience of incorporation therein.

## "THE DISTRUST OF CLASS": CHANGE & CONFLICT IN IMMIGRANT INCORPORATION & POLITICS

An exemplary figure in the period was reformer Lillian Wald, who founded Henry Street Settlement on the Lower East Side of Manhattan in 1893. Her goal was to engage the working-class, immigrant population there, many of whom were Eastern European Jews, and to work toward their stable incorporation into the city and nation. In 1896 Wald spoke about this work at the First Convention of the National Council of Jewish Women (CJW), an organization of middle- and upper-class women, predominantly second-or third-generation native-born, and of German heritage. Through the work of members such as Wald and Sadie American (by 1901, leader of the New York section), immigrant incorporation became a central dimension of the CJW's mission. In her speech, "Crowded Districts of Large Cities, Our Duty to Better Their Condition," Wald indicated the significant role that formal politics played in her work with immigrants and the construction of her own citizenship. Describing how her settlement's Russian and Polish neighbors participated in the 1894 municipal election, Wald noted "how impossible it is for these men and women to have the leisure or the strength to rear their children . . . into citizens with intelligent reasoning of how to govern themselves." She claimed that "class feeling" was intensified, and the city's institutions threatened, because the poor were inspired by "the distrust of class" in choosing "leaders of their own." Poverty bred a "dumb discontent" and "a contempt for law and order."[5]

Wald articulated a perspective on immigrants from Southern and Eastern Europe that was shared by many privileged Jewish Americans and their na- tive-born Gentile counterparts in social reform, most of whom had family backgrounds from Northwestern Europe and the British Isles. Her speech provides a telling record of the muddled ideas that such a perspective en- tailed. Notions of inferior breeding and mental capacity and the inherent criminality of the alien poor, recognition of the import of social conditions, and the perceived disorder posed by immigrant, working-class consciousness and solidarity all vied for space.

Her lament touched on three key dynamics involving immigrant incorpora- tion, politics, and ethnic and class relations in 1894: political reform, shifts in migration demographics, and intense class conflict on the local and national levels. First, Wald referred to the fact that political reformers (including herself) ran a victorious election campaign against the municipal Democratic political machine of Tammany Hall in this year. The Hall provided one of the primary vehicles for immigrant incorporation into the city through its distribution of patronage and welfare, its policy adaptation of some organized labor demands, and its facilitation and protection of immigrant citizenship. However, reformers such as Wald, were intent on attacking Tammany as an illegitimate apparatus for municipal rule, in part because of its close relation with the foreign born.[6]

Second, through her own native-born identity and her work with Eastern European immigrants, Wald aptly represented contention around linked contemporary changes in transnational migration, immigrant incorporation, and municipal politics. One motivating factor in the intensification of campaigns against Tammany was the fact that the Irish, who had recently come to dominate the Hall, were now selectively integrating into the machine newer immigrants, most importantly from the Eastern European, Jewish working classes. The percentage of foreign born in the city's population was high but relatively stable between 1860 and 1920. What changed after 1880 was *who* was arriving. While the population emigrating from Ireland and Germany remained steady between 1890 and 1910, the numbers for immigrants from Eastern and Southern Europe tripled both from 1880 to 1890 and from 1890 to 1900 and doubled again from 1900 to 1910. If the municipal political influence of working-class Irishmen was offensive to some native-born, white Protestant members of the upper classes, they found the characteristics of the new immigration more threatening. A reform focus on the links between Tammany corruption and sexual morality in poor immigrant districts coincided precisely with this shift. As George Chauncey has noted in analyzing the context for New York moral reform in this era, this altered migration meant that class conflict was "construed in ethnic as well as class terms."[7]

Italians were sporadically demonized in campaigns against politically protected prostitution. However, as I have analyzed elsewhere, it was no accident that anti-Semitism was a stronger, though contested, thread. The United States had a connected history of anti-Semitism and paranoia about conspiracy. The former provided a flexible language for the stigmatizing narratives central to anti-prostitution efforts. Working-class Jewish immigrants (including a small minority in the prostitution trade) were an important target for politicized campaigns against vice because they achieved a greater degree of integration into the machine. Jewish New Yorkers were strongly politicized across the class spectrum. Numerically and in terms of leadership, Eastern Europeans were central to radical politics, and ordinary Jewish working-class voters were known for their independent voting patterns, particularly on the Lower East Side. Perceived class and cultural interests and anxieties around the racialized construction of U.S. citizenship and status motivated elite naturalized and native-born Jews (who were, as noted, predominantly of German heritage) to join efforts to regulate the behavior of working-class, Eastern European Jewish immigrants. Both anti-Semitism and alliance with native-born and immigrant Jews were crucial to the municipal anti-prostitution and reform politics of the native-born.[8]

The third dynamic that Wald touched on with her reference to "the distrust of class" encompassed the broader political struggles swirling through immigrant incorporation and municipal politics. The 1894 election took place in the midst of an economic depression. In the years leading up to it, radical orators stumped across the Lower East Side for working-class organization, resistance, and revolt. In addition to incorporation via the machine, working-class immigrants (Lower East Side Jews prominent among them) envisioned radical change as a viable solution to the dilemmas of migration, settlement, and American economic and political problems. In comparison with earlier working-class militancy, that of the 1880s and 1890s was wider in scope, better organized, and under-girded by more coherent revolutionary ideas. In New York, militancy among the native-born working classes was infused by translocal elements such as radical Irish nationalism and the anarchism and socialism of Eastern European Jews. The Irish leaders of the radical nationalist Land League joined with German-American socialists and union men in 1882 to organize a municipal federation of labor unions. The Central Labor Union (CLU) ran a candidate for mayor in this year and, along with the Knights of Labor, was active through strikes, producer co-operatives, and consumer boycotts. As the nation experienced an economic downturn between 1884 and 1886, these sorts of working-class actions rippled across the land.[9]

The national publicity received by the Haymarket tragedy and its aftermath in 1885 and 1886 fired a generation of radicals with the ideas of anarchism and socialism. In the spring of 1886 alone 350,000 workers struck for an eight-hour day, including 25,000 in New York who led a torchlight procession along Broadway. The Knights and the CLU represented 80,000 workers in the city. Joining a national trend, in 1886 the CLU allied with socialists, Knights, American Federation of Labor (AFL) affiliates, and other radical and reform organizations to form an Independent Labor Party (ILP) for the municipal election. Henry George was their mayoral candidate. The ILP campaign was mounted to protest the state's repression of labor, but it also reflected dissatisfaction with Tammany Hall's relatively conservative political and immigrant incorporation mechanisms. It is ironic that George's candidacy, and the unprecedented level of workingclass militancy behind it, effectively shifted the long-term power balance in municipal politics in Tammany's favor. After the gradual consolidation of the political machine, fortified under Irishman John Kelly's leadership, segments of the elite previously aligned with Tammany faced a radical working-class opposition unintegrated into the Hall. Elite Democrats were no longer guaranteed the upper hand that had encouraged their alliance with Tammany for years. In 1886 elite mayoral candidate Abram Hewitt was forced into coalition with Tammany in order to avert the electoral uprising represented by George. Hewitt pulled off a victory through this alliance with Tammany. However, running well ahead of elite Republican candidate Theodore Roosevelt, George garnered thirty-one percent of the vote and did especially well among Irish immigrants, second-generation Germans, and Lower East Side Jewish immigrants.[10]

The spirit of radical militancy displayed in electoral politics in 1886 actually became more visible in the late 1880s and early 1890s, through the Populist movement and organized labor's increasing disruption of industry. Violent and legal repression by both the state and employers inspired further radical protest. By the early 1890s assassinations and such militant political philosophies as anarchism were the stuff of daily news in New York. Five days after Russian immigrant and anarchist Alexander Berkman attempted to assassinate Carnegie Steel chairman Henry Clay Frick in July 1892, a sensational *New York World* account of "Anarchy's Den" publicized a portrait of Berkman's current life partner, Russian anarchist Emma Goldman. She was presented as a "queen" surrounded by "swarthy, half-clad and grimy Anarchists" who appeared to "consider Emma Goldman as a superior being" and guarded her "with an ice-pick." In 1893 and 1894 Goldman was a prominent orator on the Lower East Side, mobilizing the native born and German and Eastern European immigrants. This kind of immigrant radicalism was widely publicized not just through popular tabloids, such as Joseph Pulitzer's *New York World*, but also via the *New York Times*.[11]

The 1886 electoral uprising from the left also spurred Tammany's leaders to further consolidate the integrative mechanisms of the machine. David Hammack has concisely assessed the years between 1886 and 1903 as the definitive "Transition Period" between New York as a "merchantdominated polity" and New York as "the Tammany-managed city."The successful Tammany mayoral candidacy of Hugh Grant in 1888 further solidified Tammany's self-sufficiency through its facilitation of greater control of municipal management and patronage. The conditions under which the Hall became an increasingly autonomous institution with support rooted in working-class, immigrant districts were also importantly informed by changes in the city's economy that affected the city's elite. By the late 1880s the greater complexity of the New York economy created several economic and cultural elites with competing interests and views, which fragmented elite participation in municipal politics.[12]

While members of the city's upper classes found the prospect of governance by a radicalized working class horrifying, they found little solace in a consolidating political machine supported by working-class immigrants. In unstable times New York elites faced in Tammany an organization that won elections through physical intimidation, bribery, and graft, but that also had a previously unparalleled degree of financial and political independence. The range of fiscal malfeasance engaged in by Tammany and the police—including the extraction of commercial vice profits— was not simply the fruit of sin. It funded the machine's newly developed autonomy. Despite elite efforts, including civil service and charity reform, through patronage and informal welfare Tammany continued to redistribute tax revenue to the working classes. With the Hall's consolidation of an immigrant working-class electorate, the distribution of patronage and social welfare in these communities could not be openly criticized by the city's elites. In fact privileged men's early attempts to undermine immigrant men's sway in municipal politics through a late-1880s Lower East Side campaign "to clean up the streets and fight the power of the local political boss" failed.[13]

Here we have conflicting approaches to immigrant incorporation and municipal governance, the fault lines of which were formed through the convergence
of local, national, and international change and contention. At a time when Tammany Hall was consolidating its hold on municipal politics, the interdependency
of native-born and immigrant citizenship and politics became highly visible.
The city's native-born reformers, including naturalized or second-generation
Americans such as Wald, advocated "intelligent reasoning" to improve the city's
institutions, but not alter them in a radical way. This would involve elite men
(and some fortunate women) governing the city and immigrant assimilation into
bourgeois respectability. Many ordinary people sought governing configurations
other than those advocated by both elite reformers and Tammany Hall. Elite
New York City reformers attempted to channel working-class immigrant radicalism through elite-led ventures, for example, social settlements, the Women's
Trade Union League, and eventually state-level Progressive legislation. They
also devoted considerable energy in these years of Tammany's consolidation to
wresting control of municipal governance from the machine.[14]

Working-class immigrant radicals, notably Goldman, were incarcerated for
threatening to "raise insurrections," but this sort of rallying cry and brute electoral demographics formed through mass migration suggested to the city's elites
that coalitions with segments of the immigrant working classes were essential to
any attack on the machine. By 1900 the percentage of foreign-born white males
18–44 years of age in New York County's population outstripped that of native-
born white men. By 1910 anxiety around the political implications of this was
evident in the U.S. Census tabulations, which reported that native-born white
males of native parentage made up only 14 percent of the total males of voting
age in New York County (Manhattan). Naturalized foreign-born white males
made up 21 percent of the total men of voting age. Another 8 percent of the total
males of voting age were foreign-born white males with their "first papers."
Having declared their intention to become citizens, the latter were eligible to
vote in New York at least until 1906, when standardization of the naturalization
process was attempted via the Naturalization Act of 1906. Native-born white
males of foreign parentage made up another 17 percent of men of voting age.
Culminating in the two election victories of 1894 and 1901, crusades against
the alleged links between the Hall and commercial vice in immigrant neighborhoods, such as the Lower Eastside, afforded opportunities for elite reformers to
ally with and attempt to regulate working-class immigrants through a common
but hierarchical moral citizenship. This entailed the mobilization of native-born
men and women and a range of immigrant responses.[15]

## "INOCULATING FOREIGN-BORN RESIDENTS": ELITE
## REFORMERS & POLITICAL ANTI-VICE CAMPAIGNS

The primary actors in turn-of-the-century municipal reform were native-
born Anglo-Protestants and native-born and naturalized Jewish men. These

predominantly genteel Republican Party men were members of, and circulated among, the city's elites. Through political reform campaigns, they attempted to construct what the Reverend Charles Parkhurst termed a new "civic manhood." This was defined in contrast with the identity of immigrant, working-class men who influenced and were represented through an immoral Democratic machine. Parkhurst preached in his sermons that the city's voice of purity spoke in "honest, ringing Saxon."

The City Vigilance League that he founded to unseat Tammany Hall described its mission as counteracting "drift" in the municipal administration by "inoculating foreign-born residents with American impulses." In 1901 the Reverend publicly accused the Catholic Church—renowned for its Irish immigrant congregants—of being "in league with Tammany," and told the city press that immigrants of "less advanced races" were "lowering the tone of . . . national life."[16]

This exclusive and racialized construction of masculine citizenship was significantly informed by the fact that white elite men—who dominated state and federal politics—actually held a tenuous position in municipal governance. When in 1882 Theodore Roosevelt was elected as a Republican legislator to represent Manhattan's wealthy twenty-first district, he was dismayed at the lack of "respectable" young men in local politics. In his *Autobiography*, he commented bluntly about his motives in politics and political reform: "the people I knew did not belong to the governing class . . . I intended to be one of the governing class." However, because of mass male suffrage, the size of the immigrant population, the influence of the immigrant and working-class dominated machine, and the evident threat of more radical politics, elite male reformers had no choice but to incorporate immigrants (even as they denigrated them) into their political and citizenship practices. In order to defeat Tammany Hall, they needed immigrant, working-class voters and the immigrant incorporation methods deployed by the machine.[17]

In fact, elite male reformers' municipal citizenship was so tenuous that they also depended on the labor networks and techniques of their female peers. By the 1890s Tammany Hall and privileged women's organizations had for decades attempted to formally and informally govern immigrant, working-class populations in the city. The importance of political machines and unions to the U.S. incorporation of working-class immigrants has been well detailed by scholars, in particular Martin Shefter. Bourgeois women's parallel roles in the organizations and networks of charity, social settlements, the Women's Trade Union League, and political and moral reform are less acknowledged in this regard outside of explicitly feminist scholarship.[18]

Beginning in the 1850s, white, Anglo-Protestant women in New York City had led attempts to morally manage the working classes and to mold the state's functions towards that end. This involved their development of everything from private-state partnerships in reformatories, industrial schools, and the New York

Infirmary & College for Women to Josephine Shaw Lowell's 1870s campaign to privatize and limit, via the Charity Organization Society, distribution of public relief by Catholic institutions and Tammany Hall. Lowell was from a sixth-generation American family and pioneered an array of institutional arrangements to incarcerate, discipline, and monitor members of the working classes. The COS distributed limited material relief, but by 1895 it had case files on "at least 500,000 individuals": one fifth of the city's total population. New York women reformers were involved in incorporating immigrants and fighting the machine through precisely this kind of information gathering and welfare-distribution. By the 1890s this included explicitly political networks for campaigning, strategizing, and coalition building. A new focus on the machine's links with prostitution allowed privileged, native-born women of various backgrounds to bring their governance efforts more formally into the electoral realm. When the People's Municipal League ran an unsuccessful reform ticket in 1890, one thousand women signed a petition heralding the imperative for women to battle against the immorality of Tammany Hall. In the elections of 1892, 1894, 1897, and 1901, native-born women played crucial parts in the political reform movement both as individuals and in various organizations.[19]

In their efforts to undermine Tammany, male political reform organizations, especially the Citizens' Union, the Committee of Seventy, and the Committee of Fifteen, directly adopted the methods of the political machine and women reformers. Beginning in 1892, Reverend Parkhurst's City Vigilance League combined the organization of a shadow political machine with the sort of social investigation networks that women in the COS and settlements pioneered. The League mapped the characteristics of the population, institutions, and practices in each assembly district with politically strategic information: residents and voters and their nationality and citizenship, the provision of social services, and the operations and police connections of vice establishments. In the successful 1894 campaign, reformers deployed the resultant voter profiles and used the information gathered to produce and distribute political propaganda.[20]

Male reformers tied in with women's politically strategic reform efforts in immigrant neighborhoods. In the midst of the depression and lead-up to the 1894 election, Josephine Shaw Lowell worked with male political reform leaders to set up the East Side Relief-Work Committee. This elite-controlled relief organization modeled on the COS was a response to working-class immigrants' protest and organization in the city's most politically volatile district. Settlement reformers later turned the Relief-Work Committee into an East Side Civic Club intended to educate local immigrants into proper citizenship in a more direct manner.[21]

Again, in the successful 1900–1901 municipal campaign male reformers depended on the immigrant incorporation techniques of Tammany Hall and women reformers, and women's direct labor as campaigners among what we

would now call "swing voters" in both privileged and working-class households. Women of the upper classes had credentials as arbiters of moral virtue
and social concern in communities of privilege, but they also had crucial
access to working-class immigrant neighborhoods where native-born, elite
Republican or Independent men were unwelcome. A 1900 *Evening Post*
article is worth quoting at length. It demonstrates how native-born women
built bridges to the immigrant working classes that facilitated reform political victory, the cultural and political incorporation of immigrants, and
formal naturalization:

> Visits are made to . . . foreign settlements. The number of men old enough to vote
> and the number of the unnaturalized are learned. The women of the Republican
> Club get this information from their foreign sisters rather than from the men. . . . But
> sometimes a wife does not know her husband's politics. . . . The visitor . . . returns at
> meal-time. If she can gain his confidence, [the husband] will listen to her respectfully,
> and even seek enlightenment upon questions of the day, which it would lower his
> dignity . . . to ask from another man. . . . A daily report is sent to State headquarters,
> whence agents are dispatched to the . . . unnaturalized men. . . . His naturalization
> accomplished, it is easy enough to persuade the regenerated foreigner . . . "to vote
> right". . . . Meanwhile the feminine campaigner is making herself agreeable to the
> woman of the tenement. . . . . If want is apparent, it is met with temporary relief. .
> . . A woman with half-a-dozen small children in need . . . will use all her influence
> for the first person who alleviates her sufferings, and can usually be counted upon
> to control her husband's vote.[22]

The document suggests that women reformers mapped eligible working-class
voters and those requiring naturalization, primarily through communication with
immigrant women. The latter were also viewed as actors in forming immigrant
electoral practices. Native-born women were less threatening to some immigrant men than native-born men unconnected with the machine. The document
also illustrates how political reformers deployed the long-standing methods of
women reformers and Tammany Hall around such matters as welfare provision,
family intervention, and naturalization, all with the aim of mobilizing votes and
new party loyalties.

White, Anglo-Protestant, native-born women, particularly Josephine Shaw
Lowell, dominated early efforts in the city to regulate the native-born poor and
immigrants from Northwestern Europe and the British Isles, especially Irish
Catholics. By the 1890s, the demographics of reformers and their targets had
diversified, as naturalized and native-born groups, such as Jews of Northwestern European background, joined their Gentile sisters in reaching out to newer
immigrants from countries such as Russia, Poland, and Italy via the New York
Council of Jewish Women (NYCJW) and social settlements.[23] Lowell founded
the Woman's Municipal League (WML), but its members included NYCJW
members Lillian Wald and Maude Nathan. The League stumped for political
reform through "parlor meetings" in privileged homes and "public meetings"

in immigrant districts. On behalf of the WML, Consumers' League founder Maude Nathan addressed Eastern European women on the Lower East Side as what she termed "a co-religionist." She was able to do so because Minnie Rosen, a working-class Jew who was not a member of the WML, simultaneously translated Nathan's speeches into Yiddish.[24]

The League also engaged in political fund-raising and gathered information for the pamphlet that reform leaders considered the most influential piece of political propaganda in their victorious 1901 campaign, *Facts for Fathers and Mothers*. Through a compilation of information from experts—judges, religious leaders, police matrons—the leaflet catalogued the complicity of the machine in prostitution, a string of "white slavery" and prostitution cases involving Jewish immigrant villains and victims, and the threat that these presented to the city's daughters. Nine hundred thousand were printed. The League mailed the pamphlet to every registered voter, and it also was distributed through Republican women's clubs, clergymen, Working Girls' Societies, and settlements. League campaign literature with wide distribution appealed to working-class, immigrant interests. *Facts for Fathers and Mothers* reminded immigrant parents that their daughters were morally vulnerable. Police corruption also was framed with reference to its impact on street vending, an important form of employment in immigrant neighborhoods.[25]

Native-born women were also unacknowledged contributors to political reform platforms and policies that served to build alliances with immigrant, working-class voters. A Committee of Seventy spearheaded the 1894 campaign. Its leaders were some of the city's most privileged and powerful men, but they framed their campaign as "a citizens' movement . . . solely in the interest of efficiency, economy, and the public health, comfort, and safety." This was contrasted with the "corruption, inefficiency, and extravagance" of Tammany Hall and its threat to the very "life and liberty" of the populace. The platform, crafted to appeal to multiple constituencies, advocated improvements in political process and a "businesslike" administration, but also public schools and parks, baths and lavatories, and street cleaning and garbage disposal. Efficiency alone implied exclusion. The Seventy's Progressivism deployed a more sophisticated strategy, emphasizing expertise and a claim to represent social needs. No women were officially affiliated with the Seventy. Yet the portions of its platform emphasizing social needs appropriated (like Tammany Hall) measures advocated by organized labor, as well as the moral high ground associated with bourgeois women, the "private" sphere of the home, and native-born women's long-standing efforts in municipal housekeeping and immigrant incorporation. Reformers uncritically presented the integrity and shared interests of the private sphere as a model for a new body politic: "a city, like a well-ordered household, should be managed solely in the best interests of its people." The social was the middle ground on which native-born elites built a reform coalition with immigrant, working-class voters.[26]

## "WOMEN, NATIVES, . . . TAXPAYERS": RECONFIGURING GENDER VIA CLASS, ETHNICITY, AND RACE

It has been argued that male Republicans allowed for a more extensive political mobilization of (native-born) women than did the Democratic Party. New York City moral reform campaigns and their links with immigrant incorporation suggest that male political leaders allied with, appropriated, and constrained women's contributions. Through his sermons and communications with the press, the Reverend Parkhurst encouraged elite women to participate in the 1894 *moral* campaign against Tammany's Halls links with vice. He was also a vocal critic of the woman suffrage amendment proposed at the New York State Constitutional Convention that year. Parkhurst publicized women's quest for the vote as "manhoodmania." Privileged native-born women in moral reform accepted virtue as their socially appropriate public entry point and explicitly based women's foray into electoral campaigns on "moral" rather than "political" grounds. Although many supported it, members of the Woman's Municipal League and Republican women's clubs assiduously avoided the issue of suffrage in the electoral arena.[27]

Josephine Shaw Lowell, it has been said, was one of the "chief political managers" of this era's electoral reform campaigns. In their private correspondence that informs his conclusion, male political reform leaders acknowledged the advisability of allying with women like Lowell but they urged caution about appearing to do so. Male reformers advised 1897 campaign manager James Bronson Reynolds that women's political labor could be utilized as long as the campaign avoided "the criticism perhaps of being a women's movement."[28]

Despite their appropriation of native-born women's labor, networks, and knowledge to defeat the machine, most men in political reform defined *gender* as the primary determinant of citizenship, not class, ethnicity, nativity, or even race. Women of privilege sought to expand the ground for their citizenship beyond gendered virtue and to increase their common ground for citizenship with men by reproducing hierarchies around class, ethnicity, nativity, and race. This most visibly involved them in unequal power relations, not with their male peers but rather with immigrant working-class men and women. Native-born women's political work with immigrants and their engagement in the moral surveillance and discipline of immigrants provide a counterpoint to the analysis of how bourgeois women entered the political realm by capitalizing on "the expansion of political opinion." In urban U.S. settings, particularly New York City, privileged, native-born women expanded their public roles through efforts to shift, redefine, and *contract* publics, political opinion, and citizenship, particularly involving the immigrant working classes. Suffragists who argued along nativist and white supremacist lines similarly participated in the linked expansion and constriction of politics.[29]

Native-born women reformers' pronouncements to their class peers often framed working-class, immigrant politics through both elitism and references to European feudalism, Orientalism, racialized unfreedom in the United States, and other contemporary racialized and nativist vocabularies. With formal participation closed to them, a primary aim of women active in New York politics was, in the terms of the Woman's Municipal League, "to create sound public opinion." The organization itself had an elite, white, native-born membership of what Lowell dubbed "Social Register" women, both Gentile and Jewish.[30] Mrs. Alfred Bishop Mason spoke at a League meeting in a way that clarified the organization's vision of creators versus followers of sound opinion. She asserted that League members might influence many votes if they could "instruct the ignorant people of the slums what right and purity of politics are." When the League called on men and women "who love the right" to work against a government that encouraged "vice and crime," they presented themselves as "women, natives, inhabitants, and taxpayers."[31]

These women worked with an interpretation of political interests and process that was consistent with long-standing elitist and racialized strains in American republicanism that legitimized property requirements for voting and demonized those framed as weak and dependent. In an 1898 speech entitled "What Can Young Men Do For the City?" League founder Josephine Shaw Lowell criticized Tammany Hall as a "despotic government." Tammany supporters were "slaves" because they were influenced in their voting by money, position, or more powerful men. Lowell referred to Tammany Hall's system of welfare and patronage for working-class immigrants that she had worked against for decades. Those who were "dependent" socially and economically, who were enmeshed in "the struggle for existence," could not be politically "independent." Lowell advocated that New York's privileged must be politically active for the sake of "the mass of tenement dwellers" who are "dependent for everything."[32]

This was a remarkable assessment from someone whose family of four depended on inherited wealth and the labor of seven servants. As a woman Lowell could be framed as the ultimate dependent in a formally masculine republic. Like many U.S. republicans before her, rather than interrogating the fundamental contradictions through which that republic operated, Lowell slid from condemning dependency to condemning those (other than herself) who were "dependent." She transformed classist interpretations of dependence, and dominant gender-based ideas about *women's* dependence, into nativist gender- and class-based ideas that carved out public space for elite, native-born women. In an 1899 YWCA address on the "Relation of Women to Good Government" Lowell asserted that the perception and love of "the right" was accessible to women because they were detached from "the struggle for existence." The implication was that *privileged native-born women* were uniquely suited for political independence.[33]

Native-born women's attempts to use nativism, racialization, and ethnic hierarchy to correct the ambiguities of hierarchy and dependence between different groups of immigrant and native-born New Yorkers were particularly complicated for Jewish Americans. Yet this dynamic was evident in Lillian Wald's 1896 Council of Jewish Women address that dismissed the possibility of Russian and Polish immigrants raising "citizens with intelligent reasoning." In a later speech on "The Interpretive Value of the Settlement," Wald engaged in a dialogue with Chicago settlement pioneer Jane Addams over the latter's recently published article. Demonstrating that privileged, native-born Jewish women envisioned their immigrant incorporation efforts as paralleling those of white Gentile women, Wald concurred with Addams that a key function of settlements was "interpreting foreign colonies to the rest of the city." The speech reveals how Wald the reformer disassociated herself from her European ancestry, while seeking to contain and assimilate immigrants and facilitate urban tourism for the native-born:

> Unexpected charm has been revealed in . . . the lovely customs transplanted with the people of Europe . . . the immigrant within boundaries has the same poetry and color and life that so charm the traveler when he sees him in his European home. It is the Settlement people who are largely responsible for interpreting this phase of their life to the community, and some day we will see the wild orgy of noise that usher [sic] in the new year or celebrate [sic] the Fourth of July give place to something lovely.[34]

Wald's presentation of the incorporation of immigrants as a domestic form of colonialism between native- and foreign-born was echoed in the vocabulary of native-born male reformers. Prominent political reform strategist James Bronson Reynolds explicitly conceived of his University Settlement on the Lower East Side as a colonialist project to civilize the immigrant working classes. He wrote, "We have in fact before us a question of Colonial Administration, the colony having established itself with us instead of being established by us." Reynolds's domestic urban colonialism depended on a racialized construction of "colony" members, and he emphasized the "essential oriental quality" of both Eastern European Jews and their "extremest [sic] idealism." Like Josephine Shaw Lowell, he also denigrated the receptivity of working-class immigrants to the material benefits offered by Tammany Hall as a "temptation to political serfdom." Underlying all of this denigration of the immigrant working classes was the reality that native-born reformers were dependent on immigrants for effective municipal citizenship and politics. In this way municipal reformers resembled colonizers engaged in inter-national forms of exploitation, who deployed racial and moral hierarchies to reframe their institutionalized dependence on colonized populations for labor, resources, and identity construction.[35]

## IMMIGRANT CONTRIBUTIONS TO MUNICIPAL
## REFORM CAMPAIGNS

### 1. "Jew Haters" and "the Cry of Parents":
### The Moral Politics of Jewish Immigrants

The complex politics and identity formation at play in the New York City context were further illustrated by the fact that it was not just such privileged Jewish Americans as Wald who cooperated in the production of nativist, classist, and often anti-Semitic hierarchies through moral and political reform. It was Abraham Cahan—Lithuanian editor of the *Jewish Daily Forward*, the Lower East Side's most prominent Yiddish-language socialist newspaper—who publicized Reynolds's Orientalist ideas in an *Atlantic Monthly* interview with the latter on "The Russian Jew in America." We need to take a closer look at how various immigrants engaged with native-born attempts to reconfigure political dependence and enact reform.[36]

Given the conservative and stigmatizing elements that punctuated these municipal campaigns, and their prominent leadership by elite Anglo-Protestants, it is unsurprising that some working-class Jewish immigrants were suspicious of the election timing of moral crusades and criticized Gentile reformers who emphasized links between Jews and prostitution. During the 1901 campaign, the City Vigilance League—founded by Reverend Parkhurst—held a meeting at the Educational Alliance, a Lower East Side settlement established and led by elite German Jews, notably Jacob Schiff, Isidor Straus, Edwin Seligman, and the Council of Jewish Women's Julia Richman. Some local residents who attended the gathering interpreted Vigilance League President Frank Moss's ideas about moral governance as racist, and he was verbally "assaulted" with cries of "Down with the Jew Hater." Moss was chief counsel for the Lexow and Mazet Commissions on municipal corruption in the 1890s. Meeting attendees may thus have been familiar with his official role in scapegoating immigrants, particularly Jews, for that corruption.[37]

On the other hand, elite Jewish reformers, especially Lillian Wald, presented Lower East Side immigrants as a major force in the 1900–1901 campaign against Tammany Hall and its alleged links with vice. In the history of her Settlement, Wald wrote, "They comprehend the hideous cost of the red-light district and resented its existence in their neighborhood, where not even the children escaped knowledge of its evils." Wald's reference to children is key, because reformers deployed "the cry of parents" to legitimize their intervention in immigrant, working-class neighborhoods, and there is a range of documentation to indicate that immigrant, working-class parents were indeed concerned about their offspring's indirect exposure to the trade.[38]

When the elite-led anti-vice Committee of Fifteen's investigators interviewed tenement dwellers in the spring of 1901, they encountered, for example, Allen Street residents who resented both having to protect their children from the open practice of prostitution and the clear connections that practice had to the eighth ward political machine. Some feared the might of the ward boss if they testified against him, but testimony before the 1901 New York State Tenement House Commission also included that of several residents who perceived prostitution as a problem in tenements.[39] Contemporary newspaper coverage of the prosecution of forced prostitution or "white slavery" cases suggests that working-class parents' concerns about the coercion of their daughters were most likely to translate into police action if both victim and accused were young and the accused was also a working-class immigrant (and thus more vulnerable to prosecution than someone like an employer).[40]

The practice of prostitution did occur openly on the Lower East Side. This was informed by the socio-economic dynamics of working-class, immigrant participation, the consolidation of the machine's links with vice, and by earlier campaigns against brothel prostitution in relatively segregated vice districts.[41] The visibility of prostitution in this neighborhood was lamented by local Jewish reformers, including Wald and the Educational Alliance's David Blaustein, along with prominent representatives of the immigrant Jewish press, such as Abraham Cahan.[42]

A mix of influences shaped the world-view of the young immigrant men whom Wald credited with leading the charge against the "hideous" practice of vice. Wald noted that "every one" of them had been "members for many years" of local settlement clubs. The individual leading this group was Henry Moskowitz, a Romanian Jew whose family emigrated when he was a child. He grew up on the Lower East Side, but his maturation into manhood unfolded in the bosom of the district's reform institutions—Henry Street Settlement, University Settlement, and, through the latter, Felix Adler's Ethical Culture Society. In 1898 Moskowitz and other men enrolled at City College founded the Downtown Ethical Society (DES) on Madison Street "with the moral and financial assistance" of Adler's Society.[43]

In late 1900, the DES organized Lower East Side meetings around the problem of prostitution. These may have provided a forum for residents to express grassroots sentiments, but the ideas motivating the organization that arranged them are relevant. Like the Ethical Culture Society, the DES aimed to build "self-government." However, like local settlements run by native-born, Gentile and Jewish reformers, the approach of the DES had strong assimilationist and moralistic components. According to DES literature, the Society had two primary purposes: "the thorough Americanization of the residents of the lower East Side," and "the ennobling of the family life." The organization presented these aims as linked and grounded in morality: "It [the society] stands for the supremacy of the moral life and tries to emphasize the moral aspects of complex problems. . . . In a quarter where the lack of necessary creature comforts is so tremendous, there is great danger of underestimating the importance of moral demands."[44]

Not all Lower East Side residents in 1900 held a vision of immigrant incorporation that overlapped so clearly with that of native-born reformers. Mary Kingsbury Simkhovitch was active in attempts to regulate the morality of immigrant women and families through her Greenwich House settlement and as a member of multiple organizations. Her settlement memoir indicates that there were mixed sentiments on the Lower East Side about politicos connected with vice. Although critical of one Tam-many leader, Martin Engel, who was under fire in 1901 for his vice links, she had this to say about the Irish district leader who was also under attack: "Precious were the days of Big Tim Sullivan, who drew tribute from a whole region. His large picnics and outings, his crowded clubrooms, his ability to keep a crowd of henchmen together, his sense of the group and his knowledge of what could be accomplished through political organization based on meeting ordinary social needs, made of him a truly notable figure."[45]

Sullivan's popularity aside, by early 1901 the Committee of Fifteen's Lower East Side tenement investigations and the local press documented that the anti-vice and anti-machine message of the DES and elite crusaders was resonating with local residents. Some working-class, immigrant Jewish men particularly perceived it to be in their interests and that of their families to join these campaigns. Because of their important role as voters and the politicization of campaigns against prostitution, Lower East Side men's resistance to, as well as participation in, vice was particularly visible in the press. The efforts of native-born reformers to protect immigrant youth were embedded in unequal power relations. Jewish immigrant men's role as protectors of daughters, sisters, and wives entailed a linked but distinct set of power relations. Consequently, when in 1901 district attorney candidate William Travers Jerome campaigned on the Lower East Side, he appealed to Jewish immigrant voters *as men*, crying for Jewish manhood to protect the "honor of Jewish women sold for brass checks." Jerome implied (and Lower East Side votes affirmed) that their masculine citizenship must involve the assertion of gender and generational authority and a renunciation of anti-Semitic assumptions that emasculated and demonized Jewish men.[46]

This call for male guardianship must have been resonant for Eastern European men who experienced status anxiety in connection with their emigration, which often involved downward occupational mobility. These men, who had traditionally operated through economic partnership with their wives, also confronted a strong male breadwinner ideology in the United States. Meanwhile, as Susan Glenn has demonstrated, wage earning became a key component in the development of Eastern European women's version of "New Womanhood." Eastern European Jewish women had a stronger tradition of "public" work than other groups (such as Italians), but emigration brought even greater opportunities and need for women to undertake public wage labor. Wage-earning daughters became more crucial to the family economy and increasingly worked with and under the supervision of men from outside their families. Glenn notes that extramarital sex was not socially acceptable in the old country or the new but argues that, traditionally, the sexuality of *married*, Eastern European, working-class women was more strictly regulated than that of single women. The dynamics exposed by Jewish immigrants' relations with antiprostitution campaigns suggest the influence of conditions specific to their urban incorporation in the United States. A concept of "white slavery" muted young women's agency and legitimized regulation of their voluntary conduct. It elevated husbands, brothers, and fathers into the role of protector. They might not be in charge in the workplace or a hostile cultural environment but at least they were in charge in their own homes. The context and spur for this was a contest over municipal citizenship, involving the eligibility to vote and political empowerment more generally at the local level. The fact that anti-vice campaigns were formally politicized, and thus suitably masculine, encouraged immigrant men to join them.[47]

Further research is required with regard to the gender distinctions that shaped how working-class, immigrant family members were involved in politicized contention around sexual exploitation and misbehavior.[48] The role of immigrant Jewish *mothers* in political campaigns against vice is far less clear than that of male family members, in significant part because they were not made visible (for example, via the press) through their participation in political campaigns. It is slightly easier to trace working-class women's reactions to anti-prostitution campaigns generally. Judging by the relative visibility of their public agitation around these issues, Eastern European, immigrant women identified less with an activist framework centered on sexual morality than their native-born and more privileged German Jewish counterparts. Lower East Side women also provided clear instances of resistance to anti-vice investigations in this neighborhood during the campaign of 1900–1901. At times, this resistance appeared to be influenced by local business relationships external to (but dependent on) prostitution. For example, in May 1901 the women who did the laundry of those working in the trade "would say nothing to the snoopers of the crusading Committee of Fifteen." Mrs. Hoffman, a candy store proprietress across the street from the laundress, seemed to express a measure of moral acceptance when she told the same snoopers: "If I would not like them whores I would not live in this neighborhood." Michael Gold's recollections of growing up on the Lower East Side (he was born in 1894) included his mother beating him when he slurred a local prostitute.[49]

One additional explanation for this attitude can be seen in women's "citizens' complaints" to the anti-vice Committee of Fourteen (which took up the Fifteen's work in 1905). They provide evidence that working-class women were intent on controlling the behavior of their *male* relatives. This was most frequently undertaken when women felt a threat to the family economy because their husbands or sons were squandering money on vices. Immigrant husbands may have entered into the realm of moral citizenship construction through electoral politics, but these working-class women sought moral reformers' assistance in governing entitlement dynamics within their families. The ethnicity and nativity of most complaint writers are unclear, but some appear to have been Eastern European women. One woman, for example, lamented her husband spending his wages on women and gambling at a "polish society." With regard to perceived neighborhood immorality, women's complaints revealed as much concern with male seducers as they did with prostitution or "fast women."[50]

## 2. Germans, Immigrant Incorporation, and Politicized Moral Reform

The complex cultural processes that shaped the links between immigrant incorporation and politicized anti-prostitution campaigns raise interesting questions about how Germans, and "German" cultural elements, were influential therein. Native-born and naturalized German Jews have been examined primarily in the U.S. context in contrast with working-class, Eastern Europeans. The German-ness of German Jews has been analyzed with reference to class and cultural distinctions associated with *Northwestern* Europeans. What needs to be researched more closely is how German Jewish experiences in U.S. cities were shaped by cultural processes that had roots in *Germany* and in the experiences of Germans who settled in New York.[51]

This is especially pertinent with regard to the involvement of Germans in both immigrant incorporation and moral and municipal politics. In the nineteenth century German New Yorkers had ties to the Democratic and Republican parties. The development of Irish dominance in Tammany Hall brought about a diminution of German influence in the municipal machine, and that meant that Germans were available for alliances against Tammany from 1869 on. In the 1897 campaign, German men were known for both their opposition to the state regulation of Sunday leisure and liquor consumption (which had an impact on their own masculine pursuits) and their gender conservatism in the face of women's involvement in politics. Male reformers' resistance to formal political and reform roles for native-born bourgeois women was importantly strengthened by concerns about alienating immigrant voters, particularly Germans. The role of women in the 1897 municipal reform campaign did reportedly offend German men, and this was one of many factors that contributed to the reform election loss that year. Elite reform candidate Seth Low (who became mayor through the 1901 reform campaign) did particularly poorly in districts with significant German populations in 1897. The Woman's Municipal League was active in the 1901 and 1903 campaigns, but women campaigners were kept at a physical distance from German immigrant districts, where messenger boys delivered League materials.[52]

Aside from these strategic concerns about German immigrant voters, how did particularly German constructions of gender and moral regulation inform German Jewish men and women's participation in anti-prostitution agitation and their linked work around immigrant incorporation? How did these dynamics combine with German Jewish men's reaction to the shift in responsibility for moral and religious duties to women under Reform Judaism? There is evidence of both conflict and cooperation between German Jewish men and women in these regards, but more research is needed on gender relations among German Jewish reformers. How did these dynamics influence class and cultural relations with Eastern European Jews, and the incorporation of both sets of groups into New York City and the United States?[53]

It is also unclear how German influences affected New Yorkers' engagement in moral and political reform struggles in immigrant neighborhoods. The sort of gender conservatism among German men that affected political campaigning may have made them receptive to crusades against prostitution. Working-class support for anti-prostitution campaigns on the Lower East Side generally has been attributed to Eastern European Jews. However, at least as late as the early 1890s there was still a higher concentration of Germans than any other ethnic group in the areas on Allen, Chrystie, and Forsyth streets, which abutted the "red light district."[54]

While all classes of German men mobilized against attempts to limit their access to beer and Sabbath leisure, contemporary political strategists also appealed to working-class Germans' concerns about prostitution. Bourgeois reformers may have stopped sending women campaigners into German immigrant neighborhoods but they continued to deliver their campaign literature on the machine's alleged links with vice. Emma Goldman was critical of bourgeois moralist approaches to prostitution. However, when she sought to mobilize workingmen during the 1893 depression she variably deployed moralist and race- and gender-conscious vocabularies—not only to appeal to working-class solidarity but also to underscore how capitalism threatened hierarchies *within* the working classes. Speaking to a large demonstration by the unemployed in August 1893, Goldman's German-language address melded the languages of radical political economy and moral reform. She railed against the destruction of working-class manhood and womanhood and the generational and gender order within families: "your daughters and sons are like flowers who lose their freshness. They wither in the factories and your women are compelled to sell themselves in the street because you are not able to support your families." Goldman appealed to "the American workingmen" in the audience by highlighting the shared plight of American- and foreign-born white wage laborers and the unemployed under capitalism. However, she constructed this solidarity among native- and foreign-born men of European heritage by linking their unfreedom with the racializing stigma of chattel slavery, proclaiming: "You are not free citizens. You are worse than black slaves." Goldman's solutions to these dilemmas did not involve immigrant or native-born incorporation into bourgeois moral respectability but rather social revolution and "a distribution of private property," as she urged workingmen "you must demand what belongs to you. Go forth into the streets where the rich dwell."[55]

It is important to note that Goldman, as a Russian immigrant anarchist, drew large crowds of working men and women with her oratory in New York's immigrant neighborhoods and across the country. Undoubtedly, Goldman encountered resistance to her activism because she was a woman and an exceptionally charismatic leader. However, her wide appeal raises the possibility that German immigrant men, working and middle class, were likely resistant to reform women's politics for some of the same reasons that privileged, native-born male reformers met with only temporary victories in municipal politics through their alliances with the immigrant working classes. The fact that German immigrant men had a history of activism in radical politics and mixed views generally on moral campaigns suggests that they may have resented bourgeois women reformers because of their nativist, classist, and moralist politics and the politics of the men with whom they aligned.[56]

Finally, the relative visibility of Eastern European, German, and Jewish-American women in politicized campaigns against vice foregrounds interesting questions about gender relations within both their own communities and the dynamics of immigrant incorporation more broadly. While the documentation of the campaigns addressed here indicates less extensive participation for Jewish immigrant women than for men, German immigrant women are largely undetectable. Certainly, Jewish immigrants were a much more significant policing and political target of anti-prostitution campaigns for the reasons outlined above. Reformers targeted German immigrant men primarily as voters, while German immigrant women's relative invisibility in the documentation stands in stark contrast with the prominence of native-born, bourgeois reform women of German Jewish heritage. Within and between these groups, how did ethnicity, nativity, class, and religion differentially shape the intersecting relations of gender and sexuality, municipal politics and citizenship, and the migration and incorporation of immigrants?

## CONCLUSION

Exploration of the complex relations of gender and sexual morality among various groups of native-born and immigrant women and men reveals that immigrant incorporation and the mobilization of municipal politics and citizenship were fundamentally interwoven in New York City at the turn of the last century. Despite native-born reformers' attempts to channel and constrict municipal politics and citizenship in ways that reproduced hierarchies of class, ethnicity, race and nation, immigrant cultures and activism profoundly shaped native-born identities and politics, and the character and life of New York. In turn, engagement in political and moral activism and conflict shaped how Eastern European and German immigrant men and women produced translocal politics, their municipal and national citizenship, family and community relations, and New York as a city of immigrants. A focus on sexual morality as a conduit for formal and informal politics allows us to analyze how groups participated in this contention by recreating and subverting institutionalized hierarchies. We have only begun here to investigate how transnational and post-settlement dynamics of culture and power particularized this experience for different groups of immigrant women and men and the native-born.

## NOTES

1. The author would like to thank Elliott Barkan, Donna Gabaccia, and Franca Iacovetta for the contribution of their insights to this piece. Small portions of this paper were first published in "Protection, Virtue, and the 'power to detain': the Moral Citizenship of Jewish Women in New York City, 1890–1920," *Journal of Urban History* 31 (2005): 655–84.

2. For Barkan's discussion of the "translocal" and a summary of work around transnationalism see "America in the Hand, Homeland in the Heart: Transnational and Translocal Immigrant Experiences in the American West," *Western Historical Quarterly* 35, no. 3 (Autumn 2004): 331–54. For an analysis of how immigration intersected with the reform of immigration law and with policing tactics targeting migrating and settled immigrants, see Val Marie Johnson, "'Arriving for immoral purposes': Women, Immigration, and the Historical Intersection of Federal and Municipal Policing," in Stacy K. McGoldrick and Andrea McArdle, eds., *Uniform Behavior: Localism, Reform, and Police-Community Relationships in Modern America* (New York, 2006), 25–54.

3. For feminist critiques of gender myopia in histories of immigration, and feminist responses to it, see the following: Donna Gabaccia, "Immigrant Women: Nowhere at Home?" *Journal of American Ethnic History* 10, no. 4 (Summer 1991): 61–87; and "The Transplanted: Immigrant Women and Families," *Social Science History* 12, no. 3 (Fall 1988): 243–53; Franca Iacovetta, "Manly Militants, Cohesive Communities and Defiant Domestics: Writing About Immigrants in Canadian Historical Scholarship," *Labour/ Le Travail* 36 (1995): 217–52; Elizabeth Ewen, *Immigrant Women in the Land of Dollars: Life and Culture on the Lower East Side, 1890–1925* (New York, 1985); Susan Glenn, *Daughters of the Shtetl: Life and Labor in the Immigrant Generation* (Ithaca, NY, 1990); Rita Simon and Carolyn Brettell, eds., *International Migration: The Female Experience* (Totowa, NJ, 1986).

4. For an analysis of these issues in New York City see Johnson, "Defining 'Social Evil': Moral Citizenship and Governance in New York City, 1890–1920" (Ph.D. diss., New School for Social Research, 2002). See also Marc Connelly, *The Response to Prostitution in the Progressive Era* (Chapel Hill, NC, 1980); Glenn, *Daughters Of The Shtetl*; Meredith Tax, *The Rising of the Women: Feminist Solidarity and Class Conflict, 1880– 1917* (New York, 1980); Nancy Cott, *The Grounding of Modern Feminism* (New Haven, CT, 1987); and Sara Deutsch, *Women and the City: Gender, Space, and Power in Boston, 1870–1940* (New York, 2000). For exploration of these issues in Canada see Iacovetta, "The Sexual Politics of Moral Citizenship and Containing 'Dangerous' Foreign Men in Cold War Canada, 1950s–1960s," *Histoire sociale/Social History* 66 (November/novembre 2000): 361–89; and Mariana Valverde, *The Age of Light, Soap, and Water* (Toronto, 1991).

5. Lillian Wald in *Proceedings of the First Convention of the National Council of Jewish Women. Held at New York, Nov. 15, 16, 17, 18 and 19, 1896* (Philadelphia, 1897), 260, 261, 265. Lillian D. Wald (1867–1940) was born in Ohio to wealthy, German-Jewish immigrant parents. After completing a nursing degree, her economic security allowed her to volunteer as a nurse on the Lower East Side. With the help of other wealthy Jews (particularly Mr. and Mrs. Jacob Schiff), she estab-

lished the Visiting Nurse Society of New York and the Henry Street Settlement. See Wald, *The House on Henry Street* (1915; New York, 1971); Clare Coss, ed., *Lillian Wald, Progressive Activist* (New York, 1989); and Doris Daniels, *Always a Sister: the Feminism of Lillian D. Wald* (New York, 1989). On the CJW and immigrant incorporation see Johnson, "Protection, Virtue, and the 'power to detain.'" See also Faith Rogow, *Gone to Another Meeting: The National Council of Jewish Women, 1893–1993* (Tuscaloosa, AL, 1993); and Linda Gordon Kuzmack, *Woman's Cause: The Jewish Woman's Movement in England and the United States, 1881–1933* (Columbus, OH, 1990). Rogow provides biographical sketches of women who worked through the CJW (224–40).

6.  For contemporary critiques of immigrant voters as the primary support for Tammany Hall see the following: G. K. Turner, "Tammany's Control of New York City by Professional Criminals," *McClure's* (June 1909): 117–34; S. S. McClure, "The Tammanyizing of Civilization," *McClure's* (November 1909): 117–28; Turner, "The Daughters of the Poor," *McClure's* (November 1909): 45–61; and Henry A. Chaney, "Alien Suffrage," *Michigan Political Science Association* 1 (1894): 130–39. For the history of the machine and its relations with immigrants see Amy Bridges, *A City in the Republic: Antebellum New York and the Origins of Machine Politics* (New York, 1984); David Wilson, *United Irishmen, United States: Immigrant Radicals in the Early Republic* (Ithaca, NY, 1998), Chapter 3; Steven Erie, *Rainbow's End: Irish-Americans and the Dilemmas of Urban Machine Politics, 1840–1985* (Berkeley, CA, 1988); and Eric Foner, "Class, Ethnicity, and Radicalism in the Gilded Age: The Land League and Irish America," *Marxist Perspectives* 2 (1978): 6–55.

7.  A long history of settlement and a North-Western European culture gave the Germans more in common with the Irish than any other immigrant group and allowed them to overcome a barrier to assimilation they did not share with them—language. While the Irish and the Germans were the largest incoming populations in 1890 and 1900, by 1910 their numbers were surpassed by those of Russians and Italians. Immigration figures are from New York County and then Manhattan. C. Groneman and D. Reimers in Kenneth T. Jackson, eds., *The Encyclopedia of New York City* (New Haven, CT, 1995), 582, 584; and George Chauncey, *Gay New York: Gender, Urban Culture, and the Making of the Gay Male World, 1890–1940* (New York, 1994), 137. For more on Germans, see below.

8.  The Irish were the only immigrant group over-represented (versus their percentage in the general population) in the documentation on prostitution and this was in the nineteenth century. Johnson, "Defining 'Social Evil,'" 218–20. For Tammany's selectivity with immigrants see Vos in Jackson, ed., *Encyclopedia*, 1150. Hofstadter analyzes the Greenback-Populist tradition of paranoia about conspiracy and anti-Semitism (*The Age of Reform*, 70–82). New York histories of Eastern European Jewish radicalism include Glenn, "Uprisings," in *Daughters of the Shtetl*; and Annelise Orleck, *Common Sense and a Little Fire: Women and Working-Class Politics in the United States, 1900–1965* (Chapel Hill, NC, 1995). For working-class, especially Lower East Side, voting in this era see David Hammack, *Power and Society: Greater New York at the Turn of the Century* (1982; New York, 1987), 155–56, 175–76; M. Angel and J. Gurock, "Jews," in Jackson, ed., *Encyclopedia*, 621. Relations between German and Eastern European Jews are analyzed in Jack Glazier, *Dispersing the Ghetto: the Relocation of Jewish Immigrants across America* (Ithaca, NY, 1998); and Moses Rischin, *The Promised City, New York's Jews, 1870–1914* (Cambridge, MA, 1962), Chapter 6. See also (particularly on racialization) Johnson, "Protection, Virtue, and the 'power to detain'"; and "Defining 'The Social Evil,'" Chapter 3.

9.  Martin Shefter, "Trade Unions and Political Machines, The Organization and Dis-
    organization of the American Working Class in the Late Nineteenth Century," in Ira
    Katznelson and Aristide R. Zolberg, eds., *Working-Class Formation: Nineteenth-
    Century Patterns in Western Europe and the United States* (Princeton, NJ, 1986),
    270, 220–21; K. Candaele and S. Wilentz, "Labor," in Jackson, ed., *Encyclopedia*,
    646; and Hammack, *Power and Society*, 173.

10. Howard Zinn, *A People's History of the United States* (New York, 1990), 263–68;
    Nell Irvin Painter, *Standing at Armageddon: the United States, 1877–1919* (New
    York, 1987), xxvii–xxviii; Hammack, *Power and Society*, 174, 134–35, 137, 173–80;
    Erie, *Rainbow's End*, 11; and Shefter, "Trade Unions and Political Machines,"
    270–71. Shefter refers to the labor party as the United Labor Party. On the Haymar-
    ket protest, bombing, and its aftermath see Robert W. Glenn, *The Haymarket Affair:
    An Annotated Bibliography* (Westport, CT, 1993); and Bruce Nelson, *Beyond the
    Martyrs: A Social History of Chicago's Anarchists, 1870–1900* (New Brunswick,
    NJ, 1988).

11. Ronald Takaki, *A Different Mirror: A History of Multicultural America* (Boston,
    1993), 225–30, 236–38; Zinn, *A People's History*, 280, 289; Michael Kazin, *The
    Populist Persuasion: An American History* (New York, 1995); and "Anarchy's
    Den," *The New York World* (28 July 1892). Goldman's quote and information on
    her mobilization of the working-class are in *People of New York v. Emma Gold-
    man*, 28, 31, 29 (Court of General Sessions of the Peace, City and County of New
    York, 4 October 1893), Government Documents, in *The Emma Goldman Papers: A
    Microfilm Edition*, ed. Candace Falk et al. (Alexandria, VA, 1990), reel 56 [hereafter
    cited as EGP 56]. In 1893 the *New York Times* voiced its terror of how Goldman's
    "appalling nonsense" might impact the "rat-eyed young men of the Russian-Jew
    colony." See Edwin G. Burrows and Mike Wallace, *Gotham: A History of New York
    City to 1898* (New York, 1999), 1187.

12. Shefter, "Trade Unions and Political Machines," 271. For analysis of the "Transition
    Period," the fragmentation of the political elite, and the consolidation of Tammany's
    working-class electorate see the following, respectively, in Hammack, *Power and
    Society*, 110–11, 137–39, 114–15, 131, 138–45, 164–65, 125–27.

13. Herbert Gutman, "Work, Culture, and Society in Industrializing America, 1815–
    1919," in Herbert Gutman, *Work, Culture, and Society in Industrializing America:
    Essays in American Working-Class and Social History* (New York, 1975), 69–71;
    Richard Hofstadter, *The Age of Reform: From Bryan to F.D.R.* (New York, 1955),
    174–85, and Douglas V. Shaw, "The Making of an Immigrant City: Ethnic and
    Cultural Conflict in Jersey City, 1850–1877" (Ph.D. diss., University of Roches-
    ter, 1972). See also James Weinstein, *The Corporate Ideal in the Liberal State,
    1900–1918* (Boston, 1968); and Samuel P. Hays, "The Politics of Reform in
    Municipal Government in the Progressive Era," *Pacific Northwest Quarterly*, 55
    (1964): 157–69. Casey uses the term "social welfare" in reference to Tammany (in
    Jackson, ed., *Encyclopedia*, 600). Takaki refers to machines as "Robin Hoods" (*A
    Different Mirror*, 162). For critiques of the machine vis-à-vis the working classes
    see Erie, *Rainbow's End*, 57–66, 85–91, 241–44; Shefter, "Trade Unions and Po-
    litical Machines." Machine connections to vice were unique to neither New York
    nor the Democrats. Edward Bristow, *Prostitution and Prejudice: The Jewish Fight
    Against White Slavery, 1870–1939* (New York, 1983), 176; Nicola Beisel, *Imper-
    iled Innocents: Anthony Comstock and Family Reproduction in Victorian America*
    (Princeton, NJ, 1997), Chapter 6. The elite men of the Neighborhood Guild (later
    University Settlement) led the first campaign against the Hall. The quote is from
    Niermann, Introduction, 5, *University Settlement Society of New York City Papers*

(Madison, WI, 1972) Microfilm, reel 1. For the limits of civil service reform and other attempts to limit participation in formal politics see G. Benjamin in Jackson, ed., *Encyclopedia*, 237; Hammack, *Power and Society*, 140–41, 128–29, 344, notes 15 and 16.

14. Johnson, "Defining 'The Social Evil,'" Chapters 1–3; Elisabeth Israels Perry, *Belle Moskowitz: Feminine Politics and the Exercise of Power in the Age of Alfred E. Smith* (New York, 1987); Ruth Crocker, *Social Work and Social Order: The Settlement Movement in Two Industrial Cities, 1889–1930* (Urbana, IL, 1992).

15. *People of New York v. Emma Goldman*, 28, 31, 29 in EGP 56. All Census Data retrieved from Historical Census Browser, Geospatial & Statistical Data Center, University of Virginia Library, on-line at <http://fisher.lib.virginia.edu/collections/stats/histcensus/>. The data and terminology in the Browser are drawn directly from volumes of the U.S. Census of Population and Housing. With regard to the enfranchisement of immigrant men with first papers, nativist Samuel Orth suggested that this was a widespread practice in the city until passage of the Naturalization Act of June 29, 1906. Samuel P. Orth, *The Boss and the Machine, A Chronicle of the Politicians and Party Organization* (New Haven, CT, 1919), Chapter IV. See also discussion below about Jo Freeman's evidence from the 1900 *New York Evening Post*. For analysis of the gradual development of prostitution as a focus for both political reform and immigrant incorporation see Johnson, "Defining 'The Social Evil,'" Chapters 1–3.

16. William Howe Tolman, *Municipal Reform Movements in the United States* (New York, 1895), 185–97; Parkhurst Autumn 1892 League circular in Tolman, 196, 192–3. "Saxon" references in the February 1892 sermon are found in Parkhurst, *Our Fight*, 16, 23. The quote about the Catholic Church is from Press Abstracts (23 September 1901), box 3, Committee of Fifteen Records 1900–1901, Rare Books and Manuscripts Division, New York Public Library. The quote about immigrants is from a 1911 *New York Evening Journal* article cited in Pamela Ann Roby, "Politics and Prostitution: A Case Study of the Formulation, Enforcement and Judicial Administration of the New York State Penal Laws on Prostitution, 1870–1970" (Ph.D. diss., New York University, 1971), 76. See Johnson, "Defining 'The Social Evil,'" Chapter 1; and Jeremy P. Felt, "Vice Reform as a Political Technique: The Committee of Fifteen in New York, 1900–1901," *New York History* 54 (1973): 24–51.

17. Beisel, *Imperiled Innocents*, 111; R. Skolnick in Jackson, ed., *Encyclopedia*, 1019; Martin Schiesl, *The Politics of Efficiency: Municipal Administration and Reform in America, 1880–1920* (Berkeley, CA, 1977), 13; Roosevelt, *Autobiography* (New York, 1913), 63. See also Hammack, *Power and Society*; and Johnson, "Defining 'Social Evil,'" Chapter 1. On Roosevelt see Gail Bederman, *Manliness and Civilization: A Cultural History of Gender and Race in the United States, 1880–1917* (Chicago, 1995), Chapter 5.

18. Shefter, "Trade Unions and Political Machines." Sarah Deutsch has demonstrated that Boston male reformers helped to integrate native-born bourgeois women into the state because of the tools they offered for battling machines, "in particular their privately funded welfare system" operated through settlements. Deutsch, *Women and the City*, 280. See also S. Sara Monoson, "The Lady and the Tiger: Women's Electoral Activism in New York City Before Suffrage." *Journal of Women's History* 2, no. 2 (Fall 1990): 100–35; Maureen Flanagan, "Gender and Urban Political Reform: The City Club and The Woman's City Club of Chicago in the Progressive Era," *American Historical Review* 94, no. 4 (October 1990): 1032–50; Gary E. Endelman, *Solidarity Forever: Rose Schneiderman & the Women's Trade Union League* (New York, 1981).

19. On women's institution building and the state from the 1850s see Lori Ginzberg, *Women and the Work of Benevolence: Morality, Politics, and Class in the Nineteenth Century United States* (New Haven, CT, 1990). On Lowell and relief see Waugh, *Unsentimental Reformer*, 105–06, 260, note 19. For critical histories of Lowell's career see Ginzberg, George Fredrickson, *The Inner Civil War, Northern Intellectuals and the Crisis of the Union* (New York, 1965); Paul Boyer, *Urban Masses and Moral Order in America, 1820–1920* (Cambridge, MA, 1978). For a flattering portrait see Waugh, *Unsentimental Reformer*. For COS figures see Tolman, *Municipal Reform*, 147. The population for the five boroughs that now make up New York City was 2,507,414 in 1890. N. Krantowitz, "Population," in Jackson, ed., *Encyclopedia*, 923. The 1890 women's petition, and Lowell's connection with the PML, is discussed by Waugh, 222–23. On women's campaigning see Monoson, "The Lady and the Tiger"; Jo Freeman, "'One Man, One Vote, One Woman, One Throat': Women in New York City Politics, 1890–1910," *American Nineteenth Century History*, 1, no. 3 (Autumn 2001): 101–23; Johnson, "'Defining 'Social Evil,'" Chapters 1–2.

20. Tolman, *Municipal Reform*, 185–97.

21. On the ESRC see Lowell, Letter to the Editor; and "For System in Giving Alms," both *New York Times* (25 December, 1893 and 22 March, 1894); "Five Months' Work for the Unemployed in New York City," *Charities Review* 3 (1894): 323–42; Burrows and Wallace, *Gotham*, 1188–90; Waugh, *Unsentimental Reformer*, 219–20; Robert A. Woods and Albert J. Kennedy, eds., *Handbook of Settlements* (1911; New York, 1970), 194.

22. See Lowell's (JSL) correspondence as follows: JSL to George Morgan, 11 March, 12 March, and 6 May, 1901, *Committee of Fifteen Records 1900–1901* (Wilmington, DE, 1998), Microfilm, reel 1, frames 0230, 0236, 0242 [hereafter cited as C15M 1: 0230, 0236, 0242], JSL to Felix Adler, 18 March 1901, C15M 1: 0232. Women's mass meetings are noted in "WOMEN TO ATTACK VICE," *New York Sun* (16 March 1901), Press Abstracts (25 June 1901) and Press Abstracts (9 October 1901) box 3, C15R. For a summary of the Women's Municipal League's participation see Monoson, "The Lady and the Tiger," 110–14. For Republican women see Freeman, "'One Man, One Vote.'" The quotation is from *New York Evening Post* (October 18, 1900).

23. On Jewish reformers and the Council of Jewish women see Gordon Kuzmack, *Woman's Cause*; Rogow, *Gone to Another Meeting*; Johnson, "Protection, Virtue, and the 'power to detain.'" The collections of Lillian Wald and Mary Kingsbury Simkhovitch both document Gentile and Jewish women reformers' regulatory and incorporation work with Southern and Eastern European immigrants in Greenwich Village and on the Lower East Side. See *Lillian Wald Papers, 1889–1940* (New York: New York Public Library), microfilm [hereafter cited as LWP2], Lillian Wald Papers (1889–1940), Rare Book and Manuscript Room, Butler Library, Columbia University [hereafter cited as LWP1]; *Greenwich House Records, 1896–1956* (New York: Tamiment Institute Library Microfilm, 1995).

24. Tolman, *Municipal Reform*, 177–79. See also Monoson, "The Lady and the Tiger," 101, 104, 108–09, 110–12, 114, 129, note 21, 130–31, notes 41 and 57; Nathan, *The Story of an Epoch-Making Movement* (New York, 1926), 19; Waugh, *Unsentimental Reformer*, 228; and William Rhinelander Stewart, *The Philanthropic Work of Josephine Shaw Lowell* (New York, 1911), 417.

25. Monoson, "The Lady and the Tiger," 101, 104, 108–09, 110–12, 114, 129, note 21, 130–31, notes 41 and 57; Woman's Municipal League, *Facts for Fathers and Mothers* (New York, 1901); Tolman, *Municipal Reform*, 177–79.

26.  The official platform is printed in Larocque in Parkhurst, *Our Fight*, 260–63. The quote about Tammany is from *New York Times* (5 October 1894), in Hammack, *Power and Society*, 151. The Committee of 70 is also quoted in Tolman, *Municipal Reform*, 28. See Hammack, 101–02, 155–56; Schiesl, *Politics of Efficiency*, 63.

27.  Prominent men in political reform besides Parkhurst were avidly anti-suffrage, as was Woman's Municipal League Board member Mrs. Parkhurst. Suffragists criticized women reformers for cooperating with anti-suffrage forces. Freeman, "'One Man, One Vote'"; Monoson, "The Lady and the Tiger," 104–05. For Parkhurst on the Constitutional amendment see *New York Times* (21 April and 14 May, 1894).

28.  Hammack, *Power and Society* 116, 143, 347, note 53. The advice quote is from reformer Nicholas Murray Butler. For Lowell's work see Stewart, *Philanthropic Work*, 563.

29.  Walkowitz, *City of Dreadful Delight: Narratives of Sexual Danger in Late-Victorian London* (Chicago, 1992), 7, 250, note 19. On suffragism and white supremacy see Rosalyn Terborg-Penn, *African American Women in the Struggle for the Vote, 1850–1920* (Bloomington, IN, 1998); and Louise M. Newman, *White Women's Rights: The Racial Origins of Feminism in the United States* (New York, 1999). See also Rebecca Edwards in Gustafson, Miller and Israels Perry, eds., *We Have Come to Stay: American Women and Political Parties, 1880–1960* (Albuquerque, NM, 1999). She argues along the following lines with regard to bourgeois women's campaigns for purer elections: "This effort was, in part, an attack on male privilege. It was also antagonistic to working class traditions. In movements to reform electoral campaigns, the gender identities of women served to reinforce, rather than bridge, class differences" (14). For a contemporary example of the intersection between nativism and white women's suffragism see Carrie Chapman Catt, *Woman Suffrage By Federal Constitutional Amendment* (New York, 1917).

30.  League members included Mrs. G. H. Putnam, Mrs. William Rhinelander Stewart, Mrs. E. L. Godkin, Maude Nathan, and Lillian Wald. Waugh, *Unsentimental Reformer*, 225; WML material in Tolman, *Municipal Reform*, 177–79. For the elite membership and working-class targets of the WML see Monoson, "The Lady and the Tiger," 101, 104, 108–09, 110–11, 112.

31.  The Mason quote is from *New York Times* (October 31, 1894), in Freeman "'One Man, One Vote'" 202; Waugh, *Unsentimental Reformer*, 225; WML in Tolman, *Municipal Reform*, 177–79.

32.  Lowell, "What Can Young Men Do For the City?" (28 March 1898), in Stewart, *Philanthropic Work*, 432–33; Waugh, *Unsentimental Reformer*, 124. David Roediger discusses the long-standing republican fear of the weak and dependent in relation to the demonization of African Americans. See Roediger, *The Wages of Whiteness: Race and the Making of the American Working Class* (New York, 1991), 35–36, 44. See also the sources he cites in note 61.

33.  Lowell, "Relation of Women to Good Government" (1899), in Stewart, *Philanthropic Work*, 435–45. See also Lowell's 10 September & November 1903 Letters to the Editor of the WML Bulletin in Stewart, 420, 421.

34.  Lillian Wald, "The Interpretive Value of the Settlement," box 34, LWP2.

35.  Wald, "Crowded Districts of Large Cities," 260, 261, 265. Reynolds' "colonial" quote is in "Annual Report 1900," 14, from *University Settlement*, reel 4. The Orientalist material is from an interview with Reynolds by Abraham Cahan, "The Russian Jew in America," *Atlantic Monthly* 82 (July 1898): 263–87. Cahan was also a critic of prostitution on the Lower East Side (Bristow, *Prostitution and Prejudice*, 148). On the racialization of radicalism generally, see James Barrett and David Roediger, "Inbetween Peoples: Race, Nationality and the 'New Immigrant'

Working Class," *Journal of American Ethnic History* 16, no. 3 (1997): 12. The views of Wald and Reynolds confirm the immigration scholarship of Matthew Frye Jacobson, which demonstrates how the heavily foreign demographic of U.S. cities in this era produced parallels between colonialist accounts and tales about the urban immigrant poor. See Jacobson, *Barbarian Virtues: The United States Encounters Foreign Peoples at Home and Abroad* (New York, 2000), 121–27. The Reynolds material on "political serfdom" is from July 1906 and is found in Irwin Yellowitz, *Labor and the Progressive Movement in New York State, 1897–1916* (Ithaca, NY, 1965), 183.

36.  Abraham Cahan (1860–1951), born in Vilna, Lithuania, immigrated to the United States in 1882. He settled on the Lower East Side. In addition to becoming the first editor for the *Forward* in 1897, Cahan was a leading English-language journalist and novelist, best known for his authorship of *The Rise of David Levinsky*. Biographical information from the Jewish Virtual Library, on-line at: <http://www.jewishvirtuallibrary.org/jsource/ biography/cahan.html>. See Cahan, *The Education of Abraham Cahan*, tr. Leon Stein et al. (Philadelphia, 1969); Sanford E. Marovitz, *Abraham Cahan* (New York, 1996).

37.  On the Educational Alliance see Israels Perry, *Belle Moskowitz*, 14 ff. On Richman see Selma C. Berrol, "When Uptown Met Downtown: Julia Richman's Work in the Jewish Community of New York, 1880–1912," *American Jewish History* 70 (September 1980): 35–51; and Johnson, "Defining 'Social Evil,'" 245, 255–57, 294. For Moss's reception, see Press Abstracts (24 July 1901) box 3, C15R. For the anti-immigrant and anti-Semitic sentiments in the Lexow and Mazet Commissions, and Moss's role in blaming immigrant Jews for crime and corruption see Connelly, *The Response to Prostitution*, 60–61, 118–19; Arthur Goren, *New York Jews and the Quest for Community: The Kehillah Experiment, 1908–1922* (New York, 1970), 134; and Bristow, *Prostitution and Prejudice*, 46–47, 175.

38.  Wald, *The House on Henry Street* (New York, 1915), 174. There are conflicting accounts around whether the 1901 campaign was initiated by Jews or Protestants, and members of the working or the upper classes. See Johnson "The 1901 Campaign Against Vice," in "Defining 'Social Evil,'" Chapter 2. The "cry of parents" quote is from "THE FIFTEEN APPROVE THE PROPOSED TENEMENT LAW," unidentified (25 March 1901), Newspaper Clippings File, C15M reel 16, frame 0387 [hereafter cited as Clippings 16: 0387, C15M].

39.  Report of Max Moscowitz, 16 March 1901, box 7, and "41 First St." on Kreisworth, Conklin, and Moscowitz, box 15, both C15R. Resident testimony before the Tenement House Commission is cited in Wagner, "Virtue Against Vice," 81.

40.  See Press Abstracts for the following dates: 17 November 1900, 24 November 1900, 24 January 1901, January 25 1901, 16 July 1901, 23 August 1901, 26 January 1901, 29 November 1901. All are in box 3 of C15R. See also "RED LIGHT CADET'S CRIME," *Sun* (15 February 1901), "VICTIMS COMPLAIN," *Sun* (16 March 1901) clippings C15M 16: 0317.

41.  As noted above Eastern European immigrants were not over-represented in the practice of prostitution in comparison with their percentage of the general population. For reformer acknowledgment that repression relocated prostitution within the city see James B. Reynolds cited in Press Abstracts (26 February 1901) box 3, C15R; "VICE NOW REDOMICILED," *New York Post* (9 February 1901); May 1901 press coverage of Reynolds' comments in Clippings, C15M 16: 0033, 0673–76. See also Committee of Fourteen, *Annual Report* (New York: Committee of Fourteen, 1914), 19; and Madge D. Headley (Secretary of the COS Tenement House Committee) to Frederick Whitin, 24 June 1914, THD Prior to 1915-i folder, box 21, Committee of

Fourteen Records (1905–1920), Rare Book and Manuscripts Division, New York Public Library [hereafter cited as C14]. For geographical shifts in prostitution, and their connections with gender control of institutions of prostitution, Gilfoyle, *City of Eros*, 336–37, note 11, 384, note 3, 394, note 2, 417, 296–97.

42. For Blaustein and Cahan see Bristow, *Prostitution and Prejudice*, 148.

43. Wald, *Henry Street*, 174. On Moskowitz and the DES, see Woods and Kennedy, eds., *Handbook*, 196; Perry, *Belle Moskowitz*, 99–101, 239, note 6; Gordon Kuzmack, *Woman's Cause*, 66; and Johnson, "Defining 'Social Evil,'" Chapter 2.

44. Downtown Ethical Society material, quoted in Woods and Kennedy, eds., *Handbook*, 196.

45. Simkhovitch, *Neighborhood*, 64–66; Bristow, *Prostitution and Prejudice*, 146–47, 148; Daniel Czitrom, "Underworlds and Underdogs: Big Tim Sullivan and Metropolitan Politics in New York, 1889–1913," in Raymond Mohl, ed., *The Making of Urban America*, 2nd ed. (Wilmington, DE, 1997), 139–41.

46. "RED LIGHT CADET'S CRIME," *New York Sun* (15 February 1901); "VICTIMS COMPLAIN," *New York Sun* (16 March 1901) clippings C15M 16: 0317. Angel & Gurock, in Jackson, ed., *Encyclopedia*, 621; Rudolf Glanz, *The Jewish Woman in America: Two Female Immigrant Generations 1820–1929, Volume I, The Eastern European Jewish Woman* (New York, 1976), 111; Hammack, *Power and Society*, 156; Felt, "Vice Reform as a Political Technique," 48.

47. Bristow, *Prostitution and Prejudice*, 42; Susan A. Glenn, *Daughters Of The Shtetl: Life and Labor in the Immigrant Generation* (Ithaca, NY, 1990), 69–70, 79–82, 116–17. For male family members' involvement in policing "white slavery" cases see "RED LIGHT CADET'S CRIME," *New York Sun* (15 February 1901); "VICTIMS COMPLAIN," *New York Sun* (16 March 1901), clippings C15M 16: 0317.

48. Ruth Alexander, Mary Odem, and Flora Rothman have analyzed the participation of working-class parents in the policing of female sexuality with different emphases. Alexander focuses on parents' efforts to control daughters. Odem highlights parents' resistance to the state and reformers. Rothman presents mothers as initiators in the incarceration of daughters and assigns a fairly benign role to reformers. Alexander, *The Girl Problem: Female Sexual Delinquency In New York, 1900–1930* (Ithaca, NY, 1995); Odem, *Delinquent Daughters: Protecting and Policing Adolescent Female Sexuality in the United States, 1885–1920* (Chapel Hill, NC, 1995); Rothman, "Bad Girls/Poor Girls: A New York History Of Social Control From The Alms House To Family Court" (Ph.D. diss., City University of New York, 1989), 344–49, 307.

49. Glenn, *Daughters of the Shtetl*, 213–14. The Committee of Fifteen reports are cited in Bristow, *Prostitution and Prejudice*, 147; Michael Gold, *Jews Without Money* (New York, 1930), cited in Glanz, *The Jewish Woman in America*, 189, note 33.

50. A careful reading of fourteen women's complaints revealed that nine were concerned with controlling the leisure pursuits of their family men. Six of the nine stressed a threat to the family economy. Six complaints concerned husbands, three sons. In addition to the complaint about the "polish society" another involved a husband patronizing an establishment rented by Louis Strieckman at Broom and Orchard Streets. The remaining complaints involved one clearly about prostitution, one about "fast women" in a leisure space, two about male seducers, and a woman who had been seduced wrote one. Most citizens' complaints were anonymous and undated. The earliest dated one considered here was from 1908, the latest 1917. Citizens' Complaints folder, box 22, C14. For working-class women's emphasis on regulating their male family members' economic roles see Johnson, "Defining 'Social Evil,'" Appendix B: New York City's Other Social Courts.

51. Rischin, *The Promised City*, Chapter 6, especially 96–98. Stanley Nadel briefly addresses the German-ness of German Jews. *Little Germany: Ethnicity, Religion, and Class in New York City, 1845–80* (Urbana, IL, 1990), 99–103. For a related argument about the Russian-ness of Russian Jews see Steven Cassedy, *To the Other Shore: The Russian Jewish Intellectuals Who Came to America* (Princeton, NJ, 1997).

52. Nadel, *Little Germany*, 147–54,132–36: Monoson, "The Lady and the Tiger," 113; Hammack, *Power and Society*, 115–19, 144, 151–54, 168. For women's involvement in the 1901 campaign see Press Abstracts box 3, C15R; and Clipping, C15M 15 and 16.

53. Johnson, "Protection, Virtue, and the 'power to detain,'" 655–84; and "Defining 'Social Evil,'" Chapter 3. Rogow touches on conflict and cooperation between German Jewish men and women (*Gone to Another Meeting*, 44–53, 57). Gordon Kuzmack emphasizes how German Jewish women's approach to these matters differed from that of male leaders (*A Woman's Cause*, 63, 68–69, 73). See also Perry, *Belle Moskowitz*; and Cahan, *Education of Abraham Cahan*, 218–19, 400.

54. For Jewish immigrants' involvement in anti-prostitution, particularly on the Lower East Side see Felt, "Vice Reform as a Political Technique"; Bristow, *Prostitution and Prejudice*, 48; Arthur Goren, *New York Jews and the Quest for Community: The Kehillah Experiment, 1908–1922* (New York, 1970). For the "red light district" see Bristow, 146. The 1890 densities for Germans in the two districts surrounding the Stanton Street mission of Rev. Paddock (who initiated the 1901 campaign) are illustrative. These were Sanitary Districts A and B of Ward 17 (A was bounded by E. 4th to Rivington, and 1st Ave. to Bowery [including Allen St.], B was bounded by E. 4th to Rivington, and Ave. B/Clinton to 1st Ave./Allen). The density for Germans in District A was 201–300 per acre. The density for Germans in District B was over 300. See also Map No. 1 of City of New York Showing Densities of Population in the Several Sanitary Districts, 1 June 1894, from F. E. Pierce, *The Tenement-House Committee Maps* (New York, 1895 [from 1890 Census]). Ward 10, Sanitary District B (Rivington to Grand, and Norfolk to Bowery) had German, Russian, and Polish densities at 101–200 per acre. Ward 11, Sanitary District A (2nd Ave. to Ave. B and Clinton to Rivington) had a German density of 201–300 per acre, and a Russian and Polish density of 51–100 per acre. Ethnic density is calculated via the nationality of mothers, from Map of the City Of New York, N.Y. Showing the Density of Population Born of German Mothers, by Sanitary Districts (Subdivisions of Wards), 1 June 1890, prepared by Kate Holladay Claghorn from data in *Vital Statistics 1890*, New York Public Library, Map Division. The figures would have decreased by the time of the 1894 and 1901 campaigns with the movement of Germans out of this neighborhood, but it seems likely that some Germans would have remained. Nadel asserts that Germans abandoned the Lower East Side by the 1880s ("Germans," in Jackson, ed., *Encyclopedia*, 463), but the 1890 census data outlined here contradict this. There was a slim possibility that some of these Germans were Protestant (Nadel, *Little Germany*, 91, 92, 95–97). Were they Catholics, Jewish, secular?

55. Goldman framed prostitution and the persecution of prostitutes as produced by "the property morality." Goldman, "Victims of Morality" in A. K. Shulman, ed., *Red Emma Speaks: Selected Writings and Speeches by Emma Goldman* (New York, 1972), 126–32. The quotations are from Goldman's trial transcript, *People of New York v. Emma Goldman*, 28, 31, 29 in EGP 56. For the history of comparisons between chattel slavery and wage labor, including the deployment of the term "white slave," see Roediger, "White Slaves, Wage Slaves, and Free White Labor," in

Roediger, *The Wages of Whiteness*; and Johnson, "Defining 'Social Evil,'" Chapter 3.

56. When Emma Goldman was released after her imprisonment for "threaten[ing] to raise insurrections" in 1893, thousands welcomed her home to the Lower East Side. For evidence of Goldman's popularity and the threat it was perceived to pose by the powers that be, see Burrows and Wallace, *Gotham*, 1187; "Anarchy's Den," *New York World* (28 July 1892); and *People of New York v. Emma Goldman* (Grand Jury Indictment, 1893), and Government Documents (1884–1916), both in EGP, reel 56. On German-American women see Christiane Harzig, "The Ethnic Female Public Sphere: German-American Women in Turn-of-the-Century Chicago," in Eldersveld Murphy and Hamand Vent, eds., *Midwestern Women: Work, Community, and Leadership at the Crossroads* (Bloomington, IN, 1997).

# 4

# Immigration Policy in a Time of War: The United States, 1939–1945[1]

*ROGER DANIELS*

THE ARGUMENT OF THIS ESSAY is that the World War II years were crucial in setting the direction for American immigration policy for the rest of the twentieth century, even though during the war immigration from outside the hemisphere fell to the lowest levels ever recorded.[2] I will discuss these changes topically in four categories: 1) internment, registration, and incarceration; 2) naturalization; 3) refugees; 4) non-immigrants.

## INTERNMENT, REGISTRATION, AND INCARCERATION

Internment, which had first been used by the United States during the War of 1812, was applied during fall 1939 to German seamen picked up on the high seas or on German vessels interned in American ports. Before Pearl Harbor hundreds of German, and later Italian, seamen and some Italian employees of the Italian Pavilion at the New York World's Fair of 1939–40, were interned, first at Ellis Island and later at facilities run by the INS in New Mexico and Montana.[3] With the fall of France in June 1940, nativists and others feared that Nazi agents, the largely mythical fifth columnists, would be hidden among immigrants or pose as refugees.[4] That month a presidential directive transferred the INS from the Department of Labor to the Department of Justice, pleasing nativists and conservatives who felt that Secretary of Labor Frances Perkins's policies were too soft.[5]

Amidst a flurry of bills aimed at making deportation easier—one of which had been vetoed by the president in April 1940[6]—Congress passed and Roosevelt signed the harsh Alien Registration Act of 1940 at the end of June. Also known as the Smith Act, it was a complex measure of forty-one sections organized into three largely unrelated titles. Title I was a peacetime sedition act that later provided the statutory basis for the conviction of a few Trotskyites during the war and in the postwar years was used to jail many of the leaders of the American Communist Party. Title II expanded the grounds, most of them involving subversive activities, under which aliens could be deported. Title III required all aliens fourteen years of age and older to register and be fingerprinted, usually at a post office, to advise the INS in writing of any change of address, and to confirm their address, in writing, every three months.[7] Allowed to fall into desuetude by the government but never repealed, the change-of-address provisions were enforced, selectively, by John Ashcroft's regime in the Department of Justice in the aftermath of 9/11 as a means of deporting large numbers of otherwise law-abiding resident aliens of Middle Eastern and South Asian origin.

More than a million resident aliens encountered serious restrictions as soon as the United States actually went to war. In December 1941, a series of proclamations based on existing statute law declared non-citizen Japanese, Germans, and Italians, "being of the age of fourteen years and upward" alien enemies and "liable to be apprehended, restrained, secured, and removed as alien enemies."[8] In mid-January 1942, all alien enemies were required to re-register and receive new identification certificates and carry them at all times.[9] This covered more than a million persons in the United States and in hemispheric territories—chiefly 600,000 Italians, 300,000 Germans, and 90,000 Japanese—but the Department of Justice had relatively modest intentions. During the course of the war it arrested fewer than 2 percent—about 16,000 persons—and interned less than half of those in INS camps: 7,459 individuals, 4,092 Japanese, 2,384 Germans, 794 Italians, and 199 "others."[10] These numbers do not include 6,610 citizens and residents of Peru and fourteen other Latin American nations: 4,058 Germans, 2,264 Japanese, and 287 Italians. These men, women, and children were deported from their homes at the behest of the United States (whose agents helped to select them) and brought into the United States, without statutory authority and in violation of American law, and interned in INS camps.[11]

What is usually called, improperly, the "internment of the Japanese Americans" will only be noted here. It was an incarceration, not based on statute law, which deprived more than 110,000 persons of Japanese birth and ancestry living on the Pacific Coast of their liberty. It made no distinctions for either citizenship or age.[12]

## NATURALIZATION

The most significant changes in naturalization law broadened the largely arbitrary "racial" categories of those eligible for naturalization but narrowed the ideological boundaries. The Nationality Act of 1940 did both. On the one hand, it clarified the status of Mexicans and others of Amerindian heritage. All Indians born in the United States had been made citizens in 1924; the 1940 statute expanded the rights of naturalization from "white persons and persons of African descent" to include "descendants of races indigenous to the Western Hemisphere." On the other hand, echoing the anti-subversive provisions of the

Smith Act, it greatly expanded the existing anti-radical provisions barring the naturalization of "persons opposed to government or law."[13]

A further and little understood change was the ending of Chinese Exclusion in 1943. The repeal statute, supported by a special message from Franklin Roosevelt, was presented as a kind of good-behavior prize for wartime allies. The campaign for it largely ignored Chinese Americans. The repeal statute was a relatively simple three-part measure. Part one repealed some or all of fifteen statutes enacted between 1882 and 1913 that had enforced Chinese exclusion. Part two gave a quota to "persons of the Chinese race," set at 105 annually, with a preference of up to 75 percent given to persons "born and resident in China." This meant that a Chinese born anywhere in the world—say, Canada—had to be charged to the tiny Chinese quota, a stipulation that applied to no other group. Part three amended the nationality acts so that "Chinese persons or persons of Chinese descent" were eligible for naturalization on the same terms as other eligible aliens.[14]

Critics, then and now, have stressed the obvious racist limitations of the reform by focusing on the tiny quota. Gilbert Woo, a liberal San Francisco Chinatown journalist, denounced it as a token gesture and an insult to Chinese Americans. But as scholars K. Scott Wong and Xiaojian Zhao separately have pointed out, the naturalization provisions, coupled with so-called War Brides Acts, enabled thousands of Chinese American men not only to become citizens but also to bring both brides and wives of long-standing into the United States. The legal immigration of nearly 10,000 Chinese women changed significantly the demographic structure of the Chinese American community, no longer a bachelor society.[15] In addition, although promoted as a special wartime case, the repeal of Chinese Exclusion was a clear sign that the days of "racial" exclusion in naturalization and immigration were numbered and can be seen as the hinge on which American immigration policy turned. As FDR himself noted prophetically in his message, passing the bill would "be an earnest of our purpose to apply the policy of the Good Neighbor to our relations with other peoples." Less than three years later separate bills extended the right of naturalization to Filipinos and "natives of India"; and in 1952, in the generally reactionary McCarran-Walter Act, naturalization was made colorblind.[16]

## REFUGEES

As is notorious, Franklin Roosevelt long refused to take political risks on behalf of European refugees who were predominantly Jewish. For example, the New Deal's most prolific legislator, Senator Robert F. Wagner of New York, co-sponsored a bill in 1939 to admit 20,000 German children outside of the quota. It had important bi-partisan support—including ex-president Herbert C. Hoover—but the White House, uncharacteristically, kept hands off. FDR was willing to allow some administration officials— Frances Perkins and Children's Bureau head Katherine Lenroot—to testify in favor of it. He even told his wife, in February 1939, that "it is all right for you to support the child refugee bill, but it is best for me to say nothing [now]." Now became never. In June 1939, as the bill was dying without ever having emerged from committee, the president annotated a memo asking for his support "File No Action, FDR." In addition, some of his personal and official family viciously opposed the bill: one of his favorite cousins, Laura Delano, wife of Commissioner of Immigration and Naturalization James Houghteling, told people at cocktail parties that the "20,000 charming children would all too soon grow up into 20,000 ugly adults."[17]

France's defeat triggered the first of several small refugee rescue actions by the United States. Roosevelt asked his Advisory Committee on Refugees to make lists of eminent refugees and then instructed the State Department to issue temporary visas in the names of those individuals. The State Department, whose reports on refugees are not always reliable, said that it issued 3,268 such visas but only about a third of them were used. A veritable galaxy of cultural superstars including Lion Feuchtwanger, Heinrich Mann, Franz Werfel, Anna Mahler Werfel, Marc Chagall, Jacques Lipchitz, Marcel Duchamp, and Wanda Landowska were brought to the United States, many of them by that most improbable secret agent, Varian Fry, who operated in Vichy Marseilles from August 1940 until September 1941.[18]

Late in 1940, two administrative measures eased the position of some refugees who had already escaped from Germany and German-occupied Europe. First, American consuls outside of Germany were allowed to issue visas to refugees who had gotten to places like Portugal, French Africa, and China and charge them to the German quota established in the 1924 immigration act, little used after the war broke out. In fiscal year 1941, only 4,028 spaces were used and in fiscal 1942 about half that number. Had this kind of administrative ingenuity been used earlier, many more refugees could have been admitted. Then, in January 1941, an agreement with Canada set up a system whereby a refugee in the United States on a temporary visa would be allowed to enter Canada briefly, apply for a quota number from there, and re-enter the United States as a regular immigrant. At that time, American law forbade a visitor from changing status without leaving the United States.[19]

Only after Secretary of the Treasury Henry Morgenthau's staff prepared its "Report to the Secretary on the Acquiescence of this Government in the Murder of the Jews" and he brought it to Roosevelt—under the less jarring title of "Personal Report to the President"—on January 16, 1944, was further action taken to bring refugees to the United States. From its blunt first sentence—"One of the greatest crimes in history, the slaughter of the Jewish people in Europe, is continuing unabated"—to the end, it was a damning indictment of American policy in general and of the State Department in particular. The report not only attacked the Department's visa policy, which, under the cloak of "national security," had kept immigration well below quota levels but also argued that some of its officials— Breckinridge Long in particular—had deliberately failed to rescue Jews. Prodded by the report, Roosevelt undertook additional actions on behalf of Jewish and other refugees but was reluctant to believe that Long, an old friend, was the deliberate saboteur of rescue plans.[20]

FDR issued an executive order creating the War Refugee Board, whose bills were paid by a combination of the President's discretionary funds and money donated by Jewish organizations. Although the language of the executive order stated that "it is the policy of this Government to take all measures within its power to rescue the victims of enemy oppression who are in imminent danger of death and otherwise to afford such victims all possible relief and assistance consistent with the successful prosecution of the war,"[21] the truth of the situation had been, was then, and continued to be at variance with that inflated claim. In fact, the War Refugee Board was not authorized to bring even one refugee to the United States. It initially placed the people it rescued in camps in North and West Africa, the Middle East, Switzerland, and Sweden.[22]

A further step was taken in June 1944. FDR cabled Ambassador Robert Murphy in Algiers on June 9 that:

> I have decided that approximately 1,000 refugees should be immediately brought from Italy to this country, to be placed in an Emergency Refugee Shelter to be established at Fort Ontario near Oswego, New York, where under appropriate security restrictions they will remain for the duration of the war. These refugees will be brought into the country outside of the regular immigration procedure just as civilian internees from Latin American countries and prisoners of war have been brought here. . . . It is contemplated that at the end of the war they will be returned to their homelands.[23]

Three days later Roosevelt informed Congress of the program.[24] He claimed that "notwithstanding this Government's unremitting efforts, which are continuing, the numbers actually rescued from the jaws of death have been small compared with the numbers still facing extinction in German territory."

Sharon R. Lowenstein, the historian of this episode, has rightly called the program a "token shipment." It brought 987 refugees, mostly Jewish, from camps in Italy to the United States. All but sixty-nine would remain in America when the camp was emptied in February 1946, President Truman having issued a directive allowing them to adjust their status. Although the few brought to Oswego were truly a token insofar as the surviving victims of the Holocaust were concerned, the precedent of presidential parole authority would become an important part of American refugee policy during the Cold War and beyond.[25]

## NON-IMMIGRANTS

Finally, there is the phenomenon of what immigration officials now call "nonimmigrants," defining that curious term as aliens "admitted to the United States for a specified purpose and temporary period but not for permanent residence."[26] It currently embraces such traditional categories of arrivals as "visitors for pleasure" and "students," but also a bewildering array of individuals who come to work or do business and enter with a complex series of visas differentiated by letters and numbers such as "H1B." In 2003 more than 2.6 million such persons were admitted as "nonimmigrants" in categories that are potentially adjustable to immigrant status. This is almost four times as large as the number of immigrants who were admitted in 2003. Those 705,827 immigrants were almost equally divided between "new arrivals" and those who had entered in some previous year and adjusted to immigrant status in 2003.[27]

There was no such category during World War Two, but a variety of persons did come to America in those years whose presence is not reflected in the INS reports. In addition to the Latin American civilians brought for internment and more than 400,000 Axis prisoners of war,[28] there was the Bracero Program (from the Spanish "*bracer*" [arm]). Begun by an executive agreement between the United States and Mexico in July 1942 and revised in April 1943, it was legalized by Congress in 1943 and extended to cover West Indian and Bahamian workers who toiled largely in eastern agriculture, as did some Canadians and Newfoundlanders. Government data report just over 225,000 agricultural workers imported during the war years, nearly three-quarters of them from Mexico.[29] A separate wartime bracero program provided about 50,000 maintenance workers for western railroads.[30] And, to be sure, there was considerable informal border crossing, especially in Texas, which the Mexican government had excluded from the formal program.

In addition, the government also made it possible for educated Chinese to study in the United States. Beginning in 1942 the Cultural Division of the State Department provided grants to enable many Chinese to study at American universities; in 1949, when Chinese Communists led by Mao Zedong (Tse-tung) drove the Chinese nationalists off the mainland to Taiwan and began the People's Republic of China, there were some 5,000 Chinese, many of them students, in the United States on non-immigrant visas. Many, perhaps most, of these "stranded Chinese" received immigrant visas and eventually became U.S. citizens.[31]

The foregoing demonstrates that the wartime experience was predictive of the path that American immigration policy pursued from World War II until the end of the century. The renaissance of mass immigration in the second half of the twentieth century, encompassing nearly twenty-seven million legal immigrants as opposed to just over twenty million in its first half, was not solely the result of the 1965 immigration act. Journalists and scholars who so describe it seriously misinform their readers. That experience also seems to have a predictive quality for some post-9/11 events, but until many currently closed files are opened it will be impossible to spell those matters out in any detail.[32]

## NOTES

1. An earlier version of this material appeared in Roger Daniels, *Guarding the Golden Door: American Immigration Policy and Immigrants since 1882* (New York: Hill and Wang, 2004), 81–97.
2. In 1943, 1944, and 1945 immigration from the Eastern Hemisphere totaled 5,513, 5,467, and 8,473 respectively. The lowest previous figures were for 1822, 1823, and 1824 when 6,911, 6,354, and 7,912 immigrants were enumerated, almost all of them Europeans.

3.    For 1812, see for example Charles Lockington, petitioner, *The case of alien enemies, considered and decided upon a writ of habeas corpus, allowed on the petition of Charles Lockington, an alien enemy, by the Hon. William Tilghman, chief justice of the Supreme Court of Pennsylvania, the 22d day of November, 1813. Reported by Richard Bache, esq.* (Philadelphia, 1813). Early American imprints. Second series; no. 28085, Microfiche 1242, Readex Microprint Corporation. For early World War II, see John J. Culley, "A Troublesome Presence: World War II Internment of German Sailors in New Mexico," *Prologue* 28 (Winter 1996): 279–95; and Louis Fiset, "Return to Sender: U.S. Censorship of Enemy Alien Mail in World War II," *Prologue* 33 (Spring 2001): 21–35.

4.    See, for example, the State Department-inspired article by Samuel Lubell, "War by Refugee," *Saturday Evening Post* (Mar. 29, 1941).

5.    Reorganization Plan No. V, 5 *Federal Register* 2223; George W. Martin, *Madam Secretary, Frances Perkins* (Boston, 1976), 442.

6.    The veto message is in *Congressional Record*, 86: 4157.

7.    54 *Stat.* 670.

8.    Presidential proclamations 2525, 2526, 2526, and 2563 of Dec. 7, Dec. 8, 1941, and July 17, 1942. Later, Hungarians, Bulgarians, and Rumanians were added to this category. Austrian and Korean resident aliens, who had German and Japanese nationality respectively, were not declared enemy aliens.

9.    Presidential proclamation 2527, Jan. 14, 1942.

10.   These numbers are very "iffy" and come from two FBI documents and the Department of Justice's annual report for 1943.

11.   Max Paul Freidman, *Nazis and Good Neighbors: The United States Campaign against the Germans of Latin America in World War II* (New York, 2003) is a superb account of the process. For the Japanese see C. Harvey Gardiner. *Pawns in a Triangle of Hate: The Peruvian Japanese and the United States* (Seattle, 1981); Seiichi Higashide, *Adios to Tears: The Memoirs of a Japanese Peruvian Internee in U. S. Concentration Camps*, 2d ed. (Seattle, 2000) is a memoir by a Peruvian Japanese, while Karen L. Riley, *Schools Behind Barbed Wire: The Untold Story of Wartime Internment and the Children of Arrested Enemy Aliens* (Lanham, MD, 2002) is an account of the INS family camp at Crystal City, Texas, in which many of the Latin Americans were held. John K. Emmerson, *The Japanese Thread: A Life in the U.S. Foreign Service* (New York, 1978) is a memoir by an official involved in the deportation of the Peruvian Japanese. There has been little scholarly analysis of the Latin American Italians involved. Friedman has provided the following table, not in his book, showing where the internees from Latin America came from.

**LATIN AMERICAN INTERNEES, BY COUNTRY, WW II**

| Country | Germans | Italians | Japanese |
|---|---|---|---|
| Bolivia | 221 | 27 | 57 |
| Br. Honduras | 12 | 0 | 0 |
| Chile | 5 | 0 | 0 |
| Colombia | 646 | 23 | 12 |
| Costa Rica | 379 | 13 | 27 |
| Cuba | 13 | 5 | 5 |
| Dominican Republic | 68 | 7 | 1 |
| Ecuador | 463 | 24 | 11 |
| El Salvador | 96 | 29 | 6 |
| Guatemala | 479 | 10 | 0 |
| Haiti | 77 | 4 | 0 |

| Honduras | 144 | 4 | 1 |
|---|---|---|---|
| Mexico | 266 | 8 | 84 |
| Nicaragua | 177 | 16 | 6 |
| Panama | 247 | 52 | 247 |
| Canal Zone* | 4 | 0 | 0 |
| Paraguay | 17 | 0 | 0 |
| Peru | 702 | 49 | 1799 |
| Venezuela | 42 | 16 | 8 |
| Total | 4058 | 287 | 2264 |

* Does not include seamen interned in 1939–40.

12. For details see Roger Daniels, *Prisoners Without Trial: Japanese Americans in World War II*. 2d ed. (New York, 2004); and Roger Daniels, "Words Do Matter: A Note on Inappropriate Terminology and the Incarceration of the Japanese Americans," in Gail Nomura and Louis Fiset, eds., *Nikkei in the Pacific Northwest: Japanese Americans and Japanese Canadians in the Twentieth Century* (Seattle, 2005), 183–207.
13. *54 Stat.* 1137.
14. The campaign for exclusion is the subject of Fred W. Riggs, *Pressures on Congress: A Study of the Repeal of Chinese Exclusion* (New York, 1950). For Congressional discussion, see U.S. Congress, House, Committee on Immigration and Naturalization, *Repeal of the Chinese Exclusion Acts, Hearings.* . . . (Washington, DC, 1943). FDR's message is in Samuel I. Rosenman, comp., *The Public Papers and Addresses of Franklin D. Roosevelt* (New York, 1950), 429–30 (in the volume for 1943). The law, technically an amendment to the Alien Registration Act of 1940, is 57 *Stat.* 600.
15. Gilbert Woo, "One-Hundred-and-Seven Chinese," appears in a trail-blazing anthology called *Chinese American Voices: From the Gold Rush to the Present*, ed. Judy Yung, Gordon Chang, and Him Mark Lai (Berkeley, CA, 2006). K. Scott Wong, "War Comes to Chinatown: Social Transformation and the Chinese of California," in R. Lotchin, ed., *The Way We Really Were: The Golden State in the Second Great War* (Urbana, IL, 2000), 164–86; Xiaojian Zhao, *Remaking Chinese America: Immigration, Family, and Community, 1940–1965* (Philadelphia, 2002).
16. *66 Stat.* 163.
17. For the Wagner-Rogers bill see Barbara McDonald Stewart, *United States Government Policy on Refugees from Nazism, 1933–1940* (New York, 1982), ch. 12. The Laura Delano quotation is from the manuscript diary of State Department official Jay P. Moffat, May 25, 1939, as cited by Stewart, 532. This, and all other references to Jewish refugee matters, were omitted from the published version of the diary. Nancy H. Hooker, ed., *The Moffat Papers: Selections from the Diplomatic Journals of Jay Pierrepont Moffat, 1919–1943* (Cambridge, MA, 1956).
18. Robert A. Divine. *American Immigration Policy* (New Haven, CT, 1957), 102–3; Cynthia Jaffee McCabe, "'Wanted by the Gestapo: Saved by America'—Varian Fry and the Emergency Rescue Committee," 79–91, in Jarrell C. Jackman and Carla M. Borden, eds., *The Muses Flee Hitler: Cultural Transfer and Adaptation, 1930–1945* (Washington, DC, 1983); Varian Fry, *Surrender on Demand* (1945; Boulder, CO, 1997, also available as an e-book).
19. Divine, *American Immigration Policy*, 103.
20. John Morton Blum, ed., *From the Morgenthau Diaries: Years of War, 1941–1945* (Boston, 1967), 220–7; and Blum, *Morgenthau and Roosevelt* (Boston, 1970), 531–33.

21. Rosenman, *FDR Public Papers* (1944 volume), 48–53.

22. There is no monographic study of the War Refugee Board. Volume 11 of David S. Wyman, ed., *America and the Holocaust* (New York, 1989–91) is devoted to *War Refugee Board "Weekly Reports."* Verne Newton, ed., *FDR and the Holocaust.* (New York, 1996) contains essays by scholars representing a broad spectrum of opinion.

23. Rosenman. *FDR Public Papers* (1944 volume), 163–5.

24. Rosenman. *FDR Public Papers* (1944 volume), 168–72.

25. Sharon R. Lowenstein, *Token Refuge: The Story of the Jewish Refugee Shelter at Oswego, 1944–1946* (Bloomington, IN, 1986). See also the memoir by Ruth Gruber, *Haven: The Untold Story of 1,000 World War II Refugees* (New York, 1983). She was a special assistant to Interior Secretary Harold L. Ickes. Lowenstein seems not to have seen FDR's cable to Murphy.

26. U.S. Immigration and Naturalization Service, *1996 Statistical Yearbook of the Immigration and Naturalization Service* (Washington, DC, 1997), 104.

27. U.S. Department of Homeland Security, *2003 Yearbook of Immigration Statistics* (Washington, DC: GPO, 2004), Tables 25 and 5. There were almost 28 million "nonimmigrants" in 2003, most of them temporary visitors not normally eligible for adjustment of status: more than 20 million were tourists and more than 4 million "temporary visitors for business." Counting entrants is not precision work. For example, in 2003 the DHS admitted 117,583 "nonimmigrants" whose particulars are "unknown," and for years it has been unable to differentiate between entrants from tiny Dominica and the Dominican Republic, one of the major sources in recent years.

28. George C. Lewis and John Mewha, *History of Prisoner of War Utilization by the United States Army—1776–1945* (Washington, DC, 1955), 91.

29. The World War II Bracero Program was initially ratified by 57 *Stat.* 70. The literature is very large. A place to begin is Wayne D. Rasmussen, *A History of the Emergency Farm Labor Supply Program, 1943–1947* (Washington, DC, 1951.) A table showing annual numbers and nationalities is printed in Congressional Research Service, *U.S. Immigration Law and Policy* (Washington, DC, 1979), Table 3, p. 40.

30. Barbara A. Driscoll, *The Tracks North: The Railroad Bracero Program of World War II* (Austin, TX, 1999).

31. For State Department programs see Wilma Fairbank, *America's Cultural Experiment in China, 1942–1949* (Washington, 1976). For the stranded Chinese see Daniels, *Guarding the Golden Door*, 152–54.

32. I have made some tentative speculations about post 9/11 policy in Daniels *Prisoners Without Trial*, 2d ed., 119–21.

# 5

# Ties of Affection: Family Narratives in the History of Italian Migration

## *DIANE VECCHIO*

AT THE AGE OF SEVENTEEN, Giuseppe Verrico left the village of his birth, Santi Cosma e Damiano for America. He had been called to the United States by a half-brother living in Cortland, a small town in central New York. In that same year, 1921, Donato Vecchio emigrated from Castle-forte, a neighboring village of Santi Cosma e Damiano, bound for the same American destination. Donato had been called by his sister Angiolina, who had immigrated to Cortland in 1915, to join another emigrant from Castle-forte, her future husband.

Theorizing migration as a process that connects people in social networks with personal and economic motives has great potential for personalizing the immigrant experience. In this essay I reconstruct the motives, strategies and experiences of immigrant families by tracking the social networks created by male migrants from two villages in south-central Italy to a community in central New York. Similar to Samuel Baily's "village outward approach"[1] that focused on Italian immigrants to Argentina, this study employs a "family outward approach" of Italian immigrants to the United States.[2]

By recreating the social networks that brought Italians to America as well as their patterns of settlement and community building in the United States, my essay explores the role of social networking in migration, transnational links with the homeland, and the role of gender in creating Italian identity in American society. Transnational connections created and maintained not only social networks of migration but also social networks that forged employment opportunities in America where male-female partnerships assumed responsibilities for earning money for the family.[3]

This community study, focusing on regional patterns of migration, demonstrates that Italian males shaped social networks of labor migrations to Cortland,

while Italian females developed family and communal life by creating a culturally transformed Italian identity in America.

The research for this paper is based on analysis of ship manifests and other
records of nearly two thousand passengers emigrating from Santi Cosma e
Damiano and Castleforte to the United States.[4] Research was conducted on both
sides of the Atlantic using Italian records housed primarily in the *comune* of
Santi Cosma e Damiano, as well as oral interviews conducted with members
of the Verrico and Vecchio families in Italy and in the United States.

## SOCIAL NETWORKS AND MIGRATION

Scholars of immigration have investigated the possibility that Italy's migrants
formed an evolving collection of transnational multi-sited social networks that
resembled diasporas. Most of these networks emanated from particular village
communities, where the decisions to emigrate were made.[5] Strong village attachments help explain the evolving social networks that brought Giuseppe Verrico and Donato Vecchio to the United States in 1921. Giuseppe's half-brother,
Bernardino, had been one of the first Italians born in Santi Cosma e Damiano
to immigrate to central New York.[1] "Come to Cortland," he wrote, "you can
find a job here—there is a factory that is hiring."[6]

The letters received from Bernardino drew Giuseppe and other family and
fellow villagers to Cortland, where a colony of Sancosmesi[7] had been developing since 1900. The letter that linked Giuseppe with Bernardino across two
continents involved a process that was repeated time and again in an international context of labor migration during the late nineteenth and early twentieth
centuries. In a similar pattern of migration identified by John Briggs in his
seminal work on Italian emigration to three American destinations,[8] brothers
connected with brothers, uncles with nephews and sisters with sisters, as word
of factory employment spread outward, in this instance, from Santi Cosma e
Damiano to the neighboring village of Castleforte.

Bernardino resembled thousands of emigrants who played a crucial role in
migration systems that were sustained for years, even decades. Determining
where the first link in chain migration begins is like piecing together a puzzle,
but it appears that Bernardino was originally summoned to New York City by
an older brother who was called by an uncle in 1898. Bernardino became instrumental in extending the chain of immigration to Cortland, starting with his half-
brother, Giuseppe, their *paesani*[9] from Santi Cosma e Damiano and Castleforte,
as well as other family members from the nearby town of Minturno.

Sailing with Giuseppe Verrico on the *Argentina* in the spring of 1921 were
three fellow villagers who made up part of the network of migrants heading
for Cortland to work in one of the numerous factories that manufactured tools,
machinery, boats, and sheet metal. The Wickwire Brothers Wireworks employed
the largest number of immigrant workers of all Cortland establishments, with
Poles, Ukrainians, Irish, and Italians manufacturing wire mesh, galvanized fenc-

ing, barbed wire, and nails. Silk mills and factories that produced bloomers and corsets, overalls, and fishing line employed large numbers of immigrant women, while both genders worked seasonally for the Cortland Canning Company.

Arriving at the train station in Cortland in 1921, Giuseppe's traveling companions, Rocco Gaetano and Cosmo Porchetta, were met by, respectively, their uncle and father, a mason who left Santi Cosma e Damiano in 1903 and eventually settled in Cortland after initially migrating to New York City. Giuseppe was met by Bernardino, who took him into his home and helped him get a job at Wickwire's, where they paid an Irish foreman $25 for the job.[10]

During the late nineteenth and early twentieth centuries, the village of Santi Cosma e Damiano and the neighboring village of Castleforte became the center of social networks of migrants creating colonies in New York State that would continue until the 1960s.[11] Emigration to the United States can be traced to 1883, but significant numbers of immigrants did not leave until 1898. During that year, fifty individuals left Santi Cosma e Damiano for the United States, with the largest group departing on March 22. On that day, twenty-four male "laborers," ranging in age from 20 to 58 years, the majority of whom were married, departed Italy for New York.

The immigrants were representative of the majority of Sancosmesi who were *contadini*; only a few villagers could boast of a higher status. *Comune* records dated 1898 list several artisans and merchants who provided specialized services for the local villagers, including several tailors, barbers, a midwife, a *fabricatore* (manufacturer), and several *possidente*—wealthy landowners who employed several of the young village women in their homes as domestic servants.[12]

A growing number of *contadini* continued to emigrate from Santi Cosma e Damiano and Castleforte until World War One brought a temporary halt to European immigration. While many of the immigrants were agricultural laborers, others, particularly those from San Lorenzo[13] and other areas in the vicinity of Castleforte, were small landholders who hoped to improve their family's economic and social position through labor migration. During these years there were also a small number of male migrants from both villages who were tradesmen and skilled laborers, working as barbers, tailors, shoemakers, bakers, and masons. Similar to many other Italian migrants during the two principal decades prior to World War One, the immigrants from the two villages were overwhelmingly male and never intended to remain in the United States.[14]

Donato Vecchio was one of those many immigrants who never planned to remain. As noted, he had been called to Cortland by his sister, Angiolina, who had immigrated six years earlier. Angiolina promised him a place to live, while her future husband promised help getting a job at the Wickwire Wireworks.

Donato's journey demonstrates the intricacy of migration through transnational-type connections of kin, in-laws, and fellow villagers. Sailing with Donato in 1921 was his brother-in-law, Giuseppe Vozzole, a cousin, Raffaele Romanielli, and another fellow villager, Giuseppe Colletta.[15] With the exception of Romanielli, who was linking up with "relations" in Ellwood, Pennsylvania, the other migrants were journeying to Cortland.[16]

The decision to emigrate reflects a collective choice made within the province of kinship networks in the Vecchio-Vozzole-Romanielli family. Their strategies were moneymaking ventures that reflect what Loretta Baldassar has described as *sistemazione*, setting oneself up (and one's family).[17] This was likely the plan implemented by the three families. However, the men migrating in 1921 were not the first in their families to engage in labor migration abroad. From at least 1900, kin members of the three interrelated families were involved in labor migration and repatriation. Social networking to the same American destination continued for decades. Many returned to Italy, others did not. Enough of them kept a foot in both Italy and the United States to sustain transnational networks for years to come.

The Italian immigrants worked in the United States for a decade and invested their American earnings to improve their lives and social position in Italy. Vozzole and Romanielli eventually returned to Italy, built impressive homes in San Lorenzo, and remained there for the rest of their lives. That had also been Donato's plan, to return with the money he earned in the United States to increase his landholdings in Italy, but the rise of Mussolini and the Fascist state prompted him to rethink his family's future in Italy.[18]

Bernardino Verrico continued sponsoring relatives and fellow villagers from Santi Cosma e Damiano. In June 1913, sixteen-year-old Pietro Laurelio listed the home of his uncle Bernardino in Cortland as his American destination. In that same year, Carmine DiLanna also left Santi Cosma for Cortland to reconnect with his brother, Luigi. Their sister, Cecilia, was Bernardino's wife.[19]

Italian males were instrumental in organizing social networks of labor migration to Cortland that continued for six decades. While males led migrations of future American laborers to the United States, the Italian women who followed them helped establish family and communal life, reflecting a culturally transformed Italian identity in America.

## GENDER AND MIGRATION

In the early years of Italian immigration to Cortland, women made up a very small percentage of migrants. Transnational social networks initially established by male migrants helped connect future immigrant women with jobs in Cortland. And yet, unlike Italian males, the women who migrated from the two villages probably would not be considered "labor migrants," since they initially came as wives, sisters, or daughters of immigrants already established in the United States. Examining the status of women and their relation to men as well as their relation to labor is complex because, while many women initially emigrated to reunite with male relatives, they nonetheless became laborers soon after arriving in the United States.

Several examples from Cortland illustrate this point: Bernardino Verrico's wife, Cecilia DeLanna, left Santi Cosma e Damiano in 1907 to join her husband in Cortland, but only after he was settled with a steady job and a place to live.[20] Cecilia may not have come over as a labor migrant, but she became a laborer after she arrived. In fact, Cecilia became one of the few women who worked in the predominately male Wickwire mill.[21] She was later joined by Filomena Cinquanta, who left Castleforte in 1911 with her daughters to join her husband in Cortland. Filomena, who had worked in the fields in Italy during her husband's absence, made the transition from agricultural labor to factory labor in the United States. The transition of women from domestic or field work in Italy to factory labor in the United States also raises important questions about the concepts of femininity and masculinity in Italian American life and suggests that life in America often altered traditional Italian notions of gender.

South Italian women typically left their native villages in far smaller numbers than did men. For example, in a random sampling of 1,762 immigrants coming from Castleforte and Santi Cosma e Damiano to the United States between 1892 and 1924, only 131 (7%) were women (fourteen years of age and older).[22]

When they did leave, most women left as permanent migrants following the paths of fathers and husbands who had emigrated earlier. In 1913, Filomena Mignano and her daughters left Santi Cosma e Damiano for Cortland. After years as a *vedove bianca*,[23] she joined her husband who had left Italy ten years earlier. Their lengthy time apart was a result of Raimondo's years of sporadic employment. Finally settled in Cortland with a permanent job and a prospect for his family's future, Raimondo reunited with his wife, and Filomena took a job at Wickwire's[24] to help provide for the family. Emilia Palazzo and her three children finally rejoined with husband and father Donato Vecchio in 1937, after Donato had spent fifteen years in the United States as a labor migrant, making frequent trips back home.[25]

Not all female migrants were married, however, and it is hard to know what opportunities and advantages they saw in emigration. Regina Cinquanta was twenty-three and single when she left Castleforte to join her brother in Cortland, and Fiorenza Vozzole was only eighteen when she left Italy in 1912 to join her sister who had emigrated earlier. Both women worked in the United States, but it is not known whether they, too, like their male counterparts, sent money back home to help support their families. It is worth speculating whether migration motives were gendered, or if women, too, had aspirations of earning money in America to assist needy families back in Italy.

Angiolina Vecchio's motives for migrating may have been typical of some young women who left Italy alone. In 1915, she emigrated, unaccompanied by either kin or friends, to be with the man she loved. When she arrived in Cortland, she moved in with her future husband, an act that defied traditional Italian values and concepts of honor and shame. Interestingly, Angiolina and Antonio Giungo became wife and husband two weeks prior to the arrival of Angiolina's mother, who traveled alone from Italy to the United States to reunite with her daughter in Cortland.

## GENDER AND COMMUNITY BUILDING

Material about family life and women's activities in particular challenges some aspects of social roles and gender dichotomies in immigrant life. The role of women in creating ethnic communities in American society has been, in many ways, overlooked. Certainly, families were important in the adjustment process of immigrants to American life, but stable family life and community building among Italians did not begin to take shape in Cortland until the arrival of Italian women. Life for Italian migrant men was characterized by temporary and transient patterns of living.[26] With the arrival of women, immigrant homes were established, creating a foundation for family life and community building.

Immigrant women transformed the physical and private location of home to accommodate the physical and public location of business, reflecting how migration often prompted cultural change.[27] In Cortland, as in many other towns and cities across the nation, women provided boarding services to immigrant males, ran small grocery stores that provided ethnic foods to the Italian community, and established neighborhood restaurants that recreated Italian food ways. Italian women's activities affected both communal and economic life and demonstrate how "migrants were tied by bonds of shared residence and mutual assistance."[28] This is particularly evident by the number of Italian males who found housing by boarding with Italian families.

In Cortland, several immigrant men boarded in the home of Angiolina Vecchio and her future husband, located on the south end of town. It was only blocks away from Wickwire's, where the majority of Italian men were employed. By 1925, Angiolina was providing boarding and lodging services to five men, three of whom were either related to her or from her native village.[29] Immigrants from Santi Cosma e Damiano and Castle-forte lived together in homes of *paesani* in a residential clustering on both the south and east ends of Cortland, where Italians had settled. Most Italians who immigrated to Cortland were from Italy's southern regions of Molise, Sicily, Lazio, Campania, Abruzzi, and Apulia. There were six wards in Cortland by 1925, and 98 percent of the Italians lived in the Third, Fifth, and Sixth wards. Italians from Castleforte and Santi Cosma e Damiano settled in the Third and Sixth wards and were clustered at the south end of town, on Crawford Street, Pine Street, Scammell Street, and South Main Street. On the east end of Cortland they grouped together on Hyatt Street, Bartlett Avenue, and Comando Avenue. Boarders followed networks of kin and paesani who preceded them. They lived in their homes and in neighborhood clusters.[30] In Cortland, this led to brothers, sisters, aunts, uncles, cousins, and *paesani* all living in the same neighborhoods.

Italian women began taking in boarders in 1905 when there were only twenty-seven assembled Italian households[31] in Cortland. In that year twenty-five of twenty-seven households of Italian women (93 percent) provided lodging to boarders, ranging from one to twelve boarders per household.[32] The practice of taking in boarders was one of the most common ways immigrant women could earn money at home. The needs of newer migrants for room and board before their own families were established meant that women could be economically productive through extending the services they were already providing for their own families.

Taking in boarders reveals a literal blurring of public and private spheres of activity in the daily lives of Italian women. This economic enterprise was, in fact, a sharp break with the Italian past and reflects Italian women's willingness to adapt to a new economic environment in the United States. The practice of taking in boarders did not exist in Italy or Sicily, since a household and its house was defined by the nuclear or extended family, usually consisting of grandparents.[33]

Closer scrutiny of this business venture also suggests the risks involved to a family's honor by taking in boarders. With the majority of boarders either single males or men whose wives remained in Italy, prospects for unwanted sexual advances or romantic relationships between boarders and the women who provided these services were heightened.

Sources reveal that clandestine affairs often occurred in boarding households. Cecelia Verrico, Bernardino's wife, took in boarders from Santi Cosma e Damiano for many years. A romantic relationship evolved between her daughter and a boarder that, fortunately, resulted in marriage. However, many parents would not allow such relationships in their homes. The daughter of one immigrant recalled that "the father of the household told the boarder he had to move out before he could consider courting his daughter."[34] In another instance, "Francesca," who lived in rented rooms with her immigrant parents on Cortland's south end, recalls that her father moved the family into their own home because he feared that his wife and daughter would be vulnerable to sexual advances by males boarding in the same household.[35] In 1918, at the age of sixteen "Antonia" was forced into marriage by her father, a Castlefortani, after a romantic tryst with a boarder from their home village ended in pregnancy.[36]

Taking in boarders fell strictly within the woman's domain. She offered room and board, which included meals and laundry services. For immigrant women who took in boarders the toil seemed endless. Cecilia Verrico's daughter recalled her mother's responsibilities:

> She would have to wash all of their clothes by hand, and they worked at the wire factory or at the railroad. Their clothes were filled with grease.
>
> Meals were nothing special. They ate what we ate; beans, greens, homemade bread, and my mother would often have to bake four or five loaves of bread a day to feed the family and the boarders. She washed dishes late into the night while my father and the boarders drank homemade wine and played cards.[37]

The number of boarders a woman took in could contribute substantially to the family's income. Rose Verrico (Giuseppe's wife) recalled that in 1925 a single male paid approximately fifteen dollars a month for room and board. The same male was a wire weaver earning twenty-four dollars a week at Wickwire's. Therefore, a woman taking in three to four boarders might earn nearly two-thirds of a working-class male's full-time salary.[38] As the number of single male transients in Cortland declined, fewer women took in boarders: in 1915, 40 percent of Italian households were taking in boarders, but by 1925, only 12 percent of Italian households did so.[39]

Providing services for these boarders was more than an economic venture for women; it served an important social and cultural function for the Italian community as well. The same women who took in boarders often acted as matchmakers for the single boarders who shared their homes. Immigrant wives and their husbands hosted Saturday night parties where "greenhorns" were welcomed into the larger community of transplanted Italians. Many single migrants who never intended to remain in the United States did so because of matchmaking efforts by Italian women, who introduced daughters of earlier migrants to newer immigrants from their *paese*.[40] Young men attending Saturday night parties were introduced to eligible young women in hopes that a romantic interest might be sparked. That is precisely what happened when Cosmo Porchetta, who immigrated to Cortland in 1921, was introduced to, and fell in love with, Bernardino Verrico's daughter. A year later they were married.[41]

The recreated community of Sancosmesi and Castlefortani helped integrate newly arrived immigrants into a fusion of Italian-American identities. Migrants arriving in Cortland joined a tightly-knit, well-organized community of *paesani*, who boarded together, worked together, and socialized together. In a very short time, the Italians in Cortland had established largely homogeneous ethnic neighborhoods. Italian streets blossomed with ethnic grocery stores and Italian restaurants. Through all these entrepreneurial endeavors, immigrant women played an important role that ultimately maintained Italian ethnic identity in Cortland.

Very little has been written about Italian women's business enterprises and how they served the immigrant community.[42] Though boarding was an important way of earning money, immigrant women also engaged in other forms of commerce, including grocery and restaurant operations. Most grocery businesses were conducted at home, while the family lived above or behind the grocery store. Some women also ran businesses that were not home-based, though still located within the ethnic community. Carmela Ferro's grocery store was located on the corner of South Main and Scammell Streets, while Mary D'Angelo's grocery was located a block south of Ferro's store. Both women converted the front rooms of their homes into business ventures, blurring the private and public spaces of domestic life with economic activities. Canned tomatoes, pasta, and fresh loaves of Italian bread lined the shelves of Carmela Ferro's front-room store, and Mary D'Angelo offered her customers salami, capicola and imported cheeses that she cut to order.[43]

Italian women in Cortland participated in the family and community economy through food enterprises and working as proprietors and cooks in their own restaurants. Women who operated neighborhood restaurants assumed multiple chores, combining cooking with serving patrons and dishwashing. Neighborhood restaurants occupied a small space, with a few tables and chairs, similar to Italian trattorias. Typically, there were no menus, and women served whatever they happened to cook that day or what was fresh, according to the season. Pasta with a simple tomato sauce was a staple of all neighborhood restaurants. Women often prepared greens, such as escarole sautéed in garlic and olive oil and minestra or pasta fagioli with homemade bread.

Italian restaurants in Cortland were located on nearly every street in the Italian neighborhoods. Maria Di Iorio (Giuseppe Verrico's aunt and Carmela Ferro's sister-in-law) emigrated from Santi Cosma e Damiano to join her husband, Gaspare, who had settled in Cortland several years earlier. Eventually, Maria started a small neighborhood restaurant on the first floor of her home with the family's living space located on the second floor of the building. The Melodyland Restaurant originally was established when Gaspare decided to turn his butcher shop into a restaurant and bar. But Gaspare could not get a food and liquor license because he had been convicted of bootlegging during Prohibition. Maria applied for the restaurant and bar license in her name. With that license and family recipes, the Melodyland opened in 1932 and seventy years later was still serving the Cortland area five days a week.[44] It is one of the few remnants of Italian identity still alive in Cortland's south end.

Maria Patriarco, an emigrant from Castleforte, also ran a bar and luncheonette several blocks south of the Melodyland. Male laborers employed by the railroad, the wire factory, and a nearby sheet metal factory regularly met at the Owego Restaurant for lunch with other working-class Italian men.[45] On Saturday night, Maria opened her restaurant to Italian musicians, who shared their music with *paesani* from the surrounding neighborhoods.

Italian restaurants were essential to the development of the ethnic community. Through their cooking, Italian women sustained food traditions that had originated in their local *paese* and provided "a structure upon which a coherent group identity could be built and maintained" in America. Italian women, while preserving regional and ethnic food traditions, were instrumental in creating an important part of communal life and ethnic identity.

## WAGE-LABOR AND WORKING-CLASS IDENTITY

Transnational communications linked Italian women in Italy with job opportunities in the United States much the same as it did for males, revealing that social networks were gendered as were employment opportunities. When Angiolina Vecchio first arrived in Cortland she found employment as a corset worker.[46] Located three blocks north of the Wickwire factory, on the south end of town, the Crescent Corset Company provided employment opportunities for female migrants. Angiolina was one of the first Italian-born women working at the Crescent (as it was commonly called) to communicate with other women in Italy about jobs in the factory. The Crescent Corset Company was established in the early 1900s and specialized in women's undergarments and foundations. The jobs consisted mainly of sewing, a skill most Italian women brought with them from Italy.

Italian women who found employment at the Crescent Corset Company created a group solidarity that was pervasive for decades. Italian women, more than any other ethnic group, dominated the work force at the company, which had grown to seven hundred workers by the early 1920s. Nearly every Italian woman who immigrated to Cortland and worked outside of the home did so at the Crescent Corset Company.

The use of the Italian language was one of the important strategies in which Italian women engaged to generate a sense of solidarity and identity, marking them off from other workers.[47] For example, Assunta Curri (the American-born daughter of Bernardino Verrico) was employed by the Crescent as a floor supervisor from 1925 to 1971. In an interview she explained that the Crescent was a perfect workplace for Italian women "right off the boat." Assunta was an ideal floor supervisor because she could speak Italian. Whenever an Italian immigrant appeared for a job, she would be directed to Curri, who would put the newly arrived immigrant on her floor where Curri could act as an interpreter.[48] The use of the Italian language by so many of the women who worked at the Crescent created a sense of solidarity among them, fusing working-class values with ethnic identity.

Kinship networks were instrumental in creating employment opportunities for immigrant women as they were for men. Most young Italian women seeking employment at the Crescent did not appear alone to apply for a job. Rather, they were introduced by a friend or relative who worked there who requested the company to hire the niece, sister, or cousin. Nicolina Giuliano, who emigrated from Castleforte in 1952, arrived in Cortland on a Friday afternoon and started working at the Crescent on Monday morning. Her cousin, Maria Patriarca, had emigrated from Castleforte several years earlier and helped her get a job on the day of her arrival.[49] These patterns of securing employment for other family members were common among immigrants who maintained strong ties of kinship in the United States.

While Italian women workers dominated the Crescent Corset Company, Italian male workers dominated the Wickwire Brothers Wireworks. The company, which began operations in the 1870s, installed a continuous rod rolling mill, and in 1902 an open hearth steel plant and blooming mill were added. The large output of this new mill made possible the production of nails and coarse wire. By 1910, Wickwire's became the largest factory in town, employing fifteen hundred persons. By the time of World War One, the manufacturing facilities consisted of forty buildings. At its peak in the 1920s, the firm was producing one-quarter of the world's wire cloth.[50]

The labor force of Wickwire's was made up of native-born Americans and immigrant Germans, Irish, Slavs and Italians. Solidarity among Italian working-men was reinforced by their numbers—by 1938, 75 percent of the workforce was made up of Italians.[51] However, American-born men as well as the Irish held the better positions, and the Irish were usually the shop foremen.[52] Wickwire's wages were lower than other factories in Cortland, but the work was steady. During the Depression, for example, factory owners reduced the workweek but kept almost the entire work force employed. Nonetheless, a potential source of friction between immigrants and other factory workers evolved with the move to organize skilled and unskilled labor. In 1938, the CIO organized Wickwire workers, and the Italian immigrants joined the effort, although interviews revealed that some immigrants were hesitant to affiliate with the labor movement because they did not feel hostile toward the Wickwire family.[53]

Wickwire's labor difficulties were becoming a real problem by the late 1940s and second-generation Italian Americans became leading figures in strikes that continued for a three-month period during 1949.[54] When the strike was over, Wickwire's agreed to provide six paid holidays annually instead of two, and, more importantly, to offer a pension plan and health insurance to its employees.[55] Labor agitation continued throughout the 1950s and 1960s, however, as employees demanded better wages. In 1968, employees charged that Wickwire's was paying not even the minimum wage. By this time, the factory's workforce had been reduced to four hundred workers. No longer able to compete in a global market, Wickwire's closed its doors in 1972. For a large number of Castlefortani and Sancosmesi who immigrated to Cortland, Wickwire's had been the major link to a labor market that provided immigrants with a reason for coming to America.

## KIN, SOCIAL RELATIONS, AND TRANSNATIONAL NETWORKS

The connections among the people of Santi Cosma e Damiano and Castle-forte and their sons and daughters abroad reveal how migrants developed and maintained familial, economic, and social ties between their country of origin and their country of settlement. One way this was done was through personal correspondence. The exchange of letters between migrants and their families was an aspect of transnationalism that was widely employed in the nineteenth and twentieth centuries. Historian David Gerber characterizes the letter as a type of "early transnational social field that lifted people out of conventional time-space and rendered the national borders that separated them insignificant."[56] It was the letter that acted as a conduit for forging links in migrant networks and it was the letter that transmitted remittances back home.

Italy desperately needed the remittances sent home by emigrants, and remaining family members often relied on money transmittals to supplement meager wages.[57] Giuseppe Verrico sent monthly remittances to his mother until the time of her death in the 1950s. The arrival of American money in Santi

Cosma e Damiano during and after World War II, in particular, helped sustain not only Giuseppe's widowed mother but also his nieces, who were orphaned when their parents were killed during an air assault. In addition, the money he sent back home helped to pay funeral expenses when his father passed away and it contributed to rebuilding the village church that was partially destroyed during the war. Though he never returned to Italy, Giuseppe provided support for his mother and other family members through the regular remittances he sent back home.

During the war and immediately thereafter, Sancosmesi and Castlefortani aided their families back in Italy by sending them bundles of clothing, shoes, and non-perishable food items. Interviews conducted with Italians who immigrated to Cortland in the 1950s and 1960s reveal that these remittances literally kept Italian families alive. Sandy Panzanella recalls that "my mom traveled to Naples in a horse and carriage and sold clothing at the open market that was sent to her from relatives in Cortland."[58]

Immigrant women facilitated the maintenance of social relationships between members of their home villages and newly constructed communities in America. This became part of Italian women's kin responsibilities. Marriage was another important bond in maintaining these relationships. Well into the 1960s, immigrants and their children living in Cortland intermarried with members of families from the same villages.

Church records show that high endogamy rates existed as immigrants and second-generation Sancosmesi and Castelfortani intermarried. Social connections that linked members of the Verricos of Santi Cosma e Damiano (Giuseppe Verrico) with the Vecchios of Castleforte (Donato Vecchio) in the 1920s, for example, resulted in the next generation marriage of their children, Marie Verrico and Alex Vecchio.[59]

Prospective matches were made between Italians in Cortland with those in Italy through letter writing, picture exchanges, and social networking. And if there were no eligible matches in Cortland, female-centered kin networks arranged marriages with the children of fellow villagers who had settled in other towns and cities in the United States.[60] After a series of introductions and visits in New Jersey, Emilia Vecchio's efforts came to fruition with her daughter's marriage to the son of *paesani* from Castleforte.[61]

The roles of immigrant women reveal how gender helped sustain social relations between the country of origin and the country of settlement. Because she was literate, Emilia Vecchio was an important link between immigrant women in Cortland and their families in Castleforte. She read and wrote letters for Italian women, some of whom paid her for her services.[62] The informal institutions of family, household, and neighborhood served the Italian immigrants well as they reconstructed new lives in Cortland.

By recreating the social networks that brought Italians to America as well as their patterns of settlement and community building in Cortland, this essay demonstrates the role gender played in forming social networks of labor migration and facilitating the adjustment of migrants to life in America. Italian communities were established by males and females alike, but gender defined specific roles in migration and settlement and in these ways links were forged with homeland communities. These links demonstrate transnational aspects of the lives of these newcomers, aspects sustained at the same time that they were beginning to incorporate elements of American society and culture into a transformed Italian American identity.

## NOTES

1.  See Samuel Baily, *Immigrants in the Land of Promise: Italians in Buenos Aires and New York City, 1870–1914* (New York, 1999), 10.
2.  The "family outward approach" reveals the immigrant experiences of my maternal grandfather, Giuseppe Verrico, and my paternal grandfather, Donato Vecchio.
3.  Susan Glenn, *Daughters of the Shtetl: Life and Labor in the Immigrant Generation* (Ithaca, NY, 1990), 208.
4.  Ship manifests with passengers sailing from Santi Cosma e Damiano, Castleforte, and other nearby villages were taken from Ellis Island records dating from the late 1890s through 1924. See www.Ellisisland.org.
5.  Donna Gabaccia and Franca Iacovetta, *Women, Gender, and Transnational Lives: Italian Workers of the World* (Toronto, 2002), 6.
6.  The Cortland factory hiring large numbers of immigrants was the Wickwire Brothers Wireworks. Interview with Giuseppe Verrico, January 1978, Cortland, New York.
7.  "Sancosmesi" and "Castlefortani" refer to the people from Santi Cosma e Damiano and Castleforte, Italy.
8.  John W. Briggs, *An Italian Passage: Immigrants to Three American Cities, 1890– 1930* (New Haven, CT, 1978).
9.  People from the same village.
10. Giuseppe Verrico interview.
11. Other New York State destinations include Utica and Gloversville.
12. Birth and marriage registry, comune of Santi Cosma e Damiano, Italy.
13. San Lorenzo was part of Castleforte, but on the outskirts of the village proper, closer to Santi Cosma e Damiano.
14. These patterns have been documented by many scholars of Italian immigration. See, for example, John Briggs, *An Italian Passage*; and Donna Gabaccia and Fraser Ottanelli, *Italian Workers of the World: Labor Migration and the Formation of Multiethnic States* (Urbana, IL, 2001).
15. I have found no evidence thus far that he was related to Donato Vecchio, so I am considering him a fellow villager.
16. Ship Manifest, 1921.
17. "Setting oneself up" is explained by Baldassar as the process by which families purchase land and/or homes. See Loretta Baldassar, *Visits Home, Migration Experiences between Italy and Australia* (Melbourne, 2001), 71.
18. Donato Vecchio, a staunch anti-fascist, decided not to return to Italy and, instead, called for his family to join him in the United States. His wife and children emigrated in 1937.
19. Ship Manifest, 1913.
20. Bernardino immigrated first to New York City, which must have proved fruitless. After returning to Italy a second time, Bernardino joined members of the DeLanna

family (his future wife's brothers) for Johnsonburg, Pennsylvania. By 1907, he was in Cortland where he settled permanently.

21. Only a handful of Italian women worked in the Wickwire Brothers Wireworks, a factory dominated by heavy industry. However, immigrant women from Russia and the Ukraine tended to work there in far greater numbers than did other immigrant groups.

22. Analysis of Ship Manifests between 1892–1924.

23. *Vedove bianca*, or white widow, is the term used for women who were left behind when husbands emigrated. An excellent study of Italian women left behind is Linda Reeder, *Widows in White: Migration and the Transformation of Rural Italian Women, Sicily, 1880–1920* (Toronto, 2003).

24. The common reference to the factory as "Wickwire's" will be used hereafter.

25. This information was compiled by examining ship manifests and oral interviews with members of the Vecchio family.

26. Italian males boarded with already-established Italian families or in boarding houses where twenty or more men lived together. They frequently moved from one household to another until they either left Cortland for good, or married, or were reunited with recently-arrived spouses.

27. Savita Nair, "Gender, Space, and Power: Indian Immigrant Women in Colonial East Africa (c. 1920–1940)," unpublished paper presented at Furman University Faculty Forum, September 2005.

28. Baily, *Immigrants in the Land of Promise*, 146.

29. 1925 Manuscript Census, Cortland, New York.

30. Louis M. Vanaria, "Settlement Patterns of Cortland Italians: The First Generation, 1892–1925," in *From Many Roots: Immigrants and Ethnic Groups in the History of Cortland County, New York*, ed. Louis M. Vanaria (Cortland, NY, 1986).

31. Household consisting of a husband, wife and children.

32. Diane C. Vecchio, "The Influence of Family Values and Culture on the Occupational Choices of Italian Immigrant Women in Cortland, N.Y., 1890–1935," in *From Many Roots*, ed. Vanaria, 36–45.

33. Donna Gabaccia, *From Sicily to Elizabeth Street. Housing and Social Change among Italian Immigrants* (Albany, NY, 1984), 27–28. Gabaccia also refers to anthropologist Charlotte Gower Chapman, who reported that in Milocca, Sicily, "boarding was unheard of."

34. Interview with Rose Carini, August 26, 1992, Milwaukee, WI.

35. Interview with "Francesca", January 2, 2000, Cortland, NY.

36. I learned of this incident when I discovered a gravestone in St. Mary's cemetery in Cortland with the mother and child buried together. After tracing birth and marriage certificates, census data, and other documents, I was able to piece together the information.

37. Vecchio, "The Influence of Family Values and Culture," 37–38.

38. Ibid. 38.

39. Statistics compiled from analysis of the New York State Manuscript Census for Cortland County.

40. Their home village.

41. Tragically, Porchetta died a year later in an industrial accident at Wickwire's.

42. This is a topic that I discuss in my research of Sicilian women who owned and operated grocery stores and restaurants in Milwaukee, Wisconsin. See Diane Vecchio, "Gender, Domestic Values, and Italian Working Women in Milwaukee: Immigrant Midwives and Businesswomen," in *Women, Gender, and Transnational Lives: Italian Workers of the World*, ed. Donna Gabaccia and Franca Iacovetta (Toronto,

2002), 160–85; and Diane Vecchio, *Merchants, Midwives, and Laboring Women: Italian Migrants in Urban America* (Urbana, IL, 2006).

43. Memories of these grocery stores are a recreation of my own experiences as a child visiting my grandparents on the south end of Cortland.

44. *Cortland Standard*, July 2002.

45. Interviews with Marie and Alex Vecchio, September 2000, Skaneateles, NY.

46. Alex Vecchio interview.

47. Carol McKibben, "Beyond Cannery Row: Sicilian Women and Identity Formation in Monterey California," paper presented at the SSHA, November 2005, Portland, OR.

48. Vecchio, "The Influence of Family Values," 39.

49. Interview with Nicolina Giuliano, August 2005, Cortland, NY.

50. John Smith, "A History of the Wickwire Brothers Wire Factory of Cortland, New York," unpublished paper, State University of New York College at Cortland, 1972.

51. Janie Welsh, "A History of Wickwire Brothers, Inc., 1873–1972, Cortland, New York," unpublished paper on file at the Cortland County Historical Society, 23, MS M678 no. 106.

52. American-born men were usually the highest paid males in the factory and held skilled positions as wire-weavers.

53. Interviews with Louis Adessa, August 1978; Giuseppe Verrico, January 1978; and Charles Abdallah, January 1979, Cortland, New York.

54. Italian immigrant men were often hesitant to go on strike fearful they would "lose everything." Most of these men were homeowners and many of them were the sole breadwinners in the family. However, second-generation Italians were more likely to go on strike and demand concessions from the factory. Leading labor activists at Wickwire's during the strikes of the late 1940s and 1950s included men from large Italian families who had fathers and brothers employed at the factory, such as the Berardi family and the Montello family. Interviews with Giuseppe Verrico; Alex and Marie Vecchio.

55. Welsh, "A History of Wickwire Brothers," 25.

56. David Gerber, "Theories and Lives: Transnationalism and the Conceptualization of International Migrations to the United States," *IMIS-Beitrage: Transnationalismus und Kulturver-gleich* (December 2000): 31–53.

57. Ibid, 44.

58. Interview with Sandy (Santina) Panzanella, August 2005, Cortland, NY.

59. Giuseppe Verrico and Donato Vecchio boarded together in the early 1920s and worked together at Wickwire's. They provided support for each other as well. When Donato purchased his first home, Giuseppe helped him with the down payment. New York State Manuscript Census for Cortland County, 1920; and interviews with members of the Vecchio and Verrico families.

60. Micaela di Leonardo discusses the significance of Italian women's kinship networks in the context of family, labor, and community in California in *The Varieties of Ethnic Experience: Kinship, Class, and Gender among California Italian-Americans* (Ithaca, NY, 1984).

61. Maria Carmine (Mary) Vecchio married Philip Coviello, the son of my grandparents' *paesani* in 1947. Marie and Alex Vecchio interview.

# 6

# Interracial Marriages and Transnational Families: Chicago's Filipinos in the Aftermath of World War II

## *ROLAND L. GUYOTTE AND BARBARA M. POSADAS*

ON OCTOBER 22, 1946, 54-year-old, Philippine-born Cesario Agudo Buensuceso filed a petition for naturalization and signed an "Oath of Allegiance" pledging to "support and defend the Constitution and laws of the United States of America against all enemies, foreign and domestic."[1] Unlike most other Filipinos seeking U.S. citizenship in the aftermath of World War Two, Buensuceso had previously sought naturalization. Twenty-two years earlier, on May 2, 1924, Buensuceso's first petition for naturalization had been denied because, as a Filipino, Buensuceso was found to be ineligible by reason of race. Buensuceso had made his 1924 petition almost five years after arriving in the United States and settling in Chicago in July 1919.[2]

In this respect—an earlier petition for citizenship—and in others, Buensuceso is atypical of Filipinos who arrived in Chicago prior to the mid-1930s, when the Tydings-McDuffie Act of 1934 limited previously unrestricted immigration from the Philippines to a fifty-per-year quota. Rather than coming to a West Coast port, as did most Filipinos, Buensuceso entered the United States on July 20, 1919, through the port of New York aboard the U.S. Army transport "Plattsburg" and likely caught sight of the Statue of Liberty, as did many European immigrants. Buensuceso's second petition for naturalization also reveals yet another unusual facet in his story. Buensuceso's wife of less than six weeks had traveled with him. Twenty-seven-year-old Cesario Buensuceso and his twenty-twoyear-old, British-born wife, Elsie, had exchanged their vows on June 7, 1919, in London, the city of her birth. Thus, unlike most of his countrymen, Cesario Buensuceso did not begin life in the United States as the typical bachelor Filipino or, far less commonly, as a Filipino husband who had left his Filipina wife at home in the Philippines. Buensuceso had served in the U.S. military during World War One,[3] and, probably on this ground, he sought U.S. citizenship in 1924, albeit unsuccessfully, for reasons that cannot be ascertained. By 1924, he and Elsie had been married for almost five years and had lived in Illinois continually since July 30, 1919, ten days after their landing on the East Coast. A daughter, Viola, was born to them on February 27, 1922, and another daughter, Dolores, arrived on June 3, 1924, one month and one day after Buensuceso's unsuccessful attempt to become a naturalized citizen.[4]

Buensuceso's story is atypical in these respects—arrival on the East rather than the West Coast, marriage in London to a British-born spouse, and an earlier petition for citizenship, as well as residence in a Chicago suburb. In other ways, however, his life after his arrival parallels that of other Filipinos living in Chicago during these years. This essay examines the lives of Filipinos resident in Chicago in the years immediately following World War Two through the lens offered by petitions for naturalization filed in 1946. It also focuses on the dominance of interracial family life among Chicago Filipinos.[5] Thus, it offers a caveat to important themes stressed in others' research on Filipino immigration to the United States before World War Two and in immigration history more generally.

First, this essay contrasts with the dominant image of Filipinos as quasi-migratory bachelors along the West Coast in work ranging from Carlos Bulosan's classic *America Is in the Heart* (1943) to Dorothy Fugita-Rony's *American Workers, Colonial Power* (2004). Two-thirds of Filipinos captured via post-World War Two naturalization petitions filed in Chicago *did* settle *and* marry.[6] Thus, the portrait of a predominantly Filipino bachelor society does not hold in Chicago, especially after World War Two, for the admittedly most stable element of the Filipino community in Chicago— those who sought citizenship immediately after naturalization became possible. In this, our work joins a growing literature that emphasizes the importance of conjugal families in Asian American history.[7]

Second, Filipinos who settled in Chicago were *not* typically members of "transnational" families in which husbands and wives remained an ocean apart for decades. In this, the Chicago story diverges from the findings of Xiaojian Zhao and Madeline Y. Hsu, who have traced patterns of marriage across the Pacific among Chinese Americans.[8] Approximately ninety-six percent of Filipinos naturalizing in Chicago at the end of World War Two swore (or affirmed) that they did not have a wife in the Philippines. Thus, our research also highlights the diversity *among* Asians settling in the United States in the early twentieth century.

Finally, almost all of the 441 Filipinos who joined Buensuceso in rushing to naturalize during the last six months of 1946 did so for specific reasons flowing from the lives that they had established in Chicago. Only in July 1946 had Filipinos living in the United States escaped their previous categorization as "aliens ineligible to citizenship" through passage of a law permitting their naturalization.[9] Filipinos sought naturalization not because U.S. citizenship promised full inclusion but rather because it precluded outright exclusion. As citizens and as Filipino Americans, Filipino Chicagoans might anticipate visiting the Philippines without fear of being denied re-entry into the United States. Those who held employment as public employees at post offices, hospitals, or research facilities no longer need dread dismissal because of their alien status. And, as husbands and fathers, their political status would now be the same as that of their mostly American-born wives and children. Filipinos knew that U.S. citizenship would make them voters but little more in the political arena. They knew, too, that naturalization would not make them white. But naturalization made clear that, if they so chose, they were in the United States to stay.

To file the petition, each applicant traveled, most likely by streetcar or subway, to the Federal District Court of the United States in Chicago. Each brought two witnesses who would swear that the petitioner was "of good moral character, attached to the principles of the Constitution of the United States, and well disposed to the good order and happiness of the United States. . . ." With their petitions for naturalization, Filipinos claimed in law what they had long been en route to becoming—Filipino American Chicagoans.

*    *    *    *    *

From the outset, Filipinos had been anomalous among immigrants of Asian descent. Unlike the Chinese, they effectively had neither a nineteenth-century U.S. presence nor any history of conflict with white Americans. Unlike the Japanese, they did not hail from a powerful nation that sought in the twentieth century to rival the United States in the Far East. Even though the Constitution did not follow the flag to the Philippines after U.S. conquest at the turn of the twentieth century, the Filipinos, as colonial subjects, were not "aliens" in the sense of "aliens ineligible to citizenship," as were those from the Asiatic Barred Zone from 1917 onward. Instead, as "nationals" of the United States, they could travel back and forth freely and enjoy other rights of Americans, such as passports if they traveled to Europe, but they could not become citizens. Once the Tydings-McDuffie Act of 1934 put the Philippines on the path to independence, however, Filipinos became "aliens."[10] This fact would spur their drive to naturalize as soon as citizenship became an opportunity.

The Filipinos naturalizing in Chicago in 1946 diverged substantially from their counterparts in Hawaii and on the West Coast, where agricultural labor remained the norm. Their community's roots dated to the earliest days of the twentieth century. Between 1903 and the mid-1910s, the first Filipinos arrived in Chicago as students, either as "pensionados" under a government program that paid their way or as family-supported students. This first generation of Filipinos educated in the United States utilized their training to fill job openings in the Philippines after the Wilson administration "filipinized" the colonial civil service. "Student" numbers grew during the 1920s when young, male Filipinos trekked to Chicago seeking similar educational benefits that they believed would advantage them upon their return to their homeland. Unlike the earlier students, these Filipinos were largely self-supporting and, as we noted in an earlier article, found themselves caught between "aspiration and reality."[11]

While some of the students of the 1920s and 1930s achieved their educational objectives and returned to remunerative employment in the Philippines, most did not. Combining school with work and the distractions of the city proved more than many could handle. Others learned from returned countrymen that the window of opportunity for white-collar employment back home had largely closed, for the Philippine economy failed to provide expanding opportunities well before the onset of the Great Depression. Initially, many did not worry, as attested by their lively sociability and substantial organizational life. Unsuccessful in finishing school, some moved on, either to the West Coast or into full-time work in Chicago and its surrounding areas.

From the outset, Chicago's Filipinos discovered the burden of race. While not as severe as the anti-Filipino race riots or anti-miscegenation laws of the Southwest and Pacific slope, the racial barriers in the Midwest informally restricted many Filipinos to poorly paid service employment with little job security. Many put in time as dishwashers, waiters, cooks, and bellhops in Chicago's restaurants, hotels, and clubs, while others served as butlers, chauffeurs, and gardeners for some of the city's elite. Steady industrial employment for those trained as draftsmen, engineers, and machinists proved harder to come by, especially as Filipino numbers in Chicago grew in the 1920s and early 1930s. The number of Chicago Filipinos practicing law and medicine or teaching in these years can be counted on two hands, though far more had aspired to those professions.

Two occupations proved an exception to this rule of insecurity and provided occupational stability for a large portion of the Filipino community that would naturalize in 1946. In 1926, Chicago's Pullman Company responded to the unionizing challenge of A. Philip Randolph's Brotherhood of Sleeping Car Porters by opening Pullman employment to several hundred Filipinos. By comparison to other forms of service work, a job as an attendant, waiter, or bartender on the railroad with Pullman promised better pay and steady work, though spending a week on a run to Seattle or Los Angeles made even part-time schooling unlikely. In addition, Filipinos found employment as postal clerks at the Post Office, initially during the holiday season and on the night shift so as to be able to attend class during the day. By 1946, some Pullman and postal workers had put in more than twenty years of service, as a settler community replaced the student community.

Though almost invisible in Chicago's polyglot metropolis, Filipinos stood out in one particular way. They crossed the boundaries of race in romance and marriage. A cohort of "students" almost ninety-five per cent male, they frequented the city's taxi dance halls.[12] They dated and often married young women of

European descent. When they married, they clustered in apartment buildings where landlords would rent to interracial couples and they raised their families. Very few contemplated returning to the Philippines with a "white" wife, mostly because of a perceived unwillingness on the women's part, although the stories of Sophie Schmidt Rodolfo and Phyllis Tiongco, both married to Filipinos who successfully completed their college work, supply exceptions to this rule.[13]

Thus constituted, the stable core of Chicago's Filipino community survived the Great Depression and World War Two. The Depression created serious hardships and taxed the resources of the community and the various, mostly Protestant, charitable organizations that offered assistance. While transience remained high, so did persistence. A measure of their unwillingness to leave Chicago is the small number of Filipinos who took up the U. S. government's efforts each year during the late 1930s to recruit them for a paid, one-way ticket back to the Philippines. Because this "repatriation" program, enacted following the passage of the Tydings-McDuffie Act, promised only a severely constrained right of return to the United States, settled Filipinos viewed it with fear and skepticism, if not outright disdain.[14]

Likewise, World War Two did not diminish Filipinos' attachment to Chicago. While some members of the community enlisted enthusiastically and served in the armed forces, others had passed the age for active duty. There is some evidence that Filipinos who enlisted were promptly discharged back to their former occupations, possibly deemed essential civilian wartime work.[15] During wartime years of labor scarcity, some Filipinos may have gained jobs in areas such as skilled factory work from which they had previously been excluded during the Depression.

\*    \*    \*    \*    \*

Citizenship for those born in the Philippines followed the breaching of the Asiatic Barred Zone in 1943, when, as a means to reward a World War Two ally, Chinese living in the United States became eligible to naturalize.[16] Filipinos in the United States who had joined the U.S. military after the war began also became eligible for naturalization. Almost immediately, supporters of Filipino Americans staked out a claim that "the denial of such possibilities to [all] Filipinos would not be consistent with a fair-minded American policy."[17] By November 1944, the House Committee on Immigration and Naturalization had before it half a dozen pieces of legislation providing for Filipino citizenship. Those testifying in favor of one or another bill included a California Congressman, the delegate from the Territory of Hawaii, several federal officials, a Filipino American veteran of World War One, and representatives from the National Federation of Post Office Clerks, the Veterans of Foreign Wars, and the American Legion. Also testifying, Dr. Diosdado Yap claimed to represent "37 Filipino organizations in the United States and Hawaii." No one appeared who opposed Filipino citizenship.[18]

Two arguments on behalf of naturalization legislation highlighted the special case of Chicago's Filipinos and their families. Labor leader E. C. Hallbeck warned that Filipino postal employees, some of them with twenty-five years service, would lose their jobs unless citizenship legislation was enacted prior to the scheduled date of Philippine independence on July 4, 1946. He noted that "the Chicago Post Office Clerks Union . . . has by far the largest Filipino representation of any organization affiliated with the American Federation of Labor." In a passionate plea, Ramon P. Pobre, a postal worker and Executive Secretary of the Filipino National Council of Chicago, declared, "Those of us who have married here and have become heads of families fear that we will be forced to leave this, our chosen country, and thus disrupt, if not break up altogether our families with all their tender ties and loving affections." In a similar vein, Interior Secretary Harold L. Ickes remarked that "There is a special need to remedy the situation of divided family citizenship . . . which has resulted from marriages between Philippine citizens and citizens of the United States."[19]

\*    \*    \*    \*    \*

Who were the Filipinos that constituted what we call the "stable core" of their community in Chicago in 1946? How, speculatively, might their experiences cast light on the sources of their presumed differences from Filipinos as conventionally depicted in the historical literature?

By the time they petitioned for naturalization, many of the 442 Filipinos had lived in Chicago for twenty years or more, often having shown up in the Windy City soon after their arrival in the United States. By this point in time, Pullman and postal work supplied the largest and steadiest source of employment among those who filed petitions, totaling 39 percent (52 men with Pullman and 120 with the Post Office). Those who had married inter-racially were almost invariably more likely to work for the Pullman Company and the Post Office than those who had not, 88.5 percent of the former (46 of 52) and 68.3 percent of the latter (82 of 120), respectively. By contrast, more than two-fifths of the unmarried (42.4 percent, or 45 of 106) were concentrated in the less secure service sectors of hotel and restaurant employment or personal service work—cooks, busboys, bartenders, butlers, chauffeurs, and elevator operators. Overall, this service grouping captured 120 (27.2 percent) of the petitioners.[20] Less than one in five (19.6 percent, or 32 of 163) of the interracially married with children held these sorts of jobs in 1946.

Possibly owing to wartime labor shortages, fifty-three worked in a range of industrial sector jobs, surpassing those employed at Pullman by one. These Filipinos earned their livings as machinists, tool and die makers, punch press operators, and welders, as well as a few employed in meatpacking. A somewhat smaller cohort of forty-eight worked for others in semi-skilled occupations that may have reflected a scaling down of their earlier educational aspirations: draftsmen, laboratory technicians, commercial artists, and a lone registered male nurse. Also included in this group are several barbers, musicians, and photographers, who were likely self-employed. More than a third of these (35.4 per cent, or seventeen of forty-eight) hailed from intact interracial families with children. Despite the relatively high educational attainment of Chicago's Filipinos, only ten practiced professions when they applied for naturalization in 1946: two physicians, two chemists, two Protestant clergy, a dentist, a lawyer, a research engineer, and a high school Spanish teacher.

Although Filipinos in Chicago had by no means left service sector employment behind, the diversification of their occupations combined with presumed job stability to foster a commitment to settled residence.

&ast; &ast; &ast; &ast; &ast;

Perhaps of even greater importance, marriage and the birth of children enhanced ties to place. Table 1 (below) summarizes presence and/or absence of family ties among the Filipino petitioners for naturalization by examining marital status, presence or absence of a spouse in the United States, and the birth of children. Of 442 petitioners, 289 (65.4 percent) had a wife and/or children in the United States, probably living with or near them in Chicago (See Table 1, Section A). By contrast, 153 petitioners (34.6 percent) of petitioners were single, widowed, or divorced, and had no children in the United States (See Table 1, Section B).

The marital patterns of ever-married Filipinos naturalizing in Chicago during the last half of 1946 offer additional evidence of the importance of marriage to a non-Filipina wife in encouraging stability and naturalization.

Among 338 currently or formerly married Filipinos who naturalized in 1946, 296 (87.6 percent) had chosen a spouse across racial lines. Among non-Filipina spouses, 110 (37.2 percent) claimed Chicago as their place of birth (not shown in tables). A substantial number were likely the U.S.-born daughters of immigrant parents. Emphasizing the pull of the nation's Second City for young, unattached women, thirty-two (10.8 percent) who married Filipinos came to Chicago from elsewhere in Illinois; sixty-seven (22.6 percent), from the nearby states of Indiana, Iowa, Michigan, Minnesota, Missouri, and Wisconsin; and sixty-three (21.3 percent), from elsewhere in the United States. Among the nineteen foreign-born spouses, Canada supplied four; Czechoslovakia, Germany and Poland, two each; and England, France, Ireland, Italy, Lithuania, Scotland, Sweden, Grenada, and Jamaica one each.

Although the race of spouses cannot be determined from the naturalization petitions, Filipinos in Chicago typically wed white women.[23] A brief colloquy between New York Congressman Samuel Dickstein, chair of the House Committee on Immigration and Naturalization; Filipino immigrant Diosdado Yap; and Louisiana Congressman A. Leonard Allen during the 1944 naturalization hearings explained the racial attitudes underlying Filipino marital choices. After ascertaining that Filipinos had married "Caucasians," Rep. Allen inquired: "Has

## TABLE 1
### FAMILY TIES AMONG PETITIONERS FOR NATURALIZATION

|  | Number | Percent | Percent of All |
|---|---|---|---|
| A. *With Family Ties in Chicago* | | | |
| 1. Interracial— Intact[a] with Children | 163 | 56.4 | 36.7 |
| 2. Interracial—Intact without Children | 78 | 27.0 | 17.5 |
| 3. Interracial—Broken[b] with Children | 26 | 9.0 | 5.9 |
| 4. Filipino—Intact | 22 | 7.6 | 5.0 |
| **Total** | **289** | **100.0** | **65.1** |
| | | | |
| B. *Without Family Ties in Chicago[c]* | | | |
| 1. Single—Never Married | 106 | 68.3 | 23.9 |
| 2. Interracial—Broken without Children | 29 | 18.7 | 6.5 |
| 3. Filipino—Broken | 1 | .7 | .2 |
| 4. Filipino Transnational[d] & Intact | 11 | 7.1 | 2.5 |
| 5. Filipino Transnational & Broken | 8[e] | 5.2 | 1.8 |
| | | | |
| **Total** | **155** | **100.0** | **34.9** |
| **TOTAL** | **444** | | **100.0** |

[a]Intact marriages are those not broken by divorce or the death of a wife.

[b]Broken marriages are those ended by divorce or the death of a spouse. The category also includes those who indicated on a petition for naturalization that they were separated from their spouse.

[c]Although without a wife or children in Chicago, some Filipinos in this category did have brothers and/or cousins who also lived in Chicago.

[d]"Split" marriages are "transnational"—meaning divided by geographical separation. One spouse was in the United States at the time of the petition for naturalization, while the other was in the Philippines.

[e]Includes two petitioners also included among interracially married Filipinos.

there ever been an instance to your knowledge—your people do not marry or intermarry with the Ethiopian race[?]" "No, sir,"Yap answered, "thousands have married white American citizens." "You are using good sense," Dickstein replied. Yap added: "We found that out, Mr. Chairman; and many of us have raised American children—boys and girls."[24] Filipinos recognized that they would never be perceived as white in the United States, nor enjoy the privileges of white status. Born of white mothers and citizens by birth, the Filipinos' children might experience a more fluid identity, and that, according to Yap, gave some Filipino fathers vicarious comfort.

The naturalization petitions capture these interracial marriages at a fixed moment in time that, for some couples, occurred years after their marriage and for other couples, only months after they said their vows. Despite the absence of anti-

## TABLE 2
### INTERRACIAL & FILIPINO MARRIED COUPLES INTACT,[a] BROKEN,[b] & TRANSNATIONAL[c]

| | Interracial Couples in Chicago | | Filipino Couples in Chicago | | Filipino Transnational Couples | | Filipino Transnational > Interracial Couples[d] | | TOTAL | |
|---|---|---|---|---|---|---|---|---|---|---|
| | N | % | N | % | N | % | N | % | N | % |
| **Intact** | | | | | | | | | | |
| With children | 162 | 54.7 | 21 | 91.3 | 7 | 41.2 | — | — | 190 | 56.2 |
| w/o children | 79 | 26.7 | 1 | 4.3 | 4 | 23.5 | — | — | 84 | 24.8 |
| **Total Intact** | **241** | **81.4** | **22** | **95.6** | **11** | **64.7** | **—** | **—** | **274** | **81.0** |
| **Broken** | | | | | | | | | | |
| With children | 26 | 8.8 | — | — | 4 | 23.5 | [2[21] | 100.0] | 32 | 9.5 |
| w/o children | 29 | 9.8 | 1 | 4.3 | 2 | 11.8 | — | — | 32 | 9.5 |
| **Total Broken** | **55** | **18.6** | **1** | **4.3** | **6** | **35.3** | **[2** | **100.0]** | **64** | **19.0** |
| **TOTAL** | **296** | **87.6** | **23** | **6.8** | **17** | **5.0** | **[2** | **.6]** | **338[22]** | **100.0** |

[a]Intact marriages are those not broken by divorce or the death of a wife.

[b]Broken marriages are those ended by divorce or the death of a spouse. The category also includes those who indicated on a petition for naturalization that they were separated from their spouse.

[c]Transnational marriages are those in which the spouses are separated by geography. One spouse was in the United States at the time of the petition for naturalization, while the other was in the Philippines.

[d]This category includes two petitioners who divorced a Filipina wife and subsequently married interracially.

miscegenation legislation targeting Filipino-white unions in Illinois throughout the period under study, only 44 (18.3 percent) of 241 intact marriages[25] between a Filipino husband and a wife of another race began *prior* to 1935 (not shown in tables). By contrast, 144 (59.8 percent) took place between passage of the Tydings-McDuffie Act and the beginning of World War Two, while fifty-two (21.6 percent) began after the start of the war. One may speculate that, during the years prior to Tydings-McDuffie, many Filipinos in Chicago continued to harbor dreams of going home and perhaps resisted the lure of marriage more than they did after passage of the legislation that changed their status from "national" to "alien." Choosing to journey to the Philippines after Tydings-McDuffie, for however brief an intended stay, risked denial of re-entry into the United States for all but those who had respected sponsors willing to vouch for the temporary nature of their trip to their homeland.[26] Reluctant to relinquish the lives that they had built in Chicago, especially during the Depression and as they grew older in the Windy City, Filipinos found spouses where they could.

The interracial marriage of longest duration in 1946 took place twenty-six years earlier, on February 19, 1920, when twenty-one-year-old Quirino Gilbolenga Polanco, who had arrived in the United States in 1917, married his Chicago-born wife, Ruth, the daughter of Swedish immigrants, in Chicago.[27] Like the Buensucesos in 1930, the Polancos spent the 1920s establishing their family. Two daughters, Juanita and Ruth, were born to the Polancos in 1921 and 1924, and ten years after the couple's marriage, in 1930, Quirino Polanco was employed as a bacteriologist at the Veterans Administration's Hines Hospital that had been established in Maywood in 1921. In 1930, the family lived a little over a mile away at 1902 St. Charles Road in a dwelling rented for fifty-five dollars per month. By 1946, one year beyond their silver wedding anniversary, Quirino and Ruth Polanco had added a third daughter, Dolores, in 1930, and the family had moved to a location 2.3 miles southeast of the VA hospital. By 1946, the two older Polanco daughters were twenty-five and twenty-two years of age and married, but neither had chosen a husband of Filipino heritage. Juanita, now Mrs. Hanson, lived in Oak Park, Illinois; Ruth, Mrs. Stitzel, in Minot, North Dakota. Although we cannot ascertain whether the Polancos owned a home in 1946, Quirino had clearly survived the Depression and World War Two without disruption of his employment. On his petition for naturalization, Polanco listed his occupation as "chief, clinical laboratorian."[28] Like Filipino postal workers, Polanco, too, had reason to fear the loss of his government job if he remained an "alien." This was an especially frightening prospect for Filipinos who had established families in Chicago.

Although the naturalization petitions offer only a snapshot taken in 1946, they do give a portrait of childbearing among both intact and broken couples in that year (see Table 3, below). Childbearing among interracial couples will later be contrasted with childbearing among couples with Filipino husbands *and* wives.

As had Quirino Polanco, slightly more than two-thirds (163 or 67.6 percent) of 241 Filipinos in intact interracial marriages had become fathers by 1946, as had twenty-six (47.2 percent) among the fifty-five Filipinos whose interracial marriages were broken. Seventy-eight (32.4 percent) of the Filipinos in intact interracial marriages had no children,[29] as did twenty nine (52.7 percent) of fifty-five Filipinos whose interracial marriages had ended. One hundred and sixty-two intact couples with children produced 297 offspring by 1946, an average of 1.83 children per family. Twenty-nine couples became the parents of three or four children. Only two couples exceeded four; one couple produced seven, and another had twelve.

The Carbonell family—parents Roman and Violet and their twelve children born between the couple's marriage on July 25, 1928, and Roman's October 2, 1946, naturalization petition—offers an extraordinary case for several reasons and not just their dozen children. Roman Carbonell arrived in the United States in June 1922 and came immediately to Chicago, likely to go to school. In the census of 1930, now a head of household and living in an apartment at 1715 West Adams on Chicago's near West Side, Carbonell listed his occupation as "student." This, in itself, is not surprising, since those without employment often continued to portray themselves as students. More often, however, such Filipinos were single, whereas Carbonell was a married man and already the father of his first child, a daughter, Josephine, called "Dolly" in the census.

However, Violet Carbonell's ethnicity and the composition of their "household" reveal interethnic dimensions that are rarely encountered. Seventeen years old when she married the then twenty-seven-year-old Roman, Violet was the daughter of Italian immigrants who undoubtedly lived in the neighborhood. Given the animosity between young Filipino and Italian men on the near West Side and the reputation that Italian families had for sheltering their unmarried daughters, one can only speculate about how young Violet came to meet and marry Roman Carbonell. In 1930, four others lived with the fledgling family of

TABLE 3
INTERRACIAL COUPLES AND CHILDBEARING

| Number of Children | Intact | | Broken | |
| --- | --- | --- | --- | --- |
| | N | % | N | % |
| 0 | 79 | 32.8 | 31 | 56.4 |
| 1–2 | 131 | 54.4 | 23 | 41.8 |
| 3–4 | 29 | 12.0 | 1 | 1.8 |
| 7 | 1 | .4 | — | — |
| 12 | 1 | .4 | — | — |
| TOTAL | 241 | 100.0 | 55 | 100.0 |

three: Roman's twenty-two-year-old cousin, Florantino Aquino, who also called himself a student, and another young couple, Dionisio and Virginia Hernandez, and their fifteen-month-old daughter Dolores. Despite the couple's surname, Hernandez, they were not Filipino but rather Mexican. Mexican-born Virginia was a nurse at a hospital, and her husband and child had both been born in Texas, as had his parents.[30]

Sixteen years later, the Carbonell family still lived on the near West Side, at 1430 W. Congress, and Roman had found secure employment with the post office. With the exception of the Carbonells' eldest son, Roman, Jr., one can only wonder whether some of their other children's names— Josephine, Patricia, Salvador, Bonifacia, Anita, Nicolas, Modesta, Robert, Shirley, Susana, and Luis—were drawn from the family's Filipino or Italian background, or both. One wonders, too, how Violet's Italian family reacted to her marriage, initially and by 1946.

\*  \*  \*  \*  \*

In contrast with the substantial portion of naturalizing Filipinos who had married interracially, only forty-two had married a spouse who was also Filipino. For purposes of analysis, we separate these Filipinos into two groups. Twenty-two petitioners lived in Chicago with a spouse born in the Philippines (Table 1, Section A, Line 4). Nineteen petitioners were geographically divided by the Pacific Ocean with the Filipino husband living in Chicago and filing for citizenship while his Filipina wife resided in the Philippines. Each of these petitioners can therefore be considered a participant in a "transnational" marriage (Table 1, Section B, Lines 4 and 5).

Among the twenty-two Chicago-based Filipino couples, fourteen had married in the United States, and eight in the Philippines (not shown in tables). Of the fourteen couples who married in the United States, five likely had known each other in their homeland; in these five instances, a marriage took place between six days and three months after the bride's arrival in the United States. Romance probably blossomed in the United States for the other nine couples; eight wed more than a year—sometimes years—after the woman's migration. The ninth couple's marriage resists classification; it took place more than six months but less than a year after her arrival.

In eight instances of vows said in the Philippines, five husbands returned to their homeland for a period of less than six months[31] and married during the visit. For example, thirty-two-year-old Alfonso Bacalzo wed his twenty-seven-year-old bride, Maxima, during a visit to his home province of La Union in 1928 and immediately brought her home to Chicago where he had lived since July 1924, less than a month after he first landed in the United States. Five children were born to the couple in Chicago between January 1929 and January 1945.[32] Similarly, in January 1935, Florentino and Ambrosia Ravelo married in the Philippines. He had spent almost fifteen years living in Chicago as a bachelor, having arrived in the Windy City in September 1920, less than four months after docking on the West Coast. Florentino returned to Chicago with his wife less than a month after they said their vows, thus beating the deadline for Filipino immigration restriction set under the Tydings-McDuffie Act. Their family ultimately would include four Chicago-born daughters.[33] In *only* three instances of a marriage contracted in the Philippines did the husband initiate migration to the United States *after* his wedding. In two instances, the couple journeyed to the United States together; the other couple was reunited within three years after the husband left for the United States. Thus, irrespective of where they married, long separations after marriage did *not* characterize the lives of Chicago-based Filipino couples.[34] In contrast with childbearing among interracial couples who produced an average of 1.8 children per family, Filipino couples in Chicago averaged 3.7 children.

Nineteen petitions for naturalization offer evidence of marriages that can be defined as "transnational." Each husband married and left a Filipina wife in the Philippines prior to his migration to the United States. Eleven petitioners maintained that their bonds of marriage were intact in 1946, whereas eight termed them broken. Among the eleven intact couples, eight experienced years of separation and might, therefore, be considered "transnational" in the way that Chinese couples often were prior to the end of the Second World War. Seven husbands left a wife, and a total of sixteen children born between 1914 and 1927 in the Philippines and apparently never returned to their homeland in the years between their migration and 1946. Because all seven men had arrived in the United States between 1920 and 1929, they had endured an average of 19.86 years— almost two decades—apart. As naturalized citizens, they might finally return to the Philippines to see their wives and children, as well as the grandchildren born during their absence.

The eighth case of a "transnational" couple deviates from the above pattern. Roman Urebio Baladad arrived in the United States in 1919 at the age of nineteen aboard the U.S. army transport *Sheridan*. During a trip to the Philippines of less than six months, Roman, then thirty-two, married Filomena who was six years his junior on April 27, 1932, in his hometown. Interestingly, Filomena, too, had been in the United States, having arrived in 1930, and the pair must have traveled home to wed. Within nine months of the ceremony, the couple lived in Chicago where their eldest son, Rodolfo, was born on February 1, 1933. Two more sons, Alfredo and Roman, Jr., were added to the Baladad family in Chicago in 1934 and 1938. But in October 1939, the Baladads left San Francisco aboard the *President Coolidge*, bound for the Philippines. One cannot know from Roman's 1946 petition for naturalization exactly what the couple intended in 1939. Was their trip to the Philippines to be a visit home, despite the restrictions on reentry imposed by the Tydings-McDuffie Act, or a permanent move?

Roman Baladad *might* have been able to re-enter the United States with his three sons who were United States citizens by birth. If he held postal service employment in 1939, as he did in 1946, he had probably taken a year's leave of absence from his federal job and traveled with the certification needed to ensure his re-admission. But the departure of Filomena Baladad, who presumably had no such guarantee, likely meant that the Baladads, or at least Filomena, wanted to stay in the Philippines. On September 21, 1940, one day after the birth in the Philippines of the couple's fourth son, Juanito, Roman Baladad arrived back in San Francisco. The timing of his son's birth and his return to the United States suggests that, despite Filomena's pregnancy, Baladad's leave of absence from the post office was about to expire. He had to choose between waiting for the birth of their child in the Philippines and losing his job in Chicago. Probably without comparable employment in the Philippines, he took both the security of his job with the Chicago post office and the prospect of relinquishing his right to return to the United States so seriously that he and Filomena chose to divide their family. When war came in 1941, Roman no doubt lost contact with Filomena and their sons, but by 1946, on his naturalization petition, he reported his family as living in the Philippines. With

U.S. citizenship in hand, Roman Baladad finally could go home again and could choose whether his stay in the Philippines would be temporary or permanent.[35]

While the couples just discussed made decisions leading to their separations prior to 1940, three "transnational" couples were affected more directly by World War Two, although in different ways. Guillermo Gonzales Pardo arrived in San Francisco on July 29, 1941, presumably leaving his wife Elenore in the Philippines. Exactly one year later, on July 29, 1942, while living in Boston, the twenty-seven-year-old Pardo enlisted in the U.S. army and served overseas from December 1945 to July 1946. On August 2, 1946, when Sergeant Pardo petitioned for naturalization, Corp. Lloyd Bollenbacher and Corp. Charles Shoemaker accompanied him from Fort Sheridan as his witnesses. Given the date of his arrival in the United States, he had been parted from his wife for five years.[36]

By contrast, Justo Belo Cardenas used his service in the Philippines during World War II to end his bachelor days. Living in the United States since 1929, Cardenas joined the army in Detroit and served overseas from June 1944 through March 1946. On August 1, 1945, during his time in the Philippines, thirty-five-year-old Justo wed a twenty-one-year-old Filipina bride, Josefa. After their marriage, Cardenas remained in the Philippines for approximately eight months. He arrived back in the United States on March 31, 1946, and was discharged from the army five days later. At the time of his petition for naturalization on September 6, 1946, Cardenas was working as an elevator operator and likely hoping that his separation from his new wife soon would be over.

In the final case related to service in World War Two, Sabino Jose Aguila used his service in the military to claim citizenship despite no evidence of prior residence in the United States. Born in 1908, Aguila, a lawyer, married his

Filipina wife in 1938 and a daughter was born to the couple in 1940. Ten days after the Japanese attack on the Philippines, Aguila was inducted into the U.S. Army of the Far East at Manila. Having survived the war, he was discharged on April 1, 1946. Leaving his wife and daughter in Manila, Aguila flew to San Francisco seven months later, arriving on October 29, 1946.[37] Less than a month later, he petitioned for naturalization, thus becoming one of a relatively small number of Philippine veterans able to do so before expiration of the law permitting their application for naturalization at the end of 1946.[38] The U.S. Congress closed the window of opportunity to their citizenship and possible migration in 1948.[39]

As opposed to the eleven intact "transnational" couples discussed above, eight of the nineteen "transnational" Filipino marriages were broken in 1946. Each husband had left a wife in the Philippines between 1924 and 1929; six with children as well. One husband claimed to be "separated" from his Filipina wife. Despite the absence of divorce under Philippine law and the legal limbo into which their Filipina wives would be consigned, seven husbands living in Chicago had formally ended their marriages and listed themselves as divorced on their petitions. After divorcing their Filipina wives, two of these husbands had married white women.

\*    \*    \*    \*    \*

In conclusion, three points stand out. First, whether their marriages survived intact or ended prior to 1946, in the absence of anti-miscegenation legislation in Illinois, two-thirds of *all* Filipinos naturalizing in Chicago during the last six months of 1946 had forsaken bachelor status in favor of interracial marriage. And, these interracially married Filipinos were almost eighty-eight percent of Filipinos who were then or ever had been married. Thus, as it emerged, Chicago's Filipino community was numerically defined in large measure by couples consisting of Filipino husbands, white wives, and interracially mixed or *mestizo* children—families whose culture was never solely Filipino. Second, only about eight percent of married Filipinos lived in Chicago with a Filipina wife, but even this small number, like the larger number of interracial couples, had settled into lives in the Second City with American-born children. Finally, "transnational" couples—those whose existence might have given solace and purpose to those Filipinos perceived incorrectly to be "bachelors"—were *very* few. At the end of World War Two, only eleven of four hundred and forty-two Filipinos in Chicago acknowledged a wife back in the Philippines.

This should not be taken to mean that transnational connections were unimportant to Chicago's Filipinos, even those interracially married. The re-opening of contact among family members divided not only by the Pacific Ocean but also by World War Two brought news unheard for half a decade, and with it both joy and sorrow. Many families in Chicago would use their own limited prosperity after the war to send money and goods home to relatives in the Philippines. Letters resumed, and after citizenship was secured, trips back home to the Philippines became feasible. Yet most Filipinos, whatever their marital status, considered such visits temporary respites from the very real lives that they had built during long years in Chicago.

Chicago's Filipino community had weathered the hardships of depression and war, the indignities of racial discrimination, unwanted "repatriation," alien registration, and uncertainty and worry during the Japanese occupation of their homeland.[40] The stable core of the community that has been the focus of this article had evolved over time from a transient mix of students and service workers into an aggregate of intact, mostly interracial families, many with children, whose breadwinners held steady work in a wide range of occupations. In the 1950s after passage of the McCarran-Walter Act of 1952, some of the Filipino bachelors who applied for citizenship in 1946 would travel to the Philippines and return with often much younger Filipina wives to form families with American-born children in Chicago. Others would marry late and interracially. Phillip Lontoc, a forty-year-old bachelor and petitioner for naturalization in 1946, married his wife Frances, the Polish American widow of Ruperto Genciana, another Chicago Filipino, in 1957, one year after Genciana's death.[41] While some Filipinos in Chicago probably delayed applying for naturalization until after 1946 or declined ever to naturalize for nationalistic or other reasons, those most interested in staying took advantage of the opportunity to claim citizenship in the first six months after it became available. With immigration from the now independent Philippines still very limited, Filipinos such as these would comprise Chicago's Filipino American community into the 1960s.

The predominance of interracial marriage among Filipinos who settled in Chicago prior to World War Two undoubtedly shaped not only the manner of their incorporation into the United States, but also that of their American-born children. Although these families were bi-cultural, and typically preserved elements of the ethnic heritage of both parents, emphasis on the American as defining the children's future success was paramount. In this sense, some Filipino American fathers could point to the educational successes of their children as validating their own original goals. But few Filipino American children learned a language other than English at home. Few displayed more than a passing interest in absorbing the nationality-based cultures and customs of either of their parents. Few dated or married other Filipino Americans or Filipino immigrants, for those whom they knew seemed too much like family—or far too "foreign." Hence, it is not surprising that in the later decades of the twentieth century, when revalidating one's ethnic heritage became a passion and a pastime for many, the Filipino American Historical Society of Chicago was organized primarily by Filipino Americans who had *both* Filipino fathers *and* mothers or, like one of the authors of this article, developed a "professional" interest in her father's history.[42]

# NOTES

This essay was presented at "Immigration History and the University of Minnesota: Where We've Been, Where We're Going," an invitational conference honoring Professor Rudolph J. Vecoli on the occasion of his retirement, Elmer L. Andersen Library, University of Minnesota, Twin Cities, May 13, 2005. The authors wish to thank Professors Roger Daniels and Elliott Barkan for their comments on this work and for the support and encouragement that they have provided over time.

1. United States of America, Petition for Naturalization by Cesario Agudo Buensuceso, No. 324592, Oct. 22, 1946, Naturalization Records for U.S. District Courts (RG 21) in Illinois, Indiana, Michigan, Minnesota, Ohio, and Wisconsin, National Archives and Records Administration, Great Lakes Region, Chicago.

2. Petition for Naturalization by Cesario Agudo Buensuceso, No. 324592, Oct. 22, 1946.

3. United States, 15th Census of the United States, Population Schedule, ED#2308, Proviso, Cook, Illinois, "Zesario Buensvuas," Roll 506, p. 24A. Buensuceso [Buensvuas] joined the U.S. armed services in 1914.

4. Petition for Naturalization by Cesario Agudo Buensuceso, No. 324592. Even in 1946, Elsie was not a naturalized citizen.

5. See Barbara M. Posadas, "Crossed Boundaries in Interracial Chicago: Pilipino American Families Since 1925," *Amerasia Journal* 8 (Fall 1981): 31–52; Posadas, "The Hierarchy of Color and Psychological Adjustment in an Industrial Environment: Filipinos, the Pullman Company and the Brotherhood of Sleeping Car Porters," *Labor History* (Summer 1982): 349–73; Posadas and Roland L. Guyotte, "Unintentional Immigrants: Chicago's Filipino Foreign Students Become Settlers, 1900–1941," *Journal of American Ethnic History* 9, no. 2 (Spring 1990): 26–48; and Guyotte and Posadas, "Celebrating Rizal Day: The Emergence of a Filipino Tradition in Twentieth Century Chicago," in Genevieve Fabre and Ramon A. Gutierrez, eds., *Feasts and Celebrations in North American Ethnic Communities* (Albuquerque, NM, 1995), 111–28.

6. This essay is based on our analysis of 442 petitions for naturalization filed by Filipinos with the U.S. District Court in Chicago between July 23, 1946, and December 31, 1946. These petitions constitute the *entire* population of Filipinos applying for citizenship in these months, *not* a sample, and are 18.55% of all petitions filed during the period. United States of America, Petitions for Naturalization, Nos. 322217–324599, July 23, 1946–December 31, 1946, Naturalization Records for U.S. District Courts (RG 21) in Illinois, Indiana, Michigan, Minnesota, Ohio, and Wisconsin, National Archives and Records Administration, Great Lakes Region, Chicago.

7. See, for example, Roger Daniels, *Asian America: Chinese and Japanese in the United States since 1850* (Seattle, WA, 1988), 198–99; Xiaojian Zhao, *Remaking Chinese America: Immigration, Family, and Community, 1940–1965* (New Brunswick, NJ, 2002).

8. See Zhao, *op. cit.*; and Madeline Y. Hsu, *Dreaming of Gold, Dreaming of Home: Transnationalism and Migration Between the United States and South China, 1882–1943* (Stanford, CA, 2000). The extent and meaning of transnationalism among Filipinos in these years has yet to be explored systematically through attention to such indices as remittances, letters to family members, visits to the Philippines, and sponsorship of immigrant relatives when allowed by U. S. law.

9. In 1943, Filipinos in the United States armed forces who had been living in the United States prior to their service were permitted to become citizens, but Filipinos in the United States who were not in the military continued to be barred.

10.  Sec. 8 (a) (1) of the Philippine Independence Act [Tydings-McDuffie Act] declared that during the interim Commonwealth period before the final withdrawal of U.S. authority, "For the purposes of the Immigration Act of 1917, the Immigration Act of 1924, this section and, all other laws of the United States relating to the immigration, exclusion, or expulsion of aliens, citizens of the Philippine Islands who are not citizens of the United States shall be considered as if they were aliens." Passage of Tydings-McDuffie did not, however, preclude ongoing residence in the United States by Filipinos who had arrived prior to passage of the legislation, nor did it specify regulations for their treatment while in the United States.

11.  Barbara M. Posadas and Roland L. Guyotte, "Aspiration and Reality: Occupational and Educational Choice among Filipino Migrants to Chicago, 1900–1935," *Illinois Historical Journal* 85, no. 2 (Summer 1992): 89–104.

12.  Paul G. Cressey, *The Taxi-Dance Hall: A Sociological Study in Commercialized Recreation and City Life* (Chicago, 1932), especially Chapter 7, "The Filipino and the Taxi-Dance Hall"; Posadas, "Crossed Boundaries."

13.  Sophie Schmidt-Rodolfo, *Goodbye to Winter: The Autobiography of Sophie Schmidt-Rodolfo*, ed. Dolores S. Feria (Quezon City, 1987); interview with Phyllis Tiongco, Manila, October 1982. Tiongco, the Chicago-born daughter of Polish immigrants, survived World War Two in Manila by pretending to be German when dealing with Japanese occupation forces.

14.  Barbara M. Posadas and Roland L. Guyotte, "Why Go Home? Repatriation and Filipinos in the Midwest in the 1930s," Biennial Conference of the Midwest Chapter of the Filipino American National Historical Society, Springfield, IL, October 25, 2003. Although those who repatriated could, technically, return to the United States under the fifty-per-year quota that the Tydings-McDuffie Act allocated to the Philippines during the Commonwealth period (after independence, the Philippines would become part of the Asiatic Barred Zone), Filipinos living in the United States felt this an unrealistic possibility, not only because of the tiny size of the quota, but also because of their own poverty.

15.  During the war, Chicago employers eagerly sought wartime replacements for workers in military service, ultimately happily employing Japanese Americans released from incarceration camps in the West and South. See: Charlotte Brooks, "In the Twilight Zone Between Black and White: Japanese American Resettlement and Community in Chicago, 1942–1945," *Journal of American History* 86, no. 4 (2000): 1655–87; Roger Daniels, "Words Do Matter: A Note on Inappropriate Terminology and the Incarceration of the Japanese Americans," in Louis Fiset and Gail Nomura, eds., *Nikkei in the Pacific Northwest: Japanese Americans and Japanese Canadians in the Twentieth Century* (Seattle, WA, 2005), 183–207.

16.  On the repeal of Chinese exclusion, see Roger Daniels, *Guarding the Golden Door: American Immigration Policy and Immigrants Since 1882* (New York, 2004), 91–93.

17.  Emory S. Bogardus, "Citizenship for Filipinos," *Sociology and Social Research* 29 (Sept.–Oct. 1944): 53.

18.  "Naturalization of Filipinos," *Hearings before the Committee on Immigration and Naturalization, House of Representatives, 78th Congress, second session, on H. R. 2012, H. R. 2776, H. R. 3633, H. R. 4003, H. R. 4229, and H. R. 4826*, November 22, 1944.

19.  "Statement of E. C. Hallbeck," *Ibid.*, 3–4; Ramon P. Pobre to Hon. Samuel Dickstein, August 9, 1944, *Ibid.*, 55; Harold L. Ickes to Hon. Samuel Dickstein, June 13, 1944, *Ibid.*, 30. Although Filipinos living in the United States had become "aliens" after passage of the Tydings-McDuffie Act, the U.S. government permitted them to

continue in federal employment during the commonwealth period. Hence, Filipinos employed by the post office had been able to retain their jobs from the mid-1930s through World War Two. They and their supporters feared that this no longer would be possible after the Philippines became independent if, at the same time, Filipinos were barred from becoming naturalized citizens. As "aliens" incapable of even declaring their intention to naturalize, they would likely be dismissed from federal jobs.

20. Not surprisingly, the unmarried also comprised the largest number of those who served in the military during World War Two (23.5 percent, or 25 of 106).

21. The bracketed couples also are counted among interracial intact couples. Each husband had one child by his Filipina wife whom he left in the Philippines. Subsequently, as part of an interracial couple, one had two children; the other, none.

22. Two couples appear in *both* the "Interracial" and the "Filipino Transnational Interracial" columns.

23. Only one instance of a Filipino-black marriage has been found in Chicago during over twenty years of research on this population. Married to a black woman, Cypriano Samonte, a mainstay of Brotherhood of Sleeping Car Porters' efforts to organize Filipinos employed by the Pullman Company in the 1930s, does not appear in the 1946 naturalization petitions.

24. *Hearings*, 17.

25. Intact marriages are those not broken by divorce or the death of a wife.

26. See, for example, Patricia Justiniani McReynolds, *Almost Americans: A Quest for Dignity* (Santa Fe, NM, 1997), 151–202.

27. In 1946, Cesario Buensuceso was divorced from his wife, Elsie. He had moved from Forest Park, where their daughters were raised and where his ex-wife continued to live, was living on Chicago's near West Side, and was working as a draftsman. Petition for Naturalization by Cesario Agudo Buensuceso, No. 324592, Oct. 22, 1946.

28. United States of America, Petition for Naturalization by Quirino Gilbolenga Polanco, No. 322860, Sept. 5, 1946, Naturalization Records for U.S. District Courts (RG 21) in Illinois, Indiana, Michigan, Minnesota, Ohio, and Wisconsin, National Archives and Records Administration, Great Lakes Region, Chicago; United States, 15th Census of the United States, Population Schedule, ED#2921, Proviso, Cook, Illinois, "Quirino Polanco," Roll 507, p. 7A; http://www.mapquest.com (accessed 4/6/05); http://www.va.gov/NFS/ HinesVAInternship/history.htm (accessed 4/6/05).

29. Twenty-six of these marriages were of five years or less duration.

30. United States of America, Petition for Naturalization by Roman Carbonell, No. 324290, Oct. 2, 1946, Naturalization Records for U.S. District Courts (RG 21) in Illinois, Indiana, Michigan, Minnesota, Ohio, and Wisconsin, National Archives and Records Administration, Great Lakes Region, Chicago; United States, 15th Census of the United States, Population Schedule, ED#944, Chicago, Cook, Illinois, "Roman Carbonell," Roll 457, p. 16B. Although the census of 1930 lists Dionisio Hernandez as a "female" employed as a "saleslady," the context of the household makes these errors evident.

31. On a petitions for naturalization, an applicant was required to list any absence from the United States of over six months duration since arrival in the country.

32. United States of America, Petition for Naturalization by Alfonso Bacalzo, No. 323251, Sept. 5, 1946, Naturalization Records for U.S. District Courts (RG 21) in Illinois, Indiana, Michigan, Minnesota, Ohio, and Wisconsin, National Archives and Records Administration, Great Lakes Region, Chicago.

33. United States of America, Petition for Naturalization by Florentino Ravelo, No. 323329, Sept. 5, 1946, Naturalization Records for U.S. District Courts (RG 21) in Illinois, Indiana, Michigan, Minnesota, Ohio, and Wisconsin, National Archives and Records Administration, Great Lakes Region, Chicago.

34. In 1946, all of these couples, save one, were intact. The lone exception, Dionisio Gacilan, married his Filipina wife in 1940 and was divorced by 1946.

35. United States of America, Petition for Naturalization by Roman Urebio Baladad, No. 323805, Sept. 25, 1946, Naturalization Records for U.S. District Courts (RG 21) in Illinois, Indiana, Michigan, Minnesota, Ohio, and Wisconsin, National Archives and Records Administration, Great Lakes Region, Chicago.

36. United States of America, Petition for Naturalization by Guillermo Gonzales Pardo, No. 323297, Aug. 2, 1946, Naturalization Records for U.S. District Courts (RG 21) in Illinois, Indiana, Michigan, Minnesota, Ohio, and Wisconsin, National Archives and Records Administration, Great Lakes Region, Chicago.

37. United States of America, Petition for Naturalization by Sabino Jose Aguila, No. 325040, Nov. 20, 1946, Naturalization Records for U.S. District Courts (RG 21) in Illinois, Indiana, Michigan, Minnesota, Ohio, and Wisconsin, National Archives and Records Administration, Great Lakes Region, Chicago. Among those seeking naturalization, Aguila was the only Filipino who arrived by airplane.

38. The Second War Powers Act, enacted on March 27, 1942, amended the Nationality Act of 1940 and provided for the naturalization of non-citizens serving in the U.S. military during the war. The law permitted naturalization of those who did not meet requirements regarding residency in the United States or literacy in English and directed the Commissioner of the Immigration and Naturalization Service to facilitate such naturalizations by verifying eligibility overseas. Congress subsequently set December 31, 1946, as the cut-off date for such applications. In the Philippines, however, the ability of Philippine veterans to apply for naturalization was limited prior to the end of 1946 by the absence of an official able to verify the eligibility of applicants during the last nine months of 1946. See, United States, House of Representatives, Committee on Veterans' Affairs, Subcommittee on Health, Hearing on the "Health Care for Filipino World War Two Veterans Act," Statement by Senator Daniel K. Inouye, June 13, 2002, http://veterans.house .gov/hearings/ schedule107/jun02/6-13-02/dinouye.html. Aguila undoubtedly understood that if he was unable to file for naturalization in the Philippines prior to the December 31, 1946, cut-off date, his only alternative was a trip to the United States for that purpose. Why he chose Chicago as his destination is unknown.

39. "Besides the explicit cutoff date in the 1940 Act [as amended in 1942], Congress in 1948 adopted a liberalized citizenship program that excluded Filipino servicemen and specifically provided that even applications timely filed under the 1940 Act and still pending would be adjudged under the new provisions. Act of June 1, 1948, Ch. 360, 62 Stat. 281." See, U.S. Supreme Court, INS v. PANGILINAN, 486 U.S. 875 (1988), http:// caselaw.lp.findlaw.com/scripts/getcase.pl?courtus&v ol486&invol875.

In the late 1980s, as reflected in the above cited U.S. Supreme Court case, the issue of citizenship for Philippine veterans of World War Two became a major political cause for Filipino Americans. The Immigration Act of 1990 re-opened the window for a several year period, but the fight continues for equity in veterans' benefits. See Barbara M. Posadas, *The Filipino Americans* (Westport, CT, 1999), 43–44.

40. *Hearings*, 18.

41. United States of America, Petition for Naturalization by Phillip Aguedo Lontoc, No. 324685, Oct. 29, 1946, Naturalization Records for U.S. District Courts (RG 21) in Illinois, Indiana, Michigan, Minnesota, Ohio, and Wisconsin, National Archives and Records Administration, Great Lakes Region, Chicago; United States of America, Petition for Naturalization by Ruperto Camacho Genciana, No. 323652, Aug. 23, 1946, Naturalization Records for U.S. District Courts (RG 21) in Illinois, Indiana, Michigan, Minnesota, Ohio, and Wisconsin, National Archives and Records Administration, Great Lakes Region, Chicago; Interviews with Phillip A. Lontoc, Chicago, August 10, 1979, and Frances Lontoc, Chicago, April 23, 1981.

42. See, Posadas, "Crossed Boundaries," and Barbara M. Posadas, "Mestiza Girlhood: Interracial Families in Chicago's Filipino American Community Since 1930," Judy Yung, ed., *Making Waves: Writings about Asian American Women* (Boston, 1989), 273–90.

# 7

# At Home in America?:
# Revisiting the Second Generation

## DEBORAH DASH MOORE

*"By the turn-of-the-century Russian-Jewish time
clock, it is now about 1925."[1]*

My book, *At Home in America: Second Generation New York Jews*, appeared in 1981, not quite midway between its subject—New York Jews in the interwar decades—and today's children of immigrants now coming of age after three decades of renewed immigration to the United States. Their visible presence in New York City invites reconsideration of an earlier generation that lived in the 1920s and '30s. *At Home in America*, written in the 1970s, sought to extend the history of American Jews beyond the immigrant era and reframe then current conceptualizations of American Jewish history. Regnant frameworks for interpreting the second generation, especially models of assimilation propounded by sociologists, seemed to lack historical contextualization. Developed after World War II, these theories imagined the United States divided along religious lines—i.e., the triple melting pot made famous by Will Herberg in *Protestant Catholic Jew*.[2] An alternative analysis of assimilation posited the substitution of a "symbolic ethnicity" for the real thing, an argument developed by Herbert Gans.[3] Such interpretations, Werner Sollors argued, could be understood as visions of declension, especially if viewed from the perspective of ethnic groups working to retain their distinctive identity.[4]

By contrast, historians of immigration who looked at subsequent generations proposed the idea of "third generation return." Often referred to as Marcus Lee Hansen's "law," this interpretation identified the second generation as transitional and marginal.[5] But what would happen if one set the second generation free from its position in an unbroken line moving toward assimilation? How could a historian come to understand the second generation in its own terms, view it in its historical situation? *At Home in America* suggested that the second generation innovated in religion, philanthropy, education, and politics. New York Jews created a new form of urban ethnicity, a master pattern for American Jews. Making homes for themselves in the city's diverse neighborhoods, New York Jews discovered that they had rooted themselves as well in America.

But the subject of the second generation failed to excite much interest.[6] Most American Jewish historians preferred to rework the fascinating subject of mass immigration. Gifted scholars, stimulated by new trends in historical research, revisited the era of immigration to explore these questions. Looking at Jewish immigrants in their urban setting, they examined such topics as women and gender, popular culture and consumption, labor and urbanism, politics and public culture, even foodways and folk practices.[7] Most recently, scholars have discovered that the Lower East Side offered rich possibilities to probe the theme of nostalgia, historical memory, and the invention of tradition.[8] And each return to New York's Lower East Side, or to the immigrant worlds of Chicago, Philadelphia, and other cities, proved eminently worthwhile. So, although *At Home in America* took its place in a chain of scholarship that started with Moses Rischin's *The Promised City* and continued with Arthur Goren's *New York Jews and the Quest for Community*, some time passed before Beth Wenger published *New York Jews in the Great Depression*, adding another link to the chain. Even more years elapsed until Eli Lederhendler's *New York Jews and the Decline of Urban Ethnicity* appeared.[9] Carrying the history of American Jews into the second half of the twentieth century challenged scholars. It was not easy to study the second generation.

Inspired in part by Louis Wirth and the Chicago School's history of American urbanism, I found that both the concept of generation and of urban growth would provide viable tools to usefully frame the study of American Jews subsequent to the complex conditions negotiated by immigrants. American Jewish history could successfully be located and the contours of a shared communal life explored within that intersection of family and cohort analysis amid patterns of urban expansion. But the rapid physical mobility of American Jews threatened this model. Perhaps immigrant history, defined by the transition from one place to another, suggested more useful ways of thinking about collective identity. Perhaps the movement from one home to another needed to be incorporated into any understanding of American Jewish history. "If you would know what kind of a Jew a man is," Louis Wirth once wrote, "ask him where he lives; for no single factor indicates as much about the character of the Jew as the area in which he lives. It is an index not only to his economic status, his occupation, his religion, but to his politics and his outlook on life and the stage in the assimilative process that he has reached."[10] Did suburbanization provide just another type of physical locale for Jewish society or did it fundamentally undermine the type of synthesis available in densely populated Jewish neighborhoods? In the Jewish historical imagination, external geography often expressed inner identity.[11]

Other categories of historical inquiry have sought to understand Jewish identity in terms of politics and gender. These scholars have proposed alternatives that emphasize organizational competition and public debates on the one hand as well as attention to gendered images and their socioeconomic basis on the other. [12] In each case, urbanization and generation have been less critical categories than seemed true for New York Jews in the interwar years.

Historians of other ethnic groups also have drawn upon theories of urbanism, mobility, and ethnic innovation by the second generation. [13] Despite the significant trauma sustained by second-generation Japanese Americans during World War Two, many of their postwar behaviors could be interpreted within the framework of an urban second-generation ethnicity. [14] Religious modifications, educational patterns, political activities, and even economic choices and social mobility pointed toward a determined effort to create a sense of being at home in America. Somewhat more hesitantly, historians of Polish and Italian immigrants similarly have sought to move their histories into the second generation. [15] Most recently, there has emerged a substantial literature on a very different Jewish second generation, the children of Holocaust survivors, most of it produced by that generation itself. [16]

But the largest change has come with the resumption of immigration to the United States. The arrival of hundreds of thousands of immigrants, many from Asia and South America, has produced new models of migration theory, most notably the concept of transnationalism, which in turn has raised anew questions about the children of immigrants, the second generation. [17] Scholars of transnationalism use the term in order "to emphasize the emergence of a social process in which migrants establish social fields that cross geographic, cultural, and political borders. Immigrants are understood to be transmigrants when they develop and maintain multiple relations—familial, economic, social, organizational, religious, and political—that span borders." [18] Having coined a new term to describe what is considered to be behavior characteristic of contemporary immigrants, in contrast to those who came a century ago, the question of the second generation also needs to be reframed. To what extent are the children of transmigrants also transnationals? Can transnationalism be transmitted across generations? [19]

A cluster of social scientists has answered "yes." Arguing that transnational behavior flourishes within families, Georges E. Fouron and Nina Glick-Schiller contend that children living within these households become part of a transnational generation. They define a transnational second generation "as all persons born into the generation after emigrants have established transnational social fields who live within or are socialized by these fields, regardless of whether they were born or are currently living in the country of emigration or abroad." [20] This sweeping vision expands the concept of second generation to refer less to a biological group— namely, the children of immigrants—than to an historical cohort—all those born after large-scale emigration creates a transnational field.

Working with Haitians, they recognize, however, that "the Haitian elision of self, family, blood, race, and nation is the product of a two-hundred-year history of nation-state building, so that the propensity of the second generation to embrace long distance nationalism [a product of transnationalism] is particularly strong."[21] Indeed, data drawn from surveys suggest that only a relatively small percentage of second-generation immigrants, approximately ten percent, participate in transnational behaviors, although among them may be influential figures within each group.[22] The value of "the contemporary study of second-generation transnationalism" is its ability to give scholars "a new understanding of an old process—the multigenerational trajectory of immigrants in their country of settlement."[23]

The debate on transnationalism among social scientists has provoked historians to revisit earlier periods of immigration and the classic 1916 essay by Randolph Bourne, "Transnational America."[24] Some have asked why his language did not enter the lexicon of politics and scholarship as pluralism, the melting pot, and assimilation did. Those influential terms all assumed the "overwhelming importance" of the United States as "a bounded if conflictual social field," as Barry Goldberg has pointed out. Instead, "the sociology of immigration, particularly that of the Chicago School, developed when immigration was a social problem; the historiography of immigration developed gradually after the nativists' triumph contained the perceived immigrant menace." The result, Goldberg continues, "was a more inclusive national narrative which asserted that consent to the ideals of the nation was more important than allegedly patriotic lines of descent."[25] While it is too soon for a historian to predict change, Goldberg wonders aloud whether "The global flows of labor and capital characteristic of new migration are finally calling into question" America's "racial imagination."[26] Rather than seeing a black immigrant as "an oxymoron," as Goldberg writes, concepts of immigration and second generation should be considered in parallel with the study of those who migrate within the United States, especially in the context of large-scale social upheaval. Thus the great migrations of African Americans north after both world wars could usefully be compared with immigration of West Indians to Harlem and Brooklyn.

Contemporary scholars of second-generation immigrants in New York City also have retained many older concepts, including that of assimilation. They have asked how the second generation becomes American. Their answer returns to the older sociological formulation of ambivalence regarding an American identity, making the second generation at home neither in the parental world nor in the United States. "One of the things that defines the second . . . generation experience is growing up and becoming adult in a culture and social setting that is vastly different from the one in which their parents came of age," write the editors of *Becoming New Yorkers*. "Of course," they admit, "all modern people face something like this."[27] But they argue that the second generation encounters a particularly poignant version of such a reality. Yet, these children of immigrants are far more rooted locally than their parents; their blend of cosmopolitanism (what others might call either transnationalism or translocalism[28]) and parochialism appears characteristically New Yorkish, if ambivalently American. The editors suggest that this rootedness, which could be considered a New York identity, seems open to all second-generation members because it "reflects the dynamic cultural creativity familiar to them, but not necessarily the larger white society."[29] Thus, the question of race complicates the situation facing the current New York second generation, changing the meaning of minority group. Still, there are sufficient similarities with the interwar decades to make comparisons possible.

In the mid-1980s, not long after publication of the paperback edition of *At Home in America*, I received an invitation to attend a conference at Yale University on the first and second generation from the Indian subcontinent. The organizers told me that they specifically wanted a comparative perspective. But when I arrived at the conference, I discovered that they actually desired a guidebook of how to create an Indian ethnicity in the United States based on what had worked in the American Jewish past. Descriptions of Jewish community centers and of synagogues organized around families fascinated them. I, in turn, listened in amazement as both generations aired their grievances, the youth at their parents' unwillingness to teach them the meanings of Hindu religious practices and the parents at their children's lack of interest in perpetuating a distinctive Indian identity. Then I tried to imagine such a conference with its effort at dialogue across the generations being held by Jews under university auspices. I gave up.

One question remained unforgettable. A woman asked me: "How did you whiten up?" Thinking that she spoke metaphorically, I replied with a brief discussion of Jewish acculturation. But that didn't satisfy her, and she repeated her question. She meant it literally. I had no reply, but another Jew attempted to answer by describing Jewish marriages within her own family. This answer seemed to come closer to the questioner's concern than I had. The issue of skin color was on her mind. It related not just to marriage or to acculturation but also to a perceived repositioning of second and third generations within American society that somehow physically lightened Jewish complexions. She was asking about where Jews fit into America's racial categories and how they managed somehow to change their location. A version of this question subsequently attracted scholars of American studies, who have looked at political and cultural trends after World War Two in an effort to discover when and how Jews became "white."[30] The incident at Yale raised rather sharply issues of comparability and the significance of skin color. Where do studies of being at home in America lead? The questioner assumed it led to an ethnic distinctiveness that was no longer readily visible, a communal identity whose members were considered "white." And the change, she was convinced, happened in the second or third generation.

The concept of generation relative to immigration and migration more generally invites examination of the relationship between culture and community. As
Simon Firth points out, "Each generation clearly does have a different experience
of its old and new worlds, and to explore these differences is to get at important
questions about the ways in which material history becomes cultural history
and vice versa."[31] Thus generation remains a useful term to probe cultural and
social change. *At Home in America* posited that Jewishness, a cultural expression, resided not with Judaism, a religion, but with Jews, who produced it as
part of their lived experiences of urban community. The term "community"
already suffered even then from an intellectual flabbiness and feel-good quality
that stimulated a measure of caution. What were the dimensions of a neighborhood that made it a community? How did common political and philanthropic
ideologies create a community of Jews? Although structured around the experience of the second generation, any collective Jewish attributes were grounded
in historical encounters with New York City in the interwar years. Density and
diversity as well as sheer numbers mattered. A "critical mass" allowed Jews
an unexpected freedom to innovate and experiment. Even as they incorporated
aspects of American or middle-class culture into their lives, they turned these
material elements into Jewish culture. Despite an emphasis on the social sources
of Jewishness, articulate observers, especially writers, who reflected upon the
world of their youth, received a place of privilege. Thus memoir and memory
entered into history, offering voices and visions of more intangible aspects of
the past. One could return to visit old neighborhoods, to look at the buildings
and imagine them as pristine, but it was impossible to people the areas again
with young Jewish families except largely through remembered accounts. The
memories, contradictory and contentious, helped to bring the neighborhood
to life.

Some institutions occupied a position of preeminent importance in the history of second-generation New York Jews in the interwar period. Within the
neighborhood, public schools represented American cultural aspirations. The
presence of large numbers of second-generation Jewish teachers in the schools
made them interpretive purveyors of American education to second- and third-
generation Jewish students.[32] Here symbolic ethnic recognition—of Hebrew as
a modern language to be studied or of the Jewish New Year as holy days to be
respected—accompanied acculturation into New York's versions of American
urban culture. Nor could one ignore synagogues and religious innovation.
Although they reached far fewer Jews than public schools, neighborhood syna-
gogue centers were more than symbols of Judaism. They developed indigenous
American Jewish religious practices that would become normative even for
subsequent migrations to the suburbs. Beyond the neighborhood both politics
and philanthropy formed self-conscious ideological bonds among Jews, linking
them to other Americans and to each other, as well as to Jews overseas. These
were the components of urban ethnicity that made Jews so at home in America.

Whether these bonds today could be considered either transnational, or more likely, translocal, would require additional study. Georges Fouron and Nina Glick Schiller argue that the contemporary "Zionist youth movement flourishes within a well-organized transnational institutional framework that builds long distance nationalism among people whose traceable ancestors never lived in Israel."[33] Did earlier examples of Zionist practices before there was a Jewish state, or of Communist activities, both of which encouraged imagined communities in new redemptive homelands also constitute transnational behavior and forms of long distance nationalism?[34]

Despite current trends emphasizing second-generation ambivalence about American identity, the second generation has emerged from undeserved rebuke. It no longer labors under theories of declension. In addition, the fundamental idea of "at home in America" has developed a trajectory of its own. It has provided a foil for scholars of anti-Semitism who consider the optimism of my book somewhat misplaced.[35] It has provoked historians of Judaism who find the unabashed ethnicity of the era to be a low point in American Jewish religious life.[36] Residential concentration, Jonathan Sarna has argued, resulted in "a Jewish population that gave every appearance of being 'at home' in America but that actually inhabited a largely self-contained subculture, a parallel universe that shared many of the trappings of the larger society while standing apart from it."[37] This is a pretty good description of acculturation without assimilation—the central accomplishment of the second generation.

But the idea of being at home in America also has offered younger scholars a foundation upon which to build. Certainly there is much left undone, especially historical studies that look at areas of second-generation culture.[38] The rich array of New York Jewish artistic productivity and popular culture deserve attention within the framework of second-generation urban ethnicity. Identifying with the city, Jews used New York as a convenient shorthand to label cultural movements with which they were involved. In the middle decades of the century such terms as the New York Intellectuals, New York School of Abstract Art, the New York School of Photographers suggested a type of creative kinship. These loosely linked affinity groups of Jews and gentiles shared innovative ways of seeing the world, shaped in part by their experiences of living in the city. Some participants took the city as their subject and espoused radical goals, seeking to change society, to influence attitudes, taste and mores through their collective endeavors. Thus Jews' own identification with New York affiliated them with a particular vision of American modernity. Equally urban and urbane, this sophisticated New York culture exuded élan and celebrated novel combinations of high and low.

Similarly, many of the questions that concern historians of immigration may eventually engage historians of the second generation. Certainly issues of gender and of consumption, of public culture and labor, invite research. Much that has been written on politics has focused on Jewish responses to

Nazi persecution and to the Holocaust, leaving large areas of Jewish political engagement within the United States unexplored. At the intersection of cultural studies with social history lie rich possibilities for exploring the Jewish culture industries in New York City.

Several young historians have begun to chart this terrain, drawing upon *At Home in America* to help frame their central questions. Michael Alexander's book, *Jazz Age Jews*, explicitly asks why Jews identified with outsiders at a moment when they had achieved acceptance and security. His answer posits an ongoing recreation of the central Jewish disaporic self-understanding, a consciousness of exile that focuses on outsiders to American culture and politics to compensate for feeling at home in America.[39] Less dramatically, Naomi Jackson's book on dance at the 92nd Street YMHA argues for a shift in Jewish institutional concerns with the second generation. Comfortable in America, second-generation communal leaders turned away from Americanization efforts toward modernist culture to nourish Jewish self-expression and collective imagination. In the process they encouraged new forms of Jewish creativity that bound American Jews more closely to both their American and Jewish heritages.[40] Both Jackson and Alexander take the second generation as their subject but move into new areas of historical and cultural studies.

The most important sustained critique of *At Home in America*, Lederhendler's *New York Jews and the Decline of Ethnicity 1950–1970*, sets out to test its hypotheses regarding the lasting imprint of second-generation Jews on New York City. He picks up the history in the postwar years, focusing more on the 1960s than on the 1950s. He points to the dramatic drop in Jewish population in the 1960s as well as a radical shift toward more conservative politics as evidence for a decline in urban ethnicity. The synthesis engineered by the second generation did not last. Their children refused to remain in the old neighborhoods or even to create new ones that reflected a similar mix of Jewish and American elements as in the interwar decades. Faced with demands by African Americans for integration of public schools and public housing, New York Jews abandoned both the city and their vaunted liberalism for ethnocentric politics and a culture of nostalgia. Lederhendler chooses a cultural approach to New York Jewish life, examining many of the writers who formed the New York Intellectuals as well as Yiddish writers and several religious thinkers. His conclusions not only paint a picture of declension for New York Jews but also argue for the impossibility of a viable urban ethnicity in America. If it can't survive in New York, still the largest Jewish city in the world, then it can't be done. Given the flux of American urban life and Jewish physical mobility, any American Jewish synthesis is ultimately provisional and contingent. It is a sobering portrait that stops short of the 1970s decade that is often considered the nadir of New York City in the twentieth century.

One of the figures Lederhendler discusses is the social scientist Nathan Glazer. In the late 1980s Glazer reflected upon his decision to republish

Hansen's essay on "The Problem of the Third Generation" when he was an editor at *Commentary* in 1952. Glazer knew that leaders of American Jewish organizations worried less about the third generation than about his own generation, the second generation. Hansen's essay reassured them by suggesting "not only was there no historical inevitability in the steady and monotonic decline of identity, allegiance, interest, commitment," but there was even reason to expect "a change in direction" in some of these features.[41] Glazer's own work, of course, contributed to such changes, albeit as a member of the second generation. Although unwilling to discard his negative view of the second generation, he did suggest that historical experience qualified and helped to explain what had happened. Glazer could not see the irony in his own account, one that paralleled the experience of Hansen, who spoke to an audience largely of first- and second-generation Swedish Americans when he gave his original talk.[42] Intellectuals are often poor guides to their own past. Similarly, Lederhendler's reliance upon Jewish intellectuals leads him to argue that New York Jews faced "cultural despair," a decline of community, and a loss of nerve that challenged their earlier, "utopian" optimism about urban life, its freedom, and its Jewish possibilities.[43] Perhaps these expressions of despair need to be reconsidered as jeremiads, or even as expressions of that exilic sensibility that characterizes a rooted diasporic Jewish life. Ethnicity is interactive. Jews came to understand themselves in relation to other Jews and to non-Jews among whom they lived. In the postwar decades, New York Jews had to reconfigure their identity as Americans in relation to Israel and as Jews in relation to African Americans and Puerto Ricans. But shared values, attitudes, ways of living and, yes, moral community endured among New York Jews.

"New York, New York, it's a helluva town!" So begins Leonard Bernstein's and Jerome Robbins's postwar paean to New York City in the Broadway musical, *On the Town*. The song continues: "The Bronx is Up and the Battery's Down and people ride in a hole in the ground." Short on specifics and long on exuberance, the song and the show expressed some of the enthusiasm these two Jews felt for New York City. Opinions on the possibilities of Jewish life in New York tend to diverge dramatically: either sunshine and optimism or gloom and pessimism. In truth, most of those who see the sunny side of New York's streets also see their shadows.

The experience of the second generation, the shaping of an urban ethnicity at home in America, represents a singular achievement. It is not necessarily either the task or the accomplishment of the third generation, although it does provide the ground upon which they will build. Thus, just as any study of immigration must take into account both place of origin and place of arrival, so should it recognize the second generation as actors in their own drama.

# NOTES

1. Philip Kasinitz, John H. Mollenkopf, and Mary C. Waters, "Worlds of the Second Generation," in *Becoming New Yorkers: Ethnographies of the New Second Generation*, ed. Philip Kasinitz, John H. Mollenkopf, and Mary C. Waters (New York, 2004), 9.

2. Will Herberg, *Protestant Catholic Jew: An Essay in Religious Sociology* (Garden City, NY, 1956). Herberg drew on the article by Ruby Jo Reeves Kennedy, "Single or Triple Melting Pot? Intermarriage Trends in New Haven, 1870–1940," *American Journal of Sociology* 99 (1944): 331–39.

3. Herbert Gans, "Symbolic Ethnicity in America," *Ethnic and Racial Studies* 2 (1979): 1–20. See also Milton M. Gordon, *Assimilation in American Life: The Role of Race, Religion and National Origins* (New York, 1964).

4. Werner Sollors, *Beyond Ethnicity: Consent and Descent in American Culture* (New York, 1986), 214–21.

5. A good discussion of these issues can be found in *American Immigrants and Their Generations: Studies and Commentaries on the Hansen Thesis after Fifty Years*, ed. Peter Kivisto and Dag Blanck (Urbana and Chicago, 1990).

6. Two who did are Gerald Sorin, *The Nurturing Neighborhood: The Brownsville Boys Club and Jewish Community in Urban America 1940–1990* (New York, 1990); and Carole Bell Ford, *The Girls: Jewish Women of Brownsville Brooklyn 1940–95* (Albany, NY, 1999).

7. To give an idea of the range of books, they include Elizabeth Ewen, *Immigrant Women in the Land of Dollars* (New York, 1985); Andrew R. Heinze, *Adapting to Abundance: Jewish Immigrants, Mass Consumption, and the Search for American Identity* (New York, 1990); Susan Glenn, *Daughters of the Shtetl: Work and Unionism in the Immigrant Generation* (Ithaca, NY, 1990); Stephan Brumberg, *Going to America, Going to School: The Jewish Immigrant Public School Encounter in Turn-of-the-Century New York City* (New York, 1986); Annelise Orleck, *Common Sense and a Little Fire* (Chapel Hill, N.C., 1995); Daniel Soyer, *Jewish Immigrant Associations and American Identity in New York* (Cambridge, MA, 1997); Arthur A. Goren, *The Politics and Public Culture of American Jews* (Bloomington, IN, 1999); Hadassah Kosak, *Cultures of Opposition: Jewish Immigrant Workers, New York City, 1881–1905* (Albany, NY, 2000); Kathie Friedman-Kasaba, *Memories of Migration* (Albany, NY, 1995); Hasia R. Diner, *Hungering for America: Italian, Irish and Jewish Foodways in the Age of Migration* (Cambridge, MA, 2001).

8. Hasia R. Diner, *Lower East Side Memories: A Jewish Place in America* (Princeton, NJ, 2000); and Hasia R. Diner, Jeffrey Shandler, and Beth S. Wenger, eds., *Remembering the Lower East Side* (Bloomington, IN, 2000).

9. Beth S. Wenger, *New York Jews in the Great Depression: Uncertain Promise* (New Haven, CT, 1996); Eli Lederhendler, *New York Jews and the Decline of Ethnicity 1950– 1970* (Syracuse, NY, 2001).

10. Louis Wirth, "The Ghetto," *On Cities and Social Life*, ed. Albert J. Reiss, Jr. (Chicago, 1964), 94.

11. Deborah Dash Moore, "The Construction of Community: Jewish Migration and Ethnicity in the United States," *The Jews of North America*, ed. Moses Rischin (Detroit, 1987), 107.

12. The last decade has seen excellent works in this area, including Riv-Ellen Prell's *Fighting to Become Americans: Jews, Gender and the Anxiety of Assimilation* (Boston, 1999); and Joyce Antler's *The Journey Home: Jewish Women and the American Century* (New York, 1997) in women's history and gender studies; and

Stuart Svonkin, *Jews Against Prejudice* (New York, 2000); and Michael Staub, *Torn at the Roots* (New York, 2002) in studies of political culture.

13. See for example George J. Sanchez, *Becoming Mexican American: Ethnicity, Culture and Identity in Chicano Los Angeles, 1900–1945* (New York, 1993), who adapts the model by applying aspects of it to the immigrant generation.

14. See, for example, David K. Yoo, *Growing Up Nisei: Race, Generation and Culture Among Japanese Americans of California 1924–45* (Urbana and Chicago, 2000).

15. John J. Bukowczyk, *And My Children Did Not Know Me: A History of the Polish-Americans*, Minorities in Modern America Series (Bloomington, IN, 1987); Gary R. Mormino and George E. Pozzetta, *The Immigrant World of Ybor City: Italians and Their Latin Neighbors in Tampa, 1885–1985*, Statue of Liberty-Ellis Island Centennial Series (Urbana, IL, 1987).

16. Joel Perlmann, *Italians Then, Mexicans Now: Immigrant Origins and Second-generation Progress, 1890 to 2000* (New York, 2005); Alejandro Portes, ed., *The Second Generation* (New York, 1996); Antony W. Alumkal, *Asian American Evangelical Churches: Race, Ethnicity, and Assimilation in the Second Generation* (New York, 2003).

17. Aaron Hass, *Children of the Holocaust: The Second Generation* (Ithaca, NY, 1990); Alan L. Berger, *Children of Job: Second American Generation Witnesses to the Holocaust* (Saratoga Springs, NY, 1997); Stewart J. Florsheim, ed., *Ghosts of the Holocaust: An Anthology of Poetry by the Second Generation* (Detroit, 1989).

18. Nina Glick Schiller, Linda Basch, and Cristina Blanc-Szanton, "Towards a Definition of Transnationalism: Introductory Remarks and Research Questions," in *Towards a Transnational Perspective on Migration: Race, Class, Ethnicity, and Nationalism Reconsidered*, ed. Nina Glick Schiller, Linda Basch, and Cristina Blanc-Szanton, *Annals of the New York Academy of Sciences*, 645 (New York: 1992), ix.

19. "Towards a Definition of Transnationalism," xiv.

20. Georges E. Fouron and Nina Glick-Schiller, "The Generation of Identity: Redefining the Second Generation Within a Transnational Social Field," in *The Changing Face of Home: The Transnational Lives of the Second Generation*, ed. Peggy Levitt and Mary C. Waters (New York, 2002), 194.

21. Fouron and Glick-Schiller, "Generation of Identity," 195.

22. Michael Jones-Correa, "The Study of Transnationalism Among the Children of Immigrants: Where We Are and Where We Should Be Headed," in *The Changing Face of Home: The Transnational Lives of the Second Generation*, ed. Peggy Levitt and Mary C. Waters (New York, 2002), 225.

23. Jones-Correa, "The Study of Transnationalism," 222.

24. See *Journal of American History* 86 (December 1999), special issue on "The Nation and Beyond: Transnational Perspectives on United States History."

25. Barry Goldberg, "Historical Reflections on Transnationalism, Race, and the American Immigrant Saga," in *Towards a Transnational Perspective on Migration: Race, Class, Ethnicity, and Nationalism Reconsidered*, ed. Nina Glick Schiller, Linda Basch, and Cristina Blanc-Szanton, *Annals of the New York Academy of Sciences*, 645 (New York, 1992), 203.

26. Goldberg, "Historical Reflections," 212.

27. Kasinitz, Mollenkopf, and Waters, "Worlds of the Second Generation," 12.

28. Elliott R. Barkan, "America in the Hand, Homeland in the Heart: Transnational and Translocal Immigrant Experiences in the American West," *Western Historical Quarterly* 35, no. 3 (Autumn 2004): 331–54; also <http://www.historycooperative.org/journals/ whq/35:3/barkan.html> (7 Sep. 2005). Para. 31 contrasts the "simultaneity, persistence, and intensity of contact/participation across boundaries" of

transnationalism with the "infrequent, periodic, apolitical, and casual bonds" of translocalism.

29. Kasinitz, Mollenkopf, and Waters, "Worlds of the Second Generation," 17.

30. Matthew Frye Jacobson, *Whiteness of a Different Color: European Immigrants and the Alchemy of Race* (Cambridge, MA, 1998); and Karen Brodkin *How Jews Became White Folks and What That Says about Race in America* (New Brunswick, NJ, 1998) make the case for lightening up, in part through the move to the suburbs.

31. Simon Frith, "Generation," in *New Keywords: A Revised Vocabulary of Culture and Society*, ed. Tony Bennett, Lawrence Grossberg, and Meaghan Morris (Malden, MA, 2005), 146.

32. For an excellent book that explores this issue explicitly see Ruth Jacknow Markowitz, *My Daughter, the Teacher: Jewish Teachers in the New York City Schools* (New Brunswick, NJ, 1993).

33. Fouron and Glick-Schiller, "Generation of Identity," 195.

34. Paul C. Mishler, *Raising Reds: The Young Pioneers, Radical Summer Camps and Communist Political Culture in the United States* (New York, 1999) does not use the concept of transnationalism in his analysis.

35. Leonard Dinnerstein, *Uneasy at Home: Antisemitism and the American Jewish Experience* (New York, 1987).

36. Jonathan D. Sarna, "American Judaism: A History" (New Haven, CT, 2004), 223–27.

37. Sarna, *American Judaism*, 222, titles the chapter "Anxious Subculture," and the subsection "At Home in America?" thus clearly returning to the older model of an insecure, persecuted group. As a second generation Jew, he also discounts the generational model as useful for understanding American Jewish history.

38. For example, see Ari Kelman, *Station Identification: A Cultural History of Yiddish Radio* forthcoming by the University of California Press.

39. Michael Alexander, *Jazz Age Jews* (Princeton, NJ, 2001).

40. Naomi M. Jackson, *Converging Movements: Modern Dance and Jewish Culture at the 92nd Street Y* (Hanover, NH, 2000).

41. Nathan Glazer, "The Historical Experience of Generations," *American Immigrants and Their Generations*, ed. Peter Kivisto and Dag Blanck (Urbana and Chicago, 1990), 107.

42. Peter Kivisto, "Ethnicity and the Problem of Generations in American History," *American Immigrants and their Generations*, ed. Peter Kivisto and Dag Blanck (Urbana and Chicago, 1990), 3.

43. Lederhendler, *New York Jews*, 87.

# 8

# Bridging "The Great Divide": The Evolution and Impact of Cornish Translocalism in Britain and the USA

*SHARRON P. SCHWARTZ*

THE ROLE OF TRANSNATIONALISM and diaspora in historical migration studies tends to be under-theorized and problematic. The term "transnational" began to be used by sociologists and anthropologists in the mid-1990s, having been coined by Linda Basch *et al.* in 1992. It is taken to refer to processes by which immigrants "forge and sustain multi-stranded social relations that link together their societies of origin and settlement," making the sending and receiving communities a single area of action.[1] Whether we refer to transnational social spaces, transnationalism, or transnational social formations, we are talking about sustained ties of persons, networks, and organizations bound across "international" borders in the name of ethnic, racial, religious, linguistic, locality, occupation or nation-state of origin, class, gender, or any other factor.[2] These phenomena are characterized "by a high density of interstitial ties on informal or formal levels," linking "a community in its present place of residence and its place of origin, however distant, and between the various communities of a diaspora."[3] However, it has become apparent that not all modern migrants engage in such high-level transnational connections. Some engage with their communities of origin sporadically or not at all. Indeed, Ewa Morawska has noted that assimilation and transnationalism often coexist in the lives of immigrants and their children.[4]

The concept of diaspora is as eclectic and problematic as transnationalism, for it too has a variety of meanings. It does not just describe the dispersal of a people resulting from expulsion or involuntary exile but also encompasses those who have moved from their homeland as labor migrants, for trade or imperial reasons, or as a part of a cultural diaspora.[5] It broadly refers to dispersed communities in a period of migration. However, Stephen Vertovec offers a different and intriguing new interpretation of diaspora that he contends "has arisen as part of the postmodern project of resisting the nation-state, which is perceived as hegemonic, discriminatory, and culturally homogenizing." According to him, an alternative agenda has been devised for the notion of diaspora—one that advocates the recognition of hybridity, multiple identities, and affiliations with people, causes, and traditions outside the nation state of residence.[6] Peggy Levitt takes this one step further by arguing that implicit in this interpretation is the question of whether life across borders involves resistance to the nation-state and allows previously marginalized groups to challenge the social hierarchy.[7] Moreover, she sees transnational communities as the building blocks of diasporas that may or may not take place.[8] Transnationalism highlights that significant networks exist and are maintained across borders. And by virtue of their intensity and importance, Glick-Schiller maintains that these actually challenge the very nature of nation-states.[9]

Transnationalism has taken on increased importance in recent years as migration is rapidly changing communities at both points of origin and destination.[10] The cultural repercussions of this are now being felt on a global scale: the influence of what were once migrant populations on the socio-cultural and economic life of major metropolitan centers and the linkages to "homelands" has reinvigorated debates about diasporas and placed transnationalism in the limelight. The implications of transnationalism therefore make it a key political issue. And yet, as Nancy Foner notes in her study of immigration to New York City, transnationalism is nothing new.[11] Indeed, as if to confirm Foner's observation, Randolph Bourne observed in his essay *Trans-National America* (1916), that America was becoming not a nationality, but a trans-nationality.[12] And more recently Ewa Morawska and Willifred Spohn have reminded us that migration also changed and reproduced communities in the nineteenth century.[13]

However, as highlighted by Elliott Barkan, there has to be recognition that the concept of transnationalism encompasses a whole range of behaviors, attitudes, and values that cannot be comfortably fit within most delineations of transnationalism. He suggests the need for an alternative model, that of translocalism. Arguing that immigrant experiences are— and have been—much more varied than any one model would represent, he defines translocalism as situations where immigrants do not maintain multiple, intense, routinized bonds and networks with sending communities. Instead their ties with their communities of origin are likely to be moderate and periodic, somewhat casual and uneven and not routine.[14]

This article explores a case study of a sub-nation-state migration. In doing this, the taken for granted and banal "national" flagging of trans-nationalism might be peeled away, revealing a more fluid, layered and contested picture. Using Barkan's model of translocalism, this article will argue that at the height of migration during the nineteenth century there were some examples of transnationalism among the Cornish, but as migration to the United States diminished during the twentieth century, translocalism became more the norm. It then argues that translocalism has taken on increased significance in the last quarter of a century with the Cornish in Britain making an effort towards ethnic revival for political reasons and encouraging their American cousins to become involved in this process. This has resulted in drawing attention to the presence of a global diaspora of well over six million people, most of whom are the descendants of the half a million people who left Cornwall during the "great migration" (ca. 1825–1920).[15] The Cornish case permits an investigation of the changes in the formation and dynamism of translocal relations and of the meaning and relevance of a diaspora to a small national group.

## CORNISH MIGRATION TO AND TRANSLOCALISM IN THE USA

A former independent Celtic kingdom, Cornwall is a small peninsula at the far southwest of Britain that has never been legally incorporated into Shire England. It is inhabited by the indigenous Cornish and more recent English immigrants. At no time during the first half of the nineteenth century could it boast a population greater than 375,000, yet Cornwall's size, both in terms of territory and population, is disproportionate to the impact the Cornish have made on the global mining economy.

By the late eighteenth century Cornwall had emerged as a center of technological innovation in deep-lode mining and steam engineering and was one of Britain's earliest industrial regions with a distinct and specialized extra-regional commodity export: copper ore. This, together with tin, provided the main output of Cornwall's mining industry. By the mid-nineteenth century Cornwall had established a clear comparative advantage in metal mining in a similar way that Lancashire had in cotton textile manufacture. As an expansive, confident, thrusting industrial region, it was beginning to export both its technology and its skilled labor force.[16]

This was initially to South and Central America, in response to a rapidly developing global mining market.[17] Cornish miners, confident in the belief that they were pre-eminent in the mining world, made shrewd, rational decisions when considering migration—an advancement strategy designed to maximize gain and minimize risk.[18] The 1860s heralded the long, drawn-out process of de-industrialization as Cornish copper, then tin sank into a terminal decline created by the restructuring of the global mineral economy, prompting increased migration. Thousands of Cornish miners left after the 1860s, making use of pre-existing migration networks.

Cornwall therefore witnessed one of the highest levels of migration from England and Wales during the nineteenth century, making it an emigration region comparable with any in Europe.[19] The United States was throughout the nineteenth century the most popular migration destination for Cornish migrants. Dynamic migrant networks developed, characterized by outward migration, onward migration, return and repeat migration. Cornish migration to the United States of America was significant up until the late nineteenth century, a time when vibrant communities dubbed "Little Cornwalls" emerged, but then fell away gradually from the early twentieth century. The Cornish were an important yet overlooked immigrant group that helped to settle the American West in particular.

Much of this migration was connected to mining that resulted in discrete settlement patterns. By the 1830s Cornish mining immigration was well established in the lead-mining region of Wisconsin, where by 1850 there were already as many as 4,500 Cornish, comprising half of the populations of Dodgeville, Mineral Point, and Hazel Green, three quarters that of Linden, and a quarter of the population of Shullsburg.[20] Those mining migrants who arrived during the California gold rush were soon joined by many thousands more after the commencement of deep-lode mining in the Sierra Nevada, Rocky Mountains, and other western mining fields.[21] Around five thousand Cornish migrated to Gilpin County, Colorado, between 1870 and 1914; at Central City they made up over 50 percent of the population and 70 percent of the mining workforce.[22]

By the late nineteenth century, Cornish miners and their families were to be found in virtually every state where there was mining or quarrying activity.[23] In 1898 there were estimated to have been ten thousand pureblood Cornish in the lead-mining region of Wisconsin; the 1890 census for Linden suggests that 90–95 percent of residents had Cornish ancestry.[24] By the turn of the twentieth century the Cornish accounted for 55 percent of the population of Wolverine, Michigan, almost 18 percent of that of Calumet, Michigan, and 98 percent of the population of New Almaden, California.[25] Over 60 percent of the population of Grass Valley California was Cornish in 1894, and by 1911 three-quarters of its population were noted to have been Cornish by descent. "It . . . almost seemed that [I] had stepped into a unknown country," wrote Edmund Kinyon in 1911, amazed at the odd ways of the Cornish of Grass Valley and the unintelligible dialect that they spoke.[26]

Although living in communities thousands of miles from Cornwall, many immigrants remained closely connected and involved in the affairs of their sending communities. This was made possible through newspapers and because of the repeated comings and goings of migrants, travel and communication made easier by cheaper, speedier transatlantic passages, the development of the telegraph, and a more efficient postal service. One of the obvious ways in which the sending and receiving communities were linked was through financial remittances. Rowse noted that in 1869 Cam-borne men in California and Nevada were remitting around £15,000– £18,000 to their families each year, and in 1894 the *West Briton* reported that the Idaho Mine in Grass Valley California had paid about $4,500,000 in dividends, a goodly portion of which had gone home to Cornwall.[27] The *Cornish Post and Mining News* estimated that in 1905 wages paid in Montana amounted to over two-and-a-half million dollars, a significant proportion of which was remitted to Cornwall.[28]

Homeland ties were also manifested in collective actions. In 1909 Hallesveor Chapel in the Cornish town of St. Ives received fifteen pounds from Cornish expatriates in Mohawk, Michigan, who had raised the money by choir singing at concerts there and at neighboring Calumet, the funds collected being split between the Methodist Episcopal Chapel in Mohawk and the chapel in St. Ives.[29] In 1913 Camborne Rugby Club received over seven pounds from Camborne "old boys" resident in Butte, Montana, a much-needed boost for club funds.[30] Here we have some examples of transnational behavior through regular monetary contributions of the kind manifested in many modern immigrant communities. But to suggest that this was the norm would be inaccurate. There were many immigrants who chose not to maintain close financial connections with their families and sending communities, remitting only sporadically or not at all.

Did the Cornish exhibit other manifestations of transnational behavior? It was not merely financial remittances that traversed migration networks but equally important social remittances.[31] On the American side, ideas about politics and religion influenced life in Cornwall and America. The *West Briton* of 1894 commented on the fact that Grass Valley was unlike many other western mining camps because of the number of Cornish that predominated. For example, because they were staunch Methodists, shops and mines closed on Sundays and a large number were in attendance at the Methodist chapel.[32] Visiting Methodist preachers were common on both sides of the Atlantic, and Cornishmen were encouraged to become members of friendly societies, transnational social networks that were conduits of information and mobility facilitating job opportunities. The Cornish also brought their enmity of the Irish with them to the United States, a resentment that was intricately bound up with the domination of the expanding mining labor market and compounded by sectarianism and political differences. The Cornish were mainly Republicans, and the Irish Democrats. Although both were Celtic, the similarity ended there, for the antagonism and mutual dislike each bore the other, as was manifested at Butte, Montana,[33] was the "most explosive and divisive internal threat to the mining labor movement in the West."[34]

On the Cornish homeland side, the 1885 election saw radical candidate C.A.V. Conybeare successfully contest a seat in the new constituency centered on Camborne-Redruth and known as the Mining Division. Conybeare's message with its anti-landlord stance of democracy against oligarchy struck a chord with miners newly enfranchised after the Franchise Act of 1884. Moreover, many of these recently had returned to the Cam-borne-Redruth area from the mines in Nevada, with a more defined set of ideas about what constituted fair labor relations. There, profitable mining had been carried on without miners having to pay for tools or explosives, or wait for wages.[35] In fact, Cornwall had traditionally been a Liberal stronghold, but the vote of disgruntled return migrants began to confront and challenge the older Liberal establishment.

In terms of the further flow of ideas and information between America and Cornwall, items of news and letters from mining camps in America and Cornwall were increasingly swapped in the late nineteenth century, as well as notices of births, marriages, and deaths.[36] The receipt of regular news in both sending and receiving communities lessened the tyranny of time and space to such a degree that even those who never had migrated from their native community could participate in a transnational way of life. By the turn of the twentieth century many Cornish people were so familiar with the United States that it was considered almost the parish next door, with American accents discernible in Cornwall's mining communities. Other tastes and values also revealed their contact with an American way of life. In 1891, a newspaper, the *Redruth Independent*, was described as "fairly American in character."[37]

The formation of Cornish societies, occurring simultaneously in North America, Australia, England, Wales, and South Africa, could be seen as evidence of increased enmeshment with sending communities. In the United States there were Cornish societies in many of the major cities, including Boston, Pittsburgh, Chicago, Detroit, and New York, and in such states as California, as well as Anglo-American clubs in places like Centerville, Montana. But, were these transnational organizations? At a superficial level, Cornish societies functioned as social clubs where acquaintances were renewed and new ones formed at dinners, picnics, and other functions, and they also acted as benevolent institutions to facilitate discussions on political and economic issues of the day. By becoming a member of a Cornish association, those of Cornish birth or descent were reaffirming and strengthening their links with Cornwall and also to one another as an immigrant group, exemplified by the Southern California Cornish Association on the occasion of their annual social gathering in 1934. The Reverend Burden, offering an invocation, declared: "We have joined hands with Cornish folk across the main! Hail One and All, Old Cornwall."[38] However, the size of the memberships, sometimes numbering only a few hundred, does not point to their being widely supported by the thousands of Cornish across America, and they in no way compare with modern transnational organizations of the type found among Haitians, Dominicans, and Mexicans, for example. Contact with Cornwall by Cornish organizations was at best sporadic, and, in some cases, completely absent. That pointed once more to translocal relations, where the emphasis was in reality clearly on the preservation of Cornish ethnicity and identity without the maintenance of strong transnational bonds.

## DIMINISHING MIGRATION AND DECLINING TRANSLOCALISM

Indeed, the following example from Mineral Point, Wisconsin, one of the earliest Cornish settlements, illustrates that by the early twentieth century many

Cornish immigrants and their offspring were engaging less and less with their homeland communities, and the links that did exist were sporadic, periodic, and superficial:

[W]hile many of the Cornish immigrants in their lifetime keep up a correspondence with Cornwall, the second generation has almost entirely dropped it, although an occasional Cornish newspaper is received in the region. The Cornish descendants are scattering, and have almost lost their identity as a race. They do not hesitate to marry with other nationalities. . . .[39]

This area of Wisconsin witnessed some of the earliest migration flows outside Cornwall; by the turn of the century the majority of the Cornish residents in the region had been born there and did not appear to have the same degree of psychological attachment to Cornwall that their parents and grandparents had had. Some family networks began to break down as immigrants and their children reared their own families and played out their lives in host communities far removed from Cornwall. Letters were written less frequently or not at all to relatives in Cornwall whom they had never met or had not seen for many years. Their connections to Cornwall in no way could be described as transnational but more accurately fit Barkan's model of translocalism.

Although kinship, religious, and parochial or village affiliation with Cornwall was still important, activities were increasingly focused on the United States, with investments made in the infrastructure required to support life in the receiving communities. As noted by Barkan, "preserving homeland ties involve[s] the struggle to determine how far to go in adapting to the new host society, balancing cultural maintenance with cultural retreat as well as prior social connections with new social bonds."[40] These decisions are unlikely to be accidental, as exemplified by the case of William T. George, who arrived in California in 1885: "I soon dropped my [Cornish] accent when I got to school here [Grass Valley]," he stated, "because everyone made fun of me."[41] Ashamed of their accents, some Cornish immigrants made a concerted attempt to become what Thurner has described as "un-hyphenated Americans," the more so in order to fit into a seemingly monocultural American society that was being assiduously championed, particularly after the First World War.[42]

But perhaps of greater significance was the decline of mining itself, the industry that had created close knit cohesive communities. As they had done in Cornwall, mines across the United States closed, particularly in the years after 1930. Communities began to fragment, with people moving away in search of alternative employment. Old customs began to die out as the youth jettisoned their parents' values and identities in their quest to achieve the American dream.[43] Crucially, the numbers of Cornish immigrants to the United States shrank considerably after the 1920s and the once dense transatlantic migration networks began to disintegrate. Beliefs and behaviors become unfamiliar when they are no longer used regularly, and a lack of exposure to news, ideas, and ways of doing things brought by migrants from Cornwall resulted in a diminishing of the Cornish presence in many overseas communities. One by one, the Cornish associations disbanded until only a handful remained, and those immigrants who stayed in the old mining communities often became retrospective and increasingly nostalgic about their Cornish roots and heritage.

The retrospection associated with the overseas Cornish at this time was an echo of that experienced in Cornwall, where mining was also declining and a way of life that had emerged with industrialization was passing into history. Some saw the need to look back to a period before industrialization and Cornwall's Celtic antecedents were increasingly stressed, well exemplified by the movement to *kyntelleugh an brewyon es gesys na vo kellys travyth* (gather up the fragments before they are lost) by newly formed Old Cornwall Societies beginning in the 1920s. Around the Cornish world, similar reactions occurred as people sought to record, conserve and protect what was left of Cornish heritage: "At Mineral Point the Cornish restoration and the interest in Cornish foods and customs during the 1930s came just in time to preserve an interesting chapter in the history of the lead region."[44]

Vernacular Cornish cottages constructed in the 1840s and 1850s, unique to the lead region of the Upper Midwest, were restored at Mineral Point by Americans Robert Neal and Edgar Hellum in the 1930s and given Cornish names: *Pendarvis, Polperro* and *Trelawney*.[45] At the behest of the National Folklore Society and the Library of Congress, the much-depleted Grass Valley Choir made a tape recording of Cornish carols and hymns in 1950 to record for posterity the musical contribution of Cornish pioneers in America. This was seen as "putting the town on the map," and gave Grass Valley "national and international publicity."[46] In Michigan's Keweenaw Peninsula, by the mid-twentieth century the Cornish had become more self-conscious of their vanishing culture. They saw to it that their "national dish"—the pasty—which had been claimed by Finns, Slavs, and Swedes, became a hallmark of "Copper Country" cuisine.

However, in spite of such efforts, it was clear that many Cornish cultural events were increasingly "stage-managed." Such sporadic and periodic episodes of Cornish translocalism may be viewed as a *cri de coeur* for Cornish families to maintain links with the cultural heritage of the former Cornish-American mining communities and, by association, ultimately with Cornwall itself. In 1953 the Grass Valley Methodist Church held a Christmas Festival and Homecoming, and the need for such an event was summed up in an accompanying pamphlet:

> Today we inaugurate the first Cornish Festival and Homecoming. We hope this will become an annual event which will take on greater significance with the coming years. Our Cornish families have been a vital part of Grass Valley for over a hundred years. With the passing years it will become inevitable that the rich heritage brought by the families from Cornwall will become lost with the growing American way of life. . . .[I]t becomes increasingly difficult to tell who is a "Cousin Jack" or a "Cousin Jenny". . . .[47]

Fourteen years later, this famous choir disbanded and by the mid-twentieth century those Cornish associations that had managed to survive were mere shadows of their former selves, beset by financial difficulties and comprised of small and aging memberships. In Cornwall, many families lost touch with their cousins overseas, and memories of life in communities beyond Cornwall became retrospective and mired in nostalgia. In the 1960s it seemed that the translocalism that had defined much of nineteenth and early twentieth century life in Cornish mining communities on both sides of the "great divide" was of interest to historians only.

## THE REVIVAL OF CORNISH TRANSLOCALISM AND CLAIMS FOR DIASPORA

Rather than creating a homogenous society that blurred or eroded cultural distinctions, local places and cultures in the United States were transformed in the twentieth century, a process that quickened with the arrival of new waves of non-European immigrants in the late 1900s. As predicted by Randolph Bourne in 1916, the idealized, monocultural, static conception of America proved to be impossible:

> America is coming to be, not a nationality but a trans-nationality, a weaving back and forth, with the other lands, of many threads of all sizes and colors. Any movement which attempts to thwart this weaving, or to dye the fabric any one color, or disentangle the threads of the strand, is false to this cosmopolitan vision. [48]

Globalization, an explosion of travel, migration, and socio-economic interchange, fuelled by ever more efficient transportation and communication networks, has transformed the form and shape of human communities around the world.[49] But it has not necessarily led to the cultural annihilation predicted by some observers, where regional, ethnic, or national distinctiveness vanish into a "melting pot." Rather, it has had the opposite effect, as ethnic groups seek to reconcile the local with the global, in the process rediscovering, reconnecting, re-affirming, and celebrating their various cultural heritages.[50]

Just as communities have undergone change in America, forces have been transforming communities in Cornwall, where a multicultural awareness has been gathering momentum since the Celtic Revival of the 1920s. This socio-cultural watershed, initially but no longer the preserve of the middle classes, represented an opportunity for Cornwall and the Cornish to look back beyond the crumbling mine engine houses of a failing industrial period to a perceived golden Celtic era. Affiliation with a Celtic past thus allowed the Cornish to opt out of the monocultural static conception of industrial Britain and to be included instead within a vibrant northwestern European Celtic arc, claiming a common identity with the Bretons and Galicians in northwest Europe and the Welsh, Scots, Manx, and Irish within the British Isles. But not with the Anglo Saxon

English. The Cornish language, which had ceased to be spoken in a vernacular way in the eighteenth century, was revived, along with the use of St. Piran's flag (a white cross against a black background) and the Celtic cross. Other symbols of Celtic Cornwall were invented rather than re-invented, including a Cornish Gorsedd (an annual ceremony in the Cornish language, established in 1928, that includes singing, dancing, and the awarding of Bardic titles,[51] and the use of the kilt in the Cornish national tartan, with its predominant colors of black and gold. This new Celtic iconography, which would have meant little to most Cornish people in the 1800s, was blended with established and accepted industrial icons and notions of Cornishness that coalesced around the mining industry: brass bands, rugby, football (soccer), male-voice choirs, allegiance to Methodism, and values emphasizing thrift, independence, sobriety, and hard work.

The fact that an increasing number of people are today willing to identify themselves as Cornish is attributable to many factors. It is partially a result of the increasing tolerance of multiculturalism that has followed in the wake of the European retreat from Empire, the end of the Cold War and the fall of the Berlin Wall, and the demise of apartheid, as well as increased immigration to First World nations. It is also a response to the arrival in Cornwall of many thousands of immigrants from England since the 1960s that has exacerbated the gulf in income and house prices, tipping the demographic scales against the indigenous population in many parts of Cornwall. Contact with people of a different nationality often makes others more conscious of their own nationality, as noted by S. Morse among Canadians.[52] More recently, the Blair government's decision to allow devolved power to Northern Ireland, Wales, and Scotland has led to an increased unraveling of Britain into its constituent national parts. This new political environment has allowed the Cornish another opportunity to challenge the dominant discourse of "English county." Instead, many want to see Cornwall accepted as a distinct European region. Moves have been made towards securing ethnic minority status for the indigenous Cornish. There have been calls for a Cornish Assembly, and Cornish recently has been recognized as a minority European language.

Yet, how does this new political climate affect those Cornish living outside Cornwall? Significant numbers of people worldwide are of mixed racial or ethnic origins and, as Wolfgang Welsch notes, the concept of homogenous cultures bound to a specific territory no longer can be assumed. He argues that contemporary cultures are fundamentally characterized by their hybridity and that transcultural practices are now the norm.[53] Indeed, Ulrich Beck has commented that "the individual is at the same time a member of different communities."[54] Identities are not legacies passively received but representations socially produced and, in this sense, matters of social dispute.[55] As ethnic identity has undergone redefinition in Cornwall, this redefinition has been echoed overseas, providing new opportunities for translocal connections. "What we appear to be witnessing," notes anthropologist, Amy Hale, "is a kind of cultural feedback resulting from a heightened awareness of ethnicity within the Celtic regions themselves. . . . [L]earning about the often shared experience of emigration has created new opportunities for dialogue around the Cornish world."[56] The end of the twentieth century witnessed extended social relations and the existence of cultural, economic, and political networks of connection across the world. They in turn gave rise to an increasing inter-connectedness across international boundaries that allowed for a reinterpretation and refreshing of traditional cultures and ways of life.[57]

In particular, the years since the 1970s have witnessed a renaissance of Cornishness overseas, aided by an explosion among ordinary people interested in genealogy and heritage, a process that has been ongoing and accelerated more recently through access to the Internet. This electronic forum, or "virtual community," can be viewed as an "electronic public sphere" that reflects "a hunger for community" in our modern era.[58] For, as Daniel Mato reminds us, constructions of identity inform and legitimize the practices of many organizations and individuals that are important producers and disseminators of public representations as well as producers of certain agendas—social and cultural movements, non-governmental organizations, intellectuals and artists.[59] The Cornish on both sides of the great divide are increasingly engaged in translocal behavior, refreshing, negotiating, and contesting their common heritage.

This is exemplified by the Cornish American Heritage Society (CAHS), set up in 1982 with the aim of preserving the history and culture of Cornish people and strengthening connections between Cornish communities around the world. This important organization, with an initial membership of several hundred, held its first "Gathering of Cornish Cousins" in Detroit, the first of a series of biennial meetings across North America.

Such gatherings have included merchandise stalls, *Crowdy Crawn* (traditional music and dance), Cornish sports, historical lectures and films, and workshops devoted to the Cornish language, cookery, genealogy, and folklore. There have even been, in recent years, Gorsedd ceremonies conducted in the Cornish language in which bards from both sides of the Atlantic participate.

Through its gatherings and its quarterly newsletter, *Tam Kernewek*,[60] the CAHS has been one of the main agents facilitating ethnic awareness among the Cornish in America. In 1999 there were thirty-two Cornish societies and organizations in North America, many of which have names derived from the Cornish language, including *Penkernewek* (Pennsylvania) and *Keweenaw Kernewek* (Michigan), and most have active websites and journals. The CAHS has *ipso facto* become the organ *par excellence* in the revived public sphere of modern translocal activity. *Tam Kernewek* helps to co-ordinate the activities of the various Cornish organizations throughout North America and encourages Cornish participation at Celtic festivals in the USA. These popular festivals are often organized by the descendants of immigrants "to educate others, celebrate their heritage, and promote and preserve aspects of traditional culture perceived as somehow being under threat."[61] Cornish participation at such festivals is a more recent feature than that of the Irish, Welsh, or Scots, but in 1998 the Cornish were awarded the first prize for the best tent at the Potomac Celtic Fest, an important milestone along the route of ethnic visibility for the Cornish in America. "Many were interested, even excited, to know that there is an active Cornish presence in the United States," noted Cornish-American Nancy Heydt. "The educational and public relations value of such festivals cannot be overstated."[62]

In the wake of the tragic death at Columbine High School of a young Cornish-American, Steven R. Curnow, the CAHS has established a Memorial Award. Realizing the need to encourage youth to take an interest in their Cornish culture and ancestry, an essay contest is open to high school seniors resident in North America with a first prize of five hundred dollars for a paper written on a prescribed topic pertaining to Cornish heritage.[63] It is hoped that in future this will lead to a student exchange program between North America and Cornwall. The year 1999 saw the inception of the Cornish Foundation for North America (CFNA). The creation of this new society marked an important turning point in the ethnic revival of the Cornish and was set up because its founding members "care about Cornwall and our Cornish identity."[64] Recognizing that modern Cornwall has socio-economic problems resulting from the demise of mining and related industries, this non-political organization aims to provide financial assistance for projects in Cornwall related to community regeneration, continuing education opportunities for residents in Cornwall, and the restoration and preservation of Cornwall's historical sites.[65]

Another key milestone in the resurgence of modern Cornish ethnicity was the revival of the famous Grass Valley Cornish Choir in 1990 under the musical directorship of Eleanor Kenitzer. In 1996 the choir toured Cornwall, as reported by the Grass Valley newspaper the *Union*:

> This week, the 34 singers of the Cornish Choir are taking the music of their grandfathers back to Cornwall. Time has passed in Cornwall. The Cornish hymns that once filled the air there now compete with the modern-day cacophony. For the emigrants and their children, however, the Old Country remains frozen in time, a snapshot from the day the emigrant family left home. For those in Nevada County who love the Cornish traditions, our Cornwall is the Cornwall of 1870, not 1996.[66]

Yet, the resurrection of this iconic choir was to be much more than the restoration of a vital part of the heritage of Grass Valley, for it was to transcend the retrospective and nostalgic looking back to yesteryear. The Grass Valley Cornish Choir has become a catalyst for modern Cornish translocalism that, Janus-like, can look simultaneously to the past for roots in an increasingly rootless world but also forward, to include among its ranks people from other ethnic and national backgrounds while forging new and vibrant links with Cornwall and other Celtic parts of Europe. The revival of the choir has resulted in cross-cultural and translocal musical exchanges that include new ideas and techniques as well as music, sung by choirs on both sides of the Atlantic and cemented by tours.

But perhaps it is Kenitzer herself, welcomed to the Cornish Gorsedd, who embodies the new spirit of "Cornishness," for although not of Cornish descent, she nonetheless worked tirelessly to protect the vital musical tradition of Grass Valley and to promote stronger cultural links between Cornwall and Nevada County, California, an effort that resulted in one of the most significant events in the history of the Cornish overseas since the nineteenth century. She conceived the idea of twinning that in 1997 resulted in a visit to Grass Valley of Mayor Hocking of Bodmin. The city limits of the California gold rush town now proudly announces, "Sister City Bodmin, Cornwall." Not to be outdone, neighboring Nevada City has since twinned with Penzance, while Mineral Point Wisconsin, which enjoys a thriving annual Cornish Festival, has paired with Redruth, resulting in exchanges of high-level delegations from both towns.

Cornwall, too, has played an important role in the blossoming of modern Cornish translocalism. The Cornwall Family History Society (CFHS), set up in the 1970s, has vigorously promoted the study of Cornish genealogy and heritage with its worldwide membership, its many thousands of members seeking to look beyond the branches of their own family tree to nurture an outward looking, dynamic sense of global Cornishness. Indeed, it was members of the CFHS who were responsible for setting up the CAHS, and in 1994 the influential *Cornish World* magazine was launched. This publication, often hard-hitting and unashamedly political, attempts to paint a realistic picture of contemporary Cornwall that transcends the utopian nineteenth-century view of Cornwall resplendent in its industrial zenith, or of more recent "Disneyesque" visions of Cornwall as a playground for tourists and the retired.[67] *Cornish World* has done much to alert its readers of the inescapable link with past migration history and has fostered a sense of co-ethnicity and solidarity among Cornish people around the world.

For many people, the acme in the Cornish ethnic revival and translocal relations was the first *Dehwelans* (Homecoming) in May 2002, a cultural event similar to those that had been taking place every two years in Australia (*Lowender Kernewek*) and in North America, when many hundreds of Cornish from across the world gathered for a three-day festival at Pendennis Castle, Falmouth. Cornish history, culture, and language events were showcased, and the competitions entered by those from Cornwall and abroad emphasized a common heritage. There was an ecumenical service at Gwennap Pit, which included leaders of all three main churches in Cornwall taking part with delegates from overseas. The service included the pageantry of Gorsedd Kernow, with the Lady of the Flowers participating from Winnipeg, and six new bards from overseas who were initiated by the Grand Bard. There was also a serious economic point to the homecoming. "Made in Cornwall" stalls were selling

Cornish goods, and lectures focused on the economic, academic, and social links that could be widened and deepened between Cornish associations and societies overseas and those in Cornwall.

Reporting on the festival, the local press noted that "Dehwelans 2002 emphasised that distinctiveness in culture, language, history and identity which makes us what we are and will be and gives us growing confidence in ourselves."[68] With the event an unqualified success, its future was secured by a government grant of Objective One money.[69] Carleen Kelemen, director of the Objective One Partnership, explained the importance of *Dehwelans* 2004: "One of the priorities of the Objective One programme is to deliver economic and employment benefits based on the distinctive nature of Cornwall. *Dehwelans* 2004 will contribute directly to these aims. Not only will it help enhance understanding and appreciation of Cornish culture, it will do it in a way that is also economically beneficial." She added: "There is a niche tourist market for this kind of event, both in terms of the actual additional visitors it will bring to Cornwall and in terms of the boost that the publicity generated will give Cornwall's economy and its national and international profile."[70]

*Dehwelans* has illustrated that the Cornish translocalism has reached a new and exciting level. But why is there such an interest in or need for a heightened sense of Cornishness? Adherence to the "old country," which has claims on the loyalty and emotion of the Cornish worldwide, has, according to academic Robin Cohen, "implications for the international state system. . . . [The] number of groups [like the Cornish] evincing a 'peoplehood' through the retention or expression of separate languages, customs, folkways and religions looks set to grow."[71] Cohen notes that concepts of diaspora have great variety and mutability, a negative factor if the proliferation of meanings of the word has the danger of multiplying confusion by suggesting meanings that are not pertinent to the particular group concerned.[72] In the Cornish case, mass movement of people has sometimes been interpreted as a crisis migration in the wake of mining failure: people were forced into "exile" overseas.[73] However, Stephen Vertovec's interpretation of diaspora as part of a postmodern project of resisting the nation-state—which is perceived as hegemonic, discriminatory, and culturally homogenizing—offers an intriguing new departure that recognizes and advocates the hybridity, multiple identities, and affiliations with people, causes, and traditions outside the nation-state of residence.[74]

Here, Peggy Levitt's contention that, implicit in Vertovec's interpretation about whether life across borders involves resistance to the nation-state and allows previously marginalized groups to challenge the social hierarchy, is of relevance to the Cornish case.[75] Attempts to make the Cornish ethnically visible worldwide have important implications. Although Cornish-American associations are not meant to be political organizations, by encouraging their members to acknowledge their ancestry as Cornish and not English they nonetheless are strengthening the case for the Cornish to be recognized as a national minority within the United Kingdom.

With up to two million people of Cornish descent believed to reside in the United States alone and with Cornwall's population of just over half a million (with the indigenous Cornish making up less than 50 percent of this total), the value of a Cornish population worldwide becomes apparent. This is exemplified by a twelve-point appendix to the Cornish National Minority Report of 2000 that stressed the historical importance of Cornish migration in the creation of a modern and vibrant sense of Cornishness.[76] Indeed, some overseas Cornish associations have become mildly political in recent years, *Penkernewek*, for example, providing its members with information of how to lend support to the campaign for a Cornish Assembly.

The most overtly political event, however, was *Keskerdh Kernow*, a re-enactment of the Cornish Rebellion of 1497, "Cornwall's Colloden," when thousands of aggrieved Cornishmen marched on London to be defeated by the English at Blackheath. The marches of solidarity planned in the United States to complement those in Britain clearly unsettled some, for in the collective memory of many Cornish Americans, Cornwall and its people were not seen as victims of English oppression and tyranny but as skilled migrants from a successful industrial region that had contributed greatly to the economic powerhouse that was the United States. Cornish-American historian and Bard Gage McKinney of California noted that he felt uncomfortable lending support to any activity that might be construed as a gratuitous intrusion into the internal politics of another sovereign state, the United Kingdom.[77] But not all Americans are as reticent in this respect. The 2004 Christmas edition of the American television show, *The Simpsons*, featured cult icon Lisa Simpson waving St. Piran's flag and shouting, *"Rydhsys rag Kernow lemmyn* (freedom for Cornwall now)," and, *"Kernow bys vykken* (Cornwall forever)."[78] This potentially huge international boost to the Cornish language and national movement came about after one of the show's production team had been to see a show by a stand-up comedian in the United States who remarked that he was Cornish, not English.

## CONCLUSION

This essay has demonstrated that transnationalism should not be viewed as a single phenomenon. Although there were some isolated incidences of transnationalism among the nineteenth-century Cornish immigrants, most did not maintain intense, multi-level, on-going connections with their communities of origin of the type observed in some modern communities. Instead, their connections were sporadic, limited, intermittent, monetarily irregular, and, by the twentieth century, diminishing; they better fit Barkan's model of translocalism. But this is not to underestimate the importance and significance of translocalism. For Cornish Americans today, translocal connections with their ancestors' homeland have provided them with a sense of heritage and roots in an increasingly mobile and changing world. Moreover, Cornish-Americans have ensured that the Cornish—hard-working Celts and archetypal nation builders—have their place among the many threads that constitute the rich ethnic tapestry of the United States. They also have been hugely instrumental in promoting a worldwide renaissance in Cornish ethnicity. As reservoirs of Cornish-ness, the Cornish overseas manifest an awareness of their heritage and identity and a will to keep this alive.

Such determination and activism could provide elements of a renaissance of transnationalism if they were sustained. They could be even more impressive—and significant—if shared by a greater number of those of Cornish descent who viewed such events as more than symbolic and occasional gestures of ethnicity. Moreover, the act of rendering the Cornish ethnically visible in countries such as the United States and the translocal events and organizations that cohere around this have important political implications in Britain. The resurgence in Cornish ethnicity is acting as a vehicle to accelerate the emergence of a vibrant Cornish diaspora. This has great relevance for Cornwall as its people attempt to be recognized as an ethnic minority within the British Isles. Such a campaign has wide ramifications for the concept of the homogenous British nation-state as groups, such as the Cornish, seek to legitimize their ethnic and national aspirations.

## NOTES

1.  See Nina Glick-Schiller, Linda Basch and Christina Blanc-Szanton, eds., *Towards a Transnational Perspective on Migration: Race, Class, Ethnicity, and Nationalism Reconsidered* (New York, 1992); and Linda Basch, Nina Glick-Schiller, and Christina Blanc-Szanton, *Nations Unbound: Transnational Projects, Postcolonial Predicaments, and Deterritorialized States* (Langhorne, PA, 1994), 7.
2.  See Daniel Mato, "On Global and Local Agents and the Social Making of Transnational Identities and Related Agendas in 'Latin' America," *Identities* 4, no. 2 (1997): 167–212; and Thomas Faist, "Transnationalization in International Migration: Implications for the Study of Citizenship and Culture," Working Paper WPTC-99-08 (Transnational Communities Programme, Oxford University, 1999).
3.  See Faist, "Transnationalization in International Migration"; and Paul Spoonley, "Reinventing Polynesia: The Cultural Politics of Transnational Pacific Communities," Working Paper WPTC-2K-14 (Transnational Communities Programme Series, Oxford University, 2000).
4.  Ewa Morawska, "Immigrants, Transnationalism and Ethnicization: A Comparison of this Great Wave and the Last," in *E Pluribus Unum?: Contemporary and Historical Perspectives on Immigrant Political Incorporation*, ed. Gary Gerstle and John Mollenkopf (New York, 2001), 172–212.
5.  Robin Cohen, *Global Diasporas: An Introduction* (London, 1997), x.
6.  Stephen Vertovec, "Religion and Diaspora: New Landscapes of Religion in the West," paper presented at the conference on "New Landscapes of Religion in the West," University of Oxford, 27–29 September 2000.
7.  Peggy Levitt, "Between God, Ethnicity, and Country: An Approach to the Study of Transnational Religion," paper presented at the workshop on "Transnational Migration, Comparative Perspectives," Princeton University, 30 June–1 July, 2001.

8.  Peggy Levitt, *The Transnational Villagers* (Berkeley, CA, 2001).

9.  See Nina Glick-Schiller, "The Situation of Transnational Studies," *Identities* 4 no. 2 (1997): 155–66.

10. See Thomas Faist, *The Volume and Dynamics of International Migration and Transnational Social Spaces* (Oxford, 2000); and Peggy Levitt and Rafael de la Dehesa, "Transnational Migration and the Redefinition of the State: Variations and explanations," *Ethnic and Racial Studies* 26, no. 4 (2003): 587–611.

11. Nancy Foner, *From Ellis Island to JFK: New York's Two Great Waves of Immigration* (New Haven, CT, 2000), 169–70.

12. Randolph Bourne, "Trans-National America," *Atlantic Monthly* 111, no. 1 (1916): 86–87.

13. See Ewa Morawska and Willifred Spohn, "Moving Europeans in a Globalizing World: Contemporary Migrations in a Historical-Comparative Perspective (1955–1994 v. 1870–1914," in *Global History and Migrations*, ed. Wang Gungwu (Boulder, CO, 1997), 23–61.

14. Elliott R. Barkan, "America in the Hand, Homeland in the Heart: Transnational and Translocal Immigrant Experiences in the American West," *Western Historical Quarterly* 35, no. 3 (Autumn 2004): 331–54.

15. For more on Cornwall's "great migration" see Philip Payton, *The Making of Modern Cornwall* (Redruth, Cornwall, England, 1992), chapter 5.

16. Bernard Deacon, "Proto-industrialisation and Potatoes: A Revised Narrative for Nineteenth Century Cornwall," in *Cornish Studies* 5, ed. Philip Payton (Exeter, 1997): 66.

17. Sharron P. Schwartz, "Exporting the Industrial Revolution: The Migration of Cornish Mining Technology to Latin America in the Early Nineteenth Century," in *New Perspectives in Transatlantic Studies*, eds. Will Kaufman and Heidi Macpherson (New York, 2002), 143–58.

18. For a theoretical overview of Cornish migration and particularly for a discussion of risk diversification strategies, see Sharron P. Schwartz, "Cornish Migration Studies: An Epistemological and Paradigmatic Critique," in *Cornish Studies* 10, ed. Philip Payton (Exeter, 2002): 136–65.

19. Dudley Baines, *Migration in a Mature Economy: Emigration and Internal Migration in England and Wales, 1861–1900* (Cambridge, 1985), 159.

20. L. A. Copeland, "The Cornish in Southwest Wisconsin," *Wisconsin Historical Collection* 14 (1898).

21. See F. D. Calhoon, *Coolies, Kanakas and Cousin Jacks: And Eleven Other Ethnic Groups Who Populated the West During the Gold Rush Years* (Sacramento, CA, 1995); Shirley Ewart, *Cornish Mining Families of Grass Valley, CA* (New York, 1989); and *Highly Respectable Families: The Cornish of Grass Valley California 1854–1954* (Grass Valley, CA, 1998).

22. Alan Granruth, *Mining Gold to Mining Wallets: Central City, Colorado 1859–1999* (Central City, CO, 1999), 42–43.

23. See A. L. Rowse, *The Cornish in America* (Redruth, Cornwall, England, 1967); John Rowe, *The Hard-Rock Men: Cornish Immigrants and the North American Mining Frontier* (Liverpool, 1974); A. C. Todd, *The Cornish Miner in America* (Spokane, WA, 1995); and Philip Payton, *The Cornish Overseas*, (Fowey, Cornwall, England, 1998).

24. Jim Jewell, *Cornish in America: Linden, Wisconsin* (Mineral Point, WI, 1990), 63–64.

25. Gage McKinney, *A High and Holy Place: A Mining Camp Church at New Almaden* (Sunnyvale, CA, 1997), 14.

26. Edmund Kinyon, "Cornish Migration to Grass Valley," *Nevada County Historical Society Bulletin* 3, no. 6 (1950).
27. A. L. Rowse, *The Cornish In America* (Redruth, Cornwall, England, 1967); and *West Briton*, 13 September 1894.
28. A. L. Rowse, *Cornish in America*, 166; and *Cornish Post and Mining News*,28 December 1905.
29. *Cornish Post and Mining News*, 28 January 1909.
30. *Cornubian*, 15 August 1913.
31. Peggy Levitt, "Social Remittances: Migration Driven Local-level Forms of Cultural Diffusion," *International Migration Review* 32, no. 4 (1998): 926–84.
32. *West Briton*, 13 September 1894.
33. See Todd, *The Cornish Miner in America*, 241–44.
34. Roger P. Lescohier, *Gold Giants of Grass Valley: History of the Empire and North Star Mines 1850–1956* (Grass Valley, CA, 1995), 43.
35. G. Burke, "The Cornish Miner and the Cornish Mining Industry 1870–1921" (Ph. D. diss., University of London, 1981), 108.
36. For more on friendly societies, see Sharron P. Schwartz, "Cornish Migration to Latin America: A Global and Transnational Perspective" (Ph.D. diss., University of Exeter, 2003), ch. 9.
37. L. L. Price, "West Barbary; or Notes on the System of Work and Wages in the Cornish Mines," in *Cornish Mining: Essays on the Organisation of Cornish Mines and the Cornish Mining Economy*, ed. Roger Burt (Newton Abbot, Devon, England, 1969), 130.
38. *West Briton*, 21 January 1935. "One and All" is the Cornish motto, appearing on the Cornish Coat of Arms.
39. Copeland, "The Cornish in Southwest Wisconsin," 330.
40. Barkan, "America in the Hand, Homeland in the Heart."
41. Ewart, *Highly Respectable Families*, 45.
42. Thurner, *Strangers and Sojourners*, 311.
43. See Mary C. Waters, *Ethnic Options: Choosing Identities in America* (Berkeley, CA, 1990), for more on this subject.
44. George Fiedler, *Mineral Point: A History* (Mineral Point, WI, 1986), 169.
45. Fielder, *Mineral Point*, 167–68. The Pendarvis restoration is the only officially designated Cornish heritage site in the United States.
46. Ewart, *Highly Respectable Families*, 61.
47. Gage McKinney, *When Miners Sang: The Grass Valley Carol Choir* (Grass Valley, CA, 2001): 236–37. Cousin Jack is the term for a Cornish male migrant; Jenny is the female equivalent.
48. Bourne, "Trans-National America," 86–87.
49. David Held, ed., *A Globalizing World? Culture, Economic, Politics* (London, 2000), 1–2.
50. See, for example, Geoff Mulgan, *Connexity: Responsibility, Freedom, Business and Power in the New Century* (London, 1998); Allan Cochrane and Kathy Pain, "A Globalizing Society?," in *A Globalizing World?*,ed. David Held (London, 2000), 5–45; and Hugh Mckay, "The Globalization of Culture?," ibid., 47–84.
51. The *Gorseth Bryth Kernow* (Gorsedd of Cornish Bards) meets annually. Although independent, it is allied to those of Wales and Brittany. It exists to maintain the national Celtic spirit of Cornwall and entry to the Gorsedd as a bard is by invitation to those who have encouraged and promoted this, or by examination in the Cornish language.
52. S. Morse, "Being a Canadian," *Canadian Journal of Behavioural Science* 9, no. 3 (1977): 265–73.

53. Wolfgang Welsche, "Transkulturality: The Puzzling Form of Cultures Today," in *Spaces of Culture: City, Nation, World*, ed. Mike Featherstone and Scott Lash (London, 1999), 194–213.

54. Quoted in Robert Pütz, "Culture and Entrepreneurship—Remarks on Transculturality as Practice," *Tijdschrift voor economische en sociale geografie* 94, no. 5 (2003): 554–63.

55. Mato, "On Global and Local Agents," 598.

56. Amy Hale and Philip Payton, "The Celtic Diaspora," in *New Directions in Celtic Studies*, eds. Amy Hale and Philip Payton (Exeter, 2000), 95.

57. See Mulgan, *Connexity*; Cochrane and Pain, "A Globalizing Society?": and McKay, "The Globalization of Culture?"

58. Howard Rheingold, *The Virtual Community* (London, 1995), 6.

59. Mato, "On Global and Local Agents," 611.

60. Translated from the Cornish language, *Tam Kernewek* means "a bit of Cornish."

61. Amy Hale and Shannon Thornton, "Pagans, Pipers and Politicos: Constructing 'Celtic' in a Festival Context," in *New Directions in Celtic Studies*, ed. Hale and Payton, 97–107.

62. Nancy O. Heydt, "Oatlands Celtic Fest," *Tam Kernewek* 14 (1996): 15.

63. Two students went on a shooting spree in this Littleton, Colorado, high school on April 20, 1999, causing a massacre of several of their teachers and fellow students. See Jean Jolliffe, "President's Message," *Tam Kernewek* 18 (2000): 3; Jean Jolliffe, Cornish American Heritage Society, "Steven R. Curnow, a victim of the April 1999 tragedy at Columbine High School in Littleton, Colorado, was a Cornish-American lad. . . . The Cornish American Heritage Society (CAHS) proudly recognised Steven as the youngest member of the organization." http://archiver.rootsweb.com/th/read/CORNISH/2000-04/ 0956957058, accessed 3 March 2006.

64. Cornish Foundation For North America Leaflet (1999).

65. Jean Jolliffe, "The price of success?" *Tam Kernewek* 17 (1999): 2–3.

66. *Union*, 5 September 1996.

67. Philip Hosken, "Cornwall—not what it seems," *Cornish World* 11 (1996).

68. See http://archive.thisisthewestcountry.co.uk/2002/5/24/38280.html.

69. Objective One is a European funding program that is given to areas in need of regeneration. Cornwall received Objective One status in 1999, which meant that there was over £300 million to spend in the county on projects to improve its prosperity. Cornwall can expect another seven years of European development funding when the current round of Objective One money ends in 2006.

70. See Bernard Deacon and Sharron P. Schwartz, *The Cornish Family*, 198. The second *Dehwelans* took place at Newquay in May 2004.

71. Cohen, *Global Diasporas*, ix–x.

72. Robin Cohen, "Diasporas, the Nation-State, and Globalisation," in *Global History and Migrations*, ed. Wang Gungwu, 118.

73. For a critique of this hypothesis, see Sharron P. Schwartz, "Cornish Migration to Latin America," chs. 1, 2.

74. See Vertovec, "Religion and Diaspora."

75. See Levitt, "Between God, Ethnicity, and Country."

76. Bernard Deacon, *The Cornish and the Council of Europe Framework Convention for the Protection of National Minorities* (Redruth, Cornwall, England, 2000).

77. Gage McKinney, quoted in Philip Payton, *The Cornish Overseas* (Fowey, Cornwall, England, 1999), 399.

78. *The West Briton*, 8 July 2004.

# 9

# Political Refugees or Economic Immigrants?: A New "Old Debate" within the Haitian Immigrant Communities *but* with Contestations and Division

*CAROLLE CHARLES*

"REFUGEE" CATEGORIES ARE usually understood and used as political categories that defined the status of distinct population groups. Usually, they refer to a type of forced migration. The definition presumes that the displaced people involved in the process are not the free agents of their predicaments; they are rather the victims. Moreover, these categories are rooted within the world-political system, reflecting state-to-state relations and/or states-and-citizens relationships. Thus, these political categories of political status are also categories of otherness. As such, not only are they expressions of relations of power but they also epitomized systems of exclusion and practices of marginalization. Consequently, they are subject to contention, resistance, and/or adaptation. Those in positions to define who are refugees as well as those being defined as refugees can manipulate these categories as they fit their own interests and agendas.[1]

In spite of that dynamic, the literature (in particular on Haitian refugees) tends to concentrate either on U.S. refugee policies or on the consequences of such policies on the targeted immigrant populations.[2] Few studies have looked at the ways these particular populations accept or contest these policies or the categories informed by these policies. Likewise, few analyses have examined variations and divisions that may exist within immigrant communities directly affected by these policies. This paper attempts to look at such dynamics. We look at how, at two distinct historical and political moments in the life of the Haitian immigrant communities in the United States, the responses of the immigrant communities varied.

We argue that, during the 1980s and early 1990s with the first refugee crises, there was a consensus on the need to advocate for asylum seekers and refugees status for those migrants who could claim "credible fear of persecution" if they were returned to Haiti. More recently, during the second term of the Aristide regime, such a positioning became more complex, indicating the absence of a consensus. In fact, a clear schism existed within the various Haitian communities about the admission that the political situation under the Aristide government created the conditions for a movement of forced migration.[3] The tension indeed had to do with the political assessment of the regime. For many, the Aristide government still was perceived as the most democratic administration that Haiti has known and its policies and governance did not conduce to making political refugees. For others, life in Haiti since the return of the Aristide government in 2002 meant the beginning of a path toward totalitarianism and thereby the claims of the new refugees and asylum seekers were quite legitimate.[4]

Nonetheless, these oppositional responses in explaining the political elements leading to a new refugee flow are indicative of the ways in which immigrant populations may be unintended participants in making these categories of otherness. They also point to how immigrant communities also are involved in transnational processes of nation-building. Moreover, in their positioning they also are interacting with the process of hegemonic power relationships between a strong state (the United States) and a weak state (which happens to be their country of origin), with such relationships partially shaping the immigration policies towards Haitian migrants.

## DIVERSITY IN THE HAITIAN MIGRATION
## FLOWS TO THE U.S.: THE REFUGEES

Haiti and Haitians have been part of many forms of transnational processes of migration, including forced migration flows.[5] Between 1973–1991, more than 80,000 Haitian asylum-seekers came to the shores of the United States. The first detected Haitian boat with refugees arrived in 1963. Their request for asylum was denied, and they were deported. Interestingly, this was the period of massive flows of temporary visitors who overstayed their visa and did not constituted a political problem for the government. In fact, between 1961–71 around 25,000 legal Haitian immigrants were admitted, and the number of non-immigrants who received a temporary visa amounted to 112,000. During that same period, Haiti lost between 60 and 75 percent of its highly skilled workers.[6]

The second boatloads of Haitian refugees came ten years later, in 1972. Sixty-five Haitian refugees claiming refugee status were denied asylum. This did not stop the arrival of more refugees. Between 1971 and 1977, an estimated 3,500 arrived on American shores, and a network of refugees was created, reinforced by the big business of smugglers that included both Haitian government agents and some U.S. officials.[7] For these refugees, no federal resettlements and no special status were awarded. It was really during the Carter administration that the refugee flows began to increase. Between 1977 and 1981, around 50,000 to 70,000 Haitians arrived by boat in South Florida. Parallel to the arrival of these refugees were also scenes of bloated bodies that did not make it.[8] Although during the period of 1986–90 there were fewer refugee boats, yet around 20,000 Haitians were still intercepted at sea.[9]

The uprooting of the Duvalier regime in February 1987 and the coming to power of the first democratically elected government in February 1991, with the Lavalas movement and its leader, Jean-Bertrand Aristide, did not fully stop the flow of refugees. Nine months later, a bloody military coup against the Aristide government triggered a resumption of the flows. The military seizure of power brought massive killings and the disruption of socio-political life—the creation of internally displaced people and a spike in the numbers of refugees fleeing to the United States. By the early 1992, around 34,000 Haitian refugees were intercepted at sea. This was a second wave of forced migration.

The issue of the plight of Haitian refugees became again a national event in the United States with the arrival on December 3, 2001, of a boatload of 187 refugees on Miami shores. Of that total, 167 were rescued and placed in INS custody. The remaining twenty had jumped into the water, with only eighteen of them reaching the shore. They were immediately placed in expedited removal process, although sixteen of them had met the criteria for claiming a credible fear of persecution. Again, in October 2002, around two hundred Haitian refugees jumped from a boat and swam the final five hundred yards to shore. Many in their testimonies claimed that they came to the United States for economic and political reasons. Some admitted that poverty was clearly a factor for their migration but they also testified against the political situation of fear, repression, violence, and insecurity that prevailed under the second Aristide government.[10] From January 2 to October 26, 2002, the national immigration office in Haiti recorded more than 19,778 cases of forced repatriation of Haitians by U.S., Bahamian, Cuban, and Dominican authorities. Their arrival and return would re-ignite the old debate over differing treatment for asylum seekers and refugees from Haiti.[11]

## THE MAKING OF THE CATEGORY OF REFUGEE

Refugees are a type of migrants who are forced to leave their home country primarily for political pressures. They also can be displaced people who are victims of adverse circumstances. Most international refugee laws and policies are guided by the 1951 UN Convention pact formulated by the United Nation High Commission of Refugees (UNHCR). Generally, a political refugee is a person who must leave his or her country of origin because of a well-founded fear of persecution for reasons of race, religion, and political participation. However, individuals who claim refugee status must prove that legitimate fear of persecution.

Both in 1969 and in 1984, a series of revisions was introduced in order to redefine and broaden the meanings of the category. By then, a refugee was any person or group fleeing any situation of generalized violence. "Refugee status" became for most international humanitarian institutions one that could be ascribed to any person or group victim of a situation of violence and searching for protection.

In spite of these humanitarian guidelines that are generally used to grant refugee status, state policies in many recipient societies depend on many factors and involve, as Gil Loescher and John Scanlan state, "a complex interplay of domestic and international factors."[12] Among these international factors are the political relationships between sending and receiving countries. But, regimes of political and social organization that characterize social life in the receiving societies are also crucial in making these policies. Since the 1990s, under the pressures and lobbying of many humanitarian and human rights organizations, new considerations in assessing the causes of forced migrations were introduced. Moreover, a new emphasis has fallen on scrutinizing the human rights records of many countries. The United Nations and other international organizations, such as the Organization of American States (OAS), meanwhile exhibit a new readiness to impose sanctions on countries with high rates of abuses and violations of rights.

Notwithstanding these new considerations, the making of the refugee category also can be used and exploited by governments in pursuit of larger geopolitical and ideological objectives, with states potentially applying different policies vis-à-vis different national groups of refugees. Such differentiated treatment of refugees often is shaped by many factors, among them the economic conditions in the host country, foreign policy interests, national security concerns, public opinion, and perception of refugee groups. The politics regarding the acceptance of a definite category of migrants as refugees or the patterns of incorporation of a particular group of immigrants also depend on the conception of citizenship existing in the receiving/host country as well as the ways in which citizenship is hierarchically organized. For example, within the world inter-state system, the United States has a hegemonic position and thus is able to define the terms of its relationship with other states within a dichotomist set of parameters.[13] Thus, there are allies or enemies of the United States and, consequently, policies regarding the forms of incorporation of potential immigrants from countries defined as allies or enemies vary drastically. A case in point is the treatment of Cuban versus Haitian refugees.

In the United States, immigration policy always has been one of the ways access to citizenship has been constructed. All immigration policies and regimes of incorporation of immigrants have been influenced by America's concept of citizenship. Historically, that concept has always been shaped by race. It is a pattern that in the United States has defined the differentiated access to specific sets of rights and duties for racially designated populations. Until 1952, the concept of citizenship always had meant exclusion or limitation to these entitlements for certain groups.[14] In fact, the history of U.S. immigration and refugee policies also reflected major racial, ethnic, and religious biases.[15] Up to the 1965 immigration reforms, the system of national origin quotas established in 1924 illustrated these biases, since during the nineteenth and early twentieth centuries the bulk of the immigration flows to the United States, excluding the forced migration of African slaves, came primarily from Europe. From the outset there was no desire for immigration of people of African descent. Rather, during the nineteenth century, the policy of some organizations was to encourage the emigration of the black population (especially the newly emancipated). Outward flows to Africa were encouraged, and patronage of colonization to Africa and Haiti even persisted after the Civil War.[16] Such historical practices (in terms of favoring particular groups of people as migrants, with race playing an important role in informing these practices) may have well influenced the case of Haitian asylum seekers.

## THE CONTOURS OF A U.S. REFUGEE POLICY

Until 1980 the United States had no systematic policy with respect to refugees. Before that time, different laws were enacted and different U.S. administrations used loopholes in the law to parole people seeking asylum. The 1966 Cuban Adjustment Act and the 1975 Indochina Migration and Refugee Assistance Act are cases in point.[17] In fact, up to the 1990 and the collapse of the Soviet Union, a Cold War perspective dominated U.S. foreign policy and, almost totally, its refugee policy. This meant the adoption of an ideological definition of refugee where practices of admission accorded with Cold War preferences.[18]

Opportunities and special provisions were created for refugees fleeing "communist" countries, as in the cases of Eastern Europeans and Cuban refugees. In 1956, with the Hungarians, and in the 1960s, with the Cubans, the United States defined those groups of political exiles as freedom fighters who deserved respect and solidarity in the land of freedom. Both President Eisenhower and President Kennedy used executive powers to circumvent all legal restrictions on immigration law. Decisions regarding the admission of refugees completely shifted to executive prerogatives. Most of them were initiated in the State Department to meet specific foreign policy objectives. Congress only approved these decisions.[19]

This pattern of preferential admission was established in 1956 and lasted until 1980, with preferences given to "victims" of communist regimes. As Loescher and Scanlan again indicate, "a double standard which governed the acceptability of migrants from particular countries emerged as principal features of American policies."[20] Interestingly, with the arrival of refugees from Indochina in 1975, race and ethnicity would subtly re-enter the political scene because Congress began to show some opposition to the practices. The argument of many opponents to the admission of Indochinese was that the parole process used for their admission was discriminatory because it did not apply to Chileans and the Soviet Jews who also were seeking asylum.[21] Ironically, claims of asylum seekers from authoritarian regimes like Haiti were ignored.

The 1980 Mariel boatlift from Cuba prompted a reform of immigration policies and the enactment of a new refugee act. In less than five months, the massive arrival of around 130,000 Cubans and 30,000 Haitians forced a reassessment of the asylum policy. A major piece of legislation, the Refugee Act of 1980, was adopted. Subsequently, two other reforms were enacted with the Immigration Reform and Control Act of 1986 and the Immigration Act of 1990.[22]

In order to resolve the crisis created with these flows, the Carter administration established a new category defined as "Cuban-Haitian entrants." The Haitians were included almost by default. The administration was compelled to extend a welcome to the Haitians who had arrived at the same time as the Cubans, although in smaller numbers. The 1980 Act modernized U.S. refugee policy by providing categories for refugee admission defined in accordance with the 1951 UN Convention. With the new act, the United States adhered to international legal standards that made asylum a matter of right rather than an option based on discretion and significance of a claim. The act also established a presidential privilege for deciding on annual allocation "after consultation with Congress."[23]

Nonetheless, the new act would not eliminate the double standard that was the hallmark of the admission policy since the 1950s, although it did remove all references to communism from the definition of refugee. With the Reagan administration, the double standard would continue. Claims of hardship and persecution were accepted only if provided by a refugee with the right ideological credentials. Moreover, under the allocation system the majority of admission slots went to those fleeing communist countries. Loescher and Scanlan point out that during 1984–85 out of the 70,000 slots allocated, 64,000 went to refugees from Eastern Europe, the Soviet Union, Cuba, Indochina, and Afghanistan and to some groups from Nicaragua. In contrast, refugees and asylum seekers from most other countries of the Caribbean Basin were the exclusive targets of programs of detention and deportation.[24] The Reagan administration also introduced a new measure, that of interdiction, which meant the stopping, turning back, and at times detainment by the U.S. Coast Guard of "suspicious boats."

## THE UNIQUENESS OF U.S. POLICY
## TOWARDS HAITIAN REFUGEES

Most analyses presented by scholars and activists in order to explain the uniqueness of U.S. policy towards Haitian refugees have focused primarily on foreign policy interests and on racism. It is thus important to analyze the forms of representations, the discourses about Haitians and Haiti, and their impact on the process of elaborating and implementing a U.S. policy towards Haitian refugees. In other words, it is important to look at the cultural dimensions of these policies. However, although these constructions are influenced by the dynamic of race relations in the United States, they also reflected the weak position of Haiti in the world economy and the nation-state system.

The emergence of the United States as the hegemonic power within the Caribbean area entailed new social relations in Haiti, resulting in its specialization as an exporter of labor, first within the Caribbean and later to the United States.[25] These new social relations were manifested in the partial dissolution of many sectors of the peasantry, their displacement and transformation into potential migrant labor. Likewise, the growing centralization of all activities in the capital, Port-au-Prince, forced many intermediary segments of the population to migrate to the capital. Many of these middlemen, who tended to be black, belonged to intermediate strata, which by the 1940s had emerged in the political arena. With the advent of the Duvalier regime, this black stratum of the population had consolidated its base of power, using violence and predation as a means of accumulating wealth. The result was increased migration. Moreover, the policies of various international agencies operating in Haiti—particularly USAID— have created the conditions for the maintenance and reproduction of these flows. Thus, as early as the turn of the century, Haiti had already become a regular exporter of labor, first to the Caribbean and later to the United States and Canada. This was, and continues to be, the major form of Haiti's incorporation into the world capitalist economy.

The hegemonic position of the United States in the Caribbean also had a profound impact on processes of class formation, on racial and class dynamics, and on the struggle for control of state power in Haiti. The increased political violence of the Duvalierist state, both at the political and economic levels, left many Haitians no alternative but migration. In 1963, for example, following a teacher and student strike, more than five thousand professionals and graduate students were given exit visas for the newly independent Zaire. The devastating effect of this brain drain still is felt today. Moreover, the various testimonies of Haitian refugees from different social backgrounds and the number of opposition figures residing in the United States attest to the role of the regime in creating the conditions for a social context of migration.[26]

In contrast to other societies of the Caribbean, the Haitian state has weak institutions and is still struggling to lay down the basic foundations for modernity. The Haitian state also functions more through repression and corruption. The use of state assets has been a common feature by which the ruling elite has secured for themselves political gains. The Haitian state is thus a classic model of an authoritarian regime. In order to maintain the socio-economic structure, it is necessary to deny political representation to all but a small segment of the population.[27]

The weak position of Haiti is reflected not only in its role as exporter of labor but also in some of the major macro-economic indicators. In 2002, Haiti held the 156th place in the Index of Development of the UNDP out of a ranking of 173 countries. Around 65 percent of the population worked in the agricultural sector and contributed 30 percent of GNP. Since 1987, the agricultural sector has been incapable of meeting the food needs for the population, and imports of foods increased from 10 percent in 1973 to 30 percent in 1983. Income per capita was around $250 in the 1990s. Data from the World Bank in 1998 indicated that 66 percent of the population lived below the absolute poverty line, 14 percent fell between the indigence and poverty lines, and only 19 percent were above the poverty line. The majority of the Haitian population has little access to basic human needs, such as public education, health, and potable water. To that situation of economic deprivation, poor Haitians are also subject to political and social exclusion. Since the mid-1990s, the Haitian economy has showed a real annual *negative* growth of 3.0 percent. The slight change experienced between 1994 and 1995 was due to massive external aid; there was no creation of jobs in the formal sector. In 1991, agriculture accounted for 34.2 percent of GDP, industry 19.8 percent, and services 40.5 percent. In 1998, the numbers shifted, respectively, to 42.1, 13.7, and 37.2.[28] In 1993 there were 1.6 doctors, 1.3 nurses, and 0.4 dentists for every 10,000 persons. Moreover, Port-au-Prince concentrated 74 percent of the doctors, 67 percent of the nurses, 35 percent of health institutions, and 52 percent of all hospital beds. Malnutrition was a major cause of illness and death, and the infant mortality rate was 94 per 1,000. Only 37 percent of the total population had access to safe water and 25 percent to sanitation.[29]

During the 1990s, Haiti received $135 million in aid, which represented around 6 percent of GNP. During that same period remittances from emigrants accounted for 35 percent of GNP. After the return of the Aristide government in 1994, more than five hundred million dollars was given for a recovery program.[30]

In 2000, J. B. Aristide was reelected to a second term. His governance began with a political crisis. In fact, the crisis started in 1998 with the rigged parliamentary elections, which led to the implosion of the broad coalition that made the Lavalas movement. A faction closely tied to the Aristide/Preval camp monopolized all positions of power and later organized the 2000 presidential elections. Despite evidence of electoral irregularities, the newly elected Aristide government refused to comply with demands for a rerun of seven parliamentary seats. As a result, there was a freeze in international aid and more political instability. Moreover, as many reports indicate, corruption within the government, poor spending policies, and increased flagrant human rights violations have deteriorated the political situation and worsened the economy.

Poverty and misery, compounded with violence and intolerance, were thus the structural elements inducing the new refugees flows. As an Amnesty International report in 2001 states, "[S]ince the electoral period in 2000, some of the progress achieved [in human rights] has been undone." The report also cited the "political pressures on the judiciary and the police and crackdowns on the exercise of fundamental freedoms. The report continued, "if not reversed, this deterioration could lead to even more serious violations of human rights."[31] Likewise, opposition political figures in Haiti, such as former President Leslie Manigat, blamed the Lavalas government for steering the country more deeply into despair, stating, "It is not just the poor who are fleeing. Everyone with money, education or skills wants to leave. People do not have faith in the future of this country."[32] In fact, testimonies of many asylum seekers tended to confirm such negative assessments. Yet, there was, on the part of the U.S. administration, a systematic denial of human rights violations. For the U.S. government, the value of Haiti was more its strategic geopolitical position.

## THE TREATMENT OF HAITIAN REFUGEES

Since the 1960s, U.S. policies toward Haitian refugees and asylum seekers can be described simply as denial of due process, mistreatment, deportation, and racial exclusion. Many researchers have documented the cultural discourse and the use of code words in the depiction of Haitians by state officials.[33] Haitians usually are defined as being less manageable or difficult to assimilate. In his study, Stepick also discusses how members of the political elite of Miami, including many Cubans, define Haitians as a disruptive force that can destroy the community and drain public resources. In addition, there were pressures of social institutions and social groups on INS to control the flows. The campaigns included jailing, denial of work authorization, and rejection of claims. Some INS employees even threatened to strike if Haitians refugees were allowed to make their claims.[34]

During the Carter administration, although the U.S. government recognized the existence of practices of state terror in Haiti, it refused to recognize Haitians as refugees. For the U.S. government, Haitians were not voting with their feet and there was no need to characterize them as victims of persecution. At the most, the Carter administration declared that only a handful of arriving Haitians were politically persecuted. The majority of the asylum seekers were defined as economic migrants, denied due process with no possibility to present their asylum claim, and refused refugees status.[35] During the Mariel crisis, however, around 30,000 Haitian refugees were granted asylum following the creation of the "Cuban-Haitian entrants status program." On the other hand, while Cubans could adjust their situation in one year under the 1966 Cuban Adjustment Act, Haitians had to wait until the 1986 reform act (IRCA) to apply for regular residency.[36] The arrival of drowned bodies of Haitians off the Florida coast in 1981–82 did not move the U.S. administration to act on humanitarian grounds.

In fact, the arrival of the Reagan administration saw the formulation of a new policy of interdiction that would tighten the treatment of Haitian refugees. The interdiction program was a strategy to seize and search Haitian boats within the boundaries of Haitian waters. It became part of an agreement (still active today) signed in September 1981 between the U.S. and Haitian governments. In that pact, all landing refugees were detained and were subject to the rules of the newly created "Haitian program." The objectives of this program were to deny access to lawyers and prevent any claim of asylum. Massive detentions at different U.S. centers, including Krome in Florida, Lake Placid in New York, Fort Allen in Puerto Rico, and Big Spring in Texas, became the welcoming home of thousands of Haitians. At one point there were 2,000 Haitians detained for more than a year at Krome, located in the Everglades swamps of Miami.

During the 1980s, the INS canceled all work authorizations, resumed detentions, and expedited the deportation hearings. This marked the launch of the unique "Haitian Program," a well coordinated operation in which INS and State Department officials collaborated to process and expel Haitians as quickly as possible. Loescher and Scanlan report that, with no more than five judges, the number of hearings increased from 5–15 a day to 100–150.[37] Meanwhile, the implementation of the interdiction program meant that any refugee claim had to be adjudicated on the boat by a team of State Department and INS workers assisted by a Creole-speaking interpreter. In contrast, the City of Miami kindly offered a stadium as temporary headquarters to the Cubans in 1980 and also in 1989 to Nicaraguans.[38] In 1982, the plight of Haitian refugees worsened, with the Centers for Disease Control (CDC) classifying Haitians as one of the prime group at risk for AIDS. Haiti thus became labeled the primary source of AIDS. New conditions were created for making more stereotypes of Haitians within the general population, while at the same a systematic policy, characterized by Stepick as one of persecution, legal confusion, and social isolation, was being implemented.[39] This in turn had a significant impact on the socio-economic conditions of Haitians and reinforced the myth that they were not manageable or assimilable. The making of otherness came full circle.

Nonetheless, with the arrival of the first Bush administration, the policies towards Haitians took on a new twist. The official position of the administration was that any leniency toward Haitians would encourage more flows. The real and firm commitment of the administration was to block entry to all refugees regardless of their circumstances, since all Haitian refugees were defined as opportunistic job seekers. During the early 1990s, administration policy continued to implement detention and deportation. Because the government faced a temporary restraining order barring the deportation of Haitians without due process, it began a practice to transfer Haitian asylum seekers to Guantánamo where they were screened for credible claims of potential persecution. This was the best way to downplay the claims of human rights abuses and to recognize Haitian refugees' pleas for asylum. The relocation also undermined any involvement of the UN High Commission for Refugees in the Haitian case. The temporary packing—called asylum—of Haitian refugees in Guantánamo was the application of a new concept of protection. Interestingly, that practice was approved by UNHCR. In a very compelling testimony, Yolande Jean, detained in Guantánamo because of her participation in a strike, revealed: "My experience on Guantanamo allowed me to discover that it was true. These things are their doing. I have no idea what we are to them, maybe their 'betes noires' or perhaps their devils. We are not human to them; but I don't know what we are."[40]

The Clinton administration, despite its promise during the election campaign to treat Haitian refugees differently, was rapidly converted to the policies of the Reagan and Bush administrations. Nevertheless, because of the criticism and pressure from humanitarian institutions and the Congressional Black Caucus, the government established in 1992 an "In Country Process (ICP)" through the U.S. embassy in Haiti. At the same time, the U.S. Supreme Court lifted the ban on repatriation. At the end of 1992, there were no more screenings at sea ceased; refugee processing in-country became the only option and was conducted in close proximity to the Haitian army barracks.

By 1994, there were around three thousand refugees detained at Guantánamo. After the return of Aristide to Haiti, they were given five days to return voluntarily to Haiti. Each refugee received between twenty and forty U.S. dollars as "seed money" to start a new life. Less than five hundred Haitians accepted the deal and the alternative was forced repatriation. Before the end of 1995, the U.S. Coast Guard transported daily around six hundred refugees under the control of a multinational military contingent.[41]

Although the number of Haitian refugees never represented even one percent of the total of undocumented population, there was an exaggeration of the negative impact of these migrants' flows on the U.S. economy. Using the handling of Haitians as a precedent, the U.S. administration implemented measures to detain and deport Salvadorans and Guatemalans, who arrived with vivid evidence of persecution. Even when class-action suits brought court victories, the courts never accorded a legal immigration status to Haitians; they only forced the government to reprocess claims and to follow its own rules and regulations. In 1998, Congress passed the Haitian Refugee Immigration Fairness Act. Those who lived in the United States since 1995 could become lawful permanent residents without having to apply abroad. But restrictions applied for those who arrived by plane or used false papers. As a result, 38,000 sought refuge and some of the cases are still being processed.

Since the 1990s, policies regarding Haitians have not changed. Rather, they have worsened. The new 2002 policies rest on the assumption that acceptance of Haitians will generate a magnet effect, producing an exodus. Similar to the period during the military coups in 1991, the State Department also supports policies of return because it asserts that there is no history of persecution of Haitians despite the significant reports of human rights groups, Amnesty International, and the National Coalition of Haitian Rights. Before 2001, Haitians were generally released into the community while their requests were processed.

Yet, in 2001 the INS adopted a law exclusive to Haitians. Asylum seekers could be detained and not released to their families even if they were eligible for asylum. This new policy of detaining Haitians had, as Cheryl Little points out, "a deeper discriminatory purpose."[42]

The policy was appealed. In April 2003, the U.S. Attorney General over-ruled a Board of Immigration appeal decision and ruled that immigrants can be jailed indefinitely without bail when a potential national security exists. In October 2003, a bill was introduced to include all Haitians who arrived by plane. On October 29, 2002, around two hundred Haitians landed on the Florida shores and the event was caught live on television. Of these 200 refugees, eighty were released, thirty-two were detained, and the rest were deported. Although a vast majority of the "asylum seekers" had passed the "credible fear threshold," a first step in the asylum process, they were still being detained.[43]

## THE SCHISM IN THE COMMUNITIES

During the 1970s, 1980s, and 1990s, the implementation of U.S. policy towards the Haitians perceived as discriminatory was contested not only by the Haitian community but also by many U.S. humanitarian, religious, and political organizations. Solidarity came in 1972 from black churches, and the National Council of Churches created the Haitian Refugee Center.[44] In the 1980s, many organizations launched a campaign in favor of Haitians, since Haitians were consistently denied asylum. With their legal actions and their protests, they would publicize the Haitian plight in order to counteract the policies. These humanitarian efforts, successful at the beginning, forced the release of Haitian prisoners without bond, the issuance of work authorizations, and the granting of hearings on asylum claims. Both the courts in their final decisions, particularly in the class-action suit *Haitian Refugee Center v. Civiletti* and other humanitarian institutions, such as the National Council of Churches, showed how Haitian national asylum seekers were discriminated against when compared to other groups of refugees and asylum seekers.[45]

A new organization, the National Coalition for Haitian Refugees (NCHR), was created in 1982. It was the product of a coalition of forty-two American and Haitian religious, labor, and human rights organizations. With that new organization, the community could bring their protests at the political level. For example, the issue that Haitians were primarily economic immigrants was contested on many grounds. As the community claimed, in Haiti economic misery, political repression and struggle for survival were interconnected in the migrant's decision to leave.

Up to the arrival of the new refugees during the second term of the Aristide government, the consensus was that the distinction by the U.S. government between economic and political refugees was meaningless. Yet, with new flows in 2000, schism in the community replaced consensus. Many called for the release of the new Haitian immigrants and demanded that they were given refugee status because of the political situation in Haiti. Others, however, deliberately avoided any discussion of the political crisis and its role in creating these flows. As a community leader of "Sant La," an important organization in Miami, stated, "you cannot talk about the Haitian refugee situation without considering the conditions in Haiti. We cannot have it both ways: advocate for detainees but be silent. We need to clearly express why those people are fleeing."[46] In contrast, organizations like "VeYe Yo," also based in Miami but with links to the Aristide government, reversed its usual position of rejecting U.S. policies towards Haitians and claimed that the new arrivals were economic and not political refugees. They stated that even if Haitians were political refugees, it was because of the embargo that the U.S. government and the international community had imposed on the Haitian government.[47]

Many who were silent also feared harassment by Aristide supporters in Miami and physical threats and persecution if they went back to Haiti. Breaches were evident at many meetings. For example, in October 2002 in Miami, there was a real confrontation between supporters and critics of the Aristide government at a meeting to discuss issues regarding Haitian refugees. On November 2002, various human rights activists from Miami, Boston, Washington, and New York decided to rally in their respective cities against the unjust detention and deportation policies. Yet, there were a lot of denunciations and threats made against any organization that dared name the Haitian government as a culprit. During that same period, meetings to prepare a demonstration in New York City took place. Many of the New York-based organizations represented many constituencies. Present also were supporters and members of the "10th Department," a political organization linked to the Haitian government who were the more vocal persons at the meetings. As a result, many of the collaborating organizations began to withdraw from the meetings in order to avoid a clash. On the day of the demonstration in front of INS, only three organizations participated, including the 10th Department. With fewer than fifty people, the groups marched separately, based on their political and ideological stands vis-à-vis the Haitian government. The only consensus was to have banners and to use slogans that were politically neutral without reference to Haiti, for example, "Free Haitians Now" and "We are Human Beings."[48]

While it was easier to criticize the Haitian government during the earliest flows of refugees, there was an obvious split between pro- and anti-Aristide supporters during the recent arrivals regarding the nature of the flows and their political causes. Nonetheless, both groups were also forced to demand that detainees be released to their family while their cases were being processed instead of waiting in prison with convicted criminals. In that vein, the most interesting illustration of that paradox was the position of the most prominent and articulate legal defender of Haitian refugees in the 1980s, who had become (and still is) one of the most highly paid lawyers for the Haitian government.

## CONCLUSION

This essay looks at how in two distinct historical and political moments in the life of the Haitian immigrant communities in the United States—the responses of the immigrant communities toward the plight of Haitian political refugees and asylum seekers—had varied. During the first Haitian refugee crisis, a consensus existed on the need to advocate for asylum seekers and refugee status for those migrants who could claim a "credible fear of persecution" and a threat to their lives if they returned to Haiti. With the new arrivals in 2001, such a positioning became more problematic, as there was no consensus for the use of the categories of refugees. Meanwhile, a clear division within the various Haitian communities opened regarding the admission that the political situation in Haiti during the second term of the Aristide government had created the conditions for flight. The tension indeed had to do with the political assessment of the Lavalas government.

Indeed, a homogeneous "Haitian community" never existed. In fact, there were always many Haitian communities, divided by class, gender, color, generation, political and ideological persuasion, language, and region of origin. But, during the years of the Duvalier dictatorship, all agreed that Haitian refugees needed the support and solidarity of all Haitians. Such consensus could not be reached concerning the new flows. During the second mandate of the Aristide government, political differences reached a confrontational stage, reflecting the political crisis in Haiti. Nonetheless, this inability to reach a consensus also may reflect the continuing existence of these divisions as well as a growing recognition of the need to redefine what is the Haitian community. What are its potential and its resources and how should it position itself within the United States with respect to Haiti?

Nonetheless, the opposing responses concerning the political elements inducing the formation of refugee flows were indicative of the ways immigrant populations may participate in the making of these categories of otherness. They also point to how immigrant communities are involved in transnational processes by positioning themselves in the process of hegemonic relationships between a strong state and a weaker one, which happens to be their country of origin. An interesting paradox is that Haitians, particularly during this last wave of forced migration, had become, more involved in asserting their citizenship entitlements. They have created more efficient organizations, such as the new Haitian Legal Aid Fund (HALAF), which has been instrumental in achieving the release of many detainees.[49]

Even more interesting is the development by many Haitian organizations in New York, Miami, Boston, and Chicago of citizenship campaigns, a new drive to register Haitian-American citizens but also to advocate citizenship. This clearly reflects a drastic shift in the perception of the immigration experience over the last fifteen years.[50] Indeed, Florida, the place with most Haitian refugees, has been the site of the most successful result in the Haitian immigrants' civic engagement. In 1999 and in 2001, Haitians won important positions in two local elections in North Miami and El Portal. They also elected a representative to the Florida State House. Yet, four years later, in May 2005, after the Haitian-American population had showed its power at the polls, controlling all the positions on the city council, including the election of the mayor, Joseph Celestin, politics in Haiti had an impact over recent local elections. The Haitian-American mayoral candidate in North Miami, Jean Monestime, lost to a white candidate, Kevin Burns. Part of the demise of the Haitian-American council indeed had to do with the casting of Monestime as an anti-Lavalas Party candidate.

This study of two distinct political and historical moments of Haitian immigration experiences indicates the uniqueness of their trajectory and configuration. Since the 1960s, Haitians have fled military dictatorships and recurring cycles of political violence, repression, and extreme poverty. Compared to many other immigrant groups, they have been subject to negative stereotypes and often have been the victims of harsh and (at times discriminatory) U.S. immigration policies. Yet, one of the most striking characteristics of those experiences is the resilience of these black immigrants to "beat these odds" and to redefine the terms of their incorporation into U.S. society. While resisting or opposing negative representation of otherness, they are also looking for ways where they can become part of the U.S. social mosaic. At the same time, they continue to maintain and to claim their rights to be a transnational and diasporic citizenry of Haiti, their country of origin.

## NOTES

1. It is interesting to follow the current reaction within the U.S. African American communities regarding the definition of the displaced people created with the Katrina Hurricane. There is an uproar about the use of the category "refugee" in reference to African Americans. See the article by Nina Bernstein, "Refugee Groups Reaching Out to Victims of Hurricane," *New York Times*, 18 September 2005.
2. See the works of Jake Miller, *The Plight of Haitian Refugees* (Westport, CT, 1984); Alex Stepick, "The Refugees Nobody Wants: Haitians in Miami," in *Miami Now! Immigration, Ethnicity, and Social Change*, ed. Guillermo J. Grenier and Alex Stepick (Gainesville, FL, 1992), 57–82; and Nina Glick Schiller, Josh DeWind, Marie Lucie Brutus, Carolle Charles et al., "Exile, Ethnic, and Refugee: The Changing Organizational Identities of Haitian Immigrants," *Migration World* 15, no. 1 (1987): 7–11.
3. See Jacqueline Charles, "South Florida Haitians Split on Tactics: Talk of Nation's Political Crisis at Issue," *Miami Herald*, 27 January 2003.
4. See the 2000 report of Amnesty International on Human Rights abuses in Haiti, *Haitian Abuses of Human Rights: Political Violence as the 200th Anniversary of Independence Approaches* (October 2003).
5. Since the 1960s the Haitian migration flows comprise many types of population movement from political exiles to documented/undocumented migrants. See the works of Carolle Charles, "Different Meanings of Blackness: Patterns of Identity among Haitian Migrants in NYC," *Cimarron* 3, no. 1 (1990): 129–39; "Transna-

tionalism in the construct of Haitian Migrants Racial Category of Identity in New York City," in *Towards a Transnational Perspective on Migration*, ed. Nina Glick, Linda Basch, and C. Blanc-Szanton, in *Annals of the New York Academy of Science* 645 (1992): 101–24; "Haitian Life in New York City," in *The Immigrant Left*, ed. Paul Buhle and Dan Georgakas (Albany, NY, 1995), 289–302; Josh DeWind and David H. Kinley, *Aiding Migration* (Boulder, CO, 1988); Michel Laguerre, *American Odyssey: Haitians in New York City* (Ithaca, NY, 1984); Laguerre, "Haitian Immigrants in the US: A Historical Overview," in *White Collar Migrants in the Americas and the Caribbean*, ed. Arnaud F. Marks and M. C. Vessuri (Leiden, Netherlands, 1983), 119–71; and Open Society, *Special Report: Haitian Boat People* (April 1997), online at http://www.soros.org/fmp2/html/haitian_full.html.

6. See Charles, "Different"; Stepick "The Refugees Nobody Wants"; and Miller, *Plight of Haitian Refugees*.

7. See Miller, *Plight of Haitian Refugees*, 60.

8. See Miller, *Plight of Haitian Refugees*; and Stepick, "The Refugees Nobody Wants."

9. See Michael J. McBride, "The Evolution of US Immigration and Refugee Policy: Public Opinion, Domestic Politics and UNHCR," Working Paper No. 3, New Issues in Refugee Research, *Journal of Humanitarian Assistance* (May 1999): 7.

10. The first Aristide government came into power in February 1991 with around 67 percent of the vote. His government was sent into exile until 1994 by a military coup in September 1991. Aristide was returned to power via a U.S. military occupation of 20,000 soldiers. In 1996, his first prime minister, Rene Preval, became the new president. In 2001 with less than 15 percent participating in the electoral process, Aristide came back into power.

11. See the Testimony of Cheryl Little on the Detention and Treatment of Haitian Asylum Seekers, U.S. Senate Committee on the Judiciary, Subcommittee on Immigration, October 1, 2002, online at www.hagcoalition.freehosting.net/, and click on Cheryl Little on left column. See also the "Statement on Haitian Refugees From Miami Archbishop, John C. Favalora," Florida Catholic Conference October 30, 2002. Website: www .flacathconf.org and click on Statements and January 2003.

12. Gil Loescher and John A Scanlan, *Calculated Kindness: Refugees and America's Half-open Door, 1945 to the Present* (New York, 1986), 8.

13. For a detailed analysis of the world-system concept see Immanuel Wallerstein, *The Modern World System: Capitalist Agriculture and the Origins of the European World-Economy in the Sixteenth Century* (New York, 1974).

14. See Carolle Charles, "Being Black Twice," in *Problematizing Blackness: Self-Ethnographies by Black Immigrants to the United States*, ed. Percy C. Hintzen, P. Rahier, and Jean M. Rahier (New York, 2003), 172.

15. See also the work of James Kettner, *The Development of American Citizenship, 1608–1870* (Berkeley, CA, 1978).

16. See Brenda G. Plummer, *Haiti and the United States: The Psychological Moment* (Athens, GA, 1992), 27.

17. See McBride, "The Evolution of US Immigration and Refugee Policy."

18. See Loescher and Scanlan, *Calculated Kindness*.

19. Ibid., 50.

20. Ibid, 68.

21. Ibid.

22. Grenier and Stepick, *Miami Now*; McBride, "The Evolution of US Immigration and Refugee Policy." See also Loescher and Scanlan, *Calculated Kindness*.

23. Ibid., 155.

24. Ibid, 189.
25. See Carolle Charles, "Different."
26. For an analysis of the political economy of the Haitian state with the changes entailed by the emergence of the United States as a world-capitalist economy, see Alex Dupuy *Haiti in the World Economy* (Boulder, CO, 1989); Roger Dorsinville, *Marche Arriere* (Montréal, 1986); Laennec Hurbon, *Culture et dictature en Haiti* (Paris, 1978); Michel Rolf Trouillot, *Les Racines historiques de L'état Duvaliérien* (Port-au-Prince, 1987).
27. See Trouillot, *Les Racines historiques*; and Hurbon, *Culture et dictature*, in particular.
28. Remy Montas, *Emploi et Chomage en Haiti: Analyse de la situation Actuelle et Perspectives pour 1998–2000* (Port-au-Prince, Mai 1998), 28.
29. See the various reports by the World Bank in Report No. 17242-HA, *Haiti: The Challenge of Poverty Reduction* (Washington, DC, August 1998), vol. 2. See also UNICEF, *La situation des enfants dans le Monde* (New York,1999); Pan American Health Organization (PAHO), *Health in the Americas/Haiti* (1998), Vol. 2.
30. See *Haiti: The Challenge of Poverty Reduction.*
31. See the various Human Rights reports of Amnesty among others: Amnesty International; "Haiti: Ten Years after the Coup, Some Human Rights Improvements Lost," http:www.amnesty.org/report2003/Hti. See also the various Press Releases of the National Coalition of Haitian Rights (NCHR): on July 29, 2002, "Haitian Coalition Disturbed by Recent Surge of Human Rights Violations: Recommends National Plan"; on December 3, 2002, "Haitian Coalition Expresses Grave Concern Over Violence and Growing Chaos in Haiti"; on July 28, 2003, "Haitian Coalition Condemns Recent Wave of Violence in Haiti," all at http://nchr.org/hrp/Haiti_office.
32. Interview of former President Francois Denis Manigat on Radio Tropical, a Haitian Radio Program in New York City (1 January 2003), author's translation.
33. See Stepick, "The Refugees Nobody Wants."
34. Ibid.
35. See Loescher and Scanlan, *Calculated Kindness*, 172.
36. See Stepick, "The Refugees Nobody Wants," 64.
37. See Loescher and Scanlan, *Calculated Kindness*, 175.
38. Stepick, "Miami: Los Cubanos Han Granado!" *NACLA* [North American Congress on Latin America]: *Report on the Americas* 26, no. 2 (September 1992): 39–47.
39. See Stepick, "The Refugees Nobody Wants," 65–67.
40. Testimony of Yolande Jean, cited in Paul Farmer, *The Uses of Haiti* (Monroe, ME, 1994), 4.
41. See McBride, "The Evolution of US Immigration and Refugee Policy."
42. Testimony of Cheryl Little, 2 (see note 11, supra).
43. Ibid.
44. See Stepick, "The Refugees Nobody Wants," 60.
45. See Miller, *The Plight of Haitian Refugees*, 94.
46. See Jacqueline Charles, "South Florida Haitians Split on Tactics: Talk of Nation's Political Crisis at Issue," *Miami Herald*, 27 January 2003; Madeline Baro-Diaz, "Haitian Communities in Miami Must Work on Their Unity," *South Florida Sun-Sentinel*, 7 Dec. 2002.
47. Steve Miller, in an article in the *Washington Times* on March 5, 2004, "Haitian Government spent Millions on lobbying U.S.," states that the Haitian government, while controlled by President Aristide and his party, spent $7.3 million between 1997 and 2002 lobbying the U.S. government. The paradox is that, as the article points out, most of the lobbying money, $5.38 million, went to the Florida firm of

Kurzban, Kurzban, Weinger & Tetzeli. Ira Kurzban was at the forefront in defending Haitian refugees in the 1980s and early 1990s.

48. This author was the chair of Dwa Fanm, one of the organizations that participated in the rally in November 2002.

49. See the NCHR press release of 21 February 2003, "Detainees Taste Freedom Thanks to New Haitian Legal Aid Fund."

50. During the 1970s and 1980s it was almost inconceivable to talk about naturalization. In fact, my dissertation dealt with the reluctance of Haitian immigrants "not to be black twice."

# 10

# The Creation and Maintenance of the Cuban American "Exile Ideology": Evidence from the FIU Cuba Poll 2004

*GUILLERMO J. GRENIER*

DURING THE PAST DECADES, Cuban Americans have attracted more than their share of attention from both the press and the scholarly community. Their visibility has exceeded the demographic reality. The slightly more than one million persons of Cuban origin or descent account for approximately 5 percent of the Hispanic-origin population of the United States.

Demographics aside, however, there are good explanations for the relatively conspicuous presence of Cuban Americans within the U.S. Latino population. Most of those explanations are rooted in three basis characteristics of the Cuban presence in the United States:

1. Cubans are primarily responsible for the growth and development of the third-largest Latino community in the United States. Their concentration in Greater Miami has created a Latino presence that accounts for over half of the total population of a metropolitan area that is frequently regarded as a harbinger of immigrant America in the twenty-first century.
2. The socio-economic selectivity of migration from Cuba during the past forty-plus years has created a community with relatively large numbers of professionals and entrepreneurs. This socioeconomic profile, although at times overstated, has had implications for the participation of Cubans in leadership positions within the national Latino population, especially in such visible sectors as media and government.
3. As a self-defined exile community, Cuban Americans have developed a set of political institutions and political culture that are sharply differentiated

from those institutions and cultures among other Latino groups. The political behavior of Cuban Americans has garnered considerable attention from the press, and many of the leading political figures and organizations of the Cuban-American community have been prominent at the national level in furthering the exile political agenda.

While the social science literature on this community represents a respectable bibliography, the attention has not been evenly distributed across the three basic characteristics outlined above. The first two, community dynamics and socio-economic adjustment, have attracted by far the most interest, while an understanding of many of the political dimensions of the community has largely escaped detailed analysis.

This is ironic, for political forces are at the core of the very origins of the contemporary Cuban-American presence in the United States. Furthermore, the press and the public have consistently focused much more on that third characteristic, in direct contrast to the situation in the scholarly literature. Whatever image most Americans have of Cuban Americans is probably constituted, more than anything else, by political features, such as staunch anti-Castroism, militancy, terrorism, political conservatism, and a predominant affiliation with the Republican Party. The anti-Castro characteristic of the community might well be considered to be its master status, establishing the limits and potentials for all group activity.

Yet, is this monolithic political profile of an entire community accurate? There are various attributes of the community that, upon reflection, caution us against making that assessment. First, when we speak of the Cuban-American community, we are speaking of a group that has had almost a continual flow into South Florida since 1959. This flow can be categorized into distinct waves, with different pull and push factors, that have found different receptions and acceptance in the region and that have had different modes of departure from the island. There is no reason to assume that members of all waves would harbor identical opinions. Moreover, a growing number of the members of the Cuban-American community in South Florida were not born in Cuba. If we refer to the Cubans immigrating to Miami as being composed of waves, the increasing numbers of U.S.-born Cubans are the rising tide of the Cuban community.

Despite this identifiable diversity, the community's political characteristics are considered uniform and dominated by an "exile ideology" established by the first wave of post-revolution migrants. The assumption is that the exile experience shaped the collective identity of those fleeing Castro's revolution, no matter when or how they came, and continues to shape the political identity of Cuban Americans, particularly when dealing with Cuba and U.S. Cuba policy.

There is evidence that the community is changing its political attitudes and perspectives. These changes seem to be driven by basic social characteristics of the community, which makes one think that the changes effectively constitute trends in the development of Cuban-American political cultures. Basic building blocks of the community, such as demographic composition and time of departure from Cuba, seem to be driving the forces of change while other equally significant dynamics are creating the cultural friction slowing down the process of change. In this latter category I include the political and economic dominance of the earlier waves of exiles as well as the length of time that members of the community have lived in South Florida, what I call "the enclave effect." While we have been gathering evidence for over a decade that leads us to cautiously signal a change in the ideological make-up of the Cuban-American community in South Florida, it is doubtful whether a completely politically homogenous Cuban-American community every existed. Even the early exiles had divisions among them as how best to deal with the Cuban Revolution and their role in this task.

In this essay, I will explore the issue of political diversity within the Cuban-American population of Miami-Dade (M-D) County by analyzing the attitudes of different cohorts of Cuban migrants on selected policies. We utilize data from the 2004 Cuba Poll, a telephone survey of 1,811 Cuban Americans in Miami-Dade and Broward counties conducted by the author and a colleague in the spring of 2004.[1] While the poll is broad and measures behavioral and attitudinal responses dealing with issues beyond our current concerns, it allows us to focus on a few variables that directly address some of the key elements of the "exile ideology" and its acceptance by the various waves of Cuban migrants. Following Lisandro Perez's description of the characteristics of the "exile ideology,"[2] we are particularly concerned with variables that measure 1) a commitment to an uncompromising struggle against the Cuban government, 2) the primacy of Cuba for Cuban Americans, 3) a lack of tolerance for debate and diversity of views towards Cuba, and 4) an overwhelming commitment to the Republican Party. These variables are measured using the wave-of-arrival characteristics of the respondents as the dependent variable in order to present an exploratory profile of the diversity of the Cuban-American community within the heart of the exile community.

## THEORIZING THE CUBAN-AMERICAN COMMUNITY

The first wave of Cubans, approximately 250,000, arrived from 1959 to 1964. As with most revolutions, the first people to be affected, and thus the first to leave Cuba, were those in the middle and upper classes.[3] The second wave of Cubans, about 300,000, arrived during the "freedom flights" from 1965 to 1973. The first two cohorts laid the foundation for the creation of a viable Cuban economic enclave in South Florida. The economic enclave founded by middle-class Cubans in these two cohorts accommodated all subsequent arrivals from Cuba and served as a magnet for immigrants from all over Latin America.[4]

The third cohort consists of those who came to the United States between 1974 and 1979, when the migration between the United States and Cuba was diminished. The third wave is also highly educated and includes more professionals than post-1980 cohorts.

The seven-year period of reduced migration came abruptly to an end during the Mariel Crisis of 1980. After Peru refused to turn over Cubans who, while crashing through the gates of the Peruvian Embassy, had killed a guard, the Cuban government withdrew the remaining guards and thousands of Cubans rushed into the embassy seeking asylum. Subsequently, Cuban officials opened the port of Mariel to allow all Cubans who wanted to leave the island to do so in an orderly fashion. While the exodus proceeded rather chaotically, 124,776 Cubans did leave from the port of Mariel, and most of them ultimately settled in South Florida.[5] Unlike the earlier cohorts, these 1980 Cubans lived most of their adult lives in Cuba's new revolutionary society. This has prompted some analysts to conclude that this migration included more individuals "pushed" by economic necessity rather than by political motives.[6] Although felons comprised less than 3 percent of the Mariel Cubans, this cohort received a hostile reception in the United States. Yet, in spite of the odds against them, they demonstrated patterns of adaptation similar to those of the Cubans who had arrived earlier.[7]

After the Mariel Crisis, the migration between the United States and Cuba was severely diminished from 1981–1989. The few Cuban Americans who came to the United States during this period of time constitute the fifth wave cohort. The sixth cohort consists of those who came to the United States between 1990 and 1995. After the fall of the Soviet Bloc in 1989, Cuba's importance to U.S. interests was reduced. However, in 1994 a large influx of migrants from Cuba facilitated the historic policy change that officially ended the preferential open door for Cuban immigrants and introduced the current "wet-foot/dry-foot" policy (immigrants found at sea are returned to the island, while those who make it to land are granted asylum), which characterizes the entry pattern of the seventh cohort, as well as established the minimum number of visas to be granted to Cubans on the island at 20,000.[8] The cohort is different from previous Cuban immigrants in that they left their homeland with tacit approval from the Castro government. Black and mixed race Cubans are more represented in this cohort as are many who considered themselves revolutionaries for many years until the opportunity to emigrate presented itself. Consequently, the cultural diversity within the Cuban community is now more extensive than ever.[9]

## 1. Uncompromising Attitude against Cuban Government

The embargo policy constitutes the most important uncompromising attitude against the Cuban government. The U.S. government has maintained some element of an embargo policy since 1959, despite mounting pressure in Congress to loosen it. In the view of hard-liners, the embargo has been the most important instrument for driving Cuba toward reform. But others suggest that the embargo contributes to keeping the country poor, thus hurting the people Cuban Americans are trying to help. This moderate perspective also encourages

**Figure 1**
**Cuban Migration by Wave of Arrival.**

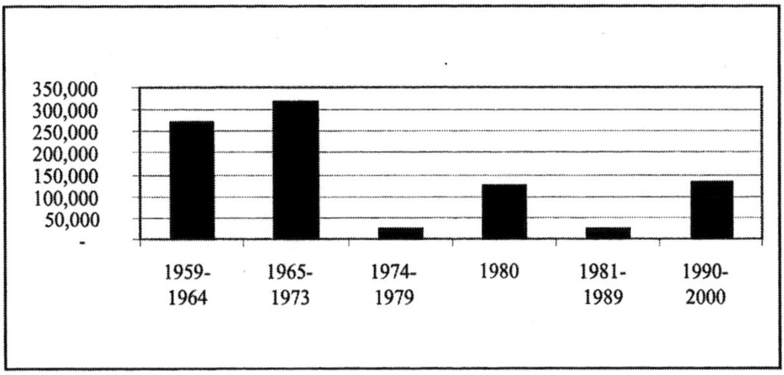

Source: Larry Nackerud, Alyson Springer, Christopher Larrison, and Alicia Isaac, "The End of Cuban Contradiction in U.S. Refugee Policy," *International Migration Review* 33 (1999): 176–92.

the initiation of a national dialogue among Cuban Americans and the Cuban government as well as the selling of medicine and food to the island. Some hard-line Cubans oppose the sale of medicine and food to Cuba, as well as starting a national dialogue, primarily because such assistance and recognition would serve only to sustain the Castro regime.

Table 1 suggests that not all Cuban Americans are in agreement about how to deal with the island, although most manifest a desire to maintain the embargo: 66 percent of all respondents favor continuing the U.S. embargo of Cuba. Yet, there are cohort differences even on this issue. The 1965–1973 sample exhibits the most intransigent views, with 78 percent supporting the continuation of the embargo, while only half of those arriving between 1990 and 1995 express a similar view.

However, there are significant differences among the cohorts in the support for some of the restrictions imposed by the embargo. Only 25 percent of all respondents oppose the selling of medicine and 35 percent oppose the selling of food to Cuba. In addition, while 56 percent of the community supports the establishment of a dialogue, strong feelings against such an initiative still exist among some cohorts. The 1965–1973 cohort weighs in with the strongest opposition to a dialogue (59%) and subsequent waves manifest a marked decrease from this highpoint. The 1995– 2004 arrivals are the most supportive of the establishment of a dialogue; only 23 percent of this group opposes the idea.

Prohibiting U.S. travel for pleasure to Cuba is another one of the restrictions imposed by the embargo. Table 2 shows that half of the respondents oppose unrestricted travel to Cuba and, as expected, there are differences among the wave cohorts. The strongest opposition is expressed by the first two waves of arrivals (72 percent and 71 percent in opposition, respectively), whereas the most recent arrivals (e.g., those who have the closest ties to the social environment of the island) are the most supportive of an open travel policy. As with other hard-line measures, far fewer of the more recent émigrés opposed unregulated visitation rights.

## 2. The Primacy of the Homeland

In the exile ideology, the affairs of the homeland represent the community's foremost priority. The public discourse is largely preoccupied with the political status of the homeland. A key element of any exile consciousness is the fact that the members of the community were forced out of their country; emigration was not a choice, as with so many other immigrants, but a survival strategy allowing them to live and fight another day. Seen in this light, emigration is part of an enduring conflict.

The importance of Cuba for the Cuban-American community is often ridiculed because, to the general public, Cuba often is seen as an issue far removed from more pressing foreign policy matters. For example, Miami-Dade County was the only county in the country with an ordinance preventing county funds from being used in any business activity involving Cuban nationals. In most situations, this prohibition was redundant given the federal trade sanctions currently in place, but the ordinance had a direct impact on local cultural organizations working within the legal limits of the federal trade sanctions. Organizations promoting cultural exchanges, musical or in the plastic arts, faced the prospect of having their county funds suspended, or at least publicly scrutinized, if Cuban artists were involved in local activities.[10]

This obsession with Cuba spills over into the political process in another way. Many Cuban Americans use the Cuba issue as a litmus test for evaluating candidates for local office. "If you want to run for dog catcher," said a Cuban-American patron at a sidewalk coffee stand, "you'd better take a hard-line position towards Cuba or you'll never get elected." While it may not be that extreme, it is true that Miami politics dances to a Cuban beat. As Table 3 demonstrates, a majority of Cuban Americans (54 percent) still considered a candidate's position on Cuba as "very" important when casting their vote. In this respect, the 1965–1973 sample exhibits the highest percentage among the various wave cohorts. The salience of Cuba falls dramatically among second-generation Cuban-Americans, only 33 percent of whom consider a candidate's position of Cuban issues as being "very important."

## 3. Lack of Tolerance for Debate and Divergent Views

The Cuban-American community has been formed by a particular set of political circumstances. Those circumstances have had a great personal impact on members of the community. Cuban Americans—as with exiles everywhere—are

## TABLE 1
## SOCIO ECONOMIC PROFILE OF CUBAN-AMERICANS IN SOUTH FLORIDA BY WAVE AND MODE OF ARRIVAL
### (CUBA POLL 2004)

| | Mean age | Median age | 1.5 Gen | College graduate and more | Household income below 20,000 | Household income 50,000 and more | Race: White | Gender: Female |
|---|---|---|---|---|---|---|---|---|
| *Wave of Arrival* | | | | | | | | |
| Before 1959 | 75 | 74 | 12% | 39% | 41% | 26% | 100% | 55% |
| 1959–1964 | 70 | 70 | 15% | 49% | 22% | 44% | 98% | 58% |
| 1965–1974 | 65 | 66 | 12% | 28% | 34% | 35% | 96% | 56% |
| 1975–1984 | 54 | 55 | 31% | 26% | 38% | 23% | 94% | 50% |
| After 1985 | 44 | 41 | NA | 30% | 38% | 17% | 91% | 47% |
| US Born | 34 | 29 | | 45% | 9% | 61% | 88% | 44% |
| *Mode of Arrival* | | | | | | | | |
| Flight to US | 57 | 60 | 20% | 32% | 36% | 29% | 95% | 57% |
| Flight from Other Country | 56 | 56 | 14% | 39% | 33% | 27% | 96% | 54% |
| By Boat | 60 | 51 | 13% | 25% | 33% | 23% | 93% | 37% |
| By Raft | 41 | 39 | 6% | 23% | 24% | 29% | 85% | 26% |

*1.5 Generation refers to those who came to the U.S. aged 1–14.

TABLE 2

MEASURES OF UNCOMPROMISING ATTITUDES TOWARDS CUBAN GOVERNMENT BY WAVE (CUBA POLL 2004)

| Measures for Exile Ideology | Cubans M-D and Broward | 1959–1964 | 1965–1973 | 1974–1979 | 1980 | 1981–1989 | 1990–1995 | 1996–2000 | Not Born in Cuba |
|---|---|---|---|---|---|---|---|---|---|
| In favor of continuing the U.S. embargo | 66% | 75% | 78% | 65% | 67% | 70% | 50% | 57% | 53% |
| Opposed to selling medicine to Cuba | 25% | 39% | 42% | 24% | 37% | 37% | 20% | 16% | 21% |
| Opposed to selling food to Cuba | 35% | 58% | 62% | 48% | 50% | 45% | 29% | 25% | 35% |
| Should not allow unrestricted travel to Cuba | 54% | 72% | 71% | 55% | 59% | 46% | 38% | 25% | 49% |
| Opposed national dialogue among Cuban exiles, dissidents, and representatives of the Cuban government | 44% | 55% | 59% | 46% | 48% | 46% | 38% | 23% | 29% |
| Against re-establishing U.S. diplomatic relations with Cuba | 57% | 71% | 75% | 66% | 57% | 63% | 45% | 29% | 44% |

## Figure 2
## Theorizing the Creation of the Cuban Community in Miami

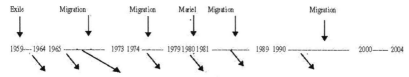

therefore not likely to be objective about the situation that has so intrinsically altered their lives and compelled them to live outside their native country. The emotional basis of the exile ideology is what makes Cubans in the United States take positions that others elsewhere judge to be irrational, as happened in the case of Elián González. Of course, many Cuban exiles will readily, and even proudly, admit to not being rational in matters that have touched them so deeply and will even flaunt their passionate lack of objectivity. One participant in a Miami demonstration carried a placard that read: *"Intransigente . . . ¿y qué?"* (Intransigent . . . so what?).

The least favorable side of emotionalism and irrationality is a traditional intolerance to views that do not conform to the predominant "exile" ideology of an uncompromising hostility towards the Castro regime. Those inside or outside the community who voice views that are "soft" or conciliatory with respect to Castro, or who take a less-than-militant stance in opposition to Cuba's regime, are usually subjected to criticism and scorn, their position belittled and their motives questioned. Liberals, the "liberal press," most Democrats, pacifists, leftists, academics, intellectuals, "dialoguers," and socialists are favorite targets. Any dissent within the community is especially difficult, since great pressure can be brought to bear on the individual or group. Moreover, intolerance of opposing views frequently has been a source of friction between Cubans and other groups and institutions in Miami. The exiles' inflexible anti-Castroism has frequently been criticized—and even ridiculed—by non-Cubans in Miami, especially when it manifests itself as attempts to censor cultural events in Miami by artists or intellectuals from Cuba.[11]

In an attempt to measure the perception of the public discourse surrounding Cuba in South Florida, respondents were asked whether they considered that all points of views on how to deal with Castro were being heard in Miami. Seventy-five percent of the total sample responded that all points of views were not being heard. As a follow-up, the respondents were asked what type of views was not being heard. Specifically, were hard-line or more conciliatory views not expressed in public discourse? Approximately 60 percent of respondents in all cohort categories perceived that the voice of stronger opposition to Castro was muted in South Florida's public arena.

**TABLE 3**

**MEASURES OF CONTINUED PRIMACY OF CUBA AND INTOLERANCE TO DIVERSE VIEWS BY WAVE (CUBA POLL 2004)**

| Measures for Exile Ideology | Cubans M-D and Broward | 1959–1964 | 1965–1973 | 1974–1979 | 1980 | 1981–1989 | 1990–1995 | 1996–2000 | Not Born in Cuba |
|---|---|---|---|---|---|---|---|---|---|
| Very Important: Political candidate's position on Cuba | 54% | 57% | 59% | 59% | 50% | 56% | 59% | 57% | 33% |
| Views Supporting Stronger Opposition Not Heard in Miami* | 60% | 59% | 58% | 52% | 68% | 52% | 58% | 65% | 65% |
| Registered Republican | 69% | 73.7% | 80.4% | 73.2% | 65.1% | 62.5% | 72.7% | 69.2% | 42.5% |

*Meaning those believing stronger anti-Castro views were being muted in Miami.

## 4. Support for the Republican Party

The primacy of the homeland explains the overwhelming preference for the Republican Party, a trait that sets Cubans apart from other Latino groups. Unlike most other Latinos, who have been traditionally Democrats, a majority of Cubans have traditionally voted Republican—due largely to the GOP's perceived strong stance against Fidel Castro.[12] Indeed, their initial attraction to the Republican Party has been motivated by their desire to influence policy towards the island, particularly during the presidency of Ronald Reagan.[13] Their high voter registration and voting rates are signaled as examples of Cuban Americans' unique political culture.[14] Their party preference stands in contrast with other Latino voters, and Cuban American voters in Miami have helped turn Florida into a bastion of Republicanism. They often play a crucial role in determining election outcomes there.

Registered Republicans far outnumber registered Democrats among Cubans in Miami in the year 2004, to the tune of approximately 69 percent Republicans versus 17 percent Democrats. In the mind of a typical Cuban American, loyalty to the Republican Party demonstrates the importance of international issues in the political agenda of Cubans. If a substantial number in the Cuban community disagreed with elements of the exile ideology, or if there were a greater balance in that agenda, with importance given to purely domestic issues, the Democratic Party would have made greater inroads.

In fact, if Cuban Americans were to view themselves as immigrants in this country, rather than as political exiles, and made judgments about political parties based upon their needs and aspirations as immigrants in the United States, they would be Democrats in overwhelming numbers. This would be true not only because of the general social agenda of the Democrats but also because of the specific experience of Cuban migration. The measures that have greatly facilitated Cuban immigration and the adjustment of Cuban Americans in the United States all have been enacted by Democratic administrations: the Cuban Refugee Emergency Program and its resettlement efforts, the assistance given to the Cuban elderly and the dependent, the establishment of the Airlift or Freedom Flights, and permission for the Mariel boatlift to take place, among others. The fact that Cubans are overwhelmingly Republican is therefore a testimony to the importance of homeland issues and the perception that Republicans are more in tune with the anti-Castro agenda.

As Table 3 shows, 69 percent of Cuban immigrants registered as Republicans, but there exist significant differences among wave cohorts. While there are some differences between the sample groups, most migrants from the island, regardless of time of arrival, exhibit an impressive level of allegiance to the Republican Party. Those Cuban Americans born outside the island, however, are less likely to register as Republicans. This could signal a significant shift in the political power of the community in the near future.

The commitment to the Republican Party by the earlier cohorts can have a significant impact on elections. Their turnout in presidential elections can be as high as 90 percent, while only between 50 and 60 percent of recent younger cohorts vote.[15] The early exiles also have an inordinate influence on the Cuba debate and policy because of their high level of registration and voting activity. Because of this, a policy like the one implemented in 2004 by the White House to curtail trips and remittances can be implemented with minimal political risks. Consider the following: 28 percent of Cubans living in South Florida arriving before 1974 have traveled to Cuba and 38 percent send money every year. Of those arriving after 1985, 45 percent have traveled to the island and 75 percent send money yearly. Now consider that 93 percent of Cubans in South Florida arriving before 1974 are U.S. citizens, and of these 94 percent are registered to vote. Of those arriving after 1985, only 23 percent are citizens, making their registration figure of 82 percent relatively insignificant.

## DISCUSSION AND CONCLUSION

Although the exile ideology persists and dominates, not all Cuban Americans can be painted with the same brush. The fact is that Cuban Americans are a diverse population or at least not the political monolith so often portrayed.

Departures from the traditional exile ideology began to manifest themselves at the end of the Cold War. With the fall of the Berlin Wall, Cuban exiles who long had struggled to overthrow an entrenched socialist regime now had in Eastern Europe an operational model of how such a thing might be accomplished. Rather than an overnight "rupture" scenario traditionally envisioned by the exiles, the new model involved an evolution that might be led by elements from within "the system," a process that could be helped by openness rather than hostility and isolation. Consequently, some Cuban Americans, including some traditional hard-liners, began to espouse a strategy of promoting a relaxation of tensions with Havana and engaging elements within Cuba. The rise of this new orientation led in the 1990s to the establishment of several organizations that, in different ways, conceptualized anti-Castro activism in more moderate terms, espousing an elimination of hostility and emphasizing constructive relations with the Cuban government. These new organizations have been committed to a peaceful transition to democracy that would not be based on confrontation and hostility.

These developments served to broaden the ideological spectrum of Cuban exile politics, creating new voices that argued against a continuation of the current U.S. policy. Although these new elements thus far have failed to gain predominance within the community, they have served to challenge what had been a monolithic image of exile politics, providing support for initiatives that challenge the traditional course of U.S.-Cuba relations.

The 1994 and 1995 migration accords between the United States and Cuba raised the ceiling for Cuban migration to the States. Since then, over 20,000

Cubans have come each year in an authorized fashion, in addition to the smaller number who arrive through unauthorized means. In addition to the new arrivals, two other important sectors of the Cuban population of the United States tend to add diversity to the political culture: the new generations and those living outside of Miami. The FIU poll shows that members of the second generation born in the United States are much more conciliatory in their views towards island politics than their parents. The same is true of Cubans who do not live within the insularity of the Miami enclave and are therefore less likely to have maintained an exile ideology. For example, according to the 1995 poll, Cubans living in New Jersey are more likely to favor a dialogue with the Castro regime than those living in Miami. Similarly, New Jersey Cubans are less likely to be influenced by a candidate's position on Cuba as they cast their vote in local and national elections. As the process of concentration in South Florida continues, the arrival in Miami of Cubans who have lived elsewhere in the United States adds still another source of pluralism to the political landscape.

And yet, despite the obvious attitudinal diversity of the Cuban-American population regarding Cuba policy, or perhaps because of this diversity, the persistence of certain hard-line attitudes still requires examination. The continued support for the embargo, for example, seems to be impervious to pragmatic policy considerations. It seems that support for the embargo underscores another trait of the political culture of Cubans in the United States: the importance of emotion over pragmatism. While admitting that the embargo may be ineffective and, further, while even recognizing that lifting it may well bring about significant changes in Cuba, a majority in the Cuban community continues to oppose any such softening of U.S. policy because of its symbolism. If the American government abandons its hard-line stance against Cuba, the argument goes, Fidel Castro will have "won" the forty-year struggle. It is therefore a struggle that is based not so much on pragmatism as it is on emotion.[16]

Ultimately, the Cuban-American story in the United States is a paradoxical one. On the one hand, Cuban Americans are held up as examples of the "immigrant success story." As an immigrant chronicle, the Cuban-American story is one of achievement and victories. It is the story of an immigrant group that has made unprecedented gains in empowering themselves in the new country. The well-documented economic success, as well as equally impressive achievements through the ballot box, has resulted in the creation of a solid ethnic enclave in a region that is often considered to be the harbinger of the multi-ethnic American future. These achievements have earned praise and respect from others and have created a positive image of Cuban Americans as strong entrepreneurs with extraordinary political influence in South Florida.

However, the Cuban-American identity is not an immigrant one, but one of exiles. As exiles, Cuban Americans often behave in ways that the rest of the country finds unreasonable and even irrational. The exile story is one of the relentless and enduring pursuit of the exile goal of recovering the homeland by triumphing over the regime, or more accurately, the person, who is responsible for their exile. That pursuit has frequently led to unfortunate episodes and behaviors, most evident during the Elián González saga, in which Cuban Americans were heavily criticized, viewed with derision, and ridiculed by many non-Cubans in Miami and throughout the nation. It is a story of frustration, misunderstandings, and resentment.

The contrast of the two stories (economic successes and the Elián González episode) is ironic. The core of the identity of Cubans in the United States, I have stressed, is as exiles, not immigrants. If the goal of exiles is to recover the homeland and the job of immigrants is to adjust economically and empower themselves in the new country, then we can reach the conclusion first formulated by our colleague, Max Castro: Cubans in the United States have been a failure at what they say they are, and a success at what they say they are not.

## NOTES

1. The 2004 Cuba Poll was conducted by Guillermo Grenier and Hugh Gladwin at Florida International University with a sample of 1,811 residents of Miami-Dade and Broward counties of Cuban descent generated from telephone survey using standard random-digit-dialing procedures that ensured that each residential phone had an equal chance of being chosen for the sample.

2. Lisandro Pérez, "Cuban Miami," in *Miami Now!: Immigration, Ethnicity, and Social Change*, ed. S. Guillermo J. Grenier and Alex Stepick III (Gainesville, FL, 1992), 1–17.

3. Susan Eckstein and Lorena Barberia, "Grounding Immigrant Generations in History: Cuban Americans and Their Transnational Ties," *International Migration Review* 36 (2002): 799–837; María Cristina García, *Havana USA: Cuban Exiles and Cuban-Americans in South Florida, 1959–1994* (Berkeley CA, 1996); Grenier and Stepick, "Introduction," in *Miami Now!*, ed. Grenier and Stepick, 1–17; and Louis A. Pérez, *Cuba and the United States* (Athens, GA, 1990).

4. Garcia, *Havana USA*, 5.

5. Grenier and Stepick, "Introduction," in *Miami Now!*, ed. Grenier and Stepick, 1–17; Larry Nackerud, Alyson Springer, Christopher Larrison, and Alicia Issac, "The End of Cuban Contradiction in U.S. Refugee Policy," *International Migration Review* 33 (1999): 176–92; Silvia Pedraza, "Cuba's Refugees: Manifold Migration," in *Origins and Destinies: Immigration, Race, Ethnicity in America*, ed. Silvia Pedraza and Rubén Rumbaut (Albany, NY, 1996), 263–79; Perez, *Cuba and the United States*; and Gerald E. Poyo, *With All and for the Good of All: The Emergence of Popular Nationalism in the Cuban Communities of the United States, 1848–1898* (Durham, NC, 1989).

6. Eckstein and Barberia, "Grounding Immigrant Generations in History."

7. Garcia, *Havana USA*; Silvia Pedraza-Bailey, Political and Economic Migrants in America: Cubans and Mexicans (Austin, TX, 1985); and Alejandro Portes and Alex Stepick, *City on the Edge: The Transformation of Miami* (Berkeley, CA, 1996).

8. Nackerud et al., "The End of Cuban Contradiction."

9. García, *Havana USA*.

10. Although the ordinance was judged unconstitutional in 2000, support for it did not go away. When asked in the FIU Cuba Poll 2000 if they supported the principles

of the revoked ordinance, 49 percent of Cuban Americans in Miami-Dade said that they did, as compared to 25 percent of non-Cubans.

11. Guillermo J. Grenier and Lisandro Peréz, *The Legacy of Exile: Cubans in the United States* (Boston, 2003).

12. Matt Barreto, Rodolfo O. de la Garza, Jongho Lee, Jaesung Ryu, and Harry P. Pachon, *A Glimpse Into Latino Policy and Voting Preferences* (Claremont, CA, March 2002); and Peréz, in "Cuban Miami," in *Miami Now!*, ed. Grenier and Stepick.

13. Rudolfo De La Garza and Luis Desipio, "Overview: The Link Between Individuals and Electoral Institutions in Five Latino Neighborhoods," in *Barrio Ballots: Latino Politics in the 1990 Elections*, ed. Rodolfo de la Garza, Martha Menchaca, and Luis Desipio (Boulder, CO, 1994), 1–42.

14. Benjamin Highton and Arthur L. Burris, "New Perspectives on Latino Voter Turnout in the United States" *American Political Research* 30 no. 3 (2002): 285–306; and Mark Hugo, "Electoral Engagement among Latinos," *Latino Research@ND* [Institute for Latino Studies, University of Notre Dame] 1 no. 2 (2003).

15. Ivan Roman, "The Cuban Vote" *Hispanic* 9 no. 8 (1996).

16. Damian Fernandez, *Cuba and The Politics of Passion* (Austin, TX, 2000).

# 11

# Relief Dollars: U.S. Policies toward Central Americans, 1980s to Present

## ESTER E. HERNANDEZ

### INTRODUCTION

Although few Central Americans ever received refugee status, as nationals of countries designated by the U.S. government as critical to its "national interest" and foreign policy aims, they have received various temporary protections short of full legal status. These temporary measures were intended to allow them to work legally in the United States, with the expectation that they would return home when the political and economic situation in their countries improved. Despite these restrictions, Central Americans have grown in numbers and have formed vibrant communities that challenge the expectation of return to their homelands. Moreover, they have become key contributors to their national economies through the monies they send home. Their respective countries seek and admire the flow of dollars, while they fear the potential disruption to their economies should there be massive deportations from the United States. Meanwhile, most of these temporary residents are denied full membership in the U.S. polity due to their ambiguous legal status.

Through immigration control procedures, state structures seek to organize the newcomers' boundaries and define a space of their "own" as well as the proper credentials to enter and occupy it (e.g., visas, passports, work permits, etc.).[1] Decisions whether to issue these credentials, then, are a primary mechanism defining who is properly authorized to enter and reside within state boundaries. In the case of Salvadorans and Guatemalans, the U.S. government initially defined them as unauthorized immigrants, whereas many others, namely sanctuary movement activists and advocates, recognized their migration as a refugee flow.[2] Within a decade of the initial inflow, the status of Central Americans multiplied into unauthorized residents, authorized residents, asylum seekers, temporary workers, foreign- and native-born so that today sizable communities throughout the United States have formed, illustrating dynamic boundary-making processes which happen as the receiving state seeks to delineate its boundaries. While unauthorized migrants both partially occupy and challenge the state, they cannot fully escape its lines of demarcation.[3] Many Central Americans in this country occupy a paradoxical position as both a transnational labor force without rights of citizenship but also as heroic citizens of their countries who provide long-distance support for their families and nation.[4]

The monies that migrant workers send to their families who remain in Central America have gained in significance over the years, reaching an estimated four billion dollars per year,[5] an amount that constitutes a significant flow of cash[6] into their national economies that made possible, in 2001, the change to the dollar as legal currency in El Salvador. It is common for government officials and Central American nationals to remark on the fact that remittances have kept national economies "afloat" for many years. Indeed, remittances exceed the amount of development aid and direct investment, and they represent 14 percent of the GDP of El Salvador, 16 percent of Nicaragua's, and 3 percent of Guatemala's. Thus, in light of high unemployment and underemployment figures in the region, remittances alleviate the poverty of many families.[7]

At the same time, a great proportion of Central Americans work in the United States with looming threats of deportation.[8] At the Summit of the Americas during the Clinton presidency, Central American presidents even declared that their countries could not absorb large numbers of deportees.[9] In their appeals for non-deportation, the presidents pointed out that the remittances migrants provide their respective countries often exceed the monies those countries obtain through international aid and some exports. Since then, the appeals for non-deportation have emphasized the catastrophic potential if massive deportation were to interrupt the flow of remittances. The presidents of the region also argued that mass deportations possibly could exacerbate unemployment in the area, causing social unrest.[10] For its part, the U.S. government has granted temporary deportation relief, in lieu of relief aid, on the basis of maintaining stability in the region. Exact numbers of how many could be deported are difficult to determine, but estimates could reach over half a million. Over a million and half Central Americans were counted by the 2000 Census (1,686,937).[11] Currently, about 330,000 have short-term work permits, which is about 20 percent of the population counted by the U.S. Census.

The policies toward each of the Central American nations have been piecemeal, and they have underscored the status of these migrants as only temporary residents until conditions in their home countries improve. Largely denied recognition as refugees and denied the right of asylum once here, Central Americans (namely, Salvadorans, Hondurans, Nicaraguans, and Guatemalans) arriving in the United States in the late 1980s and 1990s were subjected to an *extended* experience of displacement because of the inability of over half million to travel back and forth to their home countries and the uncertainty of their stay in this country. While my informants did not refer to their situation in terms of displacement, their everyday lives, social relations, and reflections are marked by discontinuities in time and in place often due to their migration, the obstacles to their return, and/or their immigration status in the United States. Many times, they are in constant communication with their families and keep abreast of their everyday concerns but lack the immediacy of face-to-face interaction; many experience long-term separations from family members.

## BACKGROUND

When Central Americans began arriving in the United States in large numbers during the 1980s, they received great attention in the U.S. media, as the U.S. government made the region central to its foreign policy. As such, the president of the United States urged Congress to approve aid packages that included military assistance to the governments of those countries as a way to prevent millions of what he called "the feet people" from arriving at this country's doorstep seeking refuge should communism prevail in the region. Thus, for years, foreign policy supportive of those governments prevented the United States from recognizing that many of those Central Americans who did make it to its doorstep had legitimate claims to asylum. Throughout the 1980s, therefore, a large proportion of Central Americans arrived through the "backdoor," joining the ranks of "undocumented" workers. Their transition into U.S. society would be accomplished largely by self-help efforts—individual and collective.

By the 1990s, political advocacy by a broad cross-section of religious and political organizations proved key to a legal victory over the high denial rates of asylum toward Salvadorans and Guatemalans, notably in the lawsuit *American Baptist Churches v. Thornburgh*, which rectified a U.S. policy regarding asylum applications and permitted several thousand Central Americans to reapply (hereafter the ABC provisions). Additionally, in 1990, the attorney general could, for the first time, grant a temporary status, in lieu of asylum or refugee status, which has become known as Temporary Protected Status (TPS) since being included in the November 1990 Immigration Act.

The TPS designation grants safe haven to people fleeing life-threatening conditions (e.g., civil wars and natural disasters) in their countries of origin. It was first granted to Salvadorans in 1991; they could get a permit to work and relief from deportation during a designated time period. Although Guatemalans were also facing the same conditions in their country, they were not granted TPS status along with Salvadorans. This underscores the fact that the U.S. government did not want to acknowledge that Salvadorans and Guatemalans were fleeing governments that it supported in civil wars that it denied were occurring. One year after TPS was granted to Salvadorans, there was a negotiated end to the civil war in El Salvador; it would take at least four more years for the civil war to end in Guatemala. Thus, the difference in treatment of two adjacent countries with similar problems in part reflects U.S. policy differences in its emphasis on resolving the armed conflict in El Salvador as opposed to that in Guatemala, which would take a few years longer to settle.

Since first granted in 1991, the TPS program that benefited Salvadorans has been renewed many times over the years under different administrative names and allowed those who registered to obtain work authorizations. Through the ABC settlement, Guatemalans who re-filed asylum applications were eligible to obtain work permits throughout the years while their cases were being processed. Recently, the TPS program was used again in 1998 and once more in 2001. This time, TPS was granted as a relief measure following the natural disasters suffered by Nicaragua, El Salvador, and Honduras (but excluding Guatemala). Since these programs have been renewed over several years, they have reinforced a sense of temporariness in terms of the recipients' residence in the United States.[12]

Ironically, through their labor earnings abroad, the émigrés earn credit for keeping their home economies afloat, while their temporary status positions them within the politics of the United States as neither refugees nor immigrants. Such countries as El Salvador, Guatemala, and Honduras increasingly rely on the high volume of remittances from émigrés, and this status, albeit ambiguous, allows Central Americans already in the United States to be economic providers, making them a national resource as exported labor at a time when their nations' economies are losing revenues from traditional export commodities, especially coffee. The case of Central America illustrates a trend toward substituting international migration to First World countries in lieu of sustainable development strategies in the Third World.[13] At the same time, through legal distinctions in U.S. immigration law, Central Americans become simultaneously subject to admission processes and instrumental to strategies of promoting development through remittances.

In the following discussion, the issue of temporary status is key to understanding the consequences of the high levels of remittances to the Central American region. To better appreciate the great importance of remittances and how they might be affected by the proportion of those without legal status who might be subject to deportation, let us look at the trajectory of the largest group of Central Americans, Salvadorans. The following summary (see Figure 1) is derived from data from the *Statistical Yearbook Immigration and Naturalization Service*. For example, for the period 1987–1997, some 326,400 Salvadorans were admitted into the country as legal residents. In prior decades, the number of Salvadorans entering the country legally had averaged about 10,000 per year, but during the years 1989 through 1990 there was a dramatic increase (five-fold in 1989 and eightfold in 1990). In 1992, however, there was a 67 percent *decrease* from the 1990 figure. This decrease was due in part to the end of the civil war in El Salvador, but even more to the sharp drop in the number receiving amnesty under

# Figure 1

## 1987-2004
## INS Statistics, El Salvador

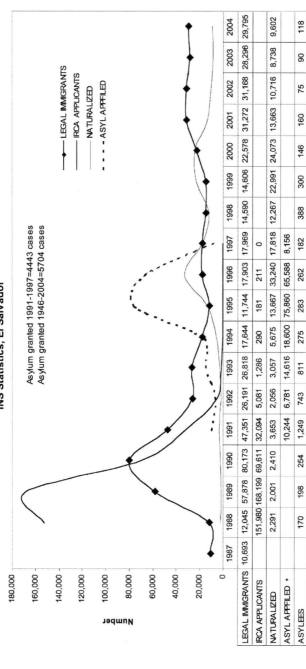

Asylum granted 1991-1997=4443 cases
Asylum granted 1946-2004=5704 cases

Legend:
- LEGAL IMMIGRANTS
- IRCA APPLICANTS
- NATURALIZED
- ASYL APPFILED

| | 1987 | 1988 | 1989 | 1990 | 1991 | 1992 | 1993 | 1994 | 1995 | 1996 | 1997 | 1998 | 1999 | 2000 | 2001 | 2002 | 2003 | 2004 |
|---|---|---|---|---|---|---|---|---|---|---|---|---|---|---|---|---|---|---|
| LEGAL IMMIGRANTS | 10,693 | 12,045 | 57,878 | 80,173 | 47,351 | 26,191 | 26,818 | 17,644 | 11,744 | 17,903 | 17,969 | 14,590 | 14,606 | 22,578 | 31,272 | 31,168 | 28,296 | 29,795 |
| IRCA APPLICANTS | | 151,980 | 168,199 | 69,611 | 32,094 | 5,081 | 1,286 | 290 | 181 | 211 | 0 | | | | | | | |
| NATURALIZED | | 2,291 | 2,001 | 2,410 | 3,653 | 2,056 | 3,057 | 5,675 | 13,667 | 33,240 | 17,818 | 12,267 | 22,991 | 24,073 | 13,663 | 10,716 | 8,738 | 9,602 |
| ASYL APPFILED * | | | | | 10,244 | 6,781 | 14,616 | 18,600 | 75,860 | 65,588 | 8,156 | | | | | | | |
| ASYLEES | 170 | 198 | | 254 | 1,249 | 743 | 811 | 275 | 283 | 262 | 182 | 388 | 300 | 146 | 160 | 75 | 90 | 118 |

Year

Number

* Includes ABC & TPS Applicants

Source: *Statistical Yearbook of the Immigration and Naturalization Service* up through 2001 and Department of Homeland Security, *Yearbook of Immigration Statistics* thereafter.

the 1986 Immigration Reform and Control Act. As of 1989, some 168,200 had applied for amnesty under IRCA, of whom 155,200 were admitted to permanent residence between 1989 and 1995. Over 145,200 were processed in the three peak years of 1989–91—making up 79 percent of all Salvadorans admitted in those three years. In 1992 the IRCA figure then plummeted from 32,000 the prior year to under 5,100.[14] From 1994–1999 there were an average of 15,743 legal immigrants and from 2000–2004 the average has been 28,621. The legal status of the population is complex and diverse.

The IRCA amnesty program established eligibility based on being in the country by January 1, 1982, or by working in agriculture for specified time periods through the Special Agricultural Workers provision, known as SAWI (1983–1986) and SAWII (1987–1988). Out of the 168,200 Salvadoran IRCA applications, the SAWI and SAWII programs received a total of nearly 25,000. Indicative of when many had begun arriving in significant numbers, there were fewer than 1,800 applicants under SAWI but over 23,200 under SAWII. As Figure 1 indicates, the high number of IRCA applicants also soon would lead to some increase in the number of legally admitted immigrants under the family reunification provisions of the Second Preference (spouses and minor children of resident aliens). The 1986 law thus provided avenues for legalization for those previously unable to avail themselves of family, employment, or refugee provisions in the immigration laws. Even so, many Salvadorans were not eligible under this law, because they arrived after the cut-off arrival date. By the time those able to get amnesty under IRCA had their status adjusted to permanent residence, they had been residing in this country for eight or more years.

As also noted in Figure 1, in addition to the IRCA applications, the INS received unprecedented numbers of asylum applications from Salvadorans and Guatemalans but approved few. The overall approval rate for asylum during the years 1973–1997 was about 23.6 percent of total cases received for all nationalities, and the great majority of those admitted involved individuals fleeing from left-wing governments.[15] For the various other organizations that advocated recognition of Central American as refugees, asylum denials seemed unjustifiable because many of the asylum claims met prima facie requirements.[16] Therefore, as noted above, the American Baptist Church, along with other advocates, filed suit against the INS, charging that Guatemalan and Salvadoran applicants were treated unfairly compared to those of other nationalities, namely those from Communist countries, who were more likely to be granted favorable asylum decisions. The 1991 agreement allowed asylum applicants from Guatemala and El Salvador to re-file their applications for asylum, with the Attorney General implementing the Temporary Protected Status program (hereafter TPS) provided for in the 1990 law.

This ABC agreement sought to address the disparities in asylum procedures for Central Americans and to acknowledge that nationals from El Salvador and Guatemala had fled civil war. The TPS recognized a temporary refugee status for Salvadorans in the country by September 1991 that lasted through 1995 under various names. After the TPS program ended, many people had the option to re-file asylum applications (note the surge in the application figures for 1994–1996), at which time they continued to obtain work authorizations.

As Figure 1 shows, from 1991–1997 asylum applications from El Salvador totaled 199,845. The INS received the highest number of applications in 1994–1996, when TPS expired and many filed asylum petitions. The asylum program has had a notorious backlog and many applications filed in the early 90s were not processed for years. To address the asylum backlog, the U.S. Congress in 1996 mandated reform that was to speed up the process of asylum applications by prioritizing them: the latest applications received were to be processed first. As a result, many Central Americans remained "in limbo" about their legal status. Nevertheless, many had work permits that were renewable every twelve or eighteen months under the TPS provisions or due to pending asylum petitions.

Therefore, in 1997, another program, called NACARA (Nicaraguan Adjustment and Central American Relief Act), was passed by Congress to address the backlog in ABC claimant cases introduced above. ABC claimants had not received timely reviews of their cases. The act tried to acknowledge the disparity in approvals, the backlog, and the fact that many ABC claimants of Salvadoran and Guatemalan nationality would be excluded under the new immigration changes legislated in the 1996 Immigration Act. Under the NACARA legislation, however, Salvadorans and Guatemalans did not receive the same benefits as Nicaraguan and Cuban nationals, who were able to adjust their status under less stringent procedures. The latter two were presumed to meet the hardship requirements as a group, while Salvadorans and Guatemalans had to show evidence on a case-by-case basis. Cubans and Nicaraguans who benefited from NACARA included people who arrived in the United States as late as 1995; moreover, it extended benefits to their family members (i.e., children and spouses). While Nicaraguans and Cubans and their families received a form of amnesty, NACARA excluded Hondurans, and initially Haitians, from benefits. Due to these uneven conditions, the Clinton administration and its INS commissioner said that they would administratively grant "extreme hardship" presumptions for NACARA applicants, stating the following:

> Their "temporary" stay has been authorized by a series of statutory, administrative and judicial actions. During this time, most have developed deep roots in and made significant contributions to the United States. These common characteristics strongly predict that the removal of individuals who are members of the ABC class would cause extreme hardship. . . .[17]

That meant that the INS would consider their applications as fulfilling the extreme hardship conditions de facto: if the applicants were granted an interview, most likely the case would be approved. Nevertheless, by 2001 this program also was plagued by backlogs because its administration fell under the asylum office of the INS (now the Citizenship and Immigration Service, or CIS).

The process of filing renewals is often perplexing for applicants. Even NACARA eligible applicants have to go through the process of work renewals while their applications are processed. Commenting on the need to renew permits every year, Gladys, a woman who was excited about the possibility of becoming a permanent resident through the NACARA program, told me:

> I've been waiting and waiting. I have been fingerprinted several times in the past three years and each time I thought the final appointment would happen soon. I give up. Who knows when I'll finally get my papers, but I think I have plenty of fingerprints!

Because they must do these renewals as long as their cases are not resolved, these experiences underscore their temporary status, reinforcing the importance of nationality inherent in processes that authorize them to take employment as laborers but deny them legal, permanent membership in the nation.

According to INS statistics for 2001, there were a total of 99,171 applications for NACARA benefits since the program began. Of those applications, 74,879 were Salvadorans (76 percent). Those 74,879 represent 37 percent of the total of about 187,000 potential beneficiaries (based on the ABC asylum applications estimates) of the NACARA program. In September 2001, according to a preliminary INS analysis, it was estimated that, in a worst-case scenario, it may take "up to 20 years" to deal with the NACARA backlog. The INS projected that, while 26,034 cases were granted between 1999–2001, in 2002 only 6,000 would be completed—although, in fact, 15,700 removals (in effect, deportations) were canceled.[18] In the meantime, NACARA did not establish an application deadline for Salvadorans and Guatemalans, and people had to continue obtaining work permit renewals every year to a year and a half while waiting for a resolution to their petitions.[19] The annual renewal ritual affected the 290,000 Central American applicants who were NACARA eligible, 82 percent of whom were Salvadoran and Guatemalan, and 10,000 Eastern Europeans. The backlog drains the resources of the applicants who must pay a fee every time their permits expire. Since the applicants often seek assistance in filling out applications, this process produces revenues to non-profit and for-profit immigrant service providers. Additionally, because these programs have been in place for years, the INS collects more fees per applicant as the backlog continues.

In addition, Nicaraguans, Hondurans and Salvadorans also have received TPS due to devastating natural disasters in their country. Hondurans (81,875) and Nicaraguans (4,309) received TPS as a result of devastating hurricane Mitch in 1998. After devastating earthquakes in El Salvador in 2001, the U.S. government extended a new TPS status provision (TPSII).[20] The Salvadoran TPS II program has 248,282 registrants whose status is also due to expire in 2006. Thus, their authorization to work will also expire in the same year. By the time these programs end, these latest cohorts of recipients will have resided in the United States for as long as seven years in the case of Hondurans and five years in the case of Salvadorans, after which they are expected to return home. An update of the data regarding Central Americans—Salvadorans especially—will shed some additional light on the impact of NACARA (1997) and yet the persistent policy discrimination against the Salvadorans and Guatemalans in particular:

1. Between 1998 and 2003, 344,796 persons born in Central America were admitted to the United States, of whom 142,510 were Salvadorans (41.3%).
2. Among those Salvadorans over 39 percent (over 56,300) were admitted under the provisions canceling removal/deportation orders (NACARA), compared with 22 percent of all Central Americans (75,200). That 56,300 equaled just 30 percent of the Salvadoran asylum applications pending in 1998.
3. In 1998 there were 185,000 asylum applications pending from Salvadorans and another 4,200 were filed between 1999 and 2003. While many were processed under NACARA, the approval rate for Salvadoran asylum applicants, 1999–2003, ranged between 7 and 11 percent versus 23 to 44 percent among all applicants. That low-percentage situation is just about the same among Guatemalans.[21]

To understand the magnitude of remittances, it is important to analyze how these monies are related to the temporary nature of a great proportion of Central American migrants. The economic impact of policies that have kept Central Americans restricted in their ability to circulate freely between where they work and live, even after conflicts in their countries removed the danger of return, is clearly evident in the volume of remittances and the market it has created. Since migrant lives and daily concerns occur in more than one geographic site, family relations and obligations traverse immediate concerns and long distance connections and relationships.[22] While migration splits families and households geographically, the linkage migrants maintain between home and host country is most evident in the aggregate amounts of money and goods or remittances sent to support family members—be it parents, siblings, children, or spouses and/or extended kin who remain "at home."[23] The proliferation of courier services, money-transfer agencies, and the market of "nostalgia" for homeland products are also indicators of these ties.

## THE CONTEXT OF REMITTANCES

The significance of family remittances is part of a larger process that began in the 1970s, and it is related to international aid as well. David Kaimowitz maintains that, along with international aid, family remittances helped transform the economies of Central America (see Figure 2). International assistance (or foreign aid) created a myriad of international actors and even affected the structure of the Salvadoran military, an institution largely financed by international aid.[24] Family remittances surpass and have even replaced economic aid from foreign governments, aid from non-governmental assistance programs, and revenue from exports, such as coffee in the case of El Salvador. Typically, on the macro level, governments keep track of official transfers and compare remittances to export revenue and to import figures. Combined, such figures affect the possibilities for investments and loans from foreign governments, multinational companies, and a host of other investors. In this way, on the micro level, the actions of immigrants on behalf of their family—or to accomplish the production and reproduction of families—are linked to national development. These remittances construct specific linkages between nationals abroad and the national economy, transforming the countries from producers for export into countries whose primary product has become migrant labor. In this process, the migrants essentially become economic resources, even if there are efforts to include them as citizens in their homelands. Their legal situation prevents their full integration in the United States and yet provisions to make them legal residents (e.g., NACARA) require that they show active involvement and employment.

In El Salvador, the income generated by coffee exports, the country's main trade product, has been declining at least since 1980. At the same time, remittance monies have been increasing. The cumulative effects of remittances are important not only for family trajectories, but also for the economic trajectory of the home country. For example, Figure 2 compares remittances (official figures only; missing comparable data for 1990–93) and coffee exports showing that coffee revenues have been in decline and that family remittances have

**Figure 2**

**Family Remittances and Export Income-El Salvador**

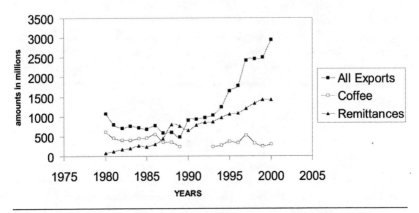

Source: CEPAL or ECLAC, Banco Central de Reserva, World Bank figures 1980–2000.

been steadily increasing for years. However, the graph does illustrate that total exports have been rising since the early 1990s.

While in El Salvador in February and March of 2001, I attended a seminar on migration issues at the Catholic University (UCA). The seminar participants and speakers were members of non-governmental and governmental organizations. One speaker, a member of the Salvadoran ministry of the exterior, said that remittance money is applied primarily toward household expenses, so it becomes difficult to earmark it for different purposes. This is a view shared by non-governmental organizations, as well. The government faces a great challenge in trying to "multiply" the remittances through projects that encourage migrants and their families to save and invest. Regardless of whether the monies are spent in investment projects, the government benefits because the macro-economic effects of the remittances—as Figure 2 illustrates—increase the circulation of cash in the country.

For immigrant families in the United States, the sending of remittances is an important activity that derives from family obligation related to notions of need, reciprocity, debt payment, and personal accomplishment. Much of the high volume of remittances is due to increasing numbers of migrants and split-family arrangements. Nonetheless, the level of individual remittances tends to decrease over time, which is likely related to the formation of new families in this country. Some studies estimate that migrants send between $700–$1,200 per year.[25] The recipients are expected to manage the monies well and to make them grow.

Remittances have changed the landscape of the country and they have even altered the economy, namely, from making possible a change to the dollar as the national currency to (re)creating entire towns linked to the flow of labor.[26] In these communities, economic activity revolves around the circulation of labor and goods made possible by the migratory movements of the 1980s that continue today. The fact that migration has transformed the economies of the sending societies is not a new phenomenon. Like earlier migrations, governments and families anxiously ask, "How long" will this flow of U.S. dollars continue? The answer, of course, depends on the dynamics of migration, family relations, the family lifecycle, and the outcome of U.S. policies regarding those present under time-limited TPS programs. In addition, while the Salvadoran government tries to figure out ways to keep remittances flowing, it seeks to define policies to confront the possible decline of such remittances, including 1) sustaining economic growth by increasing external debts; 2) moderating economic growth to keep external debt at low levels; and 3) promoting private and public savings to maintain economic growth and to limit external debt.[27]

Currently, national debates focus on how to promote sustainable small business growth from these remittances that are managed by individual recipients. These debates and anxieties about how to maximize remittances have focused on how to channel them through the banking system so that recipients can have access to credit and loans.[28] For a long time, the possible deportation of its nationals has been a major concern for the Salvadoran government should the TPS program suddenly be terminated. However, because its nationals have the longest relationship to the United States, there has been an expectation that they would get to remain either through an amnesty or other means (work visas, marriage, length of residence, etc.). Still, as the laws have begun to change and become more restrictive, it has become harder for Salvadorans to legalize their status. The possibility that these remittances might stop due to the precariousness of the legal status is of great concern given the increasing significance of the large amounts of money being transferred.

Remittances are seen as a positive fringe-benefit of migration, and even newspaper accounts describe them as a "gold mine" for the receiving governments. Douglas Massey and others have described the flow of dollars to Mexico as migradollars. For Salvadorans, a common way to discuss the same imagery is the "river of green" flowing with dollars North to South. However, this image may also be linked to less glittering and buoyant ones: The fear that the U.S. government might decide to deport undocumented workers to El Salvador, effectively cutting off the flow. Similarly, the possible return of undocumented workers is often described as an "avalanche" that surely would devastate the national economy. (In light of the devastating earthquakes in January and February 2001, the image is prescient.)

These images of money transfers contrast with how senders describe the tendency of the funds to evaporate like water, as both recipients and senders try to cover their household expenses (rent, transportation, utilities, and so on) on a monthly basis. Furthermore, for remittance senders, how much they send depends on the stability of their employment. Recipients have to carefully manage monies they receive. Alternatively, the hometown associations in Los Angeles, for example, are concerned that monies sent will not be usefully spent if directed into unproductive endeavors. The government, on the other hand, collects data on money transactions in order to acquire more investments. Thus, we can see that different actors assign a particular significance to remittances by focusing on various attributes. The impact of remittances, however, is structured by the Central American region's status as comprised of economically dependent countries and by the fact that many Salvadorans, Hondurans, and Guatemalans are participating in a transnational labor force with various levels of statelessness, ensuring that families remain spatially split for years at a time and that the flow of remittances will most likely be maintained.

Future migratory relationships between the United States and Central America will have to deal with the legacies of incorporation of unauthorized migration from the area. Incorporation has been difficult and fragmented, requiring grassroots activism and coalition building in order to overcome various forms of exclusion. Recently, the administration of President George W. Bush campaigned for the creation of a free trade agreement that would include the

Central American nations. He asserted that the trade policy would help solve the immigration problem since people who would have migrated because of the lack of opportunities now would have local jobs available to them. In support of the Central America Free Trade Agreement, he stated:

> If you're concerned about immigration to this country, then you must understand that CAFTA [Central American Free Trade Association] and the benefits of CAFTA will help create new opportunity in Central American countries, which will mean someone will be able to find good work at home, somebody will be able to provide for their family at home, as opposed to having to make the long trip to the United States. CAFTA is good immigration policy, as well as good trade policy.[29]

The challenge of the future will be to make sure that trade policies deal with migration issues simultaneously. While the North American Free Trade Agreement (NAFTA) appears to have put more people on the move, no provisions were made for migratory regulation, and in the dozen years following its inception, unregulated migration has continued to be a concern. CAFTA is likely to maintain similar patterns in the Central American region. While, at present, many Central Americans have temporary work authorizations, those temporary programs have been discriminatory in the sense that the U.S. government denied most Central Americans any legitimate claims to a refugee designation. The temporary protection programs do benefit many individuals but leave out many more. This has put the Central American governments in the position of trying to direct the massive remittances that they receive into sustainable economic results in anticipation of the eventual end of these programs. They face a great challenge because the monies go directly to recipients who in turn manage them on their own. As other scholars, notably Douglas Massey, have suggested for Mexico, structural changes need to happen that will allow for local economic initiatives, such as access to credit, loans, and investment for small business. This is highly difficult given the tremendous infra-structural problems these countries recently have experienced, even as they struggle to recover from the earlier decades of both civil war- and environmentally-related devastations.

## CONCLUSION

In summary, immigration policies position Central Americans outside membership in American society through the use of temporary programs that stop short of giving them recognition as refugees although granting them authorization to work. The U.S. government has utilized this program to be consistent with its foreign policy aims of maintaining friendly and stable governments in the Central American region while maintaining polices that exclude people fleeing such areas. The temporary protected status has allowed these workers to become providers for their national economies, in a sense becoming their countries' main export. It has turned these areas into major labor exporting regions. As the U.S. government has reduced its international aid to the region, the monies that documented and undocumented workers provide have become critical, in fact the main source of cash for families and a major fringe benefit to their homeland economies.[30]

## NOTES

1. John Torpey, *The Invention of the Passport: Surveillance, Citizenship and the State* (New York, 2000).
2. Susan Bibler Coutin, *Legalizing Moves : Salvadoran Immigrants' Struggle for U.S. Residency* (Ann Arbor, MI, 2000); Nora Hamilton, and Norma Stoltz Chinchilla, *Seeking Community in a Global City: Guatemalans and Salvadorans in Los Angeles* (Philadelphia, 2001); Cecilia Menjivar, *Fragmented Ties: Salvadoran Immigrant Networks in America* (Berkeley, CA, 2000); Sarah J. Mahler, *American Dreaming: Immigrant Life on the Margins* (Princeton, NJ, 1995).
3. Michael Kearney, "Borders and Boundaries of State and Self at the End of Empire," *Journal of Historical Sociology* 4, no. 1(1995): 52–74; Kearney, "From the Invisible Hand to Visible Feet: Anthropological Studies of Migration and Development," *Annual Review of Anthropology* 15 (1995): 331–61.
4. Ester E. Hernandez. "Power in Remittances: Remaking Family and Nation among Salvadorans" (Ph.D. diss., University of California, Irvine 2002).
5. The amounts of remittances are reported to the World Bank by the central banks of each nation. These numbers provide multilateral lending institutions a profile of credit worthiness. Therefore, it is possible that the figures may be inflated and overestimate the levels of currency entering the country.
6. See "Sending Money Home: Remittances to Latin America from the U.S," Report, InterAmerican Development Bank, 2004, http://www.iadb.org/mif/v2/files/map2004 survey.pdf, pp. 1–7. The report provides a picture of where remittances originate within the United States by state and amount sent.
7. Mario Lungo, Kay Eekhoff, and Sonia Baires, "Migracion Internacional Y Desarrollo Local En El Salvador," Report by Fundacion Nacional Para el Desarrollo (FUNDE) (San Salvador, May 1997).
8. David Lopez, Eric Popkin, and Edward Telles, "Central Americans: At the Bottom, Struggling to Get Ahead," in *Ethnic Los Angeles*, ed. Roger Waldinger and Mehdi Bozorgmehr (New York, 1996), 279–304.
9. Elizabeth Shogren, "Summit: Central Americans Will Be Treated Humanely under New Immigration Law [Clinton] Promises Region's Leaders," *Los Angeles Times*, 9 May 1997, 4.
10. Already, there are concerns about the deportation of persons with criminal records, particularly gang-affiliated deportees. Gangs have become a major social problem for El Salvador, Honduras, Guatemala, and Mexico. These gangs model and name themselves after gangs initiated in Los Angeles; and media reports depict these gangs as connected to each other and engaged in organized crime. See Robert J. Lopez, Rich Connell, and Chris Kraul, "Gang Uses Deportation to Its Advantage to Flourish in U.S.," *Los Angeles Times*, 30 October 2005, 1, 14–15.
11. U.S. Census 2002 figures show a count of 655,165 Salvadorans in the U.S., 377,487 Guatemalans, and 177,684 Nicaraguans. There are also 68,588 Costa Ricans and 91,723 Panamanians.
12. Ines M Miyares, Richard Wright, Alison Mountz, Adrian J. Bailey, and Jennifer Jonak, "The Interrupted Circle: Truncated Transnationalism and the Salvadoran Experience," *Journal of Latin American Geography* 2 (2003): 74–86.
13. See Sergio Diaz-Briquets, "Relationships between U.S. Foreign Policies and U.S. Immigration Policies," in *Threatened People, Threatened Borders: World Migration*

*and U.S. Policy*, eds. Michael Teitelbaum and Myron Weiner (New York, 1995), 160–89; and Aristide R, Zolberg, "From Invitation to Interdiction: U.S. Foreign Policy and Immigration since 1945," in ibid., 117–59.

14. Data calculated from Tables 8 and 22 in the *Statistical Yearbook of the Immigration and Naturalization Service* for 1989–1991 and Table 8 thereafter.

15. According to the *Statistical Yearbook of the Immigration and Naturalization Service* for 1989–1991, during the 1990s the largest asylum recipients were from Poland, Russia, Soviet Union, Cuba, Vietnam, Laos, Cambodia. In the 1980s and 1990s, there were more asylum recipients from China than from all Central American countries undergoing civil war.

16. Menjivar, *Fragmented Ties*; Mahler, *American Dreaming*. See also Coutin, *Legalizing Moves*; Hamilton and Chinchilla, *Seeking Community* 2001; and Aristide Zolberg, "From Invitation to Interdiction: U.S. Foreign Policy and Immigration since 1945," in *Threatened People, Threatened Borders: World Migration and U.S. Policy*, ed. M. Teitelbaum and M. Weiner (New York, 1995), 117–59.

17. U.S. Information Service, http://usembassy.state.gov/posts/gt1/wwwhimm4.html.

18. See *2002, 2003,* and *2004 Yearbook of Immigration Statistics*, Table 8. While 15,700 Salvadoran removals were cancelled in 2002, nearly 19,100 were in 2003.

19. INS Asylum Program, Preliminary Data as of 01 September 2001, "NACARA: Charts on NACARA handed out by INS Central Asylum Office at recent meeting with CBO's," NACARA listserv, the Immigrant Legal Resource Center, 09 October 2001 http://www.ilrc.org/listserv.php.

20. Ruth E. Wassen and Ester Karma, "Temporary Protected Status: Current Immigration Policy and Issues," Report of the Congressional Research Service (Washington, DC, 2005), 1–5.

21. For 1998–2001, see *Statistical Yearbook* of the INS, Table 8, as well as Table 29 (1998) and 27 (1999–2001). For 2002–2003, see *Yearbook of Immigration Statistics*, Tables 8 and 20 (2002) and Tables 9 and 18 (2003).

22. Basch, Linda, Nina Glick Schiller, and Cristina Szanton Blanc, *Nations Unbound: Transnational Projects, Postcolonial Predicaments and Deterritorialized Nation-States* (Langhorne, PA, 1994). Also see Mahler, *American Dreaming*.

23. Louis DeSipio, "Sending Money Home...For Now: Remittances and Immigrant Adaptation in the United States," Inter-American Dialogue Conference (Claremont, CA, 2000); Rick Chaney, *Regional Emigration and Remittances in Developing Countries: The Portuguese Experience* (New York, 1986); Segundo Montes Mozo and Juan Jose Garcia Vasquez, *Salvadoran Migration to the United States: An Exploratory Study* (Washington, DC: Hemispheric Migration Project, Center for Immigration Policy and Refugee Assistance, Georgetown University, 1988).

24. David Kaimowitz, "The "Political" Economies of Central America: Foreign Aid and Labour Remittances," *Development and Change* 21, no. 2 (1990): 637–55.

25. Rodolfo de la Garza, Manuel Orozco, and Miguel Baraona, *Binational Impact of Latino Remittances* (Claremont, CA: Tomas Rivera Center Policy Institute, 1997), 1–12; and see DeSipio, *Sending Money Home.*

26. Cristina Hasbun Merino, "El Salvador-Emigrantes Los Dolares De Los Emigrantes Transforman El Pueblo De Intipuca," Efe (News service), 4 August 2001.

27. Roberto Rivera Campos, "Remesas Familiares, Mal Holandes y Politica Economica" Boletin Economico y Social, Marzo 1996 FUSADES (Fundacion Salvadorena para el desarrollo social) (San Salvador).

28. Douglas S. Massey, Jorge Durand, and Nolan J. Malone, *Beyond Smoke and Mirrors: Mexican Immigration in an Era of Economic Integration* (New York, 2003).

29. U.S. Department of State, http://www.state.gov/e/eb/rls/rm/2005/48546.htm June 23, 2005).

30. As a postscript, on November 17, 2005, the U.S. Department of Justice, faced with a new surge of illegal aliens from El Salvador, filed a motion to make it easier to remove Salvadorans from the country. The Department of Justice (DOJ) sought to end an injunction requiring that the agency, before initiating deportation proceedings, notify Salvadorans fleeing civil war of their right to apply for political asylum (and thus desist from discouraging such applications). The DOJ maintains that the end of the civil war in El Salvador removes any further need to confer a protected status on Salvadorans. If granted, the action would permit the DOJ to initiate expedited removal proceedings. Anna Gorman, "U.S. Seeks to Lift Curb on Deporting," *Los Angeles Times*, 18 November 2005.

# 12

# The Social Construction of Difference and the Arab American Experience

*LOUISE CAINKAR*

## INTRODUCTION

THEORIES OF IMMIGRANT integration are a tough fit when it comes to Arab Americans. Arabs who migrated to the United States in the first decades of the twentieth century held structural positions and faced barriers of prejudice and discrimination largely similar to those of white ethnics (especially Italians).[1] Although they were barred from a broad range of institutions run by mainstream whites, they settled in urban and rural areas, ran businesses, worked in factories, built institutions, flourished artistically, held government office in a number of places, achieved a degree of economic success, and led social lives that were intertwined with members of white ethnic groups and often resulted in intermarriage. Of course there are meaningful exceptions to this simplification of history, and in specific localities, for example, the right of Arabs to naturalize was challenged.[2]

Nonetheless, the general profile of the Arab experience in the United States in the early part of the twentieth century displayed more social, political, and economic incorporation than that of racially excluded African Americans, Asians, Native Americans, and Latinos. It also was vastly better than Arab American experiences over the past thirty years, for substantial evidence indicates a widening social distance between Arab Americans and all other Americans. This social distance has been created and reproduced by institutions of power (external to Arab American communities), is measurable, and is manifested in government policies, mainstream cultural representations, public perceptions and attitudes, discriminatory behaviors, physical insecurity, and social and political exclusion. However, there are continuities between Arab communities past and present.

In both periods and throughout the intervening years, Arabs have been highly entrepreneurial, heavily engaged in retail trade, and have posted above average median incomes. Indeed, the first wave of Arab immigrants carved out occupational niches and established economic and employment patterns that continue to characterize today's Arab American communities. While from one perspective this economic stability may signal success, from another it could suggest blocked socio-economic mobility.

The differences in experience between past and present Arab American generations are due in part to religious factors. The earliest Arab immigrants more often were Christian than Muslim, while the reverse is now the case. But reducing historical changes in the Arab American experience to a Muslim-Christian dichotomy is not as analytically useful as it may appear. Currently, all major American Arab organizations, local and national, are staffed by members of both religious groups and share the same objectives: reducing discrimination, stereotyping, political exclusion, and ethnic vilification. Persons with Arabic-sounding names, whether Christian or Muslim, report experiencing job discrimination and anti-Arab comments, and persons with the "Arab/Middle Eastern" phenotype have been physically attacked regardless of religion. It is not clear that the American public has a differentiated view of the Christian versus the Muslim Arab; the utter simplicity of monolithic, anti-Arab messages has succeeded in precluding thoughtful distinctions. The negative experiences around which Arab American organizations have mobilized preceded by decades the September 11, 2001, attacks but they laid the groundwork for the collective backlash that followed them.

The deterioration in Arab American experiences over time also cannot be explained by economic factors, either of poverty or downward changes in the human capital of Arab immigrants, such as Alejandro Portes and Alex Stepick note with regard to the waves of Cuban immigrants who entered the United States.[3] The earliest Arab immigrants were predominantly uneducated Lebanese, Syrian, and Palestinian peasants, while since the 1950s Arab immigrants include highly educated Egyptians and Iraqis, predominantly entrepreneurial Jordanians and Yemenis, and better educated Lebanese, Syrians, and Palestinians. In 2000, the proportion of Arabs with high school diplomas and bachelor's degrees was higher than that of the total U.S. population, a figure that applies to every Arab nationality group.[4] Arab men and women working full-time had higher median incomes in 1999 than did the total U.S. population, a characteristic that applied to all Arab nationality groups except Moroccans and Iraqi and "Arabic" men.[5] At the same time, Arabs had higher poverty rates than did the total U.S. population (17% versus 12%). This difference, however, is explained largely by 1990s Iraqi refugees and to a lesser extent by more recent Palestinian immigrants fleeing continuing deteriorating conditions. While many newer Arab immigrants have low levels of education and job skills, the overall social class background and human capital of Arab immigrants certainly has not declined over time.

In the course of ethnographic research in metropolitan Chicago in the 1980s, I found that Palestinians who had migrated to the United States since the 1970s were more intentionally (and overtly) Palestinian than those who migrated before this time, and that cultivating a Palestinian identity was a major life theme for second-generation Palestinians born in the United States in the 1950s and 1960s.[6] These Palestinian Americans sought to reverse their parents' efforts to shed parts of their history as they achieved economic stability and accommodated to American society. Certainly, the social movements of the 1960s, the influx of new immigrants fresh from Palestine, and the expansion of Palestinian community institutions played a role in this identity formation, but they alone did not provide sufficient cause to loosen one's identification with being American. Rather, global events, the relationship of the U.S. government to them, and accompanying media depictions were more important predictors of the Palestinian American experience than were the viewpoints and customs of new immigrants or post-civil rights American institutional changes, which found Arabs largely excluded from both mainstream organizations and mobilizations of people of color. American media portrayals that have persisted since the 1967 Israeli-Arab War in depicting Palestinians as inherently savage, and the subsequent institutional silencing of Palestinian American and Arab American voices (whether Christian or Muslim), are sociopolitical projects that have fostered the institutional exclusion of Palestinian and Arab Americans and heightened their sense of otherness. Due to global events and the political agendas of powerful institutional actors, the assimilation process, as Richard Alba and Victor Nee recently redefined it, went into *reversal* as social distance and group distinctiveness became more relevant, not less, for Arab American communities.[7]

These historic achievements, continuities, and reversals of fate highlight the problem of understanding theoretically the Arab American ethnic experience over time. Evidencing neither Gans's theories of straight-line or bumpy social integration over the passage of decades and advent of new generations, nor Portes and Min Zhou's segmented assimilation, nor historic racial exclusion, Arab Americans *as a group* have experienced a major social shift from the margins of the mainstream to its outer boundaries.[8] One need only view television and film representations, consult public opinion polls, or spend time among Arab Americans, who strive to lead normal lives in the context of ever-present stereotypes and hostile images, to establish their current subaltern position. Negative perceptions of Arabs have been so widely held as to have created measurable harmful impacts on the character of the Arab American experience. At the same time, Arab Americans continue to evidence overall economic success. This seeming incongruity is explained by a combination of factors: the positive economic experiences of the earliest Arab immigrants, who did not face this type of social exclusion nor barriers of color, the high human capital of post-1950s Arab immigrants, the academic achievements of the second generation, and resources embedded in strong ethnic social networks.[9]

The Arab American experience does not fit dominant theories about ethnic integration in the United States because the conditions and variables these theories take into account were developed in earlier historic eras and largely concern domestic matters, while the Arab case is tied to more recent global political developments. Dominant theories do not, for example, consider that domestic institutional processes emerging from American global political interests can have long-term impacts on the social position of ethnic communities. This is perhaps because the negative experiences of Japanese Americans during World War II or German Americans during World War I were quite serious but relatively short-lived (compared to the many more decades-long Arab experience), and the incarceration of Japanese Americans came on the heels of decades of racial exclusion. In other global conflicts, domestic processes have centered on delegitimizing certain political ideologies (e.g., communism, anarchism, liberation theology) and establishing the hegemony of others (e.g., capitalism). Consequently, their social and policy impacts were largely felt by political organizations and activists, while the persons living under the rule of "enemy" ideologies were humanized and offered refuge. But when over a protracted period of time domestic institutions invoke essentialist constructions of human difference as their primary justifications for global political action, backed by power to assert their hegemony, their impact cannot but be felt by the human communities so construed.

The theoretical construction that best captures the Arab American experience over time is racial formation, as elaborated by Michael Omi and Howard Winant.[10] The structural exclusion of Arab Americans from a wide range of social institutions has evolved from a plethora of "racial projects"—in the media, arts, news, pedagogy, academia, civil society, political organizations, public policy, and popular culture—in which social constructions of the essential differences of Arabs (and later Muslims) have been put forth so extensively as to become widely accepted as common sense, as evidenced in public opinion polls. Winant has argued that public policies no longer can be legitimately sold to the public using racial typologies and stereotypes. Alba and Nee argue that the legitimacy of "overtly racist beliefs and practice have never been lower in the eyes of most Americans."[11] I argue that discourses, with socio-political objectives, that stress essential cultural and civilizational differences are nearly identical replacements for racist ideas and are alive and well in America.[12]

Arab Americans have been racialized using dominant discourses about their inherent violence, which are propped up with confirming images (such as angry mobs) in a process tied to the rise of the United States as a superpower and its *foreign* (not domestic) policy interests. This stigmatization threw Arab American communities off their previous course in American society as it re-created them as "others," as people who stand in opposition to Americanness because of their inherent values and dispositions. Arab opposition to Israeli military occupation and dispossession was constructed as illegitimate through recreating

Arabs as not only violent but also racist and anti-Semitic, another opposition to core American values. Later media fascinations with the question, "can Arabs be democratic?" follow in a similar vein, again positing that Arabs *by nature* hold values that clash with the essential values of the United States. Widespread American beliefs in the essential social and cultural differences of Arabs erected social boundaries around Arab Americans not of their own creation. Arab Americans conduct their lives in the context of negative representations and discourses, which intensify in parallel to U.S. involvement in the Arab region. With members of the American public they either must engage in reductionist debates about "Arabs" or keep quiet and confine their social relationships to persons who see through these omnipresent images. Arab American civic and political engagement is forestalled by this problematic situation as well as by institutional barriers erected under the pretext that their foreign policy perspectives are illegitimate and un-American. Limited social contact with persons outside of their own group further enhances social isolation.[13] Institutionally and socially isolated, their communities were easily held collectively responsible for the 9/11 attacks and then transformed into a threat to the nation.

Before turning to the Arab American experience and the process of constructing the Arab other, one final point must be made. In the 1990s, Arab American communities experienced another major shift when increasing numbers of immigrant and second-generation Arab Muslims became engaged in religious practice. While not every Arab Muslim underwent this change, which privileged religiosity over secularism, community-wide transformations in ethos and practice were dramatic and measurable and continue to this day. As with earlier shifts in identity and sense of inclusion in American society, this change was not explainable solely by the influence of new immigrants, although they gave momentum to it. Islamic revival was a global process that reached the shores of the United States through Muslim religious leaders, the Internet, satellite television, and return visits to the homeland, as well as through new immigrants. Its appeal to Arab Americans lay in its capacity to provide meaning and resilience for the Arab American experience, a historic role of religion in American life.[14]

In concordance with this global change, essentialized constructions of violent and backwards Arabs were extended nearly seamlessly to Muslims. The same representations were deployed, but instead of being about Arab culture they were about Islam and its "flawed civilization," as expressed in the clash of civilizations discourse popularized by Harvard scholar Samuel Huntington.[15] As Arab American Muslims became more religious, their differences from others in the communities in which they lived became more pronounced and more real. The evolving paradox, however, is that Muslims, as a religious group, are able to make stronger claims on American civil and political society than Arabs as a racialized ethnic group. The social inclusion of new religious groups in American society, resting on the foundations of freedom of religion, has been much easier to achieve historically than the social inclusion of negatively racialized groups, despite foundational assertions that "all men are created equal."

## CONSTRUCTING THE ARAB

Arabs have had a unique experience with social construction in America. In their one hundred plus year history in the United States, their social status has changed from marginal white to a more subordinate status that shares many features common to the experiences of people of color. Just as one can document and measure the process of becoming white,[16] a downgrading of the social status of Arabs in America through processes identified as racial formation is measurable: in public policies; mainstream representations; social patterns of discrimination, separation, and exclusion; and in self-identification. While the early Arab American experience (1880–1930) was largely similar to that of white ethnics as measured by residential, employment, and marital patterns as well as land ownership, voting, and naturalization rights (although there are some localized exceptions), the Arab American experience since the late 1960s has been decidedly different. After that moment in time, dominant themes of the Arab American experience have been exclusion, prejudice, discrimination, stereotyping, and selective policy enforcement, themes evidenced in scholarly research on Arabs produced during this period.[17] In the late 1970s, pollsters Seymour Lipset and Martin Schneider found attitudes toward Arabs "close to racist," and in the early 1980s Shelly Slade concluded that "Arabs remain one of the few ethnic groups that can still be slandered with impunity in America."[18]

Indeed, the most important, pan-Arab American organizations founded since the 1960s—the Association of Arab American University Graduates, the American Arab Anti-Discrimination Committee (ADC), the Arab American Institute, and the National Association of Arab Americans—had as their primary organizational objectives the reversal of these conditions of inequality and the dismantling of the propositions of innate cultural difference that lay at their root. One of the first historic studies of Arab American communities commissioned by an Arab American organization (ADC) noted:

At a time when the United States is more receptive to cultural pluralism, and ethnicity is no longer socially unacceptable, Arab Americans remain primary targets of defamatory attacks on their cultural and personal character. Thus, much of the activity of the Arab-American community has been directed at correcting the stereotypes that threaten to produce a new wave of anti-Arab racism in the United States and endanger the civil and human rights of the Arab-American community.[19]

The racial formation processes experienced by Arab Americans differ in both historical timing and pretext from that of other groups in the United States. Historically afforded some of the benefits and protections of whiteness, as in their eligibility for homestead lands, legal rights, and voting rights, Arab Americans' exclusion from social and political perquisites post-dates the historic exclusions of other negatively racialized groups. It cannot therefore be perfectly tied, in its genesis, to ideas about race and the superiority of whiteness that have existed since the founding of the United States. Rather, the fall of Arabs from the graces of marginal whiteness is traceable to the emergence of the United States as a global superpower. This socio-political relationship, although not framed in racial terms, is acknowledged in some of the earlier scholarship on Arab Americans. For example, Baha Abu-Laban and Michael Suleiman note that the source of bias against Arabs in the United States relates "more to the original homeland and peoples than to the Arab-American community."[20] In the 1984 ADC report noted above, domestic "images of greedy oil sheiks and bloodthirsty terrorists" are tied to political and economic events in the Middle East.[21] More to the point, "the source of today's defamation of Arab Americans might be described as the domestic counterpart of the Arab-Israeli conflict."[22]

Research on Palestinians in the United States showed how maintaining an American identity was fraught with conflict for Palestinian Americans, who were portrayed by the media as a culturally barbaric group, whose organizations were treated by the U.S. government as the enemy within, and whose story of dispossession was framed as a public discourse that was divisive, if not anti-Semitic.[23] The questions they were forced to ask themselves were: can one be American and America's enemy at the same time? Can one participate in American civil society while being excluded from its discourses? The Palestinian case exposed the racialized nature of the political discourse. Whereas the Soviet, Cuban, and Sandinista enemies were governments and political ideologies, the Arab enemy was Arabs—men and women imbued with innate cultural dispositions to violence and hatred.

The domestic transformation of Arabs from a marginal white to structurally subordinate status was facilitated by the flexibility of whiteness and the historic and "observable" racial liminality of Arabs (a concept that can be extended to South Asians and Latinos). But, at its core, the social and political exclusion of Arabs in the United States has been a racial formation process because Arab inferiority has been constructed and sold to the American public using essentialist constructions of human difference, resulting in specific forms of structural isolation. In the 1990s, when Islamist challenges to American global hegemony became more powerful than Arab nationalism, these constructions were extended more broadly to Muslims and became grander—they became civilizational. Seen as recently as 1943 by the Immigration and Naturalization Service as persons who shared "in the development of our civilization," affirming their whiteness and justifying their eligibility for naturalization, Arabs and Muslims were, by the 1990s, positioned by the "clash of civilizations" viewpoint as the cultural other—a categorization that had become an accepted scholarly perspective.[24] The seemingly race-neutral lens of essentialized cultural and religious differences became useful after blatant racism had lost its power as an effective hegemonic tool (an outcome of the civil rights movement, according to race scholars). Nonetheless, the components of racialization were there: the assertion of *innate characteristics* held by all members of a *group* and the use of power to reward, control, and punish based on these determinations.

Since race remains one of the fundamental tools for claiming rewards and organizing discipline in American society—and is something Americans know and understand—these notions of essential human difference have been corporealized, as if they were about color. Thus, race became the operant reference category for a woman voicing opposition to the construction of a mosque in her suburb, when she testified in 2004: "I have no ill remorse for the Muslim race at all. I wish we could all live in peace, but. . . ."[25] The corporealization is also evident in the actionable but sloppy phenotypic category "Arabs, Muslims, and persons assumed to be Arabs and Muslims," terms without which no analyst can accurately describe the victims of hate crimes and verbal assault in the United States after the 9/11 attacks. The phenotype became lethal when, one week after terror attacks on London's public transportation, an undocumented Brazilian immigrant was shot dead by London police for wearing a backpack, running into the subway, and "looking Middle Eastern." Similarly, in August 2005 some New York legislators called for baggage checks of persons entering New York subways who fit the "Middle Eastern" profile.[26]

Because the racialization of Arabs is tied to larger American global policies, the domestic aspect of this project is in the manufacture of public consent needed to support, finance, and defend these policies. For this reason, the most noted features of Arab exclusion in the United States are tactical: persistent, negative media representations, denial of political voice, governmental and non-governmental policies targeting their activism, and distortions of Arab and Muslim values, ways of life, and homelands (civilizational distortions). All of these actions are tied to the delegitimation of Arab claims and disenfranchisement of dissenting voices in order to assert an informational hegemony. Arab Americans have maintained their economic successes despite the context of political and social exclusion, in part because they tend to work as professionals and entrepreneurs, in occupations that are largely peripheral to power and the corporate mainstream.[27]

Since the darkening of Arabs began in earnest after the beneficiaries of the U.S. civil rights movement had been determined and the categories of "nonwhite" and "minority" had been set, Arabs have experienced the double burden of being excluded from the full scope of whiteness *and* from mainstream recognition as people of color. They are therefore still officially white and ineligible for affirmative action.[28] As Saliba notes, while Arab Americans have been victims of racist policies, their experiences have been rendered invisible by dominant discourses about race.[29] Their exclusion has been evident in political mobilizations and in multicultural pedagogy. Political exclusion of Arab voices in mainstream civil society has been reinforced by issue-control, through which organizational leaders silence discussion of issues that challenge U.S. policies in the Arab world (e.g., Palestine, Iraq) when assertion of them may frustrate other organizational objectives. In pedagogy, Arabs have been excluded from race and ethnic studies and, when mentioned, are often treated differently from other groups.[30] Consider the following quote from a race and ethnic studies textbook, which implies that, unlike other groups, Arabs are responsible for their own stereotyping:

> Perhaps more serious [than discrimination faced by Muslim women] is the persistence of negative stereotyping that has plagued Middle Easterners in the United States. The activities of *Arab terrorists* in the Middle East and elsewhere *have created* a sinister image of Arab and other Middle Eastern groups—an image that was greatly exacerbated by the attack on the World Trade Center in 2001[31] [emphasis added].

The exclusion of Arab Americans and their organizations from mainstream vehicles of dissent also left them with few powerful allies from the 1960s onward (although they have had some measurable local successes), allowing their challenges to hostile media representations, textbook biases, and selective policy enforcement to be ignored without repercussions.[32] As they stood virtually alone, discrimination and the production of negative images flourished, pointing to the importance of the organizations of civil society for halting racist activities and to the victory of strategies that ensured Arab exclusion from these groups.[33] Consequently, perpetuation and reinforcement of stigmatized views as well as political isolation left Arabs as open targets for collective punishment after the 9/11 attacks on the United States.

Because the formation of Arabs as a unique "racial" group (separate from whites as well as others) was a process with timing and purpose different from historic American racism, its objective manifestation also differs from that of traditionally subordinated groups: African Americans, Latinos, Asians, and Native Americans. Its impact is not well measured by indices of income, occupation, education, and segregation, because their racialization intervened in the ongoing trajectories of historically successful Arab American communities, and because a large percentage of post-World War II Arab immigrants came to the United States with significant amounts of human capital. These facts have allowed Arabs to overcome some of the economic outcomes that usually correlate with subordinate status; at the same time, they mask the deep impact such subordinate status has on Arab communities with low levels of human capital.[34] For similar historic reasons, some Arabs may see themselves as white (especially if they have benefited or seek to benefit from historical whiteness) while others may not, and Arab American communities may vary in their political alliances and understandings around race. Because of these unusual variations, Arab Americans may have racial options— a modification of Waters's concept of ethnic options—that members of other groups do not possess.[35] Nevertheless, these options do not alter their grounded realities as a negatively stigmatized group.[36] For these reasons of experience and aspiration, a person's racial identity may change over the course of his or her lifetime. For Arab Americans, racialization and racial identity formation should be seen as unfolding and ongoing processes.

The ways in which Arabs, Muslims, and persons assumed to be Arabs and Muslims were held collectively responsible for the 9/11 attacks (demonstrated below) should alone provide convincing evidence that their racial denouement had been sufficiently sealed before the attacks occurred.[37] The public attribution of collective responsibility for the attacks required an *a priori* understanding that Arabs and Muslims should be seen as monolithic. This perspective is reserved for persons from cultures represented as backwards or barbaric, where it is assumed that individuals operate in mechanical solidarity "in so far as they have no action of their own, as with the molecules of inorganic bodies. . . . In societies where this type of solidarity is highly developed, the individual is not his own master."[38] Allegations of primitive culture and mechanical solidarity correspond to Western racism as they have been used historically to describe communities of color. Groups described as inherently violent and unassimilable have been held responsible for their own negative fates, not the structures that denied them rights. They have been portrayed as obstacles to the progress of manifest destiny and as the white man's burden.

In contrast, a primary correlate of whiteness is the attribution of modernity, rationality, and individuality, including individual culpability. When someone who is white commits an act interpreted as wrong or reprehensible, it is depicted by the organs of power as an individual act, one that has no reflection on the values and beliefs of other members of the white population. At the same time, paradoxically, the positive virtues of whiteness are represented as shared characteristics. Thus, during World War II, Japanese Americans were interned as potential enemies, but neither German Americans nor Italian Americans were so treated. The media spoke of Hitler, Mussolini, and "the Japs."[39] Hitler and Mussolini's forces were portrayed as deviants and outliers, not reflections on white, European, or Christian culture. But the violent act of any Arab or Muslim is rendered to represent entire societies and cultures, portrayed as a mechanical, civilizational act. As with the Japanese in the United States during World War Two, these racialized ways of thinking require *a priori* stigmatization and cultural constructions.

Widespread use of the "clash of civilizations" thesis by scholars, filmmakers, publishers, the media, the Christian right, and certain members of the U.S. government—actions similar to what Omi and Winant call racial projects—cemented the social isolation of Arabs and Muslims before 9/11 and established the pre-conditions for collective backlash after the attacks. Since the backlash has been perpetrated largely by whites, it can be seen as a project further defining the boundaries of whiteness.[40] Research conducted in metropolitan Chicago shows that those who perpetrated these acts were often simultaneously displaying American flags, suggesting symbolic attempts to define the boundaries of the American nation and who lies outside of them. While there is no doubt that concerns about personal safety and national security were behind some of the backlash (as well as behind some government policies that followed the 9/11 attacks), it is in their unbridled collective nature, their inclination to target persons who *looked like group members*, that shows their racialized character. Members of groups that have been "othered" experience collective discipline and punishment, irrespective of any individual's relationship to a particular event, activity, or location.

## COLLECTIVE RESPONSIBILITY FOR THE 9/11 ATTACKS AND GOVERNMENT POLICIES THEREAFTER

Analysis of public policies and data collected in an ethnographic study of the impact of 9/11 on Arabs and Muslims in the Chicago metro area amply demonstrate the imposition of collective responsibility for the attacks on Arab and Muslim American communities, irrespective of the fact that members of them did not plan or perpetrate them.[41] Arabs and Muslims in the US have experienced, and continue to experience, forms of collective punishment as their looks and names mark them as targets.

Without much public discussion or debate, the United States government implemented a range of domestic policies in the name of national security and the war on terrorism after the attacks of September 11. Twenty-five of the thirty-seven known government security initiatives implemented between the September 12, 2001, and mid-2003 either explicitly or implicitly targeted U.S. Arabs and Muslims.[42] These measures included mass arrests, secret and indefinite detentions, prolonged detention of "material witnesses," closed hearings, secret evidence, government eavesdropping on attorney/client conversations, FBI interviews, wiretapping, seizures of property, removals of aliens with technical visa violations, and mandatory special registration. At the very minimum, at least 100,000 Arabs and Muslims living in the United States personally experienced one of these measures.[43] Furthermore, the number of Arabs and Muslims able to study, work, or attend trainings, meetings, and conferences in the United States has plummeted.[44] The profiling of Arabs and Muslims at U.S. airports via special security checks and removal from airplanes has dampened their desire to travel domestically or abroad. In a February 2002 article entitled "Flying While Arab," *Arab-American Business* magazine provided special safety tips for Arab-American travelers. While many Arabs say these selective airport procedures have ended, others remain reticent to fly.[45]

Government measures began directly after the September 11 attacks with the round-up and detention of some 1,200 citizens and non-citizens, most of Arab and South Asian descent. Although the U.S. government has never released identities, profiling based on looks, names, and being in the wrong place at the wrong time characterizes the contexts in which many were arrested and detained. More than five hundred of these detainees were deported for visa violations, after long waits under incarceration for security clearance; none were charged with connections to terrorism.[46] Subsequent measures included both mandatory holds on all non-immigrant visa applications submitted by men aged 18 to 45 from twenty-six countries (most of them Arab, subject to special security clearances) and interviews with some five thousand individuals who came to the United States from Arab and Muslim countries after January 1, 2000, on non-immigrant visas, plus a second round of interviews with an additional three thousand persons. The Justice Department asked local police departments to participate in interviewing Arab residents of their towns, placing them in the position of monitoring persons they are supposed to protect.

In January 2002, the INS (now split between two divisions of the Department of Homeland Security) launched an initiative to track down and deport six thousand non-citizen males from (unnamed) "Middle Eastern" countries who had been ordered deported but never left the country. Even though they are less than two percent of the estimated 314,000 so-called "absconders" in the United States, "Middle Easterners" were the government's target. In a meeting with members of Chicago's Arab community, government officials claimed that they were not engaging in racial profiling, since other communities would be approached next, although they never were.[47] In June 2002, the Department of Justice issued an internal memo to the INS and U.S. Customs requesting that they seek out and search all Yemenis entering the country, including American citizens. Yemeni Americans were removed from planes and boarding lines, waiting hours for security clearances. In July 2002, the INS announced that it would begin enforcing section 265(a) of the Immigration and Nationality Act, which requires all aliens to register changes-of-address within ten days of moving. Nothing prevents the selective enforcement of this rule and, indeed, an INS official from one region openly stated that this rule was not intended to be enforced for everyone.[48] In North Carolina, a Palestinian legal immigrant stopped for driving four miles over the speed limit was detained for two months and finally charged with a misdemeanor for failing to report his address change. The INS sought his deportation, but a local immigration judge ruled that the defendant could not be deported because he did not willfully break the law.

On August 12, 2002, Attorney General Ashcroft announced the implementation of the Special Registration program, requiring tens of thousands of foreign visitors from Arab and Muslim countries to be fingerprinted, photographed, and registered. The domestic call-in part of the program required non-immigrant[49] males, aged 16 to 64, from twenty-three Muslim-majority countries, plus heavily Muslim Eritrea (and North Korea), to report and register with the U.S. immigration authorities during a specified time frame in order to be fingerprinted, photographed, and questioned. They were expected thereafter to submit to routine reporting. Credit cards, licenses, and other documents were photocopied and sometimes not returned. Registrants were checked against lists for terrorist connections. Persons cleared of terrorist connections but found to be in violation of their visas or out of (immigration) status were jailed, required to post bond, and issued removal (deportation) orders.[50]

*"THIS NOTICE IS FOR YOU"* was splayed across the top of INS flyers announcing the registration call-in program, reminiscent of the notices posted for Japanese living in Pacific Coast states during World War Two. The arrest and detention in southern California of hundreds of registrants, mostly Iranians, during the first period of registration sparked a national protest, as persons seeking to voluntarily comply with government rules were handcuffed and led off to jail for visa violations. Men in leg shackles were confined to rooms holding fifty or more persons and forced to sleep on concrete floors. Most of these detainees were working taxpayers with families who had otherwise lived lawfully in the United States for decades and many had pending applications for permanent residency.[51]

In May 2003, the government phased out domestic call-in registration. According to the Department of Homeland Security, 82,880 Arabs, Muslims, and others from the selected countries had been "specially" registered through domestic call-in. Of these, 13,434 were issued removal orders for visa violations, all of them affirmatively cleared of terrorism or terrorist connections. Another 127,694 persons were registered at their port-of-entry and none were found to have connections to terrorists.[52] Of the more than 200,000 Muslims, Arabs, and persons from Muslim-majority countries registered, less than fifty were found to have criminal records. The rounding up for removal of more than 14,000 persons for visa violations—a highly select group comprising less than one percent of the estimated 3.2–3.6 million persons living in the country while "out of status" and the eight million undocumented—has few historic precedents in the United States, far outnumbering the 556 foreign nationals deported for their political beliefs during the infamous 1919 Palmer Raids.[53]

The purpose of the special registration, according to the Executive Associate Commissioner of the INS Office of Field Operations, was to facilitate the "monitoring" of aliens whose residence in the United States warranted it "in the interest of national security."[54] The Department of Homeland Security, which took over the now-divided immigration (and naturalization) functions of the former INS, referred to Special Registration (using its NSEERS acronym) as a "pilot project focusing on a smaller segment of the nonimmigrant alien population deemed to be of risk to national security."[55] These statements make explicit the government's view that Arabs and Muslims *as a group* are considered a security risk for the United States. This view is found in other Bush Administration programs, such as FBI director Mueller's January 2003 initiative to tie FBI field office goals for wire-tapping and undercover activities to the number of mosques in the field area.[56]

An examination of the legislative history upon which Attorney General Ashcroft legitimated special registration provides useful clues about its ideological and racial boundary-making. Ashcroft cited legislative authority for this program encompassing a history going back to the 1798 Alien and Sedition Acts, which were primarily aimed at restraining and deporting aliens living in the United States who were considered subversive. Ashcroft specifically cited as his authority the 1940 Smith Act, formally known as the 1940 Alien Registration Act, which was passed to strengthen national defense in response to fears of communist and anarchist influences in the United States. It required that all aliens over the age of thirteen be fingerprinted and registered, and required parents and legal guardians to register those thirteen years of age and younger. In turn, they received a numbered Alien Registration Receipt Card from the DOJ/INS proving registry and were required to carry this card with them at all times.[57] The Smith Act was built on 1918 legislation making past and present membership in "proscribed organizations and subversive classes" grounds for exclusion and deportation. The 1918 Act, in turn, was built on the Alien and Sedition Acts of 1798. The Smith Act was aimed not only at foreigners. It also prohibited American citizens from advocating or belonging to groups that advocated or taught the "duty, necessity desirability, or propriety" of overthrowing any level of government by "force or violence." It was the first peacetime federal sedition law since 1798 and was the basis of later prosecutions of persons alleged to be members of communist and socialist parties. The 2002 special registration program thus lies within the family of policies permitting the government to monitor, restrain, and remove persons whose political beliefs and ideologies it perceives as a threat.

On the other hand, because the special registration program named its targets by their country of birth, not their political beliefs, it shares features of the body of U.S. policies based on ideas about race, including slavery, abolished in 1865, and Indian removal. Other such initiatives included the 1790 Naturalization Law, denying naturalized citizenship to non-whites, the last remnants of which were repealed in 1952; the 1882 Chinese Exclusion Act, repealed in 1943; the Asiatic Barred Zone; and the immigration quotas (enacted in 1921 and revised in 1924, 1929, and 1952, whose abolition in 1965 signaled the end of an era in which U.S. immigration policies were based principally on race). Although most of these laws referred to geographies and countries, their explicit purpose was racial. After 1965, it was considered against liberal democratic principles to blatantly discriminate in immigration policies by country of birth. But, in 1981 the regulation of persons from select "foreign states" re-emerged in immigration law when the Attorney General was permitted to require "natives of any one or more foreign states, or any class of group thereof" to provide the government with address and other information upon ten-days notice.[58] Interestingly, the Iran Crisis of 1980 was specifically mentioned in the House Judiciary Committee report submitted for the 1981 law, thus connecting new geographically-based immigration policies to political Islam.[59] Attorney General Ashcroft used the 1981 law to authorize call-in special registration.[60] Selective policies by country of birth emerged again in 1991 when Attorney General Richard Thornburgh required the special registration of persons holding Iraqi and Kuwaiti passports and travel documents.[61]

In sum, since the end of quotas and the dawn of the civil rights era, punitive or controlling special immigration policies based on country of birth or nationality have been applied solely to persons from (non-European) Muslim-majority countries (with the exception of North Korea) and to Arabs. These place-based discriminatory policies flourish at the nexus of assumptions about the relationship between national origin and presumed inherent cultural and ideological traits—what we have come to label as "race." These laws and policies locate Arabs and Muslims and place them in a subordinate status, thereby reinforcing the appropriateness of maintaining essentialist ideas about members of these groups.

These post-9/11 policies and programs link back to the racialization of Arabs and Muslims because of the essentialized, undifferentiated representations of these groups. Those representations, based on the assumption that persons who inhabit the grand categories of Arab and Muslim possess certain innate characteristics making them a security risk, were institutionalized through homeland security and war-on-terror policies. Operating in tandem with Islamaphobic discourses found in American society, these policies entrench the stigmatization of Arabs and Muslims in the United States. Understanding that race is a historically located social construct that has no fixed meaning and that it differentiates between human beings using discourses of human essences, we must ask: can policies that target persons from two continents, three geographic regions, and through their messiness incorporate persons from three major religions, be considered part of a racial project?[62] The answer, I believe, is yes, because they use essentialized categories and understandings to create structural outcomes, which in turn become tied in the public's mind to a phenotype. Thus, a global project that included multiple subordinate populations has been amalgamated into a civilizational racial project.

## POPULAR SUPPORT FOR COLLECTIVE POLICIES

After the 9/11 attacks, public opinion polls showed broad support for the special treatment of Arabs and Muslims *as groups* in the United States. A poll conducted in mid-September 2001 found respondents evenly divided over whether all Arabs in the United States, including American citizens, should be required to carry special identity cards.[63] Two late-September Gallup polls found that a majority of Americans favored profiling of Arabs, including American citizens, and subjecting them to special security checks before boarding planes.[64] A December 2001 University of Illinois poll found that some 70 percent of Illinois residents were willing to sacrifice their civil rights to fight terrorism, and more than one-quarter of respondents said Arab Americans should surrender more rights than others.[65] A March 2002 CNN/Gallup/*USA Today* poll found that nearly 60 percent of Americans favored reducing the number of immigrants from Muslim countries. Five months later, a majority of the American public polled said that there were "too many" immigrants from Arab countries.[66] In December 2004, a Cornell University study found that nearly 50 percent of respondents in a national poll believed the U.S. government should curtail civil liberties for Muslim Americans.[67]

These polls indicate that the essentialized representations of Arabs and Muslims—propagated by the media and film industry, uncontested in pedagogy, and reflected in government policies and actions—have been extremely effective in garnering public support for treating Arabs and Muslims as a distinct group (often reified in the artificial concept of "Middle Easterners") possessing fewer rights than others. These views would not have emerged so quickly after 9/11 had they not been cultivated prior to the attacks. Otherwise, the hijackers would have been seen in ways similar to Timothy McVeigh, the Oklahoma City bomber, or members of the Irish Republican Army—as extremists whose actions do not reflect on an entire race, religion, or civilization.

## ARABS AND RACE FROM THE PERSPECTIVE OF ARAB MUSLIMS IN METROPOLITAN CHICAGO

Data from interviews conducted between 2002 and 2004 with Arab Muslims in metropolitan Chicago as part of a post 9/11 ethnographic study provide insight into how Arabs view their place in the racial structure of the United States. One hundred and two study participants (see Table 1 for sample demography) were asked: "There have been discussions about whether Arabs are white or not, with different points of view, do you think Arabs are white, not white, or what?" Sixty-three percent of respondents said Arabs were not white; twenty percent said they were white, while another seventeen percent gave equivocal responses. Study data indicate the elements of social life that persons bring to bear in their assessment of the "racial place" of Arabs, which could be phenotypical, experiential, observational, relational, local, national, or global. These data also point to the complexity of understanding Arab American ideas about race and the need to supplement questions about race using standardized, official categories with questions that take into account the meanings of these terms.

### TABLE 1
### STUDY SAMPLE STATISTICS (N  102)

| % Female | % Poor/ Low income | % Middle Class | % Upper Middle Class & Wealthy | % 19–29 | % 30–49 | % 50 | % H.S. or less | % Some college or BS/BA | % Post Grad. | % Born US* |
|---|---|---|---|---|---|---|---|---|---|---|
| 45 | 18 | 62 | 20 | 30 | 56 | 14 | 14 | 43 | 42 | 29 |

*Includes for sociological reasons persons who migrated to the US before age 10.

Individuals who said Arabs were not white made this assessment on the basis of, in order of frequency: their treatment in American society; skin color and other phenotypic criteria; the fact that Arabs are multiracial and possess cultural/historical differences from white Europeans; and Arab distinctiveness ("Arabs are Arabs"). Many invoked multiple criteria. A majority of persons who said Arabs are white and about one-third of persons who said Arabs were not white moved immediately into an unprovoked discourse on information and application forms (especially census forms and job and school applications). In other words, the discussion of race became a discussion of boxes, how they respond to these boxes, and the way American society boxes people into groups by color. Arabs know well that they are supposed to check the white box on forms, and a majority say they do so, whether they believe Arabs are white or not and even when they have serious problems with the concept. (Arabs who check "other" and write-in "Arab" or an Arab nationality, or who can be identified as Arabs by language, country of birth, or ancestry, are re-coded by the Census Bureau as white.)[68]

Q: There have been discussions about whether Arabs are white or not, with different points of view, do you think Arabs are white, not white, or what?

A: This confuses me every time I fill out an application. We are not White, Black, Hispanic, or Asian. We are Arab. I put white. If there is an other, sometimes I put that. But I put White because I know we are not other (Jordan-born female).

Still, some insist on checking the "other" box. This man responded to the question about race as follows:

I always choose "other." I'm not white and I'm not going to check white (Puerto Rican-born male).

A large segment of persons who said Arabs were white said they knew this because it is what they were told.

I was really surprised when I learned that we were Caucasian (US-born woman).

Geographically, Egypt is in Africa but they classify all the Arabs as white, so I write white (Egyptian-born male).

But most make a distinction between what they write on forms and what they see as their reality.

We used to report quarterly on affirmative action and I always asked my boss, "what should I do? Should I put myself as a minority or not?" He did not know either, so we called the company headquarters and they said you will be considered white. But of course in real life we are not. As far as statistics go, that's what they say, legally (Palestinian-born male).

That's one of the things I am thinking about as a student transferring colleges. They have a race question and I have to check white. We are white in this case but in all other cases we are a minority (Palestinian-born male).

Having to check the white box on forms is another form of discrimination to some.

I am resentful that I have to put down white. I don't look white. I am not treated as white (1.5 female).

I don't feel that I am white. I felt I was at a disadvantage to have to check "white." I don't think it's fair because it is not who I am. I just don't feel that I'm a typical white American, you know, Anglo-Saxon, because if you look at me I'm not. I feel that I am a minority. Why should I be grouped with these people and not have a chance to obtain a scholarship? (Libyan-born woman).

Sometimes you put other but what is other? Other could be anything. You feel like inferior, you know. Like the minority of the minorities. We're not defined. . . . Officially we are white but we're not white. Somebody can say I don't have to hire you because you are white and I have a lot of white people here. But you're not white! (Palestinian-born male).

## Arabs Are Not White: Responses Based
## on How They Are Treated in American Society

The largest response category among persons who said Arabs are not white (36%) revolved around how Arabs are treated in American society.[69] In other words, their saw their racial place as non-white because they do not benefit from the statuses, assumptions, and behaviors that accord to whiteness. The overwhelming majority of persons who gave this type of response were born in the United States, suggesting that deep understanding of the relationship between race and inequality of experience are particularly American, formed as part of an American upbringing. These responses, in that they invoke issues that existed before 9/11, support the assertion that racial projects to exclude Arabs from the benefits of whiteness were in place before 9/11.

I call the people I work with white and they ask, "what are you?" What color are we? I don't feel as a white person. People think I must be foreign. People ask me "where are your parents from?" (Chicago-born male).

We have always been told we should be classified as other, then white. But if I go to Mississippi with my brother named Ahmed, there is no way he'd be treated as white (Chicago-born female).

Arabs are definitely not white. That categorization comes from the treatment of a community by the institutions of American society. Arabs in the schools face the same institutional racism as [do] other students of color (Chicago-born male).

You understand that there is racism even if it is not personally inflicted on you. Being a first-generation Egyptian American and Muslim is a difficult thing–to form an identity of your own and feel like an American and that you fit into this country when you feel you really don't anyway. So, there's always been this sort of racism. . . . [T]hat outlook was always there, it was just exaggerated [after 9/11], making you feel like the enemy. That you're the bad one, and you're definitely a foreigner and do not belong in this country. I'm just as much American as anyone else. I feel like maybe I need to get the hell out of this country because something bad is going to happen to our people here (U.S.-born female).

The issue is are you part of a privileged group of people that can dominate others, and I do not think we are part of that. Arabs are not part of the white or European ruling structure. We are politically excluded (U.S.-born female).

Arabs are not white. When I view someone as white they are part of the majority culture. I don't get treated as white, so I am not white. I never check white (U.S.-born male).

## Arabs Are Not White: Responses Based on Skin Color and Other Phenotypic Criteria

The second most common response (28%) among persons who said Arabs are not white was about skin color and phenotypic features. These responses were found among both U.S.- and non-U.S.-born respondents, although immigrants frequently spoke of how they only learned about ideas and systems organized around skin color after arriving in the United States.

I'm not white, I'm olive. To certain people it matters if you're white (Chicago-born female).

We don't look white. What matters in the U.S. is not Caucasian blood but skin color. This has a huge impact on us. And you see nappy hair, even if blue eyes and light skin (Chicago-born female).

In this suburb, it is lilly white. We don't belong here. I am very aware of my skin color and looks (Kuwait-born female).

I am from a country that is not white, for sure (Sudan-born male).

You know it's funny, nobody ever discusses color once you step out of the United States. I think it only matters in this country. This country is very race-conscious, color-conscious I mean. My sister married a very dark man and when you look at him you would say he is Black. We never thought that was unusual. . . . I complained about my hair once at school and they said oh, yeh, you have that Semitic hair. I never thought of my hair being Semitic. Sometimes the girls would say to me, "well you are olive skinned." I don't see myself that way. So, I think in their minds they have a perception of gradations of color, and I don't have that (Jordan-born female).

Many respondents were extremely uncomfortable with the very concept of race and color. For a variety of reasons they found it useless, irrelevant, or offensive.

I don't feel comfortable classifying people by color anyway. It is against my ideology, my thinking, and my religion (Egypt-born male).

We are definitely not white. But the whole idea of color makes no sense to me. My neighbor is black according to census forms but she is lighter than I am. There are Arabs that are lighter than white people. I don't think people should be classified like that, by color. I don't agree with it at all. If I was to classify myself, I would consider myself brown. I would not consider myself white. My youngest and oldest child would be white and my middle child brown. It does not work for me (Kuwait-born female).

We do not talk about this issue in our community. We feel that we are Muslims and that is what matters to us (Palestine-born male).

### Arabs Are Not White: They Span a Range of Geographic Regions and Skin Colors

The third most common response (24%) among persons who said Arabs are not white was that Arabs cannot be a racial group because they encompass many geographic regions and skin colors.

I think Arabs should have a different category until things change. . . . If you look on the map, Arab countries cover two continents and the white white and dark black. If this is my cousin and he's dark, and he's from Africa, are you going to call him white? (U.S.born female).

It does not matter to me because in the Arab community we have white, black, and yellow. As Muslims, there is no difference between colors (Palestine-born male).

Arabs are distinct upon themselves. And the Arab world encompasses both black and white (U.S.-born female).

Arabs are a race of colors, many colors. In my family some have blond hair and blue eyes. Some have brown curly hair. All colors (Lebanon-born male).

### Arabs Are Not White: Arab Heritage Is Different from Caucasian/European

The fourth most common response (20 percent) among persons who said Arabs are not white was about culture and heritage. To them, being white means being Caucasian and European, and Arabs are neither.

Their history and culture is [sic] quite separate from Europe's. I find it a disgrace that the Arab people should be so blatantly insulted by the disregard of their history (U.S.-born female).

I do not think Arabs are white in the sense of Caucasian or white American (U.S.-born female).

White in my mind means European but since I am not European, I feel like I am lying. Why should I write white? (Egyptian-born male).

Most Arabs think Caucasians are Europeans (Kuwaiti-born male).

I have a culture and heritage, being white denies that (U.S.-born male).

The following comments from a young man living in a middle class Chicago suburb show how Arab is counterposed to Caucasian/white/American:

I was with a group of friends. These Americans, Caucasians, drove past us and yelled out remarks—racial remarks. They turned around and they ran at us and we started to fight. In Chicago Ridge everyone was Arabic mostly; our whole neighborhood was Arabic . . . white person or American would say something about us unless it was in school, but in Orland, it's a little different. Arabic are like, they are not the minorities over there (in Orland Park) (U.S.-born male).

Seventeen percent of respondents gave what may be called equivocal responses to the race question, marking the difficulty they have with the racializing of Arabs as well as the flexible character of the race construct. Along with expressing this ambiguity, the following quote reveals (along with some above) the socially-constructed nature of the way Arabs respond to the formulaic race question and the way it is interpreted through transmitted knowledge.

I don't really know. I think, for me, it's always been white because of what I look like. I consider myself white. That's probably a personal reflection because my skin color is white. I've always thought all Arabs were white. I've never really thought of them as being non-white. But, again, why do we say we're white, because we're not white. Like people say, "you put white," and I think that it just doesn't make sense. I don't know what white means in terms of technical definition. Is it people who live north of the equator? I don't know how the experts have defined it. If you ask anybody, they say to put white as a race. Do I think we're white? I don't think so (Chicago-born female).

## THINKING ABOUT THE BOX

Even though the race question used in the study was not formulated as a discussion of forms and categories, responses nearly always invoked them at some point, signaling both a learned relationship between racial identification and state categories and a deep tension between the Arab experience in the United

States and the phenomenon of racial categorization. Nonetheless, when asked whether racial identification matters, thirty percent of persons interviewed said racial position is important in American society, whether they like the concept or not, because it determines benefits. As neither white nor non-white, Arabs accrue neither the benefits of whiteness nor the protections of minority status. They feel this exclusion is unfair and further indicates their subordinate status. While quite a few respondents said Arabs should have their own category, like Hispanics, since they do not fit into any existing categories, many think the whole discussion is absurd but for the fact that American institutions work on these premises.

> Hmm. Does it matter? It might matter, actually, I'm not really sure. I guess if you're looking theoretical, it shouldn't matter, but when you look on social and political and all that stuff, I think it does matter because of the way institutions in our society run. If you have affirmative action at your university and you're African American, there are rights of having a qualified percentage. We probably wish it doesn't matter, but it does. On resume applications, they look at what your application says. I think it would be foolish to think that they don't look at what your race is (Chicagoborn female).

The formation of Arabs as a unique racial group (distinct from white) was a socio-political process with timing and purpose different from historic American racism, leaving many Arabs in the position of having no racial category (box) that makes sense. Arabs were in the midst of the process that rendered them non-white after the categories of race—White, Black, Hispanic, Asian and Pacific Islander, and Native American—had been set. Arab claims-making over the past few decades for a special category has been declined by the Census Bureau. Although largely rejecting the concept of the racial box, Arabs know that in a racially constructed society thinking inside the box matters.

At the same time, Arab Americans may have racial options that members of other groups do not possess.[70] When asked, many decide from one context to the next whether they are white or not and whether they will select the box they have been told to select, or think about color and treatment. Their own racial identity may change over their lifetime, based on their experiences, preferences, and demands. Local contexts and organized affiliations may affect Arab American understandings about their racial place.[71] Racial identity is an unfolding, ongoing, contextual, and socially constructed process for Arab Americans. As the data in our Chicago study suggest, when Arabs select the white box it does not necessarily mean that they identify with whiteness. But when they check other, they know that they have become lost, paradoxically hidden yet the object of social obsession. (They probably do not know that they will be recoded as white if they can be identified as Arab.) These options do not alter their grounded reality as a negatively stigmatized group. On the contrary, they offer proof of their racially subordinate status. Thus, the majority of Arab Muslims in the metropolitan Chicago study view their social position in American society as subordinate and translate that status to a non-white racial position in a race-based societal hierarchy. Unfortunately, one cannot conclude from these data if religious affiliation plays any role in this finding since Arab Christians were not part of the study.[72] It is notable, however, that religion and religious discrimination were rarely invoked in responses to this question, except in statements that Islam does not condone racial distinctions.

## DISCRIMINATION AND SAFETY IN THE POST 9/11 ARAB-MUSLIM EXPERIENCE[73]

Prejudice, discrimination, and a compromised sense of safety are historically correlated with racial subordination in the United States. These experiences have ranged from lynching, mass removals, quarantining, law enforcement profiling, and sentencing disparities to inferior employment, housing, and educational opportunities. Study participants were asked if they had experienced discrimination since 9/11. Fifty-three percent said yes and forty-seven percent said no. Among those who responded "yes," specific instances of discrimination were reported in the following social sectors: employment (39%), public space (22%), schools (11%), law enforcement (11%), commercial transactions (9%), government offices (9%), airports/airplanes (7%), and civil society institutions (6%). These responses are related to a specific interpretation of the meaning of the term discrimination, which is to be denied something or treated in a different way than others. Many respondents did not interpret hate speech or being watched while conducting routine activities, such as loading their trunks, as discrimination. The same applies to feeling unsafe or fearing removal from the United States, which came up in many interviews in the context of other questions.

Some respondents changed their daily life patterns to avoid placing themselves in situations in which they expected to experience discrimination. Quite a few interviewees spoke of eating separately and changing job positions, friendship groups, or their names as means of avoiding verbal harassment or abuse. Many persons who used to travel domestically have altered their travel patterns after the attacks; they either stopped traveling or drove to their destinations. These actions indicate that the policing and control of members of the group has moved inside the mind of the individual, what Hatem Bazian and Nadine Naber call "virtual policing." The overwhelming majority of our interviewees reported being verbally insulted, although these events took different forms depending upon the context in which they occurred. Insults were reported in public spaces, in the schools, in the context of commercial transactions, and in shopping malls. Many reported negative comments at work or in the process of applying for jobs. Some reported attacks on their homes, and a number of women were spit upon. "Go back to your country" was the most frequent slogan in public attacks, followed by "we want to kill you." Comments about Arab terrorists were common in work-related slurs.

Despite the fact that many interviewees said they had not experienced discrimination, the overwhelming majority said that there are places in American society in which they do not feel safe. Feelings of lack of safety in public spaces appear to be gendered, as women, especially *muhajibaat* (veiled women), express this feeling more than men. Suburban shopping centers and malls were mentioned frequently as places where women endured stares and insults. Feeling unsafe is not limited to the public sphere. The government's use of secret evidence, closed hearings, interrogations, and home invasions appears discriminatory to members of Arab and Muslim communities. Consequently, many of them feel vulnerable to a certain degree, even in their own homes. Thus, while some persons in the study said they felt safest in their homes, others said they felt the hidden eyes of surveillance, assumed their phones were tapped and computers monitored, and were concerned about the right of government agents to enter their homes at any time without having permission or leaving a trace. Such matters of collective safety and security historically are tied to racial subordination in American society. The circle of closure that Arabs and Muslims feel is not physically tangible, but many fear it could become so if another attack occurs. Most persons interviewed for this study report that they do not feel secure in the United States, and many expressed fears of mass deportation, revocation of citizenship, or internment camps.[74] Those with resources have adopted strategies to anticipate these potential outcomes: they have sent their children to universities in other countries and begun building homes in their countries of origin.

This feeling of "homeland insecurity" is exacerbated by the post 9/11 increase in discourses about civilizational differences between Arabs/ Muslims and persons holding Western values. These ideas are broadcast and published in mainstream American media, particularly by neoconservatives and Christian-right spokespersons, and are used to justify a range of government actions. Some of these spokespersons have described Islam as a religion outside the pale of human values and Muslims as "worse than Nazis."[75] A booklet entitled *Why Islam is a Threat to America and The West* argues that Muslims are a fifth column in the United States and "should be encouraged to leave" the country.[76] Televangelist Pat Robertson called Muslims potential killers on his *700 Club* program.[77] While in office, former Attorney General Ashcroft stated in an interview with syndicated columnist Cal Thomas, "Islam is a religion in which God requires you to send your son to die for him. Christianity is a faith in which God sends his son to die for you."[78] Indeed, Arabs and Muslims feel quite uneasy about the close alliance between the Bush Administration and the Christian Right.

## CONCLUSION

The racial formation processes experienced by Arab Americans differ in both historical timing and pretext from that of other groups in the United States. Unlike the historical argument of racial superiority and inferiority used to buttress the development of the United States as a country of white privilege, the fall of Arabs from the grace of marginal whiteness is traceable to the later emergence of the United States as a global superpower. The seemingly race-neutral lens of essentialized cultural differences and innate violence was promoted in the media and left to percolate by the educational system, thereby building support for government policies that targeted Arab Americans, justifying their political exclusion. This approach was effective and powerful because, while it buttressed U.S. global policies, it did not appear blatantly racist.

Racial projects that moved Arabs into subordinate status began to clearly mark the Arab American experience in the late 1960s and provided momentum for the foundation of pan-Arab American activist organizations. In the 1990s, when Islamist challenges to American global hegemony became more powerful than Arab nationalism, these essentialized constructions were extended to Muslims and became grander; they became civilizational: Both Arabs and Muslims were represented as persons of inherently different values and dispositions than "Americans." These constructions became racialized since race is a key category for organizing difference in the United States and is something Americans know and understand. It is an interpretive construct with great power in American society and one that newcomers quickly learn. Like others, Arabs are informed as to what their official racial group is, but, unlike others, many Arabs find a disjuncture between their category (white) and their experiences, since race is understood as a phenomenon with experiential correlates.

For decades, Arabs in the United States have faced challenges from the public over their beliefs, values, opinions, and culture. Their protests over negative representations have been silenced by their powerlessness, an outcome of their blocked participation in the institutions of civil society. The corporealization of the essentialized Arab/Muslim, embodied in images of dark haired, olive-skinned, and hook-nosed persons, came to life as "Arabs, Muslims, and persons assumed to be Arabs and Muslims" faced widespread attack after 9/11. Notions of collective, civilizational responsibility justified imputing to Arabs and Muslims a collective guilt for the attacks. As persons purportedly of a different civilization, Arabs/Muslims were counterposed to Americans and to whites—they were suspected, unsafe, and virtually circled.

The most noted features of Arab exclusion have been persistent, negative media representations, denial of political voice, governmental and non-governmental policies that target their activism, and civilizational distortions of Arab and Muslim values and ways of life. Since the darkening of Arabs began in earnest after the beneficiaries of the U.S. civil rights movement had been determined and the categories of "non-white" and "minority" had been set, Arabs have experienced the double burden of being excluded from whiteness *and* from mainstream recognition as people of color. Their isolation from mainstream vehicles of dissent left them with few powerful allies to contest their treatment in American society, leaving them open targets for collective punishment after the 9/11 attacks on the United States. While many Arab American activists recognized long ago that the road to their political inclusion and an end to the discrimination was in alliances with people of color, their untouchable issues (especially, Israeli military occupation of Palestinian lands) and their domestic economic role as urban shopkeepers placed strains on these relationships. Perhaps one of the positive developments in the post 9/11 America is the greater willingness of these groups to accept Arabs into their ranks.

Viewed over its one-hundred-year history, the Arab American experience is not well explained by prominent theories of immigrant integration and ethnic assimilation. The reason for this lies in a number of assumptions: that race is a special case of ethnicity rather than a discredited but still powerful social organizing tool; that the creation of racially defined subordinate groups is a legacy of the American past (although the consequences of this history endure); and that no new racial groups will be constructed. It follows from these assumptions that no new group will experience downward movement on the color line, because in post-civil rights American society racial projects asserting the essential human difference of certain groups are no longer acceptable. Those days are over. Research should therefore focus on whether the color lines are blurring, whether some groups are permeating the old boundaries of race as evidenced by upward mobility, and whether some groups continue to face racially-based subordination.

I have shown that racializing processes are not just legacies of the American past, that racist ideas composed of social constructions of essential human differences can be effectively hidden behind new discourses, and that government policies may even promote these ideas. The fact that such policies are rooted in global matters instead of the domestic distribution of power and resources does not alter the fact that they produce domestic inequality, civic and political exclusion, pedagogical stereotyping, and that they incite hate crimes, prejudice, and discrimination. Arab American experiences with these social phenomena affect how they see their place in the American racial order. Many Arab Americans have been critical of American democracy because of their very real experiences of political exclusion with regard to challenging U.S. foreign policies, civic exclusion because their issues are portrayed as "divisive," and the use of stereotypes and hostile images to support government policies. These aspects of the American political system are well known in the Arab world, affecting—in the views of many Arabs—the sincerity of American efforts to install democracy around the world.

The one-hundred-year history of Arab American communities provides clarity to this analysis, since one can compare their experiences before and after negative racialization. Arab Americans were at one time considered white, although this status was contested in some locations, and they largely benefited from marginal whiteness during the first decades of their American experience.

After they were constructed as a group at odds with American values, as inherently violent and oppressive, they lost privileges in many American social and political realms. The spread of Islamic revivalism to the United States offered resources to dispirited Arab American Muslims: hope, a way of life based on a belief in God, and social relationships that offered dignity, inspiration, and strength.[79] The capacity of religion to provide "refuge, respectability, and resources" is well recognized.[80] Unfortunately, as the Islamic revival spread across the country, so, too, were ideas about Arab barbarism extended to Muslims and evolved into a discourse of inherent civilizational differences. As the paradigm and phenotype were extended to Muslims, Arab and Muslim were conflated, making it is necessary to speak about them in one construct: the Arab/ Muslim/Middle Easterner. This consolidation will move Arab and Muslim Americans into a new trajectory that may begin to transform dominant discourses, because Muslims as a religious group may be more successful making claims on American institutions than racially subordinated Arabs, a pattern borne out in the history of race and religion in the United States.

## NOTES

1.  Early Arab immigrants largely fit into the Not-Quite-White category, which includes Italians, Poles, Slavs, Jews, and Greeks, among others. This conclusion is based on an analysis of the structural position of Arabs demonstrated in the published literature on the early Arab immigrant experience (1890–1930). I consider the legal rights (such as property ownership, voting, immigration, and naturalization), residential patterns, and employment experiences of Arab immigrants and their children as primary indicators of their marginal white social status.
2.  There is evidence that in some locations, such as Detroit, Buffalo, and parts of the South, their marginal whiteness was contested. This outcome corresponds to the notion that racial projects can have distinct local characteristics within the context of larger national structures. An examination of the racial status and positioning of the early Syrian immigrants is found in Sarah Gualtieri's work. See, for example, Sarah Gualtieri, "Strange Fruit? Syrian Immigrants, Extralegal Violence and Racial Formation in the Jim Crow South," *Arab Studies Quarterly* 26 no. 3 (2004): 63–85.
3.  Alejandro Portes and Alex Stepick, *City on the Edge: The Transformation of Miami* (Berkeley, CA, 1993).
4.  United States Department of Commerce, U.S. Census Bureau, *We the People of Arab Ancestry in the United States* (Washington, DC, March 2005).
5.  Ibid. "Arabic" corresponds to persons who described their ethnicity as Arab, Arabian, or Arabic and is different from the collective Arab category. Analysis of census data for metropolitan Chicago showed that, among Arabs, Palestinians were most likely to use this term.
6.  Louise Cainkar, "Coping with Culture, Change, and Alienation: The Life Experiences of Palestinian Women in the United States" (Ph.D. diss. Northwestern University, 1988). By "intentionally Palestinian," I mean that they defined much of their everyday cultural and political activity in reference to a specific Palestinian identity.
7.  Richard Alba and Victor Nee, *Remaking the American Mainstream: Assimilation and Contemporary Immigration* (Cambridge, MA, 2003).

8.  Herbert Gans, "Introduction," in Neil Sandburg, *Ethnic Identity and Assimilation: The Polish Community* (New York, 1973): vii–xii; and Alejandro Portes and Min Zhou, "The New Second Generation: Segmented Assimilation and Its Variants," *Annals of the American Academy of Political and Social Sciences* 530 (November 1993): 74–96. The characteristics of those experiencing Portes and Zhou's incorporation as disadvantaged minorities are becoming evident among Arabs of low socio-economic status in Chicago. This phenomenon has developed in the past fifteen years. For racial exclusion, see for example, Robert Blauner, *Racial Oppression in America* (New York, 1972).

9.  An examination of the role of social capital (ethnic and religious) and occupational niches in maintaining the economic success of Arab Americans despite other negative changes is warranted. The author has proposed such a study.

10. Michael Omi and Howard Winant, *Racial Formation in the United States: From the 1960s to the 1990s* (New York, 1994).

11. Howard Winant, *The World is a Ghetto* (New York, 2001); and Richard Alba and Victor Nee, *Remaking the Mainstream*, 15.

12. It is certainly meaningful that the editors of *Contexts*, a publication of the American Sociological Association, included this discussion in the Fall 2005 special issue on race. Louise Cainkar, "Violence Unveiled," *Contexts* 4, no. 4 (Washington, DC: American Sociological Association), 67. My argument that Arab Americans have been racialized builds on Naber's by locating its source, as well as the source of Arab American invisibility and the "racialization of Islam," in structural foreign policy interests. See Nadine Naber, "Ambiguous Insiders: an investigation of Arab-American invisibility," *Ethnic and Racial Studies* 23, no. 2 (2000): 37–61.

13. Exceptions to this pattern are found among activists and others linked to progressive organizations and low-income Arabs in multi-racial neighborhoods, where dominant stereotypes have less credibility.

14. I discuss the process of Islamic revival among Arab Americans extensively in another paper. See Louise Cainkar, "Islamic Revival Among Second-generation Arab Muslims in Chicago: The American Experience and Globalization Intersect," *Bulletin of the Royal Institute for Inter-Faith Studies* 6, no. 2 (Autumn/Winter, 2004): 99–120.

15. Samuel Huntington, *The Clash of Civilizations and the Remaking of World Order* (New York, 1996).

16. For the process of becoming white see David, Roediger, *The Wages of Whiteness: Race and the Making of the American Working Class* (New York, 1991); and Noel Ignatiev, *How the Irish Became White* (New York, 1995).

17. See, for example, Jack Shaheen, *The TV Arab* (Bowling Green, OH, 1984); Shaheen, *Reel Bad Arabs: How Hollywood Vilifies a People* (New York, 2001); Michael W. Suleiman, ed., *Arabs in America: Building a New Future* (Philadelphia, 1999); Ernest McCarus, ed., *The Development of Arab American Identity* (Ann Arbor, MI, 1994); Sameer Y. Abraham and Nabeel Abraham, eds., *Arabs in the New World: Studies on Arab-American Communities* (Detroit, 1983); Baha Abu-Laban and Michael Suleiman, eds., *Arab Americans: Continuity and Change* (Belmont, MA, 1989); M. Cherif Bassiouni, ed., *The Civil Rights of Arab-Americans: The Special Measures* (North Dartmouth, NH, 1974); Louise Cainkar, "Coping with Culture," 1988; James Zogby, *Taking Root Bearing Fruit* (Washington, DC, 1984).

18. Ronald Stockton, "Ethnic Archetypes and the Arab Image," in *The Development of Arab American Identity*, ed. Ernest McCarus (Ann Arbor, MI, 1994), 119–53; Seymour Martin Lipset and William Schneider, "Carter vs. Israel: What the Polls Reveal" *Commentary* 64, no. 5 (1977): 22; and Shelly Slade, "Image of the Arab

in America: Analysis of a Poll on American Attitudes," *Middle East Journal* 35 no. 2 (Spring 1981): 143.

19. James Zogby, *Taking Root*, 1984, 21.
20. Abu-Laban and Suleiman, *Arab Americans*, 1989, 5.
21. Ibid., 18, 21.
22. Ibid., 22.
23. Louise Cainkar, "Coping with Culture."
24. U.S. Department of Justice, Immigration and Naturalization Service, "The Eligibility of Arabs to Naturalization," *INS Monthly Review* 1 (1943): 15.
25. Field data, Orland Park mosque hearing. April 2004.
26. "Middle Eastern" is an artificial construct created in the West with varying definitions. For some, the Middle East ranges from North Africa through Muslim South Asia. For others, it is the Arab countries in Asia. Sometimes its geographic area is left undefined. Very few persons from "Middle Eastern" countries identify with the term. In Census 2000, 2.4 percent of Arab respondents gave their ethnicity as Middle Eastern. See U.S. Census Bureau *The Arab Population* (Washington, DC, 2003): 2.
27. The author examines this proposition about the relationship between income, occupational niches, and the social and political exclusion of Arabs and Muslims in current work in progress.
28. Helen Hatab Samhan, "Not Quite White: Race Classification and the Arab-American experience," in Suleiman, *Arabs in America: Building a New Future* (Philadelphia, 1999), 209–26.
29. Therese Saliba, "Resisting Invisibility," in Suleiman, *Arabs in America*, 304–19.
30. Louise Cainkar, "The Treatment of Arabs and Muslims in Race and Ethnic Studies Textbooks," paper presented at the Annual Meeting of the American Sociological Association, Atlanta, Georgia, 2002.
31. Martin Marger, *Race and Ethnic Relations* (Belmont, CA, 2003), 165. Emphasis added.
32. See Fay in Zogby, *Taking Root*, 23, where she discusses the isolation of Arab Americans and ADC's efforts to establish ties with other ethnic and racial groups in order to forge anti-racist alliances.
33. Indeed, this exclusion is invisible to many, rendering attributions of Arab blame for their own situation plausible, the very outcome desired by the crafters of stereotypes and strategies of exclusion.
34. Here we may see evidence of segmented assimilation processes.
35. Mary C. Waters, *Ethnic Options* (Berkeley, CA, 1990).
36. In other words, I argue that subjective matters of Arab American identity, including racial identification, and Arab American political alliances should be examined as outcomes of the structural processes I describe. They are not independent of these processes nor can they be used to explain the structural position of Arab Americans.
37. I am speaking domestically here, but the wars in Iraq and Afghanistan and other features of the War on Terror (Guantanamo, torture, rendering, disappearances) suggest a collective global responsibility.
38. Emile Durkheim, in Anthony Giddens, ed., *Emile Durkheim: Selected Writings* (London, 1972), 139.
39. Elliott Barkan provided this nugget of media history.
40. See Louise Cainkar, "The Impact of 9/11 on Muslims and Arabs in the United States," in *The Maze of Fear: Security & Migration After September 11th*, ed. John Tirman (New York, 2004), 215–39; and Louise Cainkar, *Homeland Insecurity: The*

*Arab/Muslim American Experience after 9/11* (New York, forthcoming), working title.

41. The study was funded by a grant from the Russell Sage Foundation.
42. Fred Tsao and Rhoda Rae Gutierrez, *Losing Ground* (Chicago, 2003).
43. Some 83,000 persons living in the United States underwent call-in special registration, according to the Department of Homeland Security. At minimum, at least 20,000 additional Arabs and Muslims nationwide have been affected by one or more of the numerous post-9/11 national security initiatives.
44. See chart in Louise Cainkar, "Global Impacts of the September 11th Attacks" *Journal of Comparative Studies of Africa, Asia, and the Middle East*" 24, no. 1 (Winter 2004): 248.
45. Data from ethnographic study.
46. United States Department of Justice, Office of the Inspector General, *The September 11 Detainees* (Washington, DC, 2004).
47. Statement made at a meeting with top regional government officials and members of Chicago's Arab community.
48. National Immigration Forum, national conference call, August 15, 2002.
49. "Non-immigrant aliens" includes all immigrants who are inspected by the INS upon entry to the United States and are not U.S. citizens, permanent residents, applicants for permanent residency, refugees, or applicants for asylum. Special registration excluded non-immigrants who are diplomats, persons working with international organizations, and a few other narrow categories of non-immigrants (categories A and G).
50. Richard Swarms, "More than 13,000 May Face Deportation," *New York Times*, 7 June 2003; Reuters, 18 December 2002; BBC News Online 19 December 2002; *News-day* 13 December 2002.
51. Reuters, 18 December 2002.
52. Carol Hallstrom, Department of Homeland Security, Community Relations, Chicago, e-mail to Louise Cainkar, June 2003.
53. 556 foreign nationals were deported during the Palmer Raids. Alex Gourevitch, "Detention Disorder," *The American Prospect Online*, 31 January 2003. Operation Wetback is another instance of mass expulsion.
54. INS Memo (undated), HQINS 70/28, from Johnny Williams, Executive Associate Commissioner, Office of Field Operations.
55. U.S. Department of Homeland Security, "Fact Sheet: US-VISIT Program, 19 May 2003. The acronym NSEERS stands for National Security Entry Exit Registration System.
56. See, e.g., Michael Isikoff, "The FBI Says, Count the Mosques," *Newsweek*, 3 February 2003. For a list of some of the earlier programs, see Louise Cainkar, "No Longer Invisible: Arab and Muslim Exclusion After September 11," *Middle East Report* (Washington DC: MERIP), No. 224 (Fall 2002), http://www.merip. org/mer/mer224/224_ cainkar.html.
57. The law requiring aliens to carry their registration documents with them at all times is still on the books. This would mean that carrying one's passport bearing registration information is mandatory, although not currently enforced.
58. Public Law, 97–116, December 29, 1981, Immigration and Nationality Act Amendments of 1981.
59. House Judiciary Committee, Report No. 97–264, 2 October 1981, "Need for Legislation."
60. 67 Federal Register 52584 (8 December 2002).
61. 56 FR 1566. This registry was during the 1990–91 Gulf War period. The government's stated reasons for registry include the Iraqi theft of Kuwaiti travel documents,

the "potential for anti-U.S. terrorist-type activities" because of "US condemnation of and economic sanctions against the Iraqi invasion of Kuwait," and "securing information on terrorists." Reno rescinded this rule in December 1993, amended the Code of Federal Regulations to make the country designation process simpler, and then published a Federal Register notice requiring "certain nonimmigrants from Iraq and the Sudan" to register. In 1996 Reno added "certain nonimmigrants bearing Iranian and Libyan travel documents. Ashcroft added Syria to this list on September 6, 2002, and at that time declared that citizens and nationals of these five countries, and persons believed to be such, were subject to the newly expanded special registration.

62. Omi and Winant, *Racial Formation*, 1994, 71, define essentialist as a "belief in real, true human essences, existing outside or impervious to social and historical context."

63. Daniel Smith, "When 'For a While' Becomes Forever," *Weekly Defense Monitor*, 2 October 2001.

64. *Chicago Sun-Times*, 2 October 2001.

65. *The News Sun* (Springfield, IL), 20 December 2001.

66. Gallup News Service, 8 August 2002.

67. Erik C. Nisbet and James Shanahan, *Restrictions on Civil Liberties, Views of Islam, & Muslim Americans* (Ithaca, NY, 2004).

68. U.S. Department of Commerce, Census Bureau, *Technical Documentation, Summary File 3, 2000*, issued March 2005. There was a popular movement among many Arabs in the United States to check the "other" box and write in Arab as an expression of non-whiteness and to push for an Arab category. This effort was largely undone through re-coding. A few Arab nationalities are curiously exempt from the white re-code.

69. Since these are open-ended ethnographic interviews, some persons offered responses that fall into multiple categories.

70. Mary Waters developed the concept of "Ethnic Options." I am extending this concept to race. See Waters, *Ethnic Options*.

71. The quite different responses to the race question in the Detroit Arab-American Survey may be the result of a number of factors, primary among them local Arab American experiences with race and with political organizing, as well as methodological. The question was formulated in a manner that replicated official categories and boxes. See Wayne Baker, et al., *Preliminary Findings from the Detroit Arab American Study* (Ann Arbor, MI, 2004).

72. Read finds some evidence that Muslims experienced more discrimination after 9/11 and that they were more likely to define and perceive themselves as a minority group than Christian Arabs. See Jen'nan Ghazal Read, "Multiple Identities and Post 9/11 Discrimination: A Comparison of Muslim and Christian Arab Americans," in *From Invisible Citizens to Visible Subjects: "Race" and Arab Americans Before and after September 11th*, ed. Amaney Jamal and Nadine Naber (Syracuse, NY, forthcoming).

73. A more extensive elaboration of this section may be found in Louise Cainkar, "Thinking Outside the Box: Arabs and Race in the U.S.," forthcoming in Amaney Jamal and Nadine Naber, eds., *From Invisible Citizens to Visible Subjects*.

74. These fears may be receding, as long as the domestic front is quiet. Fears remain about what might occur in the event of another terrorist attack.

75. Mathew Lee, "US Evangelist says Muslims 'Worse Than Nazis'," *Agence France Press* 12 November 2002.

76. William Lind and Paul Weyrich, *Why Islam is a Threat to America and the West* (Washington, DC, 2002).

77. Mohamed Nimer, "Muslims in America After 9–11," *Journal of Islamic Law and Culture* 7 no. 2 (2003): 73–101.
78. Ibid. For more documentation of these types of comments, see American Arab Anti-Discrimination Committee, *Report on Hate Crimes and Discrimination against Arab Americans: The Post September 11 Backlash* (Washington, DC, 2003).
79. The spread of Islamic revival is a complex, global process that merits extensive analysis. I discuss this process in greater detail in "Islamic Revival Among Second-generation Arab Muslims in Chicago: The American Experience and Globalization Intersect," *Bulletin of the Royal Institute for Inter-Faith Studies* 6 (Autumn/Winter, 2004): 2. This research is supported by a Carnegie Corporation Scholar Award.
80. Alejandro Portes, quoted in Charles Hirschman, "The Role of Religion in the Origins and Adaptation of Immigrant Groups in the United States," paper presented at Princeton University conference on "Conceptual and Methodological Developments in the Study of International Migration" 23–25 May 2003.

# NOTES ON CONTRIBUTORS

Elliott R. Barkan is completing his term as President of the Immigration and Ethnic History Society and is a Professor Emeritus of History and Ethnic Studies at California State University San Bernardino. For seventeen years he was Book Review Editor of this journal. His research interests have focused on inter-disciplinary and multi-ethnic approaches to the study of immigration and ethnicity. His recent works include editing *A Nation of Peoples: A Sourcebook on America's Multicultural Heritage* (1999), *U.S. Immigration and Naturalization Laws and Policies: A Sourcebook* (with Michael LeMay, 2001), and *Making It in America: A Sourcebook on Eminent Ethnic Americans* (2001). His current work is on the American West: "Turning Turner on His Head? The Significance of Immigration in Twentieth Century American Western History" *New Mexico Historical Review* (Winter 2002); "Return of the Nativists?: California Public Opinion and Immigration in the 1980s and 1990s." *Social Science History* (Summer 2003); "America in the Hand, Homeland in the Heart: Transnational and Translocal Immigrant Experiences in the American West," *Western Historical Quarterly* (Autumn 2004); and *From All Points: America's Immigrant West, 1880–1952* (Indiana University Press, forthcoming).

Louise Cainkar is a sociologist and senior research fellow at the University of Illinois at Chicago's Great Cities Institute. Her scholarly work focuses on Arabs and Muslims in the United States, about whom she has published widely. She is completing a book on the Arab/Muslim experience after 9/11 based on an ethnographic study funded by the Russell Sage Foundation. She is also studying Islamic Revival in the United States, supported by a Carnegie Corporation Scholar Award. In addition to the United States, she has conducted research in Jordan, Iraq, Kuwait, and the West Bank and has worked in the field of human rights. She is currently involved with other scholars in an Iraqi Oral History Project.

Carolle Charles is an Associate Professor of Sociology at Baruch College. Her scholarly work focuses on three interconnected areas of research: labor migration and transnational pattern of migrants' identities; the dynamic of race, culture, and history; and gender and empowerment. She has published on issues of race, immigration, citizenship, blackness, gender, and identity.

Roger Daniels was born in New York City and served in the merchant marine during the latter stages of World War Two and in the Army during the Korean War. His doctorate is from UCLA. He is Charles Phelps Taft Professor Emeritus of History in the University of Cincinnati. He has written widely about Japanese and other Asian Americans, about immigration, and about American politics. His most recent books are *Guarding the Golden Door: American Immigration Policy and Immigrants* and the second edition of *Prisoners Without Trial: Japanese Americans in World War II*, both published in 2004 by Hill and Wang. He lives in Bellevue, Washington.

Nancy Foner is Distinguished Professor of Sociology at Hunter College and the Graduate Center of the City University of New York. She is the author of numerous books, including *From Ellis Island to JFK: New York's Two Great Waves of Immigration*, winner of the 2000 Theodore Saloutos Book Award. Her recent publications include *In a New Land: A Comparative View of Immigration* (New York University Press, 2005) and *Wounded City: The Social Impact of 9/11* (Russell Sage Foundation, 2005).

Guillermo J. Grenier is a Professor of Sociology at Florida International University. Born in Havana, Cuba, he received his Ph.D. from the University of New Mexico. He is the author of *Inhuman Relations: Quality Circles and Anti-Unionism in American Industry*. Other books include *Employee Participation and Labor Law in the American Workplace; Miami Now: Immigration, Ethnicity and Social Change; Newcomers in the Workplace: Immigrants and the Restructuring of the US Economy*; and *This Land Is Our Land: Newcomers and Established Residents in Miami* (University of California Press, 2002, with Alex Stepick), and *Legacy of Exile: Cubans in the United States*, with Lisandro Perez (Allyn and Bacon, 2002). He conducts yearly surveys on the attitudes of the Cuban-American community towards Cuba.

Roland L. Guyotte is Professor of History at the University of Minnesota, Morris, and an elected member of the Academy of Distinguished Teachers of the University of Minnesota. He is History Discipline Coordinator and has served as Vice Chair of the Division of the Social Sciences. He has published widely in United States history, including works on U.S. higher education and the history of immigration. His article, "Aspiration and Reality: Occupational and Educational Choices among Filipino Migrants to Chicago, 1900-1935," co-authored with Barbara M. Posadas, received the Harry Pratt Memorial Award of the Illinois State Historical Society. His current research focuses on immigration policy and Asian American citizenship.

Christiane Harzig is an Associate Professor at Arizona State University, teaching history of migration. She has worked in Germany, the United States, and Canada and recently received the John A. Diefenbaker Research Award from the Canada Council. She has published on Canadian and U.S. social history, gender and migration, immigration policy, and German migration. Among her recent publications are *Immigration and Politics: Historical Memory and Political Culture as Resources in the Netherlands, Sweden and Canada* (Gbttingen, 2004) and, as editor with Danielle Juteau, *The Social Construction of Diversity. Recasting the Master Narrative of Industrial Nations* (New York, 2003).

Ester E. Hernandez is an Assistant Professor in the Department of Chicano Studies, California State University Los Angeles. She completed her doctoral studies in 2002 at the University of California, Irvine. Her dissertation, "Power in Remittances: Remaking Family and Nation among Salvadorans," is based on ethnographic interviews and participant observation. Her publications include *Chicanos, Latinos and Cultural Diversity*, co-edited with D. Espinoza, R. Rodriguez, and L. Maldonado (2004); and "Review of Latino/a Immigrants in Los Angeles," in *Latina/o Los Angeles: Global Transformations, Settlement, and Political Activism*, ed. Gilda Ochoa and Enrique Ochoa (forthcoming). She is currently working on "Remitting Citizenship: Inclusion, Exclusion and Exchange," to be coauthored with Susan Coutin.

Val Johnson completed her Ph.D. at the New School for Social Research and is an Assistant Professor of Feminist Criminology and Women's Studies at Saint Mary's University in Halifax, Nova Scotia. Her research interests center on the production and governance of identities, bodies, communities and space, particularly in cities. She has recently published or has forthcoming essays on "The Moral Citizenship of Jewish Women in New York City (1890–1920)" and "Women, Immigration, and the Historical Intersection of Federal and Municipal Policing." She is presently co-editing two interdisciplinary collections: one on the criminalization of poverty and one on the television franchise *C.S.I.* Her most recent research is an investigation of Canadian juvenile justice reform, 1960–1982.

Deborah Dash Moore is William C. L. Heutwell Professor of History at the University of Michigan and Director of the Jean and Samuel Frankel Center for Judaic Studies. She specializes in twentieth-century American Jewish history. Her most recent book, *GI Jews: How World War II Changed a Generation*, appeared in 2004.

Barbara M. Posadas is Professor of History at Northern Illinois University. She is the author of *The Filipino Americans* (1999) and numerous articles on Filipino American history, particularly in the Midwest. She has been a member of several editorial boards and has served as president of the Illinois State Historical Society, as a board member of the Immigration and Ethnic History Society and the Urban History Association, and as chair of the OAH Committee on the Status of Minority History and Minority Historians, among other positions. Her current research focuses on Filipinos in Chicago before 1965 and on immigration policy and Asian American citizenship.

Sharron P. Schwartz recently completed her doctorate at the University of Exeter, examining Cornish migration to Latin America. She is currently Research Fellow in Migration Studies at the Institute of Cornish Studies, School of Humanities and Social Sciences, University of Exeter. Among her most recent works are "Exporting the Industrial Revolution: The Migration of Cornish Mining Technology to Latin America in the Early Nineteenth Century," *New Perspectives in Transatlantic Studies* (2002); and "Migration networks and the transnationalisation of social capital: Cornish migration to Latin America, a case study," *Cornish Studies* 13 (2005). She presently is writing a book on the nineteenth-century migration of Cornish mineworkers to Latin America.

Diane C. Vecchio is Professor of History at Furman University in Greenville, South Carolina. She is the author of *Merchants, Midwives, and Laboring Women: Italian Migrants in Urban America* (University of Illinois Press, 2006).